S0-BDL-498

McGraw-Hill
HANDBOOK
OF ENGLISH

VIRGINIA SHAFFER

Head of English Department, Forest
Park High School, Baltimore, Mary-
land; Coordinator of Writing, Mc-
Coy College of The Johns Hopkins
University

HARRY SHAW

Formerly Director, Workshops in
Composition, New York University

Second Edition

McGRAW-HILL BOOK COMPANY, INC.

New York Chicago San Francisco Dallas Toronto London

COPYRIGHT ACKNOWLEDGMENTS

Library of Congress Catalog Card Number: 59–10723

CONTENTS

Grammar

Usage

Capitalization

Punctuation

The Word

The Sentence

The Paragraph

The Whole Theme

The Research Paper

The Précis and the Paraphrase

Writing for Special Purposes

Listening and Thinking

Appendix

PREFACE

The McGraw-Hill Handbook of English, Second Edition, is designed to help the student build the skills he needs to express himself with clarity, ease, and appropriateness. It describes American English as it is actually used by careful speakers and writers and shows why some kinds of expression are considered more effective than others. In addition to stating the facts about language that educated people must know, this book emphasizes the importance of clear thinking as an essential both to effective expression and to intelligent reading and listening. Types of faulty thinking are analyzed and exercises are provided to develop the student's ability to recognize and avoid such errors in his own writing and speaking.

This new edition of the **McGraw-Hill Handbook of English** contains a number of new features which the authors believe will enhance the usefulness of the book. A new format employing a second color gives increased prominence to rules, principles, and section numbers. Expanded sections on levels of usage, the use of the dictionary, and report writing provide materials for instruction and reference essential to the student's work in English and his other studies as well. A section on taking tests acquaints the student with the form and content of college entrance and placement tests and shows him ways in which he can improve his performance. A comprehensive review of sentence diagraming brings together in one place all of the principles of sentence analysis and provides the explanations and practice sentences the student needs to master them.

This book makes a completely functional approach to grammar, usage, and mechanics. Rules are clearly stated, illustrated, and immediately applied. Abundant drill material enables the student to familiarize himself with important principles and helps him to see how they apply to his own writing.

The natural-sounding practice sentences in the **McGraw-Hill Handbook of English** greatly simplify the task of both teacher and student. These sentences were not written solely to embody an error. They are drawn from more than seven thousand student themes analyzed for this purpose. Often these sentences appear in the form of a paragraph on safe driving, travel, or an illuminating incident from the life of a literary figure, so that the student adds to his knowledge and broadens his cultural outlook as he studies his grammar.

The authors make a special effort to provide for different levels of instruction. The drill that follows each major principle is arranged in two sections. The first begins with easy sentences and moves on to the kind of sentences that normally appear in careful student writing. The second section provides sentences of greater maturity. These may be used for superior students or for review with students who have mastered the simpler sentences. Thus, the teacher who wishes to use homogeneous grouping can readily do so.

In recognition of the fact that language changes, the authors of the **McGraw-Hill Handbook of English,** Second Edition, have scrutinized every explanation, illustrative example, and practice sentence to ensure its appropriateness in a handbook reflecting modern American usage. While making clear that the standards of English change with the needs of those who use it, the authors are careful to remind the student that at any given time there are standards. This book describes fully and accurately the standards of written English today.

VIRGINIA SHAFFER
HARRY SHAW

ACKNOWLEDGMENTS

For assistance in preparing the manuscript, the authors are indebted to a number of people. Miss Elizabeth Connelly, former Head of the English Department at the Patterson Park High School in Baltimore, and Mrs. Thea Hodes, former teacher of superior children at School No. 49 in Baltimore, read parts of the manuscript and offered valuable advice on the adjustment of the material to suit the needs of students of varying ability. Mrs. Philip Edwards, Director of Young People's Work at the Enoch Pratt Free Library, and her assistants gave invaluable help in locating illustrative paragraphs in books popular with young people. Miss Bernice Wiese, Supervisor of School Libraries in Baltimore, examined the section on the use of the library. Suggestions from Mr. Simeon Round, Mrs. Anna Bloom, and Mr. Ellis Newton on "The Theme" and "The Research Paper" have been incorporated in the revision. The authors are grateful to all these people and to the students at the Forest Park High School and at McCoy College of The Johns Hopkins University, who have made helpful suggestions while using the materials in this book.

GUIDE TO EXERCISES

Asterisks indicate key exercises and achievement tests.

Grammar

Grammar is not a static thing. It changes and grows as men put new life into it, and it has different levels for different occasions. In the casual English of informal conversation, many people today are using "It's me," or "Drive slow"; but these forms would not, of course, appear in formal writing.

Grammar is for use. The definitions and explanations given in this part of the book are valuable only when they help the student to write and speak more effectively. Because the types of words defined here function in many different kinds of sentences, it is important to remember that a given word is not always used as the same part of speech. It may be a noun in one sentence, a verb in another, an adjective in a third. How a word is used determines what part of speech it is.

> *Sailing* is my favorite sport. (Noun)
> We were *sailing* across the bay. (Verb)
> Far off we could see a small *sailing* vessel. (Adjective)

In the pages that follow, the essential principles of grammar are reviewed. If there has been some tendency to permit variations of the forms commonly accepted as correct, these variations are presented.

A glossary of grammatical terms appears on pages 52–61. If any grammatical terms used in this book are unfamiliar to you, turn to the glossary.

1

1. NOUNS

1a. Definition.

A *noun* is the name of a person, place, or thing.

> man, officer, Thomas Jefferson, park, street, desk, team, courage

1b. Kinds of nouns.

A *common noun* is the name of any one of a class of persons, places, or things. It is not written with a capital letter.

> horse, child, garden, alley, tub, book, engineer

A *proper noun* is the name of a particular person, place, or thing. It is written with a capital letter. (See Section 21g.)

> General Grant, President Lincoln, Patterson Park, Linden Avenue, Soil Conservation Service

An *abstract noun* is the name of an idea or a quality apart from any object.

> honesty, intelligence, grace

A *collective noun* names a group of persons or objects.

> class, crowd, army, fleet, family

NOTE: Abstract nouns and collective nouns are usually common nouns.

EXERCISE 1

Identify the proper nouns in the following list and write them with a capital letter on a separate sheet of paper.

company	maryland	southern high
high school	north	school
secretary	english	king

tuesday   general electric   automobile
junior   company   lincoln park
                 house of repre-   doctor
                     sentatives

1c. Number.

Nouns may be *singular* or *plural*. If a noun names *one* person, place, or thing, it is *singular* in number. If it means *more than one,* it is *plural* in number. *Field* is singular; *fields* is plural.

EXERCISE 2

Study Section 39d. Then on a sheet of paper write the correct plural form of each of the following words:

tomato	woman	pony
lady	piano	valley
sister-in-law	sheep	alumnus
phenomenon	chief	canoe
James	wolf	knife

1d. Gender.

Nouns have four genders: *masculine* (*man, boy*), *feminine* (*woman, girl*), and *neuter* (*desk, road*). When a noun may be either masculine or feminine, it has *common gender* (*person, playmate, companion*).

EXERCISE 3

Write on your paper the feminine form (or equivalent) of each of these nouns:

nephew	alumnus	tiger
executor	lion	policeman
master	duke	patron
emperor	salesman	host
king	marquis	actor
drake	poet	gander

3

1e. Case.

Nouns have three cases: *nominative, objective, possessive.*
Nouns in the nominative and objective cases have the same
form: *boy* (*nominative*), *boy* (*objective*). The possessive
case requires an apostrophe (*boys'*) or an apostrophe and *s*
(*boy's*). (See Section 26.)

1f. Uses of nouns in the nominative case.

The most important uses of nouns in the nominative case
are the following:

1. *Subject of a verb.* (See Section 3.)

> s.   v.
> The *storm* caught the ship in mid-ocean.
>
> s.   v.
> Suddenly the *winds* roared in a great blast of fury.
>
> v.   s.
> Across the deck swept huge *waves.*
>
> s.   v.   s.
> The *passengers* rushed to their cabins when the *waves*
> v.
> rolled over the deck.

2. *Predicate noun,* also called *predicate complement,
predicate nominative,* or *subjective complement.* (See
Section 14b.)

A predicate noun is a noun used in the predicate (see
Glossary of Grammatical Terms) to point back to the subject. It follows the verb *be* (*am, is, are, was, been, be, were*)
or some other linking verb (*become, seem*).

> s. v.   p.n.
> *Jerry* is the *boy* to play halfback.
>
> s.   v.   p.n.
> The *Americans* are the *people* who have led the struggle
> for liberty.
>
> s.   v.   p.n.
> Those *girls* were the *winners* of the basketball tourna-
> ment.

s.   v.   p.n.
The *man* on the witness stand seemed a *person* of honesty.

3. *Noun in direct address.* (See Section 23f.)

Bruce, will you ride to the canyon with me?

4. *Noun in an absolute expression.* (See Section 72e.)

Night having fallen, we camped near the trail.

5. *Appositive* with a noun in the nominative case. (See Section 14j.)

Melody, my *horse,* saw me from the corral.

1g. Uses of nouns in the objective case.

The most important uses of nouns in the objective case follow. (For further explanation, see Section 14. See also Section 4d for *adverbial objective.*)

1. *Direct object of a verb.*

We won the *game.* (*Game* is the direct object of the verb *won.*)

Jean gave a *party.* (*Party* is the direct object of the verb *gave.*)

2. *Indirect object of a verb* (object of *to* or *for* understood).

Shall I give *Ted* a sweater at Christmas? (*Ted* is the indirect object of the verb. *Sweater* is the direct object.)

3. *Object of a preposition.*

Mother brought some souvenirs from *Atlantic City.* (*Atlantic City* is the object of the preposition *from.*)

4. *Appositive* with a noun in the objective case. (See Section 14j.)

We met Mr. Townley, the *sheriff.*

5. *Objective complement,* or *predicate objective.* (See Section 14i.)

> We elected Walter *president.*
> I consider her a good *player.*

6. *Subject of an infinitive.* (See Section 14g.)

> I wanted *John* to go to the movies.
> Sally asked the *chairman* to take a walk with her.

7. *Object of an infinitive.* (See Sections 3g and 14h.)

> His desire to please the *voters* was great.
> The ship was anchored to save *fuel.*

8. *Object of a participle.* (See Sections 3g and 14h.)

> Waving his *hat,* Rusty galloped down Main Street.
> Emily is the girl driving the *car.*

9. *Object of a gerund.* (See Sections 3g and 14h.)

> Catching a *mustang* is not an easy job.
> Playing *tennis* is good exercise.

10. *Adverbial objective* (noun used as adverb).

> The ranch was sold last *year.*
> We stayed *home* all day.

1h. Uses of nouns in the possessive case.

There are two important uses of nouns in the possessive case:

1. Before a noun, to show ownership or some other close relationship that might be expressed by *of* or *for the use of.*

> The *child's* ball, *his* mother, a *day's* journey, *members'* lounge

2. Before a gerund. (See Sections 3g and 26h.)

> Have you heard about *Ruth's* winning the contest?

EXERCISE 4

Arrange the nouns in these sentences in two columns. Put those in the nominative case in one column and those in the objective case in another column. Beside each noun, write the reason why you have listed it as nominative or objective.

Example:

NOMINATIVE		OBJECTIVE	
leopard	subject	zoo	object of preposition

Recently a leopard escaped from a zoo in Ohio. Some hunters had caught the animal on Christmas and shipped it to the United States for display in a new zoo where the animals were not confined in cages but were allowed to roam at will over a wide territory surrounded by deep moats. The animals could not escape because the moats were too broad for even the leopard to leap. Or so thought the keepers of the zoo. But this leopard was a wily beast. He apparently figured the distance carefully and with a great bound jumped across the moat. From one end of the country to another, the newspapers carried big headlines that told of the chase. Armed groups sought him in the park near the zoo and in the surrounding neighborhood. At first the superintendent of the zoo wanted the beast to be caught alive, but after a few hours, the danger seemed so great that hunters were told to shoot the animal at sight. Because the keepers considered the leopard to be a very dangerous beast, they warned the people nearby to keep their children inside and to look for any evidence that would lead to the capture. For two days the whole country read the news avidly. Then the headlines announced that the zoo would try to trap the animal with food. By this time some people had begun to consider the zoo and the police to be very ineffectual. Then huge pieces of drugged meat were placed on the ground near a cage in which the leopard's mate was held, and the next morning the hungry animal was found hardly able to stand up because the drug was so strong. He was seized, and the country relaxed.

2. PRONOUNS

2a. Definition.

A *pronoun* is a word used in place of a noun.

2b. Kinds of pronouns.

There are several kinds of pronouns: *personal, relative, demonstrative, interrogative, reflexive, intensive, indefinite,* and *reciprocal.*

1. A *personal pronoun* is a direct substitute for a noun. Like a noun, it has number, gender, and case. It also has *person.* Person is shown in pronouns by a change of form to indicate the person speaking (*first person*), the person spoken to (*second person*), or a person or thing other than the speaker and the one spoken to (*third person*). See the following table of forms of personal pronouns:

Singular

	NOMINATIVE	POSSESSIVE	OBJECTIVE
1st person:	I	my, mine	me
2nd person:	you	your, yours	you
3rd person:			
masculine	he	his	him
feminine	she	her, hers	her
neuter	it	its	it

Plural

	NOMINATIVE	POSSESSIVE	OBJECTIVE
1st person:	we	our, ours	us
2nd person:	you	your, yours	you
3rd person:			
all genders	they	their, theirs	them

Grammatical problems frequently arise from the fact that, unlike nouns, personal, relative, and interrogative pronouns have distinct case forms. These problems are discussed in Section 14.

2. A *relative pronoun* relates or connects a clause to its *antecedent*—the noun to which it refers. The most often

used relative pronouns are *who, which,* and *that. Whoever, whichever,* and *whatever* are less frequently employed compound forms; *whosoever, whichsoever,* and *whatsoever* have almost entirely gone out of current use. *Who* and *whoever* are the only relative pronouns with complete case forms. Relative pronouns do not show changes in form for person, gender, or number. See the following table of case forms for *who* and *whoever:*

NOMINATIVE	POSSESSIVE	OBJECTIVE
who	whose	whom
whoever	whosever	whomever

The choice of a relative pronoun is determined by its antecedent; the case form for *who* and *whoever* is determined by the way the pronoun is used in the relative clause. (See Section 14.) *Who* is used to refer only to persons; *which* is used to refer to things (inanimate objects and animals), and to persons considered as a group; *that* may be used to refer to either persons or things.

> The flier *who* served in World War II is now an airline official.
> Radar equipment *which* is to be used for small ships must be installed carefully.
> The crew *which* won the race was excused from classes.
> The hat *that* I bought last summer is now out of fashion.
> The man *that* I saw was named Mortimer Taylor.

3. A *demonstrative pronoun* points out and identifies. It has number but no gender or case. The demonstrative pronouns are *this, that, these, those.*

> *This* is the way to kick a spiral.
> *That* is my new television set.
> *These* are your books; *those* on the desk are mine.

4. An *interrogative pronoun* (*who, whom, whose, which, what,* occasionally *whoever, whichever, whatever*) intro-

duces a question. The case forms for the interrogative pronoun *who* and the relative pronoun *who* are the same.

> *Who* shall demand that a pardon be granted?
> *Which* is the route we should take from Hammond?
> *What* do you have in mind?
> *Whom* do you recognize?

5. A *reflexive pronoun* is used for reference to the subject of the sentence. It is composed of one of the personal pronouns plus *self* or *selves: myself, yourself, himself, herself, itself, ourselves, yourselves, themselves.* These pronouns are also called *compound personal pronouns.* In formal speech or writing, these pronouns are not used as subjects.

Wrong: Helen, Sue, and *myself* went on a hike.
Right: His laboratory assistant burned *himself.*
Right: They appointed *themselves* as cheer leaders.

6. An *intensive pronoun* is used for emphasis. Intensive pronouns and reflexive pronouns have the same form.

Right: The nurse *herself* was at fault.
Right: We students *ourselves* are wholly responsible.

7. *Indefinite pronouns* are somewhat less exact in meaning than other pronouns. Among the more frequently used indefinite pronouns are *another, any, anyone, anything, everybody, everyone, everything, few, many, nobody, none, one, several, some, each.* The pronoun *one* and its compound forms, and compound forms built on the element -*body* form the possessive case in the same way as nouns (*anyone's, everybody's*). Indefinite pronouns involve grammatical problems which are discussed in Section 11d.

8. A *reciprocal pronoun* indicates an interchange of action suggested by the verb. This interchange may be seen in the following sentences involving the only two reciprocal pronouns in English:

> The two teams complimented *each other.*
> The members of the squad shouted at *one another.*

3. ASSERTING WORDS: VERBS AND VERBALS

3a. Definition.

A *verb* expresses action or state of being.

> Morgan *kicked* the ball with all his strength.
> *Be* ready at eight o'clock.
> Howard *became* a statesman and *wrote* a number of books.

3b. Kinds of verbs.

Verbs are classified as *transitive, intransitive,* or *linking.*

A *transitive* verb is regularly accompanied by a direct object.

> v.   o.
> The engineers *threw* a *bridge* across the river.
>
> v.   o.
> The refugees *ate bits* of bread found on the road.
>
> v.   o.
> An old woman *seized* a squawking *goose* and ran into the house.

An *intransitive* verb requires no object.

> Automobiles from Paris *crept* along the roads.
> People *ran* wildly in every direction.

Many verbs can be used in either a transitive or an intransitive sense.

> We *read* the news with great care. (Transitive)
> We *read* until late at night. (Intransitive)
> I *won* the first set. (Transitive)
> I *won* easily. (Intransitive)

A *linking,* or *copulative,* verb shows the relationship of the subject to the predicate noun.

> Washington *was* our first president.
> My favorite color *is* green.

11

3c. Auxiliary verbs.

Auxiliary, or *helping,* verbs, such as *may, can, must, would, should, do, did, shall, will,* and all forms of *be* and *have,* are often used with other verbs to express particular shades of meaning—usually of time (see Section 3f) or voice (see Section 3d). Such combinations are called *verb phrases.*

> I *have known* Jerry since the first grade. (Time)
> This theme *was rewritten* three times. (Voice)

3d. Voice.

Transitive verbs are further classified as to *voice—active* or *passive.*

A verb is in the *active* voice when its subject performs the action.

> We *built* a large house in the country.
> The engineers *have developed* new types of electrical refrigerators.
> The Marshall Plan *helps* the reconstruction of Europe.

A verb is in the *passive* voice when its subject receives the action. Notice that some form of the verb *be* (*am, is, are, was, were, been, be*) is used with another verb in the passive voice.

> A large house *was built* in the country.
> The doors *were bolted* from the inside.

3e. Mood.

The *mood* of a *verb* shows the mood or manner in which the speaker thinks of the action.

A verb in the *indicative mood* states a fact or asks a question of fact.

> The farmer *planted* his crop early.
> What time *is* it?

A verb in the *imperative mood* expresses a command.

Clean your room.
Open your books to page 10.

A verb in the *subjunctive mood* indicates a condition contrary to fact or a wish. The subjunctive is discussed in Section 17c–g.

If you *were* in Europe, you would find life very different.
I wish I *were* in the South where it is always warm.

3f. Tense.

Tense indicates the *time* of the action or state expressed by a verb.

Every verb has three *principal parts* which are used as a basis for the formation of tenses. Many mistakes are made in usage because people do not understand how to form these tenses or how to use them. (See Sections 15 and 16.)

The *principal parts* of a verb are the *present, past, past participle.**

PRESENT	PAST	PAST PARTICIPLE
talk	talked	talked
skate	skated	skated
hurry	hurried	hurried
do	did	done
sing	sang	sung
draw	drew	drawn

If the second and third principal parts of a verb add *-d, -ed,* or *-t,* the verb is called a *regular verb.* Otherwise it is an *irregular verb,* and its parts should be memorized. Notice the irregular verbs in the preceding list.

* A fourth principal part, the present participle, is sometimes also given. The present participle is made by adding *-ing* to the present tense form of a verb: talk, *talking.* The four principal parts are given in this order: talk, talked, talked, *talking.*

13

EXERCISE 5

Write the principal parts of each of the following verbs. Then write sentences using each of these verbs in the past tense. (For a discussion of tenses and their use, see Section 16.)

go	drown	lead	come
drink	speak	shrink	sneak
give	tear	show	dive
hide	do	swing	draw
ring	write	freeze	eat
choose	swim	sting	fall
twist	steal	forget	throw
begin	attack	bite	sing
blow	break	beat	wear

3g. Verbals.

Understanding the difference between verbs and **verbals** will help you to avoid one of the most serious errors in writing, the half sentence or fragment. A *verb* is used as the simple predicate of a sentence; with the subject, the **verb** may make a complete statement. A *verbal* cannot be used as a simple predicate of a sentence. (See Section 55.)

> He *kicked* the ball. (Verb)
> *Kicking* the ball (Verbal)
> *To kick* the ball (Verbal)

There are three types of verbals: *participles, gerunds,* and *infinitives.* (For help in using verbals, see Sections 14k, 16i and j, and 65.)

1. A *participle* is a word which has the function of both verb and adjective. The present participle always ends in *-ing* (*speaking, singing*). The past participle is the third principal part of the verb. The perfect participle consists of *having* or *having been* plus the past participle (*having spoken, having been driven*).

Notice the past participles in the following list of principal parts:

		PAST PARTICIPLE
walk	walked	walked
smile	smiled	smiled
drive	drove	driven
draw	drew	drawn
see	saw	seen
sing	sang	sung
bring	brought	brought

Notice that some of the past participles end in *-ed* and some in *-n;* others change the vowel (*sung*); and still others change their form completely (*brought*). The participle can take an object and be modified by an adverb. When it does, the group of words taken together is called a *participial phrase.* (See Section 6b.)

> The ball *kicked* by the player went into the stand. (Participle used as an adjective)

>   1   2
> The crowd *cheering* the *team* could be heard a mile away. (1: participle used as an adjective in a participial phrase; 2: object of participle)

>   1   2
> We followed the crowd, *cheering lustily.* (1: participle used as an adjective in a participial phrase; 2: adverb modifying participle)

2. A *gerund* is a verbal noun. Gerunds have the same form as present or perfect participles, but are used as nouns instead of adjectives. A gerund may take an object and be modified by an adverb or an adjective.

> 1   2
> *Discovering* the *plans* of the enemy was the job of the intelligence service. (1: gerund; 2: object of gerund)

15

      1   2

Working intelligently is no easy task. (1: gerund; 2: adverb modifier)

                       2   1

Our music teacher dislikes *loud singing.* (1: gerund;
2: adjective modifier)

3. An *infinitive* is the form of the verb usually preceded
by *to.*

     to walk   to observe   to have enjoyed

An infinitive may be used as a noun, an adjective, or an
adverb.

My greatest pleasure is *to travel.* (Infinitive used as noun)
We have four days *to spend* in Billings. (Infinitive used
as adjective)
Bruce was glad *to have come.* (Infinitive used as adverb)

Sometimes the word *to* is omitted from the infinitive.

Let me *go* with you.
Will you help me *pack?*

The infinitive may take an object and be modified by an
adverb or an adverbial phrase or clause.

    1   2
To reach the *mountain* we walked twenty miles. (1: infinitive; 2: object of infinitive)

               1   2
George and I tried *to walk faster.* (1: infinitive; 2: adverb
modifier)

               1   2
The snow began *to drift along the slope.* (1: infinitive;
2: adverbial phrase modifying infinitive)

           1   2
I intend *to stay* here *until you arrive.* (1: infinitive; 2:
adverbial clause modifying infinitive)

EXERCISE 6

From the following paragraph, list in one column all verbs that are used as simple predicates; in another column, list all verbals. The listing has been made for the first two sentences.

Verbs	*Verbal*
had	to go
liked	
had named	

Shelley, the English poet, had a tragic death. He liked to go out on the Mediterranean Sea in a light sailboat which he had named *Ariel.* But because he was very unskillful as a sailor, some of his friends worried about him constantly. Shelley, however, loved the beauty of the sea and the graceful fashion in which the boat slipped over the waves. One day, after visiting some friends, he set out for his home in Lerici in spite of a warning of a storm. Wishing to protect Shelley, his friend Trelawny, who was a good sailor, wanted to accompany the writer in a larger boat named *Bolivar;* but he had not obtained port clearance papers, and the port authorities kept him from leaving. Shelley was in a hurry; so he set out, leaving Trelawny fuming at the shore. The sailors on Trelawny's boat, greatly concerned about Shelley, watched the black clouds gathering. When the storm finally broke, Trelawny, worried about his friend, tried to get news of him. Meantime, Shelley's wife waited at Lerici, feeling sure that Shelley could not have been so foolish as to set out in the storm. Finally she decided to go to Leghorn to see what had happened to him. Reaching the city, she begged for news and was told that Shelley had indeed set out just before the storm. Panic-stricken, Mary made inquiries in every direction, but getting news of her husband was difficult. At last she and Trelawny learned that parts of a wreck had been cast up on the shore at Viareggio. They still did not give up hope, but several days later the body of Shelley was washed up on the shore. He was only thirty years old when he died.

17

To Drive, INDICATIVE MOOD, ACTIVE VOICE

Principal Parts: drive, drove, driven

		SIMPLE		PROGRESSIVE	
		Singular	Plural	Singular	Plural
Present Tense					
1st person		I drive	we drive	I am driving	we are driving
2nd person		you drive	you drive	you are driving	you are driving
3rd person		he (she, it) drives	they drive	he (she, it) is driving	they are driving
Past Tense					
1st person		I drove	we drove	I was driving	we were driving
2nd person		you drove	you drove	you were driving	you were driving
3rd person		he (she, it) drove	they drove	he (she, it) was driving	they were driving
Future Tense					
1st person		I shall (will) drive	we shall drive	I shall be driving	we shall be driving
2nd person		you will drive	you will drive	you will be driving	you will be driving
3rd person		he (she, it) will drive	they will drive	he (she, it) will be driving	they will be driving

Present Perfect Tense

	Singular	Plural
1st person	I have driven	we have driven
2nd person	you have driven	you have driven
3rd person	he (she, it) has driven	they have driven

	Singular	Plural
1st person	I have been driving	we have been driving
2nd person	you have been driving	you have been driving
3rd person	he (she, it) has been driving	they have been driving

Past Perfect Tense

	Singular	Plural
1st person	I had driven	we had driven
2nd person	you had driven	you had driven
3rd person	he (she, it) had driven	they had driven

	Singular	Plural
1st person	I had been driving	we had been driving
2nd person	you had been driving	you had been driving
3rd person	he (she, it) had been driving	they had been driving

Future Perfect Tense

	Singular	Plural
1st person	I shall (will) have driven	we shall (will) have driven
2nd person	you will have driven	you will have driven
3rd person	he (she, it) will have driven	they will have driven

	Singular	Plural
1st person	I shall have been driving	we shall have been driving
2nd person	you will have been driving	you will have been driving
3rd person	he (she, it) will have been driving	they will have been driving

To Drive, INDICATIVE MOOD, PASSIVE VOICE

	SIMPLE		PROGRESSIVE	
	Singular	*Plural*	*Singular*	*Plural*

Present Tense

	Singular	*Plural*	*Singular*	*Plural*
1st person	I am driven	we are driven	I am being driven	we are being driven
2nd person	you are driven	you are driven	you are being driven	you are being driven
3rd person	he (she, it) is driven	they are driven	he is being driven	they are being driven

Past Tense

	Singular	*Plural*	*Singular*	*Plural*
1st person	I was driven	we were driven	I was being driven	we were being driven
2nd person	you were driven	you were driven	you were being driven	you were being driven
3rd person	he (she, it) was driven	they were driven	he (she, it) was being driven	they were being driven

Future Tense

	Singular	*Plural*	*Singular*	*Plural*
1st person	I shall be driven	we shall be driven	I shall be being driven	we shall be being driven
2nd person	you will be driven	you will be driven	you will be being driven	you will be being driven
3rd person	he (she, it) will be driven	they will be driven	he (she, it) will be being driven	they will be being driven

Present Perfect Tense

1st person	I have been driven	we have been driven
2nd person	you have been driven	you have been driven
3rd person	he (she, it) has been driven	they have been driven

Past Perfect Tense

1st person	I had been driven	we had been driven
2nd person	you had been driven	you had been driven
3rd person	he (she, it) had been driven	they had been driven

Future Perfect Tense

1st person	I shall have been driven	we shall have been driven
2nd person	you will have been driven	you will have been driven
3rd person	he (she, it) will have been driven	they will have been driven

Verbals

Active Voice

Present infinitive:	to drive
Perfect infinitive:	to have driven
Present participle:	driving
Past participle:	driven
Perfect participle:	having driven
Present gerund:	driving
Perfect gerund:	having driven

Passive Voice

Present infinitive:	to be driven
Perfect infinitive:	to have been driven
Present participle:	being driven
Past participle:	(none)
Perfect participle:	having been driven
Present gerund:	being driven
Perfect gerund:	having been driven

To Drive, IMPERATIVE MOOD

ACTIVE VOICE

(you) drive

PASSIVE VOICE

(you) be driven

To Drive, SUBJUNCTIVE MOOD*

ACTIVE VOICE

Present Tense

	Singular	Plural
1st person	(if) I drive	(if) we drive
2nd person	(if) you drive	(if) you drive
3rd person	(if) he (she, it) drive	(if) they drive

Past Tense

	Singular	Plural
1st person	(if) I drove	(if) we drove
2nd person	(if) you drove	(if) you drove
3rd person	(if) he (she, it) drove	(if) they drove

PASSIVE VOICE

Present Tense

	Singular	Plural
1st person	(if) I be driven	(if) we be driven
2nd person	(if) you be driven	(if) you be driven
3rd person	(if) he (she, it) be driven	(if) they be driven

Past Tense

	Singular	Plural
1st person	(if) I were driven	(if) we were driven
2nd person	(if) you were driven	(if) you were driven
3rd person	(if) he (she, it) were driven	(if) they were driven

Present Perfect Tense

1st person	(if) I have driven	(if) we have driven
2nd person	(if) you have driven	(if) you have driven
3rd person	(if) he (she, it) have driven	(if) they have driven

1st person	(if) I have been driven	(if) we have been driven
2nd person	(if) you have been driven	(if) you have been driven
3rd person	(if) he (she, it) have been driven	(if) they have been driven

Past Perfect Tense

1st person	(if) I had driven	(if) we had driven
2nd person	(if) you had driven	(if) you had driven
3rd person	(if) he (she, it) had driven	(if) they had driven

1st person	(if) I had been driven	(if) we had been driven
2nd person	(if) you had been driven	(if) you had been driven
3rd person	(if) he (she, it) had been driven	(if) they had been driven

* In the place of a future subjunctive, the form (if) *I should drive* is used. The subjunctive is rarely used except in the present and past tenses.

4. MODIFYING WORDS: ADJECTIVES AND ADVERBS

4a. Definition of adjective.

An *adjective* modifies a noun or a pronoun.

4b. Uses of adjectives.

By describing or limiting, an adjective makes more nearly exact the meaning of the word it modifies. Adjectives tell *what kind of, how many, which one.* Adjectives are of two general kinds:

1. *Descriptive:* a *red* convertible, an *easy* job, a *broken* window

2. *Limiting:* the *first* day, his *former* roommate, *five* times

NOTE: A noun or pronoun in the possessive case may be considered an adjective since it limits the meaning of another noun.

The articles *a, an,* and *the* are adjectives. *A* is used before a word beginning with a consonant sound; *an,* before a word beginning with a vowel sound. Remember that it is the *sound,* not the spelling, that determines which article should be used. A word beginning with silent *h* actually starts with a vowel. The sound of *y* before a vowel is a consonant sound and calls for *a,* whether the word begins with *y* or with a vowel having the sound of *y,* such as long *u.*

> *an* apple, *an* hour, *an* opportunity, *a* hero, *a* European, *a* university

An adjective is called a *predicate adjective* or *predicate complement* when it is related to the subject by a linking verb (*be, feel, become, taste, seem, appear, look, sound,* for example).

> The water felt *warm.*
> The corn is *green.*

EXERCISE 7

In one column, list each word (including verbals) used as an adjective in this paragraph. In another column, list the noun that each adjective modifies.

Across a sea that was now turquoise, now emerald, we could watch the Venezuelan coastline with the purple Andes in the background. Flying fish stood a moment on their tails, flew a little distance, and dived back into the sea. The air was still. The fresh odor of the sea mingled with the heavy smell of sweat from the stevedores' bodies. In a few moments a dozen small boats had reached the side of our ship, and their brown-skinned occupants were slipping into the clear water to find the money that the passengers had thrown down for them.

4c. Definition of adverb.

An *adverb* modifies a verb, an adjective, or another adverb by describing, limiting, or in some other way making the meaning more nearly exact.

4d. Uses of adverbs.

An adverb tells *how, when, where, why, to what extent*. (Adverbs that tell *why* are usually in the form of phrases or clauses rather than single words. See Sections 6 and 7.)

> We saw a parade *recently*. (When)
> We *certainly* did enjoy the music played by the bands. (To what extent)
> *Here* we saw soldiers from many countries. (Where)
> The taxi drove *slowly* down the street. (How)

If we tell how slowly the taxi drove, we have an adverb modifying another adverb.

$$\text{The taxi drove} \begin{cases} quite \\ very \\ too \end{cases} \text{slowly down the street.}$$

25

The following examples show adverbs used to modify adjectives:

> When the day was over, our guide was *very* tired. (*Very* modifies the adjective *tired*.)
>
> He was *almost* sick with fatigue. (*Almost* modifies the adjective *sick*.)

Occasionally a noun is used as an adverb. (This use of a noun is called the *adverbial objective*.)

> After the game we went *home*.

Neither adjectives nor adverbs should be used profusely. Overuse of either robs sentences of conciseness and force. Both adjectives and adverbs can help to make writing specific and vivid, but writing that is heavily larded with them is weak and flabby. Particular problems in the use of adjectives and adverbs are discussed in Sections 18 and 63.

EXERCISE 8

In one column on your paper, list each word (including verbals) used as an adverb in the following paragraph. In a second column, list the word that each adverb modifies.

Have you read *The Ancient Mariner*? Many very interesting stories are told about the author of the poem, Samuel Coleridge. Among them are some particularly good tales of the poet's love for talking. One day Coleridge met Lamb walking rapidly to work and stopped to talk to him. Lamb, who was hurrying to reach his job on time, moved away; but Coleridge quickly grabbed the button of his listener's coat and insisted upon finishing his story. For a few minutes Lamb waited patiently, but Coleridge was apparently preparing for a long talk. Presently Lamb took a knife from his pocket and carefully cut off the button that Coleridge was holding. That evening Lamb, returning from work, saw Coleridge still holding the button and still talking vigorously.

5. JOINING WORDS: PREPOSITIONS AND CONJUNCTIONS

5a. Definition of preposition.

A *preposition* is a linking word used to show the relationship of a noun or pronoun to some other word in the sentence. It is usually followed by an object.

5b. List of prepositions.

Here is a list of common prepositions:

about	before	down	off
above	behind	during	on
across	below	except	over
after	beneath	for	through
against	beside	from	to
along	between	in	toward
among	beyond	like	under
around	by	near	upon
at	concerning	of	with

Some prepositions are composed of more than one word:

according to	because of	in front of
ahead of	by means of	in place of
as far as	contrary to	in spite of
back of	in addition to	instead of

The meaning of a sentence is sometimes confused if prepositions are not used correctly in combination with other words. (See Section 43.)

Between is used when two are considered.
Among is used when more than two are considered.

> I must choose *between* dancing and tennis.
> The money was divided *among* six heirs.

NOTE: In casual speech, *between* is sometimes used when more than two are considered.

Beside means *next to.*
Besides means *in addition to.*

> The most popular boy in school sits *beside* me in French.
> What are you studying *besides* English and math?

5c. Definition of conjunction.

A *conjunction* is a linking word used to connect words or groups of words in a sentence.

5d. Kinds of conjunctions.

Coordinating conjunctions join words or groups of words of equal rank; for example, *and, but, for, or, nor.*

Certain coordinating conjunctions used in pairs are called *correlative conjunctions.* Most frequently used of these are *either . . . or; neither . . . nor; both . . . and; whether . . . or.*

Subordinating conjunctions join dependent clauses to main clauses; for example, *if, as, since, because, although, while, so that, when.* (See Section 7.)

NOTE: Certain adverbs are used as connectives. They are called *conjunctive* adverbs. Examples are *however, moreover, nevertheless, therefore.* (See Glossary of Grammatical Terms and Section 24b.)

In good writing, conjunctions must be chosen with care in order that they may show the exact relationship between ideas. Often a careless writer will use *and* where the relationship of clauses needs to be more accurately expressed, probably by use of subordination. Notice how the emphasis and meaning differ in these sentences:

> The search for the chemical formula has been rewarding, and further investigation will make the rewards even greater.
> Although the search for the chemical formula has been

rewarding, further investigation will make the rewards even greater.

Common errors in the use of conjunctions are discussed in Sections 19a–c, 23a–c, and 70.

The conjunction is the seventh kind of word, or part of speech, that you have studied so far. There are eight parts of speech altogether. The seven parts of speech that you have studied are nouns, pronouns, verbs, adjectives, adverbs, prepositions, and conjunctions. The eighth part of speech is the *interjection,* which is simply an exclamatory word with little relation to the rest of the sentence. It is the least important of the eight parts of speech.

> *Oh,* must you go? (*Oh* is an interjection.)
> Here, *alas,* our good fortune came to an abrupt end. (*Alas* is an interjection.)

6. PHRASES

6a. Definition.

A *phrase* is a group of related words which does not contain a subject and predicate and which functions as a single part of speech. It is important to know how to use phrases because their position in a sentence often determines the meaning. (See Section 63b.)

> There has been much discussion of the new slum-clearing project in school.

The position of the phrase *in school* makes this sentence indicate that slum-clearing took place in school. Actually, the sentence should read:

> In school there has been much discussion of the slum-clearing project.

Understanding the use of phrases also helps one to learn to punctuate correctly. (See Section 23.)

6b. Kinds of phrases.

Phrases often contain a *preposition,* a *participle,* a *gerund,* an *infinitive,* or a *verb.* (See Section 3g.)

Prepositional phrases:	to the dance, by my club, between the boys, of the tickets, at the end of the road
Participial phrases:	running a mile quickly, playing basket-ball, scratching his head, overcome by gas, exhausted after the journey
Gerund phrases:	visiting the animals, selling tickets, kicking the ball, playing tennis, preparing a report
Infinitive phrases:	to play the game well, to sing a song, to walk a mile, to see the circus, to shout loudly
Verb phrases:	have written, would have dived, am beginning

Notice that a phrase may contain another phrase. In the prepositional phrase *at the end of the road,* the object of the preposition *at* is modified by another prepositional phrase. Also, in the participial phrase *exhausted by the journey,* the participle is modified by a prepositional phrase.

Notice, too, that phrases containing present participles and those containing gerunds look alike. The use of such a phrase in a sentence determines whether it is a participial or a gerund phrase. (See Section 3g.)

Phrases (except verb phrases) are used as *nouns, adjectives,* or *adverbs.* Prepositional phrases are generally used as adjectives or adverbs; participial phrases, as adjectives; gerund phrases, as nouns; infinitive phrases, as nouns, adjectives, or adverbs. In some types of writing, it is desirable to expand a word into a phrase; in other types it is better to contract the phrase into a word. A knowledge of phrases helps to give variety to sentence structure.

Noun phrases:

> *To manufacture automobiles* was a great undertaking.
> (Infinitive phrase as subject)
>
> *Cranking the old 1910 model* was a risky business.
> (Gerund phrase as subject)
>
> Many manufacturers tried *to develop mass production.*
> (Infinitive phrase as object of *tried*)
>
> The next step was *to invent a self-starter for the automo-
> bile.* (Infinitive phrase as predicate nominative. Notice
> that the infinitive phrase contains a prepositional
> phrase, *for the automobile.* This prepositional phrase is
> used as an adjective and modifies *self-starter.*)
>
> The plan *to develop a self-starter* caused tremendous ex-
> pansion in the industry. (Infinitive phrase as apposi-
> tive)

EXERCISE 9

On your paper, write the noun phrases that you find in
the following sentences. Beside each phrase, write the kind
of phrase (infinitive or gerund) and its function in the sentence (subject, object of verb, and so on).

Example:
1. Hearing soft music: gerund phrase—subject

1. Hearing soft music makes me sleepy.
2. Planting a garden is good fun.
3. He hates studying his lessons.
4. We decided to pay his way.
5. I want to play a harp.
6. Making a wise decision is not an easy task.
7. Collecting stamps gave Morris many pleasant experiences.
8. I always enjoyed feeding the animals at the circus.
9. Leaving her family in a foreign country worried Alice a great
deal.
10. Shirley's decision to marry David upset her family very
much.
11. Harold's greatest ambition was to make the football team.

12. To build a prosperous business had been his aim since childhood.
13. My uncle wants to go to Australia.
14. The custom here is to go to bed early.
15. Jerry's plan to start a chicken farm surprised the whole family.
16. Later, the Japanese started to make their own motion pictures.
17. Running a large farm taught him to accept life philosophically.
18. The big problem now is to provide adequate parking space.
19. The guests began to open their presents.
20. He wanted to join the club, but getting in was very difficult.
21. She soon learned to keep house, to knit, and to sew.
22. His hobby, restoring old furniture, later became a profitable business.
23. Arthur's chief desire was to be a successful farmer.
24. Some nations try to prevent psychological aggression.
25. Going to concerts in Boston gave Howard a new interest in music.

Adjective phrases:

Adjective phrases, like adjectives, modify nouns or pronouns.

> The bodies *of early automobiles* were high and open. (Prepositional phrase used as adjective modifying subject)
>
> Women *wearing long dusters and goggles* sometimes drove the cars. (Participial phrase used as adjective modifying subject)
>
> We had few opportunities then *to buy a car.* (Infinitive phrase used as adjective modifying object of verb)
>
> One day we saw an early model *stalled on the road.* (Participial phrase used as adjective modifying object of verb. Notice that the participial phrase includes a prepositional phrase, *on the road.* The prepositional phrase is used as an adverb and modifies *stalled.*)

EXERCISE 10

On your paper, write the adjective phrases in the following sentences. Classify each phrase and tell what it modifies. Do not list separately prepositional phrases used as parts of other phrases.

Example:
1. Singing a gay song: participial phrase—modifies *peasant*

1. A peasant singing a gay song trudged past us.
2. "Adonais" is a tribute to the memory of John Keats.
3. Sue bought a new dress to wear to the party.
4. Ichabod saw a strange object coming toward him.
5. There was ample time to finish the work.
6. The snowshoe rabbit has very large feet covered with soft white fur.
7. I should like a position in the saxophone section of the band.
8. Exhausted by the day's labor, he slept soundly.
9. Having beaten Southern High, we hoped to win the city championship.
10. There was a knock on the door, and a man of huge proportions entered.
11. You must break the lock on the cabinet and get the materials needed for the play.
12. The magazine made an effort to improve the morals of the community.
13. Caird, endorsed by the political machine and sponsored by liberal groups, saw his picture everywhere.
14. The election of a new legislative body has produced a shift in the balance of parties.
15. A man wearing a long, loose overcoat and carrying a cane entered the room.
16. Rex Hunter, making his start with the Royals, pitched his first game today.
17. The theater houses the Royal Players, sponsored and supported by the government.
18. We saw a number of students taking the examination for a civil service job.

19. Discussion of the controversial public-housing issue excited a committee of aldermen today.
20. People trying to get new automobile licenses formed a long line in front of the office of the Automobile Commissioner.

Adverbial phrases:

> *Adverbial phrases* modify verbs, adjectives, and adverbs.

>> Yesterday a woman fell *on our sidewalk.* (Prepositional phrase modifying verb *fell*)
>> She fell hard enough *to sprain her ankle.* (Infinitive phrase modifying adverb *enough*)
>> She was easy *to lift.* (Infinitive phrase modifying adjective *easy*)

Restrictive and nonrestrictive phrases:

If a phrase is essential in order to explain or identify the word to which it refers, the phrase is called *restrictive.* If the phrase is not absolutely necessary, it is called *nonrestrictive.* Nonrestrictive phrases are always set off by commas from the remainder of the sentence.

> The citizens' committee gains *in political stature.*

In this example the adverbial phrase is restrictive because it tells the particular way in which the committee gains.

> The citizens' committee, *gaining in political stature,* began to demand reforms within the city government.

Here the adjective phrase is nonrestrictive because it is not essential to the writer's purpose in telling what the committee began to demand. See Section 23h for further discussion and examples of punctuation for restrictive and nonrestrictive modifiers.

EXERCISE 11

On a sheet of paper, write the adverbial phrases in the following sentences. Classify each phrase and tell what it modifies. Do not list separately prepositional phrases used as parts of other phrases.

Example:
1. To South America: prepositional phrase—modifies *flew*
   in a jet plane: prepositional phrase—modifies *flew*

1. He flew to South America in a jet plane.
2. Suddenly, out of the darkness came an octopus.
3. During my spring vacation I took a trip with five friends.
4. George left home to seek his fortune.
5. I passed my driver's test and aided my father by delivering orders.
6. Lately, I have used a budget to keep my money in order.
7. Mr. Upton was walking down the street with a neighbor when the accident occurred.
8. The soldiers advanced in mass formation, while the guerrillas, concealed behind trees, fired at them.
9. On the eve of the wedding, the bridal company was entertained by Mrs. Barton Remsen.
10. In Ecuador, dogs wander through the churches and sleep on the floor on hot afternoons.
11. The natives wear hibiscus blossoms in their hair and colored leaves in their arm bands.
12. The report is too complicated to be handled by the secretary.
13. By using screens, one can protect the plants from the cold.
14. Around the house we planted a hedge high enough to keep the world outside.
15. Schools have recently introduced courses in driver education to teach boys and girls how to drive.
16. In these days, it is very important to learn driving techniques because traffic is complicated by speed.
17. Teen-age youths who take risks to show off before their friends are in many cases the direct cause of an accident.
18. At five o'clock this afternoon there was an accident near Washington Boulevard.
19. It was caused by a boy of nineteen who wanted to show some friends how fast his car could go.
20. His car was smashed to pieces, and several people were seriously injured by the collision.

6c. Achievement test on phrases.

On your paper write all the phrases except verb phrases from the following sentences. Beside each phrase, write the kind of phrase and its function in the sentence. Do not list separately prepositional or verbal phrases used as parts of other phrases.

Example:
1. Knitting socks for the Red Cross: gerund phrase—subject

1. Knitting socks for the Red Cross consumed a great deal of her time.
2. Discharged from the army, the young man decided to go back to college.
3. Airmen have found the eagle flying 9,750 feet above the earth.
4. Plastics are becoming very popular in factories producing household objects.
5. Men working on the project will be research workers of wide experience.
6. The first step in the investigation is to isolate the cold virus.
7. The company has tried to improve conditions, but it has been blind to obvious problems.
8. He practiced law for three years and then joined the editorial staff of a large newspaper.
9. The man's main objective is to write stories about ordinary people.
10. Young people driving cars must learn to respect the law.
11. Finally, exhausted from fighting, he was sent to California for a rest.
12. Besides running a candy business here, Ted Saunders has started two stores in a nearby town.
13. The company employed a group of men whose job was to look for flaws in the garments finished by weavers.
14. At that time, no school in America would admit a woman to study medicine.
15. On the second floor of the building is an auditorium seating three hundred people.

16. The house, decorated with flags and bunting, was ready for the carnival.
17. Attracted by the noise, Sue left her room and hurried into the street.
18. Annually an American mother is chosen by the Mothers' Day Foundation to set an example for other mothers in the United States.
19. The native village has bamboo houses along irregular streets, the smell of oil everywhere, derricks enveloped in a haze of smoke, and the never-ceasing throb of engines.
20. Aiming at a medium-income group, the manufacturers plan prefabricated houses to cost $10,000.
21. To build these houses is a problem in mass production.
22. Planned on a single pattern, the houses are provided with some variety through wings, porches, and garages.
23. The builders work hard to get the house under a roof in a single day, but accomplishing the task is not always possible.
24. Selling these houses often requires high-powered salesmanship, but the salesmen try to meet all objections to standardization.
25. Special lessons in selling techniques are given to all employees of the company.

7. CLAUSES

7a. Definition.

A *clause* is a group of words which has both subject and predicate. (See Section 23 for punctuation of clauses.)

7b. Kinds of clauses.

An *independent* (*main, principal*) *clause* makes a complete statement and may stand alone; that is, it makes reasonable sense if the remainder of the sentence is omitted.

> I listened to a radio program.
> Although I should have been studying last night, *I listened to a radio program.*

Sometimes there may be more than one independent clause in a sentence.

> *John studied,* but *I listened to a radio program.*

A *dependent,* or *subordinate, clause* cannot stand alone. It depends upon the rest of the sentence to complete its meaning; it is subordinate. A dependent clause usually begins with a relative pronoun (such as *who, which, that*) or a *subordinating conjunction* (such as *if, as, since, because, although, while, when, where, until*).

Dependent clauses:

> although it is raining
> when I saw him
> if I learn to drive
> who would go with us

Dependent clauses may be used as adjectives, adverbs, or nouns. According to its use as one of these parts of speech, a dependent clause is called an *adjective clause,* an *adverbial clause,* or a *noun clause.*

1. *Adjective clauses* are usually introduced by a relative pronoun (*who, which, that*) or by a subordinating conjunction (*when, where, why*). Sometimes, however, the relative pronoun is omitted. When omitted, the relative pronoun that could introduce the clause is said to be *understood.* A clause introduced by a relative pronoun is also called a *relative clause.* (See Section 23h.)

> The convertible *which you wanted* has been sold. (Adjective clause modifying *convertible*)
> I told him the reason *why I was not coming.* (Adjective clause modifying *reason*)
> The man *whom you recommended* has done an excellent job. (Adjective clause modifying *man*)
> He is a boy *I never admired.* (Adjective clause modifying *boy;* relative pronoun *whom* omitted)

EXERCISE 12

From the following sentences list the adjective clauses and tell what word each adjective clause modifies. Some sentences may contain no adjective clauses.

1. The automobile radio which I ordered on Saturday has not arrived.
2. Most of the listeners to soap operas are housewives, who take a great interest in serial stories.
3. The fire started in the hotel coffee shop, which was closed.
4. Flames were discovered coming from the elevator shaft in the rear of the hotel.
5. Today I interviewed a young woman who wishes to become a lawyer.
6. He just came back from Indiana, where he spent his Easter holiday.
7. Henry became acquainted with the soldiers who were stationed at a nearby camp.
8. Of all the good times that I had during vacation, I enjoyed our hay ride and barn dance the most.
9. In front of the stage was a pit where men stood to see the play.
10. The modern novel presents a picture of almost every aspect of human life.
11. Jane Austen wrote novels of manners, of which *Pride and Prejudice* is the most famous.
12. Mrs. Henry McClintock discussed the data which she had presented at the last meeting.
13. They must find a house in which they can live on a greatly reduced income.
14. There was a group of outlaws who endangered the lives of the people in the community.
15. A relative invited the boy to his home, where the youth found many enjoyable books.
16. This has been a period in which conversation has received little attention.
17. The road is a part of a main highway and leads eventually to the sea.

18. The time when she was to leave came quickly, and she took a boat for the country that she had never seen.
19. The motion picture advances rapidly, with little time that is not filled with mystery and intrigue.
20. The speaker urged parents to encourage a child who is skillful with his hands to become a satisfied craftsman instead of a second-rate white-collar worker.
21. The story tells of a family that inherited a house with sinister memories and of a spell which haunted all people connected with the place.
22. Dr. Downs reported briefly on the work of the jail committee which was appointed by the mayor on February 14.
23. The younger members of a Chinese family must pay every respect and show every courtesy to the older members.
24. A man who is an expert driver seldom needs to slam on his brakes, because he is alert to all driving conditions.
25. The country road where we took our driving lessons has become a broad highway filled with cars.

2. *Adverbial clauses* may express nine relationships.

Time (*when, before, while, since*):

> *When a boy drives a car,* he must learn certain rules of the road. (Clause modifies verb *must learn.*)
> He will watch pedestrians carefully *while he is driving.* (Clause modifies verb *will watch.*)

Place (*where, wherever*):

> After finding the book *where I had left it,* I hurried back to the house. (Clause modifies the gerund *finding.*)
> I am willing to go *wherever we can find good fishing.* (Clause modifies the infinitive *to go.*)

Manner (*as, as if*):

> He kicked the apple *as if it were a ball.* (Clause modifies the verb *kicked.*)

Condition (*if, so, unless, provided that*):

> *If you have the blouse in blue,* I will buy it. (Clause modifies the verb *will buy.*)

Cause (because, as, since):

> The train, three hours late *because the engine had broken down,* was crowded with troops. (Clause modifies the adjective *late.*)

Purpose (in order that, so that):

> We worked hard all day *so that the house would be pretty for the party.* (Clause modifies verb *worked.*)

Result (that, so that, so . . . that):

> The pile of driftwood mounted, *so that soon we were able to start a blazing beach fire.* (Clause modifies verb *mounted.*)
>
> We were *so* hungry *that we ate the stale crackers.* (Clause modifies adjective *hungry.*)

Degree or comparison (than, as much as, as . . . as, just as):

> John climbed farther *than you did.* (Clause modifies adverb *farther.*)

Concession (though, although):

> *Although the Socialists lost seats in the election,* they received a large popular vote. (Clause modifies verb *received.*)

EXERCISE 13

Write the adverbial clauses found in the following sentences and tell what each adverbial clause modifies. Some sentences may contain no adverbial clauses.

1. As they reached a shady spot in the road, the cars stopped.
2. Before he started on the camping trip, he bought a new sleeping bag.
3. We reached camp just as the sun was setting.
4. When school was dismissed for the summer vacation, I immediately got a job in an office.
5. If you do not want any of the colors mentioned, we shall be glad to take your order for another shade.

41

6. One day while he was taking undersea pictures off the coast of Lower California, he encountered a huge porpoise.

7. Although he has always been pleasant, I do not like him.

8. During the last few days, it has rained so hard that the wheat has been ruined.

9. I never had a bicycle until I earned the money to buy one.

10. If you wish additional information concerning my character or ability, you may get in touch with Mr. Horace Brown.

11. The mayor has been so successful that he has been elected six times.

12. We worked for ten hours in order that the job might be completed.

13. After he was graduated from high school, he entered the University of Maryland.

14. Although he did not score, he made the best play of the game.

15. Speaking with quiet confidence, the statesman urged his country to cooperate with the rest of the world.

16. In the period from 1200 to 1600, famines were common in Europe because it was difficult to transport food.

17. When the crops failed, people died because they could not get food from other countries.

18. We have wasted our resources as if we thought the supply was limitless.

19. If we are not careful in the future, we may again be without materials necessary for comfortable living.

20. In order that we may preserve some of our wildlife, the government has set aside national parks and bird refuges.

21. However, these efforts are small, so that very little is accomplished.

22. Men are more eager for money than they are for protection of the country.

23. Since we must help feed the rest of the world, we should be more careful than we have been in the past.

24. The country has been so mechanized that Americans must think also of a possible petroleum shortage.

25. When we are no longer willing to waste our resources to make money quickly, we shall have learned an important lesson.

3. *Noun clauses* perform the functions of nouns. A noun clause is usually introduced by *that, what, who, which, where, when, how, why.* It is used as:

Subject:	*Who is guilty* does not concern me.
Object of verb:	I hope *that you will be able to go to college.*
Object of preposition:	We judge a man by *what he does.*
Appositive:	He reached the conclusion *that it was wise to stay out of Newberry.* (See *Appositive* in Glossary of Grammatical Terms.)
Predicate noun:	One serious problem is *that there is no running water.* (See Section 1f, item 2.)

CAUTION: Occasionally the relative pronoun or the subordinating conjunction *that* is omitted.

> I told him I would go. (*I would go* is the dependent clause.)
>
> I told him that I would go.

EXERCISE 14

On your paper write all the noun clauses that you find in the following sentences and tell how each noun clause is used. Some sentences may contain no noun clauses.

1. I promise that I will help you.
2. I hope that I can go to the party.
3. He asked how he could get to North Avenue.
4. I do not know what I should tell Edith about the party.
5. One result of my work in literature is that I have developed better taste in reading.
6. Experiments show that music will decrease the time required for a job.
7. Success depends, in a measure, upon what characteristics we inherit from our parents.
8. The fact that it looks like rain has no effect on my decision to leave today.
9. That we shall win the pennant this year is a foregone conclusion.

10. The article says that youth should be taught to be responsible.
11. Who will inherit the money does not interest me.
12. The fact that he had learned scouting saved his life in the jungle.
13. We are judged by what we say.
14. The President's advisers feel that a cooling-off period in strike situations is highly desirable.
15. Why you like him is certainly a mystery.
16. He was born just a short distance from the place where he now lives.
17. A boy brought the message that an urgent call had come.
18. The conclusion is that international responsibility for internal affairs is cheaper than another war.
19. He said he would try to get to the party.
20. In 1798, a scientist named Malthus warned the world that the population would outgrow the food supply.
21. Nobody paid any attention to what he said.
22. Everybody thought that the abundant supply of food would last forever.
23. Now we again receive warnings that our food supply is not adequate.
24. What we can do to save our remaining resources is an important problem.
25. That we are wasting our land by bad farming methods is clear to everybody.

7c. Achievement test on clauses.

On your paper, write each dependent clause in the following sentences. Label it *noun, adjective,* or *adverb.*

1. He is one of the most skillful locksmiths that I have ever seen.
2. They moved to a farm in Iowa, where they spent fifteen years.
3. The book would be of great interest to a person who intends to become a journalist.
4. The businessmen knew what was coming.
5. Although she looked like a bright child, she found great difficulty in learning to read.

6. The truth of the matter is that he is very lazy.
7. I worked hard all morning so that I might go to the circus in the afternoon.
8. We spent the weekend at one of those charming inns where George Washington slept.
9. When a heavy load is put on the llama's back, the animal simply lies down and refuses to move.
10. She had to get up very early in the morning because she often had to cook for as many as eighteen people.
11. How the result was achieved is less important than the fact that it was achieved.
12. Training schools for nurses brought into being the efficient, immaculate nurse that we take for granted today.
13. The conditions that one found in early hospitals would not be tolerated for a minute in these days.
14. When she was nineteen, she decided to go to Europe, where she planned to study medicine.
15. Although she looked delicate and frail, she was not made of the stuff which shrinks from a disagreeable task.
16. A new plastic material which is now used in surgical dressings pleases the patients very much because it does not stick to the wound.
17. Another change which has taken place in me is that I enjoy classical music.
18. Although the field of costume design is crowded, many new opportunities are expected to develop.
19. I was thinking that we could have a fine time if we were both accepted at the same college.
20. In the eighteenth century, smallpox was so common that scarcely anyone escaped from the malady.
21. I hope that Sally will be surprised, because her mother is working very hard to make the party a success.
22. He reached the conclusion that it would be wise to go to college before going to law school.
23. Phyllis Grain found that she had married not only a spoiled husband, but all his relatives.
24. This is one of the most exciting stories I have ever read.
25. Many people who have frequent automobile accidents are emotionally childish.

8. SENTENCES

8a. Definition.

A *sentence* is a group of words expressing a complete thought.

It must have a *subject* and a *predicate*. The subject is the name of the person or thing about which the verb makes a statement. The predicate is what is said of the subject; it must contain a verb which completes an independent statement. Such a verb is called a *finite* verb. Remember: participles, infinitives, and gerunds are not finite verbs.

8b. Kinds of sentences.

Sentences may be classified according to grammatical structure as *simple, compound, complex,* or *compound-complex.*

One of the greatest problems of inexperienced writers is learning to use the type of sentence which suits the idea to be presented. They must try, also, not to use the same kind of sentence too often. (See Section 72.)

A *simple sentence* expresses *one* complete thought. The simple sentence may have a single subject or a compound subject, a single verb or a compound verb; but all of the subjects must perform the action in all of the verbs.

> Ralph plays in the school orchestra. (One subject, *Ralph;* one verb, *plays*)
> Ralph and Sally play in the school orchestra and sing in the glee club. (Compound subject, *Ralph, Sally;* compound verb, *play, sing*)

Phrases do not affect the kind of sentence. A sentence may have many phrases and still be a simple sentence.

> They sold their wedding presents in order to get enough money to travel to Europe. (One subject, *they;* one verb, *sold;* simple sentence)

A *compound sentence* contains two or more independent clauses. It is really two simple sentences combined by an appropriate connecting link. This connecting link may be a *coordinating conjunction* (*and, but, for, or nor*) preceded by a comma. It may also be a *conjunctive adverb* (*however, moreover, nevertheless, therefore, thus, then, so, yet, otherwise*) preceded by a semicolon. Or the connecting link may be omitted and a semicolon may be used. The compound sentence is useful when you wish to express two thoughts of equal value.

> Harold went to college for only a year, but his sister is a graduate of Smith. (Two complete thoughts joined by *but* and a comma)
>
> I signed an application blank from our state university; however, I am not sure of going there. (Two complete thoughts joined by *however* and a semicolon)
>
> Sue is pretty; her sister is very homely. (Two complete thoughts separated by a semicolon)

A *complex sentence* contains one independent clause and one or more dependent clauses.

The sign of the complex sentence is the dependent or subordinate clause. (See Section 7b.) A complex sentence is used when one of the two ideas to be expressed depends on the other to complete its meaning.

      (dependent)   (independent)
When she was a little girl, she was very much interested in horses.

      (independent)   (dependent)
A broken sign hung on the gate, which was partly open.

      (dependent)   (independent)
When he was ready to make the trip, he had to wait on

            (dependent)
Long Island because there was bad weather.

47

Careless writers sometimes make the mistake of using a subordinate clause as a sentence.

> Although my violin is broken.
> When the bell rang.

Clearly, these are not complete ideas. They are a part of a complex sentence.

The *compound-complex sentence* has characteristics of both the compound and the complex sentence. It has two independent clauses, as the compound sentence has, and at least one dependent clause, as the complex sentence has.

> (dependent)   (independent)
> When the legislature passed a sales tax, many people
>
> (independent)
> complained; but the Governor agreed to use much of the money for improved schools.

Knowing how to use these three kinds of sentences will help you to give variety, interest, and good form to your writing.

Sentences are also classified according to *meaning* and *purpose*.

A *declarative sentence* states a fact or makes an assertion.

> The plane has four engines.

An *interrogative sentence* asks a question.

> Do detective movies teach crime?

An *imperative sentence* expresses an entreaty or command.

> Please come as soon as possible.
> Forward, march.

An *exclamatory sentence* expresses strong feeling.

> Oh, if he were only here!

EXERCISE 15

On your paper tell whether each of the following sentences is simple, compound, complex, or compound-complex and give the reason for your decision. For example, sentence 1 is complex because it contains one independent clause and one dependent clause.

1. He belongs to a club which is composed of famous men in sports.
2. After hearing his first concert, the child wanted to study music.
3. From this point one can look across forty miles of the Great Plains on a clear day.
4. The Bastille was a strongly fortified structure used as a place of confinement for those who displeased the king or his court.
5. For six years his hobby has been chemistry, and he has even constructed his own laboratory.
6. By the end of the year, the building job was begun; but it did not progress rapidly.
7. The American soldier escaped with the assistance of a German youth, to whom he promised a large sum of money.
8. The author is very fond of moralizing and displays this interest in the book.
9. I have a very bad temper, and after an argument I am inclined to sulk and be sarcastic.
10. Your party sounds like great fun, but I'm afraid that I shall not be able to come.
11. The tickets are to be printed with a perforated section that can be torn off.
12. The old part of the city, which dates back to the Middle Ages, was built on the top of a hill; the modern city occupies the lower slopes and part of the plain.
13. The dance, accompanied by native drums, was a series of stamping steps in rhythmic patterns.
14. We drove up the mountain, shuddering at each narrow turn of the road.
15. Everyone said that it would be hard to get reservations at a hotel, but we didn't have any trouble.

16. Walking into his father's office, he calmly announced his intention to go to sea.
17. The National Institute of Health has planned a fight against the common cold.
18. After the graduation, she and her family went to Florida; they wanted to visit her brother, who is in business there.
19. Because of the confidential nature of his work, my cousin could not say much about his activities; but he did tell me that he expected to accompany the Ambassador on an important diplomatic mission.
20. The death of Pericles symbolized the end of the greatest period in Athenian history.
21. Time after time, the person who discovers a fire rushes off in a frenzy of excitement, leaving the door wide open.
22. The people had vigor enough to make an attempt to free themselves.
23. He was graduated from Notre Dame with a law degree, but immediately went into journalism.
24. The luncheon-club diet of chicken patties and canned green peas was too much for him; so he gave up his job as club reporter.
25. The highlight of the day's events will be seven races for speedboats and cruisers, for which the club will offer trophies worth one hundred dollars each.

EXERCISE 16

Follow the directions in Exercise 15.

1. The captain ordered his men to prepare to move back to the rest zone at sundown.
2. When my brother landed in Newfoundland, he was astonished to find the meadows filled with daisies and buttercups.
3. The resort was crowded with people, and the band kept up a ceaseless accompaniment to the noise.
4. The native children approached the Americans and held out their hands.
5. When Joan decided to accompany her aunt to Ocean City, she looked forward to a good time; but she was not counting on the really superb time that she did have.

6. The book is written with a subtle suggestion of satire, as if the author were trying to criticize in a mild manner the stuffiness of the period.
7. The client was ushered into the room to await an interview with the famous lawyer.
8. People who recognize the danger of potential epidemics recommend a world network of public health stations.
9. He is continually in trouble and has now spent a large part of his inheritance.
10. Although his composition was rejected for the Prix de Rome contest, this only served to make Ravel more popular; for everyone attributed the rejection to petty jealousies, intrigues, and politics.

EXERCISE 17

Use your knowledge of clauses and kinds of sentences to revise the following paragraph. On your paper, rewrite the paragraph. Remember that short, choppy, simple sentences do not make an interesting style; but when simple sentences are combined to make compound or complex sentences, you must be careful not to put too many ideas together. The ideas which appear in one sentence must be closely related, and the conjunctions used to join them must show what the relationship is. (See Sections 59, 60, and 61.)

Conservation of our resources is an important problem for the United States. Some farmers and timberland owners waste their land. They do not know how to use it wisely. Farmers plant the same crops year after year. The soil loses its richness. Wise farmers help their land. They plant special crops. These crops restore nitrogen to the soil. Range lands are another problem. They are often damaged by overgrazing. Then the animals do not get enough to eat. The owner must buy commercial feed. The overgrazed land is eroded by the wind. The topsoil is blown away. A third problem is insects. They eat the crops. They are hard to control. DDT could be used to kill some of them. DDT might kill valuable insects. Some of the valuable insects pollinate fruit trees.

EXERCISE 18

Follow the directions in Exercise 17.

Many high schools today are teaching boys and girls to be safe drivers. The instructors say a person must be an adult emotionally to drive well. Your little brother shows off for company. He is a baby. He wants to be seen. He hasn't learned to think. A person who thinks is growing up. He acts on reason. He does not act as a result of his feelings. A show-off in an automobile is a baby emotionally. He exceeds the speed limit. He takes ten people in a five-passenger car. He drives an old car. His car has bad brakes. He impatiently dashes past other cars on their right. He is like your little brother. He is showing off for a crowd. His showing off is more dangerous than that of your little brother. He may kill people. Little brother merely annoys people. Some boys are eighteen years old. They are still babies emotionally. They should not be permitted to drive cars.

9. GLOSSARY OF GRAMMATICAL TERMS

In a discussion of grammar and writing, many terms are used. Sometimes there are several terms which have the same meaning. If you have trouble with a term, consult the following pages.

ABSOLUTE EXPRESSION. An absolute expression is composed of a noun or pronoun and a participle. An absolute expression modifies no single word in the sentence; rather, it modifies the sentence as a whole or adds details to the whole statement.

> *The tire being flat,* we decided to pump it up.
> *Two hours having elapsed,* we again set out on our journey.
> The little boat hugged the shore, *its sails flapping in the wind.*

ACTIVE VOICE. A verb is in the active voice when its subject performs the action.

ADJECTIVE. A word that modifies a noun or pronoun. It may be either descriptive or limiting. (See Section 4b for examples.)

ADVERB. A word that modifies a verb, an adjective, or another adverb. It tells *how, when, where, why,* or *to what extent.* (See Section 4d.)

ALLITERATION. The use of several words beginning with the same sound. It is usually not a good device to use in prose writing. At present it is used chiefly in advertising.

> Make Money with Munder
> Sales Service Simplified
> Tasty, Tempting, Tantalizing

ANTECEDENT. The substantive (noun or pronoun) to which a pronoun refers.

APPOSITIVE. A substantive added to another substantive to identify it or explain it. The appositive signifies the same thing as the substantive it explains and is said to be in apposition with it.

> One important product, *rubber,* this country had to import. (*Rubber* is in apposition with *product.*)
> More hardy than wheat are these grains—*rye, oats,* and *barley.* (*Rye, oats,* and *barley* are in apposition with *grains.*)

An appositive agrees in number and case with the substantive to which it refers and is set off by commas or dashes unless it is so closely related to the other substantive that the two words seem part of the same expression.

> My friend *Andrew* built a sailboat. (The appositive *Andrew* is closely related to the noun to which it refers.)

AUXILIARY. A verb used to "help" another verb in the formation of tense and voice forms. *Be, can, do, have, may, must, ought, shall, will* are examples.

> He *has* gone away for a visit.
> You *will* please turn out the light.
> We *should have been* working with the stevedores on the dock.

CASE. The change of form that a noun or pronoun undergoes to indicate its relationship to other words in a sentence. There are three cases in English—nominative, possessive, and objective.

CLAUSE. A group of words which has a subject and a predicate. (See Section 7.)

COMPARISON. The change in the form of an adjective or adverb to indicate greater or smaller degrees of quantity, quality, or manner. The three degrees of comparison are positive, comparative, and superlative. (See Section 18e.)

small	smaller	smallest
little	less	least
wisely	more wisely	most wisely
quickly	less quickly	least quickly

The comparative degree is used to show relationships between two persons, objects, or ideas.

> Fred is *taller* than I.
> This box is *less attractive* than the other one.

The superlative degree is used to show relationships among three or more:

> Allan is the *tallest* one in his family.
> This sewing kit is the *most attractive* of the six available.

COMPLEMENT. A word or expression used to complete the idea indicated by another word or expression. A predicate complement may be a substantive or an adjective that completes the meaning of the copulative verb. It is also called the subjective complement, or predicate noun or adjective.

> Mr. Crawford is a *salesman*. (Substantive used as predicate complement)
> Jane is very *gay*. (Adjective used as predicate complement)

An objective complement is a noun or adjective that completes the meaning by telling something about the direct object. It is also called predicate objective.

> They called the dog *Jerry*. (Noun)
> We dyed the dress *blue*. (Adjective)

COMPLEX SENTENCE. A sentence containing one independent clause and one or more dependent clauses.

COMPOUND SENTENCE. A sentence containing two or more independent clauses.

COMPOUND-COMPLEX SENTENCE. A sentence containing at least two independent clauses and one dependent clause.

CONJUGATION. A list or table giving all the forms of a verb to show mood, tense, number, person, and voice. (See pages 18 to 23.)

CONJUNCTION. A linking word used to connect words or groups of words in a sentence. Coordinating conjunctions join words or groups of words of equal rank; subordinating conjunctions join dependent clauses to main clauses. (See Section 5d.)

CONJUNCTIVE ADVERB. An adverb used as a connective. It serves as a link between independent clauses or sentences. Some conjunctive adverbs are *however, moreover, nevertheless, consequently, therefore, thus, then, so, yet, otherwise*.

DECLENSION. A list or table giving the different forms of a substantive to indicate case, number, person, and gender. When changes in a substantive are thus shown, the word is said to be *declined*. (*I, my, me*)

DIRECT ADDRESS. A noun or pronoun in direct address is one that names or refers to the person spoken to.

> *John,* where are you?
> When we finish rolling the court, *Fred,* we'll still have time for two sets of tennis.

ELLIPSIS. The omission of a word or words necessary to the grammatical completeness of a clause or sentence. In the sentences below, the words in parentheses might be omitted in speaking and writing; without such words the sentences are called *elliptical.*

> Some of the patriots carried guns, others (carried) swords, still others (carried) clubs and sticks.
> While (we were) drifting downstream, we grounded on a sand bar.
> He was eighteen years of age; his brother, (was) twelve (years of age).

EXPLETIVE. An expletive is a word used chiefly to introduce an idea. *It* and *there* are commonly used as expletives.

> *It* was Alice whom we saw.
> *It* is a truism that men love freedom.
> *There* are four hundred people present.

FINITE VERB. A verb that is capable of making a complete and independent assertion. Finite verbs express tense.

> He *walked* to school.
> I *have finished* the job.

Verbals are not finite verbs.

GENDER. The classification of substantives according to sex. There are four genders: masculine, feminine, neuter, and common (either masculine or feminine): *boy, girl, it, individual.* Nearly all traces of grammatical gender have disappeared from modern English nouns.

GERUND. A verbal noun. A gerund has the same form as the present or perfect participle. (See Section 3g.)

> *Speeding* is the most common cause of automobile accidents.

GRAMMAR. The science which deals with words and their relationships to each other. *Rhetoric* deals with the art of expressive speech and writing, with the laws of clear, effective writing; *grammar* is concerned with the features of a language and with speech and writing according to various standards of usage.

IDIOM (idiomatic usage). The manner of expression characteristic of a language. (See Section 43.)

IMPERSONAL CONSTRUCTION. The use of the pronoun *it* in a sentence like this:

> *It* is raining.

INFINITIVE. The form of the verb that is usually preceded by *to* (*to go, to see*).

INFLECTION. A change in the form of a word.

INTERJECTION. An exclamatory word not grammatically related to the other words in a sentence.

> *Oh,* that's what you meant.
> *Heavens!* You have broken the vase.

INTRANSITIVE VERB. A verb used in such a way that it does not require a direct object. (See Section 3b and *Transitive Verb* in this glossary.)

> The poor man *trembled* as he *spoke.*

INVERTED ORDER. The arrangement of the words in a sentence so that the whole or a part of the verb precedes the subject. Inverted order is always used in questions and in sentences that start with a word expressing or implying a negative idea. It is sometimes used in sentences that start with other adverbial modifiers.

> What do you think?
> Seldom have I heard such a fine voice.
> Down from the hills came the guerrilla bands.

LINKING VERB. Verbs such as *appear, seem, smell* are linking (or copulative) verbs, which express the relation between subject and complement.

> The other man *was* his nephew.
> That *seems* inexpensive.

MOOD. The change of form that a verb undergoes to show the state of mind or manner in which a statement is made. There are three moods in English: indicative, imperative, and subjunctive.

MODIFIER. A word that describes or limits another word. (See Section 4.)

NONRESTRICTIVE MODIFIER. A phrase or clause that furnishes additional information about the word modified but does not change or restrict its meaning. (See Section 23h.)

NOUN. A word that names something—a person, a place, a thing, an idea, or a quality.

NUMBER. The change in the form of a substantive or verb to show whether one or more than one are indicated. (See Section 39d.)

> *Singular:* man, boy, lady, knife, he, is
> *Plural:* men, boys, ladies, knives, they, are

OBJECT. The substantive following a preposition, or the word, phrase, or clause indicating the thing or person affected by a transitive verb or verbal.

> He is in the *room*.
> The carpenters built a *house*.
> He said *that he would go*.

A *compound object* consists of two or more substantives used as object of a verb, a verbal, or a preposition.

> The Duanes built *the house and the barn*. (Compound object of verb)

PARALLELISM. The use of the same structural form for ideas of equal value. (See Section 68.)

PARENTHETICAL MATERIAL. Any expression that interrupts a thought and is not necessary for the grammatical completeness of the sentence in which it occurs. (See Sections 23e and 33.)

PARTICIPLE. A word which has the function of both verb and adjective. The present participle always ends in *-ing* (*speaking, going*). The past participle is the third principal part of the verb. The perfect participle consists of *having* or *having been* plus the past participle (*having spoken, having been driven*). (See Section 3g.)

PASSIVE VOICE. (See *Voice* in this glossary.)

PERSON. The quality of a substantive or verb that shows whether it relates to the speaker (first person), the person spoken to (second person), or another person or thing spoken about (third person). Nouns do not show person by changes in form. Finite verbs undergo a few changes in form to show agreement with their subjects in person.

> I read, you read, he reads

PHRASE. A group of related words which does not contain a subject and predicate and which functions as a single part of speech. Phrases are classified according to use as noun, adjective, and adverbial phrases, and according to form as prepositional, participial, gerund, infinitive, and verb phrases.

PREDICATE. The part of a sentence which makes an assertion about the subject. A *simple predicate* is the verb (or verb phrase) alone; a *complete predicate* consists of the verb with any modifier, object, or other completing word which it may have.

> Mr. Tyler drove the ball nearly two hundred yards. (*Drove* is the simple predicate; *drove the ball nearly two hundred yards* is the complete predicate.)

PREPOSITION. A linking word showing the relationship of a noun or pronoun to some other word in the sentence. (See Section 5a–b.)

PRINCIPAL PARTS. The three parts of a verb (present infinitive, past tense, and past participle) from which all other forms and uses of verbs (tense, mood, tone, voice) can be expressed. (See Sections 3f and 15.)

PRONOUN. A word used in place of a noun. (See Section 2.)

RESTRICTIVE MODIFIER. A phrase or clause that restricts or changes the meaning of the word modified. Restrictive adjective modifiers limit the meaning of the word modified to one particular person, place, or thing; they answer the question "which?" (See Section 23h.)

SENTENCE. A group of words expressing completeness of meaning. (See Section 8.)

SUBJECT OF A SENTENCE. A substantive naming the person or thing about which an assertion is made. A *simple subject* is this substantive alone. A *complete subject* is a simple subject together with its modifiers. A *compound subject* consists of two or more substantives used as subjects of the same verb.

> The green *house* is for sale. (Simple)
> *The green house* is for sale. (Complete)
> *The green house and two acres of land* are for sale. (Compound)

SUBSTANTIVE. An inclusive term for a noun and all noun-equivalents. Pronouns, gerunds, noun phrases, and noun clauses are noun-equivalents. The following italicized expressions are used as substantives:

> The *dog* was three years old.
> *They* are coming tomorrow.
> *From New Orleans to Chicago* is a long distance.
> Did you know *that he was here today?*

SYNTAX. Construction; the grammatical relations between words in sentences.

TENSE. The time of the action or of the state of being expressed by the verb. (See Section 3f.)

TRANSITIVE VERB. A verb that requires a direct object to complete its meaning.

> The player *hit* the ball.
> My brother *studied* the assignment. (See Section 3b.)

VERB. A word expressing action or state of being. (See Section 3a–f.)

VERB PHRASE. A verb together with an auxiliary: *shall take, shall have taken, will have been taken.* Distinguish between a verb phrase and a verbal. (See Section 3c.)

VERBAL. A verb form used as a noun, an adjective, or an adverb. (See Section 3g.)

VOICE. The change in the form of a verb to indicate whether the subject is the performer of the action (active voice) or is acted upon (passive voice).

Usage

Since language is a means of communication, it is important to choose the words and the grammatical forms that will carry to your listener or reader exactly the idea and emotional tone that you wish to present. Sometimes a stiff, formal language makes you seem unfriendly. On the other hand, the use of casual English in an interview for a job may give the impression that you are not serious about the work. In an informal conversation with friends, "*Who* are you going with?" is acceptable in many groups, but in a research paper, the appropriate language would be more formal. Hence, a sentence would read: "The men *whom* the Puritans sent to discuss matters with the Governor were. . . ." Language not only carries thought, but it also causes an emotional reaction. The words that you choose, the grammar that is employed in what you say, even the fashion in which your thoughts are put together affect the hearer or reader. For this reason, it is important for you to know several levels of language and be able to choose the appropriate one for each occasion. Of course, as you seek the right expressions, you will avoid those which are illiterate or vulgar.

In addition to being modified by the broad distinction between formal and informal language, many rules concerning word usage and grammatical structure are modified by considerations of time, place, and situation. Language is constantly developing. In some of your reading, you will find expressions which were correct and clear in another period but which are now outmoded. When Rosalind and Celia in Shakespeare's *As You Like It* enter the Forest of Arden, Celia says, "I cannot go no further." Today this double negative would not be used. Sometimes words appropriate in a certain section of the country may carry little meaning or sound ridiculous elsewhere. Although "tote a poke" is quite meaningful in parts of the South, few New Yorkers or San Franciscans understand the expression at all. Finally, every area of study develops its own vocabulary which may mean little to people who have not studied in the field. Technical expressions, for example, may be understood only by a limited audience experienced in industry. It is important, then, if you want your language to be correct and clear, that you use expressions which are in *current, national,* and *reputable* use.

When you choose a word or a grammatical form, be careful about your source of information. It is not enough to say that you have heard the expression used by public speakers or seen it in a reputable magazine. Advertisements, newspapers, magazines, broadcasts, or speeches may use incorrect forms of language. Several examples in print, several misuses by famous speakers or writers, several mispronunciations in a national radio broadcast do not make a word, a grammatical structure, or a pronunciation generally acceptable.

Although good dictionaries and handbooks occasionally disagree about the labels to be applied to certain expressions, they are still your best guides if you wish to learn the *standard* English of *today.* Your handbook shows you the formal structure necessary for serious or dignified writing and speaking and indicates a colloquial or informal variation when there is an accepted one. A reliable, up-to-date dictionary records and labels words and expressions. Remember that the mere entry in a dictionary does not guarantee that a word is in current reputable use. Your dictionary helps you to judge the acceptability of a word by the absence or presence of a "restrictive label" like *archaic, obsolete, illiterate, slang.* If the word has no restrictive label, it may be regarded as appropriate formal English. A word labeled "colloquial" is generally acceptable in informal but not formal speech and writing.

Although much more use is made of informal than of formal English, there are occasions when educated people who have responsible positions must write business reports, articles for company journals, minutes of club meetings, and even articles for publication. To such people, a knowledge of formal English is imperative. The drill in this section includes experience with both formal and informal English because in daily living there is a need for both.

Do you say:

> "I didn't sleep good last night."
> "Jenny met Terry and I at the station."
> "One of the pages in my book are tore."
> "I was almost froze when I came home from the game."

All these sentences are incorrect. Take the diagnostic tests in Section 10 to see where you make mistakes. Then study the pages that will help you to correct your errors.

10. DIAGNOSTIC TESTS IN USAGE

10a. Diagnostic Test I (Sections 11–14).

Here is a chance for you to check your usage habits. All the sentences in the diagnostic test appeared in the compositions of students. Most of the sentences contain at least one error. On your paper, write the number of each sentence. Beside the number, write the correction or corrections and the reason for each correction. Do not rewrite the whole sentence unless it is impossible for you to show in a few words what the correction should be. If the sentence is correct, write C beside its number. When your paper has been checked and you know which principles are giving you trouble, turn to the sections that will explain your problem.

Examples:
1. Every one of the students have bought their class rings.
2. At one place which we visited were the famous Seminole Indian Village, the parrot farm, and the monkey jungle.

Correction:
1. has   1. subject and verb agreement
   his   pronoun and antecedent agreement
2. C

1. The mailing lists contains the names of all the customers whom we think will be interested in the sale.
2. Every man, woman, and child were lost.
3. Lack of materials and modern equipment discourages nurses and doctors in many hospitals.
4. The bed of the river was shallow at some places and deep at others, which would make swimming dangerous.
5. It's hard to keep in touch with girls who you know at camp but who you do not see all winter.
6. A businessman must be careful not to offend anyone, particularly if their complaint is justified.
7. When people know little about gardening, there's many mistakes made in planting.
8. The phenomena is observed in almost every country in the world.
9. I asked Father to let John and I go to New York.
10. The tunnels, Holland and Lincoln, extends under the Hudson River and connects Manhattan with New Jersey.
11. Roads are being constantly improved so that the chances of accidents due to a faulty highway are comparatively few.
12. Before one makes up their mind, they should consider all the factors involved.
13. I shall be very glad to come to your party because they are always such fun.
14. While the line was being arranged for the processional, I was wondering who I'd walk with.

15. I think it was her who broke my locker.

16. Why don't you and Marcia meet Dad and I in New York and go to Maine with us?

17. Each of us are expected to pay for the materials that we broke.

18. A discussion between you and I will have no results because neither of us are willing to compromise.

19. Either our buyer or one of our executives is going to London to obtain English tweeds for our fall stock.

20. Every one of the businesses were taxed heavily on their excess profits.

21. With my grandmother lives my two cousins, who are four years older than myself.

22. The chief topic of discussion are the problems caused by the overcrowding of the colleges.

23. Jerry, whom I noticed was quite good-looking, was coming toward us.

24. If I had been her, I should not have approved of Bob going to Europe.

25. On the bed is the skirt and the dress which is to be packed for the trip.

26. After some deliberation, the Board of Directors reorganized the business completely, which seemed to Ralph and I a good idea.

27. Please fill in the enclosed application blank and return same by Monday, June 10.

28. Employment problems is helped by modern machinery because people who buy them need somebody to work them.

29. It says in this book that it will increase sales if you improve the English of the salesmen.

30. Either you or I are sure to be the new president of the club.

31. The stenographer who you see in my office was employed by Mr. Shriver and he in my absence.

32. The inability of an individual to face the problems of marriage sometimes cause them to put off marriage until they are middle-aged.

33. I thought that Father was going to let Sally and I go to the movies tonight, which would have pleased us very much.

34. Measles are often serious. Me and my brother had them when we were children, and they nearly killed us.

35. In the backfield at least one of our men have the experience and speed that is necessary to carry the pigskin over the goal line.

36. Most Americans read the newspapers, and it is therefore an excellent means of spreading propaganda.

37. The stewards of labor unions can write a report against the bosses which he feels is not following the contract.

38. The number of people who succeed in that line of work are very small.

39. The following description, together with the drawings, present a master plan for the development of an airport.

40. The direction of the runways have been decided after a consideration of the prevailing winds.

41. The gardener whom I hoped would do the work was sick today.

42. I'm sure it wasn't him whom you saw at the dance.

43. Mrs. Bingham is the only one of the women who have reached their quota.

44. Between you and I there will always be a friendly feeling.

45. The company thinks that whoever you choose as a representative will do a good job.

46. This is the boy whom you said you thought might do well in the job.

47. Freedom of the press and of public assembly do not necessarily mean that equal opportunity for the expression of all opinions are available.

48. Please give these books to whoever calls for them.

49. You have been here longer than her and ought to be more competent.

50. Are you one of those people who listens to a special radio program every day?

10b. Diagnostic Test II (Sections 15–19).

Follow the directions for Diagnostic Test I.

1. If the automobile test for a driver's license was a bit more difficult, teen-agers would be more better prepared to drive.

2. It's surprising how bravely some people can seem in real danger.

3. Really, if I were you, I'd get out of here in a hurry.

4. Most of the actors in the picture were unknown, but they performed like they were seasoned stars.
5. I could have shook her when she told that story.
6. Not paying much attention to where we were at, we missed our turn in the road.
7. When the boy attempted to pay his fare, he found that he left his wallet at home.
8. I suppose we all talk foolish when we are excited.
9. We should send for the doctor; Sue has felt badly all day.
10. Leaving Oklahoma City at eight in the morning, we arrived in Tulsa at noon.
11. Come quick; Mary has broke the window.
12. When I first seen you, I thought you were Dick.
13. Booth always does his work neater than Sarah.
14. Helen hasn't wore her new suit yet.
15. Moving to Delaware, we built a large stone house.
16. I am living on this same street for thirty years.
17. I wish I was able to work as rapid as you do.
18. This batch of candy doesn't taste as well as the last.
19. If he had not had the title searched, he would have lost his deposit on the house.
20. Get your *Home Magazine* by taking advantage of one of the most liberal offers they have ever made.
21. Graduating from high school in 1938, he took a job as an apprentice in a machine shop.
22. Finishing his work, he put his book away and turned on the radio.
23. The party would of been gayer if you had been there.
24. One of the first lessons taught the salesmen is how to write legible.
25. I sure was glad that you got the engine started as quick as you did.
26. The J.V. team is doing pretty good this year.
27. There must be a new trial because this one has not been handled legal.
28. After laying asleep for an hour, Toby jumped up and began to bark.
29. The radio was so low that we had to set right beside it in order to hear it.

30. John has a tremendous appetite; last night he must have eat six ears of corn.

31. That dark face powder makes you look like you have jaundice.

32. I cannot study without you turn off the radio.

33. Suddenly, this here dark-complexioned man strikes the boy in the face.

34. The manager explained to Mrs. Pentz that he already wrote her two letters.

35. Since my twelfth birthday I was able to save an average of ten dollars a month.

36. At the end of the year he planned an escape. After all the details were thought out careful, he breaks out of prison and flees to the jungle.

37. He discovered that she was a girl from his own city, who eloped years before with a guardsman in her father's regiment.

38. On the way home, we sang all the songs that we learned at camp.

39. Many times I have wished that I was able to visit the famous cities of Europe.

40. You should of saw Jake's face when the teacher sent him to the principal.

41. I intended to have gone fishing with my brothers.

42. I move that Robert sings a solo.

43. Beginning to build the house five months ago, we finally completed the job today.

44. When she returned from her vacation, I asked Edith what she did in Puerto Rico.

45. I should have liked to have gone to the play, but I sure was too sick to move.

46. I could have swore it was Hal I seen in the drugstore.

47. The cobra is the most deadliest snake in the world.

48. To compete with the railroads, airlines have lowered their rates considerable.

49. The television commentator said that the ship had sank at 9:45.

50. Byron swum the Hellespont to prove that Leander could have swam it, as the legend said he had.

11. SUBJECT AND VERB AGREEMENT

11a. A verb must agree with its subject in person and number.

A *verb* is frequently an action word like *run, go, sing.* (See Section 3.) It may, however, assert a condition or a state. The verbs *be* and *seem* assert a condition or a state. Because action words stand out clearly in a sentence, it is easy to begin the grammatical analysis of a sentence by finding the verb. Then look for the person or thing about which the verb makes a statement. When you find it, you have the subject. A subject is always either a noun, a word or group of words used as a noun, or a pronoun.

> Our *club* (subject) *gives* (verb) three dances each year.

In the preceding sentence, the subject and the verb are easy to find, but in some sentences the subject comes after the verb or is separated from the verb by other words. Before you try to make the verb agree with the subject, be sure that you have the real subject. Then decide whether it is singular or plural. Errors in verb forms are frequently made in the use of the present tense. In this tense, verbs in the third person singular end in *-s*; verbs in the third person plural do not usually end in *-s*. (If you are uncertain about the *person* and *number*, consult Sections 1c and 2b.) Remember that used as subjects, *I* and *we* are the forms for the first person; *you,* for the second person; *he, she, it,* and *they,* for the third person.

> The first dance helps us to pay for Christmas baskets for the poor. (The noun *dance* is third person singular. The verb *helps* is also third person singular.)
>
> The boys invite the pledges to the first football game. (*Boys* is third person plural. The verb *invite* is also third person plural.)
>
> I invite a different girl for each dance. (*I* is first person singular. The verb *invite* is also first person singular.)

70

NOTE: *Don't* means *do not*. It is used correctly with plural subjects and with *I* and *you* as singular subjects. Be careful not to use it with a third person singular subject like *he, the chair, the flower, Henry*. With such subjects use *doesn't*.

Wrong: He *don't* play tennis.
Right: He *doesn't* play tennis.
      The car *doesn't* need washing.
      Jack *doesn't* seem to make friends very easily.

11b. *There* and *here* are not subjects.

After *there* and *here* we usually find the verb first and then the subject.

Wrong: There *is* dances every Friday night at the community center.
Right: There *are* dances every Friday night at the community center.
Wrong: There *comes* the boys on the football team.
Right: There *come* the boys on the football team.
Wrong: Here *is* the tickets for the dance.
Right: Here *are* the tickets for the dance.

11c. A prepositional phrase that follows the subject does not affect the number of the verb.

Phrases such as *of the men, in the various groups, to my sisters* are called prepositional phrases. The important words in a prepositional phrase are a preposition (*to, for, from, with, by, in, between, of, near* are some common ones) and a noun or pronoun which is the object of the preposition. Do not make the verb agree with the object of a preposition.

Wrong: Personnel managers from the Stark Company *interviews* boys in our senior class every year. (The word *Company* is the object of the preposition *from. Managers* is the subject.)
Right: Personnel managers from the Stark Company *interview* boys in our Senior class every year.

71

Wrong: One of the boys *preside* at each meeting.

Right: One of the boys *presides* at each meeting.

Wrong: The owners of the campus store *jokes* with all the students.

Right: The owners of the campus store *joke* with all the students.

EXERCISE 1

The following sentences illustrate Sections 11a–c. Many of them contain errors in subject and verb agreement. On your paper write the number of the sentence with which you are working. Then write the subject of each incorrect verb in the sentence and the *correct* form of the verb. If the sentence contains no errors, write the number of the sentence and put C after it. Some of the sentences may have two errors.

1. Since there is over 65 million motor vehicles in the country, the problem of parking space is a tremendous one.
2. A review of our catalogues show that our new manager has improved the stock.
3. Recently the houses on our street were reassessed.
4. Smog and smoke damages to merchandise and buildings reaches a figure of five billion dollars a year.
5. Near the community center is three large department stores.
6. The lack of police protection at dangerous intersections result in accidents.
7. One of the boxes of books are missing.
8. Misunderstandings between students and players were the cause of the fighting.
9. One of our problems with night football are the behavior of the spectators who do not go to our school.
10. Eleventh-hour attempts by a local businessman to keep the team in the city has failed.
11. In these days one out of every five married women work.
12. Suddenly out of the woods comes two hunters with a powerful dog.
13. If Irving don't drive carefully, he will be arrested.

14. Movies have a much larger screen than televisions and, as a result, is easier on the eyes.
15. From the center of the city to the three neighboring towns runs a magnificent expressway.
16. One of my friends thinks that speeding in an automobile shows how grown up he is.
17. Sue ~~don't~~ think we should go to the movies tonight. *doesn* &
18. The pleasant working conditions in modern offices helps to make stenography attractive.
19. News of world events are very important to us, as is the daily happenings in our own city.
20. Large sums of money is awarded to some of the contestants on television shows.

11d. Singular pronouns require singular verbs.

These pronouns are singular: *each, everyone, everybody, anyone, anybody, someone, somebody, no one, nobody, one, many a one, another, anything, either, neither.*

Wrong: Each of the boys *play* some game well.
Right: Each of the boys *plays* some game well.
Wrong: Everyone in the United States *were* concerned about the problem of slavery.
Right: Everyone in the United States *was* concerned about the problem of slavery.
Wrong: Neither of the Senators *show* any uncertainty.
Right: Neither of the Senators *shows* any uncertainty.

NOTE: The pronoun *none* may be used with either a singular or a plural verb, according to the sense of the sentence. Like *some* and *any*, it requires a singular verb when it refers to a quantity and a plural verb when it refers to a number.

> Is there any milk? No, there *is* none.
> Are there any eggs? No, there *are* none.

In informal or colloquial speech, the plural verb is often used with *everyone* or *each* if these words are followed by

73

a phrase that seems to make their meaning plural, but careful speakers and writers follow the rule of agreement and use a singular verb with *everyone* or *each*.

Notice that *everyone* is written as one word. The expression *every one* (two words) means "each separate one." It is usually followed by an *of* phrase:

> *Everyone* is expected to come.
> *Every one* of us is required to bring a book.

11e. Words joined to a subject by *with, in addition to, as well as,* and *including* do not affect the verb.

> Our allies, as well as the enemy, *were* suffering.
> My whole equipment, including fishing rods, tackle, and knapsack, *was* lost on the trip.

11f. A collective noun usually takes a singular verb. If, however, the individuals of the group are considered, the verb is plural.

> The team *fights* for victory.
> Our class *sings* very well.
> The family *disagree* on the question of my dates.

11g. For nouns plural in form but singular in meaning, use a singular verb.

> Measles *is* sometimes serious.
> Mathematics *is* a difficult subject.

NOTE:

1. Although authorities differ in their opinions about the number of some of these nouns, the following are usually considered to be singular: *physics, economics, news, politics, ethics, mumps.*

2. Subjects plural in form, which describe a quantity or number, require a singular verb when the subject is regarded as a unit.

> Ten miles *is* too far to walk.
> **Two** from five *leaves* three.

3. A title of a book, play, film, painting, musical composition, or other such work is singular.

> *Pride and Prejudice* is my favorite novel.
> *The Frogs* is a play by Aristophanes.

11h. Fractions and words such as *all*, *none*, *some* will be singular if bulk or a total number or amount is implied, and plural if individuals are considered.

> Three-fourths of the roof *is* painted.
> Three-fourths of the members *are* here.
> All the girls *were* eager to have a beach party.
> All the food *was* gone.

11i. When the word *number* is used in the sense of "many" it is plural; when it refers to an arithmetical number, it is singular.

> A number of people *are* waiting outside.
> A number *is* printed on every ticket.
> The number of people who have subscribed *is* surprisingly small.

NOTE: When the word *number* is preceded by the article *a*, it is usually plural. When it is preceded by *the*, it usually means a unit and is singular.

11j. Be careful of the plurals of foreign nouns. Some nouns retain the plural forms of the foreign language from which they have been taken. Though they may look like singular nouns, they are plural and require plural verbs. (See Section 39d, item 9.)

Singular	*Plural*
phenomenon	phenomena
genus	genera
synopsis	synopses
alumnus	alumni

Synopses of two stories *were* submitted.
The alumni *were* in favor of building the stadium.

75

NOTE: *Data* is correctly used as a plural, though many now use it as a singular.

11k. A verb does not agree with a predicate noun.

The main thing to see *is* the beautiful gardens.

EXERCISE 2

Most of the following sentences contain errors in subject and verb agreement. Write on your paper the number of each sentence and the necessary correction or corrections. If the sentence is correct, write C opposite the number of that sentence.

1. Every one of the players on the team have good grades.
2. Mumps have caused a great deal of absence at the Liberty Heights School.
3. The number of people present for the lecture by Professor Toynbee was far larger than we expected.
4. Two-thirds of the group want a party right away.
5. A number of states has motion-picture censorship.
6. No decision can be made in the Security Council of the United Nations unless each of the five members approve.
7. Each of the hunters are permitted by the state game laws to shoot four ducks.
8. Neither of the plans presented by the committee members seem practical.
9. Don't you think that economics are harder than any other subject we study?
10. Every time that the hero comes on the stage, the audience sits breathless.
11. Each of our customers receive a monthly statement.
12. Two-thirds of our traffic regulations has been changed since we employed a new traffic director.
13. Neither of these points have anything to do with the problem.
14. Were either of Mozart's parents musically gifted?
15. Some of the girls in our class comes to school with their hair in curlers.
16. Every one of the plans seem practical, but we prefer the most economical one.

17. If you decide that either of the plans are acceptable, we are ready to sign the contract.
18. The number of orders that have been received this year are larger than ever before.
19. All of the sugar has been sold.
20. Three-fourths of the boys in our class intend to enter college.

11l. A compound subject joined by *and* requires a plural verb.

> Mathematics and chemistry *are* my most difficult subjects.
> Television and radio *have* revolutionized social habits.
> On the landing field *stand* a B-36 and a small helicopter.

NOTE:

1. When the two subjects form a single thought, a singular verb is used.

> Bread and peanut butter *is* my favorite snack.
> My comrade and friend *was* with me.

2. If two or more subjects are joined by *and* and preceded by *every*, the verb is singular.

> Every boy and girl in the auditorium *applauds* the principal when he appears on the stage.

11m. If two subjects are joined by or, *either* . . . or, *neither* . . . nor, the verb agrees with the subject nearer it.

> Neither the student president nor his friends *want* to see Jack elected.
> Either new athletic fields or a swimming pool *is* to be provided in the spring.
> Either they or I *am* at fault.

11n. If one subject is used affirmatively and the other negatively, the verb agrees with the subject that is used affirmatively.

> He, not I, *is* responsible.

EXERCISE 3

Many of the sentences in the following exercise have incorrect verb forms. Some of the sentences are correct. On your paper, write the number of the sentence on which you are working. Then write the subject of each incorrect verb and the correct form of that verb. If the sentence is correct, write C after the number of the sentence. Read carefully. Some of the sentences may have two errors.

Example:

    1. Careful workmanship combined with the best materials make our product the finest on the market.   1. workmanship makes

1. Cooking, cleaning, and tending to the baby leaves my sister little time for reading.
2. My cousin always said that my mother's hot rolls and chocolate cake was the best food he had ever tasted.
3. Neither the Governor nor his press secretary were available for comment.
4. An adolescent, as well as his parents, have ideas about growing up.
5. Speeding, overcrowding, and reckless driving causes many automobile accidents.
6. Nearly every great artist, musician, and writer has personal idiosyncrasies.
7. My parents have ideas about the family car with which neither my brother nor I agrees.
8. If neither the president's plan nor the negotiators' offers are accepted, the government may have to take over the plant.
9. Parents worry about early marriages because neither a boy nor a girl are mature at eighteen.
10. Either nose drops or an inhaler helps to relieve a cold.
11. Homes in this neighborhood, including those just across the street, is assessed at fifteen thousand dollars.
12. He is a national figure whose every word and action carry weight.
13. The efficient manner in which you handle daily routine and

the excellent showing that you made in the sales campaign shows that you are capable.

14. The express company gave a receipt acknowledging that the glider and its mattress was received in perfect condition.

15. Some people say that television appearances of election personalities and the threat of communism has caused a large turnout of voters.

16. At the time of your visit to our factory, the success of performance tests and the durability of the product was pointed out.

17. Love and comfort, as well as attention to special needs, is important to old people.

18. Facts, not emotionalism, are needed to solve this case.

11o. A relative pronoun (*who, which, that*) may be singular or plural depending upon the word to which the pronoun refers.

The only way to tell whether a relative pronoun is singular or plural is to examine the part of the sentence that precedes it and decide which word in the sentence the pronoun refers to. This word is called the antecedent of the pronoun. If the antecedent is singular, the pronoun will be singular, and the verb that goes with it must be singular.

> Our team is the only one of the bowling groups which *has* kept rigidly to the schedule. (*Which* is the subject of the relative clause. It refers to *one* and is therefore singular.)
>
> Monieka is one of the six mission stations that *are* supported by our church. (*That* is the subject of the relative clause. It refers to *stations* and is plural.)
>
> Jerry is the only one of the golfers who *has* maintained a consistently good score. (*Who* refers to *one*.)

EXERCISE 4

In the following sentences you will find errors in verb forms in both independent clauses and relative clauses. On your paper, write the number of the sentence on which you are working. Then write the subject of each incorrect verb and the *corrected* form of the verb.

Example: A number of the animals that is brought to Dickey-
ville by the circus is used in the parade through the
town.

      1. that are—number are

1. The recent hurricane caused floods which has ruined our stock.
2. Note these pieces, which we are certain represents the best buy for the money.
3. Since publishing our catalogue, we have made two changes in our circular saw which we think improves its perform- ance.
4. The same dependable parts and reliable workmanship that has made our product outstanding goes into our latest model.
5. Jack is one of the few boys who have made both the team and the honor roll.
6. As we read the papers, we cannot help thinking that the number of problems which confronts us today is tremen- dous.
7. If every one of us who are a citizen vote, we are sure to have better government.
8. Recently one of the major-league teams which have been with one city for a long time wished to make a change.
9. Two of our athletes who have been stars all season was selected to be on the all-American team.
10. Henry is the only one of the committee members who have proved really responsible.

EXERCISE 5

Write on your paper the number of each sentence. Be- side it write the subject of each incorrect verb and the correct form of that verb. Explain why you have made the correction. If no correction is necessary in the sentence, write C beside the sentence number.

1. Helen and her sister comes to school late every day.
2. Near the parking lot was several large department stores.
3. There is two or three boys trying out for each position on the team.
4. Recently there has been investigations of the injury caused to the brain by boxing.
5. Everyone in my classes are subscribing to the school paper.
6. The changes in the design of the house was made at the suggestion of the builder.
7. That don't make any difference.
8. Each of our toasters are carefully tested before being shipped.
9. The interior of the early theaters were not very attractive.
10. The revenue that is collected at the games support the teams.
11. Neither the professor nor his wife were at home.
12. The decision of the three officials were announced before noon.
13. During the last few years there has been many arguments over the place of sports in college life.
14. The cake's too sweet; it don't agree with me at all.
15. The brown puppy, as well as the black and the white ones, were sold to some tourists yesterday.
16. Mary's keen interest in life and people makes her parties a delightful experience.
17. Each of the class representatives have pledged support to the student president.
18. Coleridge's ideas of how a perfect society should be managed was very impractical.
19. Either Jane or I are going to suffer as a result of this.
20. The captain, together with all the boys on the team, were introduced from the platform.
21. Each of the amateur actors were beginning to feel stage fright.
22. The development of children depend in large measure on family training.
23. The mother, as well as the children, have been quarantined.
24. Neither the man nor his lawyers are ready to agree to that proposal.

EXERCISE 6

Follow the directions in Exercise 5.

1. The results obtained by our recent experiments with penicillin has been very gratifying.
2. First the sisters of the bride appears; then follows her aunt and uncle.
3. If one of these plans seem faulty, please discuss the issue with me.
4. Either our representatives or one of the officers of the company is going to Europe to settle the question.
5. *Gulliver's Travels* have been popular reading for many years.
6. The president of the company, in addition to several of the officers, were present at the meeting.
7. In the office of the president was a large mahogany desk, a swivel chair, and a few small straight chairs.
8. There's several questions that I want to ask you.
9. As the time of the celebrations approaches, each of the natives prepares for the dance.
10. If there is any complaints about the merchandise, please write us at once.
11. The letter, together with the advertising materials, was forwarded to him yesterday.
12. Everyone in the school have an opportunity to make some money on the side.
13. One of the men who has made great progress in the building of prefabricated houses is Foster Gunnison.
14. His development of porches, fireplaces, and garages provide variation of the standard prefabricated house.
15. The public thought that Leeuwenhoek and other scientists who believed his theory was crazy.
16. George must leave college for a while; his mother and father needs him on the farm.
17. There was no running water and no sanitary arrangements anywhere in the city.
18. Many people find that the comfort and security which comes with owning a home makes the cost seem reasonable.
19. This country, together with Canada and some of the Latin-

American countries, have the material resources for complete prosperity.

20. The structure of our politics and of our political traditions make any attempt at tariff reform very difficult.

EXERCISE 7

Follow the directions in Exercise 5.

1. Common sense, as well as economics, tell us that what a country sells to other countries must be balanced by what it buys from abroad.
2. The duties of the chief clerk includes authorization of overtime, arrangements for pay drafts, and handling the safe.
3. The material, mounted on large panels, explains the principles of advertising; it shows how good design, coloring, and lettering attracts the customer.
4. We are pleased to say that all the necessary equipment, including clamps to pack the typewriter, has been shipped to you.
5. The synopses were prepared by the same writers who wrote the stories.
6. In Fielding's work we often find little humorous touches that show the subtlety of his thinking.
7. In the laboratory, the technician is able to perform various tests which, when combined with the proper clinical examination, results in a quick and accurate diagnosis.
8. The language, the approach, and the form of the sales letter is different for the various types of sales expected.
9. Mrs. Hammond sent word that she, together with her children, were staying at the lake for another week.
10. A painting of the artist, as well as one of Borda and his priest brother, hangs on the wall at the rear of the church.
11. So far as finding the people who had been lost in the landslides were concerned, we had given up hope.
12. In 1910 there was constructed at Holtwood, Pennsylvania, a dam and a hydroelectric plant.
13. From the bottom of the Susquehanna River come deposits of fine particles of anthracite coal.

14. The full effect of the program will not be seen until a number of years has elapsed.
15. We live in one of those three-story houses that fronts on Moreland Drive and dates back almost a hundred years to Civil War days.
16. Unified control of the three armed services are maintained under a single Secretary of Defense.
17. The rubber blades of the fan not only act as a safety factor but adds to the quiet operation.
18. Mr. Eckels was one of the many people who was approached on the idea of buying a prefabricated house.
19. The rapid production methods and the mass construction used in building the prefabricated house keeps the price low.
20. Of all the women present, Mrs. Rutherford is the one who have done the best work.

12. PRONOUN AND ANTECEDENT AGREEMENT

12a. A pronoun should agree with its antecedent in gender, number, and person.

Our writing would be very dull if we repeated nouns again and again. Consequently, we use a pronoun instead of repeating the noun. But the meaning of the pronoun will not be clear unless it has the same gender, number, and person as the noun for which it stands. This noun is called the *antecedent*. (See Sections 1 and 2.)

> Orlon is an important synthetic material. It is said to be better than nylon. (*It* refers to *orlon,* the antecedent. Both *orlon* and *it* are neuter gender, singular number, third person.)

Pronouns do not necessarily agree with their antecedents in case.

12b. The words *each, either, neither, somebody, anybody, everybody,* and *nobody* are singular, and in

formal English a pronoun referring to any one of these
words should be singular (*he, his, him, she, her, it*).

In colloquial English the rule stated above has been relaxed somewhat. People who wish their language to sound
informal and casual sometimes use *their* to refer to *everybody;* but this form should not appear in formal writing.

Colloquial: Everybody took *their* heavy coat to camp.
  Formal: Everybody took *his* heavy coat to camp.
Colloquial: Each of the boxers was accompanied by *their* man-
         ager.
  Formal: Each of the boxers was accompanied by *his* man-
         ager.

**12c. A collective noun used as an antecedent takes a
singular pronoun if the group is thought of as a unit
and a plural pronoun if it is thought of in terms of its
individual members.**

> The audience was generous with *its* applause.
> The audience shifted restlessly in *their* seats.

NOTE: Once you decide whether a collective noun is to be
singular or plural, stick to your decision. If you use it as
the subject with a singular verb, make sure that all pronouns referring to it are singular; and if you use it with
a plural verb, make sure that all pronouns are plural.

Wrong: The family *was* discussing *their* difficulties.
  Right: The family *was* discussing *its* difficulties.
  Right: The family *were* discussing *their* difficulties.

**12d. A noun or an indefinite pronoun used as an
antecedent takes a pronoun in the third person.**

All nouns and indefinite pronouns are in the third person
except when they are used in direct address or in apposition with a pronoun of the first or second person. Aside
from these two uses, all nouns and indefinite pronouns
require a third-person pronoun. A phrase such as *of us,*

of you coming between the pronoun and its antecedent does not affect the person of the pronoun.

Wrong: If a man wants to achieve success, *you* must work for it.
 Right: If a man wants to achieve success, *he* must work for it.
Wrong: Neither of you has finished *your* lunch.
 Right: Neither of you has finished *his* lunch.

12e. When the antecedent is a singular noun of common gender, the masculine pronoun should be used unless it is clear that the noun refers to a girl or a woman.

Right: Each member of the dramatic club indicated *his* choice of a play for the annual production.
Right: Each member of the girls' glee club was asked to name *her* favorite Christmas carol.

12f. A pronoun agrees with the nearer of two antecedents joined by *or* or *nor*.

He loves everything or everybody *who* is connected with his work.
In this cool room, neither the gardenia nor the roses will lose *their* freshness.

12g. *Who* refers to persons, *which* refers to things, and *that* refers to persons or things.

The man *who* told me the story is your doctor.
The book *which* you lent me contains some very exciting stories.
The woman flier *that* took her plane on a round-the-world trip has been awarded a medal.

12h. *What* should not be used to refer to an expressed antecedent.

Wrong: The book *what* you sent me as a graduation present arrived yesterday.
 Right: The book *that* you sent me arrived yesterday.
 Right: I heard *what* you said.

EXERCISE 8

Most of the sentences in the following exercise contain pronouns which do not agree with their antecedents. Write on your paper the number of each sentence. Then write the correct form of any pronoun that is wrong or colloquial. In some instances a verb will also need to be changed. Beside the correct form of the pronoun (and verb, if necessary), in parentheses, write the antecedent of the pronoun you have corrected. If a sentence is correct, write C beside the sentence number.

1. Every student must be in their place at 8:45.
2. Has everyone passed in their paper?
3. The human mind has not caught up with the speed of their own inventions.
4. Everybody who goes to our camp will enjoy their summer vacation.
5. We offer a money-back guarantee to each of our customers when he buys this new paint.
6. Everyone in our family has their own household chores.
7. A business executive gets better work from their employees if they use a little kindness.
8. If next year's senior class has their way, the ruling will be changed.
9. There are many kinds of people who make pleasant guests.
10. When a company changes their system abruptly, they may cease to make money.
11. The football team has won every game they've played this year.
12. Can any state be really independent? The answer is they can't.
13. Each of us in the nurses' home had our personal problems.
14. If a boy is trusted and allowed to stay out late, you have a sense of responsibility.
15. The theater in Shakespeare's day was not so elaborate as they are today.
16. A student understands the national government better if they have a chance to participate in student government.

17. When a girl is interviewed for a job, you should wear neat clothes and avoid gaudy jewelry.
18. A person should consider carefully the background of every speaker they hear.
19. The diesel engine weighs much more than the gasoline engine, and therefore they are not used in automobiles.
20. The police department gives their support to driver education in the schools.
21. A person gets bored watching some television programs because you can tell just what will happen next.
22. Not one of my neighbors has made any improvements in their home.
23. An impudent boy sometimes sets an example for their younger brothers and sisters, and they want to imitate him.
24. When I have absolutely no time, every mother in the neighborhood asks me to baby-sit for them.
25. In our two-party political system, each party has their own platform on which their candidates run.

EXERCISE 9

Follow the directions in Exercise 8.

1. The car leaving the school grounds had boxes of books piled so high in the back that it blocked the back window.
2. During the next year each of us will meet situations that will subject us to unfamiliar pressures.
3. In the early days, people thought that man had no business to poke their noses into scientific affairs.
4. If singers can find appealing words and dramatize their songs, he will be successful even if he is unknown.
5. There were many boys besides me, and everyone was trying to get settled in their barracks.
6. The girls received as favors small keys of silver with the emblem of the club engraved on it.
7. By voting for the man of your choice, the average American has a good chance to improve his government.
8. The company voted to pay a bonus of one hundred dollars to every employee, regardless of their salary.

9. If a person works all the time and never plays, by the time they are in the prime of life they are good for nothing.

10. The great ocean waves rolled on, continually washing the sand with its salty spray.

11. Sometimes he turns on the porch light or the hall light and forgets to turn them off.

12. Any student who is interested should sign this sheet and indicate beside their name what courses they wish to take.

13. In addition to qualifications for the job, one must also consider conditions under which you are willing to work.

14. To continue education under the scholarship plan, one must have made satisfactory grades in all his courses.

15. Bacon introduced a new scientific approach to learning which would help everyone if they used it.

16. Many songs that were popular in Grandpa's day have fascinating rhythms that make it still appealing today.

17. Although I think that parties and dances are all right to a certain extent, I believe it is harmful when it is carried to excess.

18. When a person rides through our state, particularly in the industrial section, you see mostly ugly factory towns.

19. Anyone, no matter where they live, what school they go to, or what their religion may be, is welcome at the recreation center.

20. A number of producers will piously pass resolutions proclaiming their interest in free enterprise and then work hard to keep high tariff protection for ~~its~~ _their_ own product~~s~~.

EXERCISE 10

The following sentences contain errors in subject and verb agreement and pronoun and antecedent agreement. Write on your paper the number of each sentence. Then write the necessary corrections of verbs and pronouns. Write also an explanation of why you have made the changes. If no correction is necessary, write C beside the sentence number.

1. Have either of the boys finished their homework?

2. Each of the political machines are trying to put into office their chosen candidates.
3. Each of the boys have already done what they were told to do.
4. When a child returns to school, one of the things in which he is interested at once is the sports.
5. Only one who has slept on such a bed know how hard they are.
6. Have either of you written your minutes?
7. Everyone is enthusiastic over the coming election and are working to promote their candidate.
8. The attendance and spirit at the games was never so great as it is now.
9. As time went on, every village and city was obliged to surrender some of its privileges to the state.
10. Every one of the students are required to pay their dues before May 1.
11. All members of the drama club are urged to attend the meeting; and anyone else interested in taking part in the play are invited to leave their name with the secretary.
12. After their appointment each of the men are given a course in business writing.
13. The maker of the prefabricated house says that the appearance of the houses don't matter so long as they sell.
14. If any one of the employees is late, he must report at once to the supervisor.
15. Each of us, at one time or another, have expressed ourselves on the subject.
16. Only after the improvement association got their members to protest were they able to block the new zoning law.
17. Neither trouble nor expense were spared in giving each of the boys the education they wanted.
18. Not only has the value of real estate gone up, but the cost of labor and materials have risen tremendously.
19. Each teacher will report factors which in their opinion interferes with successful work in the classroom.
20. Studies of the problem seems to show that women who have had some work experience before marriage makes better wives because she knows the value of money.

13. REFERENCE OF PRONOUNS

13a. The antecedent to which a pronoun refers should be made clear.

Sometimes the thought of a sentence is clear to the writer because he has the antecedent of his pronoun in his mind. The reader, however, cannot be expected to be a mind reader. He must be able to put his finger on the word to which the pronoun is meant to refer. Otherwise, he may misunderstand what he has read. Writing which is not perfectly clear to the reader is of little value. (See Sections 2 and 12.)

13b. The antecedent of a pronoun should be expressed, not merely implied.

> Mrs. Seton told me the other day that she has taken a cottage at the seashore. *He* doesn't want to go, but she thinks the salt air will do him good.

Who is this *he?* No man has been mentioned. The antecedent is in the mind of the speaker. Changing *he* to *her husband* clears up the difficulty.

Vague: I intend to be a lawyer because *it* is interesting work. (There is no antecedent for *it*.)

Improved: Because law is interesting work, I intend to be a lawyer.

Vague: I like to travel in Switzerland. *They* are always pleasant to visitors.

Improved: I like to travel in Switzerland. The Swiss are always pleasant to visitors.

13c. Avoid the indefinite use of *it* and *they*.

Indefinite: In this magazine article, it shows that war is horrible.

Better: This article shows that war is horrible.

Indefinite: They have good roads in Delaware.

Better: Delaware has good roads.

Vague: They say that Argentina is a wealthy nation.
Better: It is said that Argentina is a wealthy nation.

NOTE: *It* is sometimes used impersonally to introduce an idea. In these cases no antecedent is necessary.

> It will be clear tomorrow.
> It was Lincoln who made the "House Divided" speech.

It is necessary, it is true, it is certain, it is likely, it is imperative are correct.

13d. Do not use impersonal *it* and the pronoun *it* in the same sentence.

Vague: We can send the refrigerator today, or we can keep it in the factory for a few days if *it* is necessary.
Better: We can send the refrigerator today, or we can keep *it* for a few days.

NOTE: In informal English, *it* sometimes refers to an idea instead of a single antecedent.

Informal: The boys were nervous, but they tried not to show it.
Formal: The boys were nervous, but they tried not to show their uneasiness.

13e. In formal writing avoid the use of *you* to mean people in general.

In colloquial or informal speech, expressions such as "You can see how important money is" or "Dancing makes you graceful" are permissible. Formal English requires the use of *one* or *anyone* in these statements.

> Anyone can see how important money is.
> Dancing makes one graceful.

13f. In formal writing avoid the use of *which, this, that* to refer to a whole clause.

Informal: The company has had our entire building air-conditioned, *which* makes working in hot weather very comfortable.

Informal: We have rearranged the entire file, *which* will make it easier to find things quickly.

In these sentences a whole statement is the antecedent of *which.* Such sentences can be improved in three ways.

1. Ahead of the word *which,* use *an act, a fact, a situation, a habit,* or *a procedure.* The noun preceding *which* will be its antecedent.

Formal: The company has had our entire building air-conditioned, a fact which makes working in hot weather comfortable.

Formal: We have rearranged the entire file, a procedure which will make it easier to find things quickly.

2. Recast the sentence, omitting the word *which.*

Improved: Because our building has been air-conditioned, we can work in comfort during hot weather.

Improved: Our new arrangement of the material in the file makes it possible for us to find things quickly.

3. Recast the sentence to provide an antecedent for the pronoun.

Improved: The company has installed air-conditioning, which makes working in hot weather very comfortable.

Improved: We have rearranged the entire file according to a new system which will make it easier to find things quickly.

NOTE: If the meaning is clear and the sentence would become awkward or stilted if it were corrected, the informal construction may be used.

13g. Avoid ambiguous reference to either of two nouns of the same gender.

Vague: Howard told Arthur that he had been elected. (Because *he* could mean either *Howard* or *Arthur,* the sentence is not clear. It could be improved by using *latter* or *former,* or by giving the exact words which Arthur said.)

Improved: Howard told Arthur that the latter had been elected.
Improved: Howard said to Arthur, "You have been elected."

Ambiguous reference can also be corrected by using a synonym for the antecedent or by changing the construction of the sentence.

> *Vague:* He took the books from the boxes and placed *them* on the floor. (The books or the boxes?)
> *Improved:* He took the books from the boxes and placed the volumes on the floor. (*Volumes* used as synonym for *books*.)
> *Improved:* He removed the books and placed the boxes on the floor. (Construction changed.)

13h. Avoid the use of *same* in place of a personal pronoun.

Wrong: Please fill out the blank and return same to us.
Right: Please fill out the blank and return it to us.

EXERCISE 11

The following sentences contain pronouns which do not refer clearly to a stated antecedent. Write on your paper the number of each sentence. Beside each number write the pronoun which has no clear antecedent. Then write your correction. If no correction is necessary, write C beside the sentence number.

1. In our new public museum they plan to feature modern art.
2. When George met Frank, he was going to the football game.
3. Mark has been unable to do his homework. May he have the weekend to complete same?
4. If the students were given control of the study hall, it would give the teachers more time.
5. The teacher in charge of the corrective gymnasium work tries to correct your posture.
6. Our organization was established to help people when they most need it.

7. I think that when an agitator is arrested, it makes him look like a martyr.

8. Edith told Sarah that she was sure to be elected president of the class.

9. When I visited Denver, I saw they have the kind of climate I like.

10. The old stable was torn down and a new theater built in its place, which improved the appearance of the neighborhood tremendously.

11. The colonel is famous for telling humorous stories, and he gets it by remembering everything he reads.

12. Sam's father was a bookseller, and he read many books in his shop.

13. My uncle Charles sent us some books which we enjoyed very much.

14. If the toaster won't work, we can't have it for lunch.

15. The lamp is very durable, which accounts for the slight loss in breakage.

16. The building is poorly designed, which causes space to be wasted.

17. In this book it says that Jackson was a great general who never made a tactical mistake.

18. We had hot baths at the hotel, which for me was enough to make Dijon a landmark.

19. It has not been twenty years since the first house was built in this town, and it now contains more than 10,000 inhabitants.

20. The little girl asked her mother how old she was.

21. When the immigrants arrived, the ground in the West was not broken, and they could not do it with the few tools available.

22. Please fill in the blanks on the enclosed form and return it to us so that we can begin serving you without delay.

23. When Jack asked Mr. Henderson for a job, he didn't know what to say.

24. We are trying to rid the city's streets of rubbish in order to make it more attractive.

25. Unless payment is made in ten days' time, we must turn it over to our attorneys.

EXERCISE 12

Follow the directions in Exercise 11.

1. He was a businessman, and all his life he tried to make his son like it too.
2. Sign the card and return same to us at once.
3. My work in the senior year is very hard, but it is worth it to know that in June I shall graduate.
4. The poet Markham must have believed strongly in God because in his poems it mentions God frequently.
5. Our policy is to give service to members first, but to give it also to nonmembers when it is possible.
6. Have your eyes examined; if you don't need them, the oculist will tell you.
7. When Mrs. Ennis told the story to my mother, she was not sure of what had happened.
8. Richard's uncle has lived many years in Tahiti, has learned to speak the language, and likes them because they are so colorful.
9. Sandy examined her notebook with bitterness, took out her paper, and tore it to pieces.
10. When you walk through the halls, you can choose the person with whom you want to talk, which was not possible in our old school.
11. In some mystery stories on television, criminals seem to be encouraged to continue their crimes, which is another reason why these programs should not be presented.
12. The grounds around the stadium are very small, and they have to walk miles from where they park.
13. We are conducting a traffic safety campaign to make it safe for school children.
14. Diggs and Haworth want the goods shipped by June 10, but we cannot do it.
15. If you are dissatisfied with the merchandise, return same at once.
16. We bought a new house, which was something we had planned to do for years.
17. Ed comes so early every morning that it makes the other employees seem lazy when they arrive at nine o'clock.

18. The staff officer's associates are supposed to be well educated, honest, and industrious, but it does not always work out that way.
19. Competing gas companies are selling a large volume of gasoline, which indicates a large potential volume of sales for our service station if we build in this section.
20. In some suburbs, civic consciousness has always been high, and the sections show it.

14. CASE OF PRONOUNS

There are three cases for nouns and pronouns: nominative, possessive, and objective. Because nouns do not change their form to show the nominative or objective case, the rules given here are important chiefly for pronouns. (Review Sections 1 and 2.)

14a. The subject of a verb is in the nominative case. The nominative forms are I, you, he, she, it, we, you, they.

> Sarah and *I* have joined a club at school.
> When Ned comes, *he* and *I* are going to build a boat.
> *We* boys can do a better job without the girls.

14b. The pronoun following any part of the verb be (am, is, are, was, were, been, be) and referring to the subject is in the nominative case. It is called a *predicate nominative*. (See Section 1f.)

> The officers of the class are Carol, Alfred, and *I*.
> It was *he*.
> Do you think it could have been *she* who sang on the radio last night?

NOTE: Colloquial English permits "It's me" or "It was us," but these forms should not appear in formal writing.

14c. The object of a verb or a preposition is in the objective case: me, you, him, her, it, us, them. (See Section 1g.)

97

Watch particularly the second member of a compound object. Both members must be in the same case.

> Mother met *Hilda* and *me* at the station. (*Hilda* and *me* are objects of the verb *met*.)
>
> Mrs. Fulton had invited *her* and *me* to a party. (*Her* and *me* are objects of the verb *invited*.)
>
> Between *Jack* and *him* there has always been a real friendship. (*Jack* and *him* are objects of the preposition *between*.)
>
> All the plans for the senior dance were made by *Fred* and *her*. (*Fred* and *her* are objects of the preposition *by*.)

NOTE: Common prepositions are *to, for, from, with, by, between, near, beside, like,* and *but* when it means *except*. (See Section 5a–b.)

> Everybody came to the party but *him*. (Except *him*)

14d. The indirect object is in the objective case.

The indirect object is the object of *to* or *for* understood.

> Uncle Fred sent *me* a bracelet from India. (*Bracelet* is the direct object; *me* is the object of *to* understood.)
>
> Save *me* a piece of that cake. (*Me* is the object of *for* understood; *piece* is the direct object.)

14e. The compound pronouns myself, herself, himself, itself, themselves, yourself, yourselves, ourselves are used as intensive or reflexive pronouns.

Colloquial: Dave, Marian, and myself went on a picnic.
   Formal: Dave, Marian, and I went on a picnic.
Colloquial: The party was for Dave, Marian, and myself.
   Formal: The party was for Dave, Marian, and me.
     Right: I'll make the sandwiches myself. (Intensive, for emphasis)
     Right: The cat washed herself. (Reflexive. *Herself* refers to *cat*.)

NOTE: There are no words *hisself* or *theirselves*. The words to be used are *himself* and *themselves*.

14f. In an elliptical clause introduced by *than* or *as*, the pronoun will be nominative or objective according to the structure of the complete clause. An elliptical clause is one with a word or more missing; the omitted word or words are understood from other parts of the sentence. Supplying the missing part will help you to decide the case of the pronoun that will be used in the clause.

My brother is taller than *I*. (*Than* introduces the elliptical clause *I am*. *I* is therefore the subject of the verb *am* understood.)

Dick is just as good an actor as *she*. (*She* is subject of *is* understood.)

Nobody cares more about your success than *he*. (*He* is subject of *does* understood.)

I shall send him rather than *her*. (*Her* is object of *send* understood.)

This television program amused you much more than *me*. (*Me* is object of *amused* understood.)

CAUTION: *Them* is a pronoun and must not be used as an adjective.

Wrong: *Them* prizefighters put on a good show last night.
Right: *Those* prizefighters put on a good show last night.
Right: I enjoyed the good show put on by *them* last night.

EXERCISE 13

This exercise contains errors in the use of personal pronouns as subjects, predicate nominatives, and objects of verbs or prepositions. Write on your paper the number of each sentence and beside it write the necessary corrections. Write also an explanation of why you have made each correction. If no correction is necessary in a sentence, write C beside the sentence number.

1. Eileen and her are both class officers.
2. Why did you run when the principal called Frank and I?
3. Her and her husband were prisoners in China during the war.
4. I saw she and her mother in New York last week.
5. On October 30, a couple of girls and myself are going to give a Halloween party.
6. My father used to send groceries from his store to she and her sister.
7. Maud married a man who was as poor as her.
8. I think you will enjoy the book as much as me.
9. Ten football players, including Dave and I, will do a mock ballet at the pep assembly.
10. Dickens wrote for social reforms because when he was a boy, his entire family except he was put in a debtors' prison.
11. It was him who rang the bell.
12. Did your class have the same test as us?
13. The guide who was employed by my brother and I did an excellent job of showing us the city.
14. Everybody but Ted and I had left the locker room when the coach and him arrived.
15. Whenever something goes wrong in our house, it's me who get the blame.
16. Although my brother is much more careless than me, my parents seldom punish either he or my sister.
17. Ben, Howard, and me are planning a trip to the Grand Canyon this summer.
18. Fred's parents have promised to give he and his brother the trip for a graduation present.
19. Although I study more than them, I never seem to get the marks that him and Nick get.
20. What are you going to give Sally and her for Christmas?
21. It must have been him who told you that Mark and me were at the dance.
22. If I were her, I should not invite Jack and he to the party after the way they treated we girls last week.
23. Give Harold and I an opportunity to explain what happened, and I am sure that you will excuse we boys for being late.

24. I can't explain just what the trouble was because I was not with Judith and she when the accident occurred.
25. There has never been any competition between you and I because you are clearly a better student than me.

EXERCISE 14

Follow the directions in Exercise 13.

1. One evening when Rosalie and me were home alone, we heard a strange noise.
2. We trembled for several minutes, but finally it was me who had the courage to investigate.
3. Sue, Phyllis, and myself were waiting for Zelda to come.
4. If anybody is late, it's always her.
5. Do not forget that the other side wants to win as much as us.
6. Last year Dad and me went to Florida for a month, and a friend of his invited he and I for a trip to the Everglades.
7. You cannot imagine what fun him and I had on that trip.
8. We have great admiration for she and her mother.
9. Our singing often brought my brother and I, before the student assembly.
10. The striking similarity between my new roommate and me ensures our getting along well.
11. Thank you for the marvelous time you gave Jim and I last weekend.
12. Larry and her were going to get married in June, but they decided to wait until Ted and me could plan a double wedding.
13. Two girls and another boy and me plan to go to the freshman dance.
14. Since my father has always traveled a great deal, my mother had the responsibility of bringing up my brother and I.
15. The glee club is the main interest of my roommate and I, but my brother won't join we boys in singing.
16. I think it was he who planned the reorganization of the business.
17. On Sunday my parents came to camp and took Allen and I for a country picnic.

18. There was no mail for Pete and I because we had failed to write to Susan.
19. My little brother always wants to go fishing with Dad and I, but we give he and Jerry a quarter and send them for ice cream.
20. If I were him, I'd appoint a new representative to meet customers like them.

14g. The subject of an infinitive is in the objective case.

The infinitive is the form of the verb that usually has *to* in front of it—*to study, to write, to sing.* (See Section 3g.)

> I wanted *him* to run for class president. (The whole group of words is the object of *wanted; him* is the subject of *to run.*)
>
> Doris expected *me* to wait for her.
>
> Jack asked *me* to go to the dance.
>
> The music teacher let *Gordon and me* sing a duet. (A verb used after *let* is an infinitive although it is used without *to. Gordon and me* are subjects of the infinitive *to sing.*)
>
> My father let *Jimmy and him* wash our car.

14h. The object of an infinitive or of any other verbal is in the objective case.

> The librarian wants to see *us.* (*Us* is the object of the infinitive *to see.*)
>
> Finding *you* here is a surprise. (*You* is the object of the gerund *finding.*)
>
> Having recognized *him* instantly, I hurried across the street. (*Him* is the object of the participle *having recognized.*)

14i. The complement of the infinitive *to be* is in the objective case when the subject of the infinitive is expressed.

This construction may cause some trouble because it requires an objective case after a linking verb. It may help to remember that the objective case will occur after *to be* only when two conditions prevail: (1) The sentence must use the infinitive form of the verb *to be;* (2) the subject of that infinitive must be expressed. Notice the difference in these examples:

> I should like to be *he*. (Here, *to be* is the infinitive, but it has no subject. As a result, the pronoun is in the nominative case.)
> I thought you were *he*. (Here, the form *were* is not an infinitive.)
> I took you to be *him*. (In this sentence, *you* is the subject of the infinitive *to be*. The subject of an infinitive is in the objective case. Then the objective case must follow.)
> Aunt Jane took Lucy to be *me*.

The construction is an awkward one and can be avoided.

14j. An appositive must be in the same case as the word with which it is in apposition. (See Appositive in Glossary of Grammatical Terms.)

> The principal wants us all—Albert, Roland, and me—to run for the office. (*Albert, Roland, me,* are in apposition with *us* and must be in the same case.)

14k. The possessive case of a noun or pronoun should be used before a gerund. (See Section 3g.)

> I do not approve of *his* playing football. (*Playing* is the gerund. It is the object of the preposition *of*.)
> My teachers were not sure of *my* winning the prize. (*Winning* is the gerund.)
> *His* singing could be improved. (*Singing* is the gerund.)

NOTE: Be sure to distinguish between gerund and participle. The latter is used as an adjective and does not have a possessive case preceding it.

> We saw him standing on the corner. (*Standing* is a participle modifying *him*.)

EXERCISE 15

This exercise contains errors in the use of the three cases of personal pronouns. Write on your paper the number of each sentence and beside it write the necessary corrections. Also write an explanation of why you have made each correction. If no correction is necessary in a sentence, write C beside the sentence number.

1. Yesterday my sister took pictures of my family and myself.
2. The guard would not permit Alfred and he to enter the building.
3. The Sherwoods want Judy and I to go with them to Atlantic City.
4. The manager gave Miss Short and I complete directions for the job.
5. Nancy and me want to thank you for a wonderful weekend at the shore.
6. I asked Dad to let Joseph and I go to Salt Lake City for a visit.
7. Yesterday Mrs. Howard invited Sue and I to come to a party.
8. I am not sure of him going to college.
9. What is the use of me studying Latin?
10. Because they had not completed their work, Mr. Harris would not permit Allen and he to leave for the game.
11. Do you remember me telling you about our new house?
12. If I were sure of him finding a job in Detroit, I'd sell the house now, when I have a good offer.
13. Our drama coach wants Hazel and I to be in the Christmas assembly.
14. For some reason I took Stuart to be him.
15. At Christmas time the company gave Ed and she a bonus.
16. It was hard for Beatrice and me to believe Dick's story.
17. Let Irving and I work on the experiment because him and myself have done some similar experiments in our laboratory.
18. Arrangements had been made for Mr. Green and I to attend the conference, but a special order prevented me going.
19. We all expected the election returns to show the winner to be he.

20. I hope the winner will be he.
21. The Starr, Davidson Company wishes the manager and I to take a course in business letter writing.
22. Please reserve for Mr. Carson and I a room on the seventh floor.
23. The firm is going to send Roger and I to the plant in Pittsburgh, but there is no indication of us being transferred permanently.
24. Although we had worked hard for a year, our employer did not wish to give Steve and I an increase in salary.
25. How did the court prove it to be he that had helped the enemy?

141. *Who* is in the nominative case and is used as the subject of a verb or as predicate nominative. (See Section 14b.)

Who and *whom* are used as relative pronouns that introduce relative clauses and as interrogative pronouns. They follow exactly the same rules as personal pronouns.

> The sportsmen *who* sailed the boat over the rapids were Californians. (*Who* is the subject of the verb *sailed.*)
> Our neighbor, *who* has just built a ranch-type house, spent years in planning the structure. (*Who* is the subject of the verb *has built.*)

The next two sentences illustrate a problem that often arises with the choice of *who* or *whom*. The words in the subordinate clause are not in natural order—that is, subject first and verb next. Arranging the clause in natural order will help you to see the relationship of the relative pronoun to the clause.

> It is difficult to see from here *who* the people are. (Relative clause in natural order reads: the people are *who*. Then it is clear that *who* is a predicate nominative.)
> We are not sure *who* the next president will be. (Natural order: the next president will be *who*. *Who* is the predicate nominative.)

Interrogative sentences will be clearer if they are arranged in natural order.

> Question: *Who* shall I say called?
> Natural order: I shall say *who* called. (*Who* is subject of *called.*)

14m. *Whom* is in the objective case and is used as the object of a verb or a preposition and as an indirect object.

Current usage studies indicate that the distinction between *who* and *whom* is breaking down. In formal English and in cases where a preposition or verb immediately precedes the pronoun, the objective case (*whom*) is retained. In informal conversational English, when the pronoun precedes the verb or preposition of which it is the object, *who* is accepted; but in writing anything but the most informal, chatty paper, one should observe the rule for the objective case.

> *Right:* Every person with *whom* Mr. Sanford works considers him a very conscientious person. (*Whom* is the object of the preposition *with* immediately preceding it.)
>
> *Informal conversation:* My mother always wants to know where I am going and *who* I'm going with. (*Who* is really the object of the preposition *with*, but informal English accepts *who* in this case. Notice that *who* precedes the preposition of which it is the object.)
>
> *Informal conversation:* *Who* do you wish to speak to? (*Who* is the object of the preposition *to*, but informal English accepts *who* in this case. Notice that *who* precedes the preposition of which it is the object.
>
> *Formal:* The bank handles every overdrawn account in the same manner, no matter

whom it concerns. (*Whom* is object of *concerns.*)

Formal: Clerks are instructed to handle courteously all requests for information, regardless of *whom* they are from. (The whole relative clause is the object of the preposition *of*. *Whom* is the object of *from.*)

14n. Whom is used as the subject or object of an infinitive and as a complement of the infinitive *to be* when its subject is expressed. (See Section 14i.)

Whom are you going to send as a delegate to the convention? (Natural order: You are going to send *whom; whom* is the object of the infinitive *to send.*)

Some people *whom* the world considers to be good thinkers are really appealing to emotion, not logic. (Natural order: The world considers *whom* to be good thinkers; *whom* is the subject of the infinitive *to be.*)

Whom did you think him to be? (Natural order: You did think him to be *whom? Whom* is the complement.)

NOTE: In sentences containing relative pronouns, follow these directions if you have trouble:

1. Be sure to work only with the subordinate clause.
2. Omit semiparenthetical expressions such as *I think, do you consider, we regard, you know* if the thought of the clause remains complete without them.
3. Arrange the subordinate clause with subject first and then verb.
4. If you are still in doubt, substitute *he* or *him* for the relative pronoun. In general, where *he* makes sense, *who* can be used. If *him* seems correct, use the relative pronoun *whom.*

Example: He is a man $\left\{ \begin{array}{l} \text{who} \\ \text{whom} \end{array} \right\}$ I am sure everybody admires.

1. The subordinate clause is: $\left\{ \begin{array}{l} \text{who} \\ \text{whom} \end{array} \right\}$ *I am sure everybody admires.*

2. Omit the parenthetical expression *I am sure*. We have remaining: $\left\{ \begin{array}{l} who \\ whom \end{array} \right\}$ *everybody admires.*

3. In natural order the clause reads: *everybody admires* $\left\{ \begin{array}{l} who \\ whom \end{array} \right\}.$

4. *Everybody admires him.*
   Everybody admires whom.

5. Conclusion: He is a man whom I am sure everybody admires. (*Whom* is the object of *admires.*)

14o. Whoever and whomever follow the same rules as who and whom.

> The medal will be given to *whoever* has the highest grade in English. (The object of *to* is the whole clause *whoever has the highest grade*. *Whoever* is the subject of *has.*)
>
> Send to the main office *whomever* you employ this morning. (*Whomever* is the object of *employ.*)
>
> He tells the same old story to *whomever* he meets. (*Whomever* is the object of *meets.*)

EXERCISE 16

On your paper, write the number of each sentence. Beside it, write the correct form of the relative pronoun as it should appear in formal English. Explain why you have selected this form. If any sentence would be acceptable as informal English, write X beside your correction.

1. Please send us the names of three firms who you have accounts with.
2. This is the boy who we met at the game.
3. I have not yet decided who I shall vote for.
4. Of all the characters in Dickens, who do you like best?
5. When I reached the office, I forgot who I had been told to ask for.

6. Who do you think we took on our camping trip?
7. The guide who we hired in Washington showed us the Lincoln Memorial.
8. We could not decide who had made the best play.
9. I tried to get in touch with the carpenter who you recommended.
10. Has William told you who the class elected as president?
11. Whom could it have been?
12. Please let me know whom should be notified in case of accident.
13. The woman has a child who she has not seen for five years.
14. Who did you apply to?
15. Do you know who the two women quarreled over?
16. Your organization will be responsible for all students, no matter who they are housed by.
17. Because the border was being changed constantly, the people did not know who the land belonged to.
18. The speaker at the conference was a historian who our committee has always disagreed with.
19. Who the committee selects as speaker is a matter of complete indifference to me.
20. Who did you say it was?
21. Who do we play next week?
22. I am sure that I can get along with whoever you put in charge.
23. If the card was unsigned, how could you tell who it was from?
24. Of all the people in history, whom would you prefer to be?
25. Mr. Henderson has never mentioned who he works for.

EXERCISE 17

Follow directions in Exercise 16.

1. Today people often know who the winning candidate is before they go to bed on election night.
2. Before the invention of the telegraph, the voters didn't find out who they had elected until days or even weeks later.
3. Please make a list of all those whom you think will contribute.

4. This is the man whom I believe has promised to speak at our assembly.
5. Our son wants to marry a girl who we think is not worthy of him.
6. We shall sell our antiques to whomever will pay the highest price.
7. The Gorgon turned to stone whoever she looked at.
8. I will call this problem to the attention of our Senator, whom I know well.
9. Mrs. Corcoran is a very capable woman, whom we think is doing a good job.
10. We had a long argument over who we would ask to the party.
11. I can't imagine who you think will be willing to help you do such a thing.
12. Who did you say this package was for?
13. The notice was sent to all of our customers whom we found to have a good credit rating.
14. When he opened the door, he was not sure who he expected the visitor to be.
15. In Beatrix the author has created a character whom the reader feels is alive and real.
16. Whoever the company accepts will be sent to Brazil.
17. Let me know who you think you could use on the team.
18. Ted is so proud of his television set that he wants to show it to whoever comes to the house.
19. The book is by Hardy, whom, you know, has written both novels and poetry.
20. No matter who I mention in conversation, Stan always pretends to know him well.
21. There is no pleasure in arguing with a person whom you know counts on emotion to win his point.
22. My roommate, whom I feel sure will be very exciting, has not yet returned from Europe.
23. Please let me know when you will arrive and who you would like me to invite.
24. In many countries people have so few privileges that they cannot marry who they please.
25. Who did you think him to be?

EXERCISE 18

Follow the directions in Exercise 16.

1. Whom did you say will ride your horse in the race?
2. How can a toad have the power to cause the growth of a wart on whomever touches it?
3. I should like to communicate with Major Eric Holdon, whom I understand is with the 95th Division.
4. We carried word of the meeting to all the ranchers who we found at home.
5. We can secure coaches for whomever needs help with his work.
6. The firm was worried about whom should be in charge of sales when Mr. Benton and him resigned.
7. Betty sat down near Frances and I and struggled with her Latin, but us girls refused to help her because she doesn't listen in class.
8. I don't know who to invite to the card club when Helen and her go to the luncheon next week.
9. I have known some teachers who were very severe in their handling of students, I included.
10. Think of all the immigrants whom you know have traveled across the ocean to get a free education such as you and me have.
11. Mr. Sutton Ames is an honorable man respected by all those who he has any business with.
12. There was no doubt in the minds of the people about whom should be elected.
13. Can you recommend the man as one who I can trust?
14. We challenged the students of Newton High, who we thought we could beat easily.
15. Are you sure it was him who you saw downtown?
16. Whom do you consider to be the best writer in the senior class?
17. The bus driver was very rude to my mother and I.
18. Choose whoever you want; I am tired of the whole question.
19. Our firm will not let we employees have a coffee break.
20. Two great women who the world will always remember are Florence Nightingale and Marie Curie.

21. Einstein said Marie Curie was the only one of all celebrated people who fame has not corrupted.
22. Marie Curie was one of a group of Polish girls for who learning had a great appeal.
23. She married Pierre Curie, whom everybody knows later won the Nobel prize with her.
24. When she was about to be married, a friend who she was very fond of offered to give Marie a wedding dress.
25. The young scientist asked the friend who had made the offer to give her a dress that could be used later in the laboratory where her and her husband worked.

15. PRINCIPAL PARTS OF VERBS

Every verb has three *principal parts:* the present, the past, and the past participle.* If you know these parts of any verb, you can form all of its tenses. (See Section 3f.) The *past* and the *past participle* of many English verbs are formed by adding *-d, -ed,* or *-t* to the present. These are called *regular,* or *weak,* verbs.

PRESENT	PAST	PAST PARTICIPLE
save	saved	saved
talk	talked	talked
ask	asked	asked
mean	meant	meant
spend	spent	spent

There are, however, other verbs, which do not follow this pattern. These are called *irregular,* or *strong,* verbs, and they form the past tense and past participle in several ways. Although it is impossible to establish a rule for these changes, groups of these words do often fall into a special pattern. One group has a vowel change in the past tense, and in some cases in the past participle as well.

---

* Often the present participle, a form made by adding *-ing* to the present tense form, is considered one of the principal parts: swim, swam, swum, *swimming.*

PRESENT	PAST	PAST PARTICIPLE
drink	drank	drunk
sing	sang	sung
cling	clung	clung
fight	fought	fought
sit	sat	sat
shoot	shot	shot
come	came	come
run	ran	run
find	found	found

Some verbs in this group, in addition to the vowel change, add -*n* to the past participle.

PRESENT	PAST	PAST PARTICIPLE
grow	grew	grown
break	broke	broken
fly	flew	flown
freeze	froze	frozen
drive	drove	driven
write	wrote	written
eat	ate	eaten
ride	rode	ridden
fall	fell	fallen

Another group changes its form completely in the past tense and past participle.

PRESENT	PAST	PAST PARTICIPLE
bring	brought	brought
think	thought	thought
buy	bought	bought
stand	stood	stood
go	went	gone
do	did	done
lie	lay	lain
catch	caught	caught
wind	wound	wound

113

A few verbs change the last consonant, but not the vowel.

PRESENT	PAST	PAST PARTICIPLE
make	made	made
have	had	had
build	built	built

A few others have the same form for all three principal parts.

PRESENT	PAST	PAST PARTICIPLE
burst	burst	burst
hurt	hurt	hurt
set	set	set
spread	spread	spread
cast	cast	cast

If you are uncertain about the correct verb form, consult your dictionary.

NOTE: A word labeled *slang, obs., dial.,* or *archaic* in the dictionary is not appropriate for formal speaking or writing.

PRINCIPAL PARTS OF SOME TROUBLESOME VERBS

PRESENT	PAST	PAST PARTICIPLE
ask	asked	asked
arise	arose	arisen
bear	bore	borne or born
beat	beat	beaten
become	became	become
begin	began	begun
bid	bid	bid (as in an auction)
bid	bade	bidden, bid (as in a command)
bite	bit	bitten
blow	blew	blown
break	broke	broken
bring	brought	brought

15

PRESENT	PAST	PAST PARTICIPLE
build	built	built
burn	burned or burnt	burned or burnt
burst	burst	burst
cast	cast	cast
catch	caught	caught
choose	chose	chosen
climb	climbed	climbed
come	came	come
cut	cut	cut
deal	dealt	dealt
dig	dug	dug
dive	dived, dove (colloq.)	dived
do	did	done
drag	dragged	dragged
draw	drew	drawn
drink	drank	drunk
drive	drove	driven
drown	drowned	drowned
drug	drugged	drugged
eat	ate	eaten
fall	fell	fallen
feel	felt	felt
find	found	found
flee	fled	fled
flow	flowed	flowed
fly	flew	flown
forget	forgot	forgotten, forgot
freeze	froze	frozen
get	got	got, gotten
give	gave	given
go	went	gone
grow	grew	grown
hang (to execute by hanging)	hanged	hanged
hang (other meanings)	hung	hung

115

PRESENT	PAST	PAST PARTICIPLE
happen	happened	happened
hear	heard	heard
help	helped	helped
hide	hid	hidden, hid
know	knew	known
lay	laid	laid
lead	led	led
lend	lent	lent
let	let	let
lie (to tell a falsehood)	lied	lied
lie (to recline)	lay	lain
lose	lost	lost
mean	meant	meant
meet	met	met
pass	passed	passed
pay	paid	paid
prove	proved	proved, proven
put	put	put
raise	raised	raised
rise	rose	risen
ride	rode	ridden
ring	rang	rung
run	ran	run
say	said	said
see	saw	seen
set	set	set
shine	shone	shone
show	showed	shown, showed
shrink	shrank, shrunk	shrunk
sing	sang	sung
sink	sank, sunk	sunk
sit	sat	sat
sleep	slept	slept
speak	spoke	spoken
spend	spent	spent
spring	sprang, sprung	sprung
stand	stood	stood
steal	stole	stolen

PRESENT	PAST	PAST PARTICIPLE
suppose	supposed	supposed
swim	swam	swum
swing	swung	swung
take	took	taken
tear	tore	torn
think	thought	thought
throw	threw	thrown
use	used	used
wake	waked, woke	waked
wear	wore	worn
win	won	won
wind	wound	wound
wring	wrung	wrung
write	wrote	written

15a. Do not misuse the past tense and the past participle.

The past participle, the third principal part, makes a compound tense of the verb only when it is accompanied by some part of *have* or *be*.

The past form, or the second principal part, of a verb is used without an auxiliary.

PRESENT	PAST	PAST PARTICIPLE
see	saw	seen
do	did	done

Wrong: I *seen* the flames reach the top of the building.
 Right: I *saw* the flames reach the top of the building.
Wrong: The fireman *done* something very brave.
 Right: The fireman *did* something very brave.

Seen and *done* are past participles and form tenses only with the aid of some part of the verb *have* or *be*.

Wrong: I *have saw* several cock fights.
 Right: I *have seen* several cock fights.
Wrong: Herbert was praised because he *had did* a good job on the yearbook.

Right: Herbert was praised because he *had done* a good job on the yearbook.

Be careful not to write *of* for *have.*

Wrong: I could of gone to the circus.
Right: I could have gone to the circus last week.
Right: I could've gone to the circus.

15b. Do not confuse an irregular verb with a regular verb.

It is easy to make the mistake of adding *-ed* to certain irregular verbs.

Wrong: He *drawed* a bucket of water from the well.
Right: He *drew* a bucket of water from the well.
Wrong: Last night the wind *blowed* at thirty miles an hour.
Right: Last night the wind *blew* at thirty miles an hour.

EXERCISE 19

Most of the following sentences contain errors in the use of the past tense and the past participle. Write on your paper the number of each sentence and the correction or corrections necessary. If no correction is necessary in a sentence, write C beside the sentence number.

1. We went to the hospital to see Mary, who had broke her arm.
2. Yesterday I swum across the lake at its widest point.
3. I never done a thing like that in my life.
4. She has tore the whole sleeve out of her dress.
5. I seen him go down the street just a few minutes ago.
6. I should of told you the whole story.
7. The letter was wrote on thin white paper.
8. I had already bit into the apple when I seen that it was rotten.
9. The boys had drunk all the milk that was in the icebox.
10. You should of gave him enough money.
11. Sue had never wore the dress before, and now it was tore to pieces.

12. The old woman taken a huge basket and set out for the store.
13. If you have broke the test tube, you must pay for it.
14. I have hid him in the closet so that Jerry cannot find him.
15. We rung and rung, but nobody came to the door.
16. We are worried about Anna because she hasn't ate a thing all day.
17. His balloon lay on the floor, bursted and tore.
18. "How far have you drove in this car?" asked the policeman.
19. We were sure that Angelo had not stole the money.
20. When you have wrote the letter, please show it to me.
21. Jack was badly beat by another boy in the neighborhood.
22. When I heard of him again, he had become a great physician.
23. Have you ever rode in an airplane?
24. You must of knew that the chair would break.
25. He done the work so carefully that no corrections were needed.

EXERCISE 20

Follow directions in Exercise 19.

1. Our team was beat badly last Saturday.
2. His suit had shrank until it was almost unwearable.
3. Enterprising citizens have built new homes, tore down trees, and made a beautiful residential section.
4. We drove out to Essex Inn for the reunion and seen a lot of our old classmates.
5. When my mother seen my wet hair, she knew I had went swimming.
6. Because my clothes had been soaked in the rain, I wrang them out and hanged them up to dry.
7. When I had had a few directions, I begun driving the tractor as if I had drove it for years.
8. A small shop near school serves the best milk shakes I have ever drank.
9. We had poor preparation last year, for we seldom gave book reports or done any outside reading.
10. When you come to see us, we'll show you the lot we have chose for our new home.

11. When the balloon bursted, the child was frightened and run to his mother for protection.
12. If I had worked last summer, I could of went to camp this summer.
13. When I ran into the garden, I saw that Bill had fell from the tree and probably broke his leg.
14. Several times the leash was bit into two pieces by my playful dog, but I never done anything to punish him.
15. Betty was pointing excitedly at something in the water, but the whistle drownded out her voice.
16. We thought we had drove about five hundred miles, but the road sign said we had come only three hundred.
17. He swung the bat and hit the ball over the fence.
18. The book could not have been wrote by a reputable author, even though one critic has spoke highly of it.
19. When I past Charlie on the street, I thought I had never saw a person so thin.
20. They lead us into the woods, where they would have stole our equipment if we had not been careful.

15c. Learn to use correctly *lie* and *lay, sit* and *set.*

The principal parts of *lie, lay, sit,* and *set* are as follows:

PRESENT	PAST	PAST PARTICIPLE
lie	lay	lain
lay	laid	laid (There is no word *layed*.)
sit	sat	sat
set	set	set

Lie and *sit* mean "rest" or "recline." They do not take an object.

> I have been *lying* on the beach all day.
> Yesterday I *lay* on the beach for only a short time.
> Mother *lies* down every afternoon for an hour.
> I had just *lain* down when the telephone rang.
> Please *sit* here.
> How long have you *sat* there?

Lay and *set* mean "place." They take objects.

> Mr. Burke *laid* the notes on the desk before me.
> I *set* the can of paint on the window sill.

NOTE: *Set* has some meanings in which it does not take an object. For instance:

> The sun, moon, and stars *set*.
> Jelly *sets* when it becomes firm.
> A *setting* hen is a hen that has been placed on eggs.

EXERCISE 21

In the following sentences, choose the correct form of the verb *lie* or *lay*. On your paper write the number of each sentence and beside it write the correct verb form, if an incorrect form has been used. Write an explanation of every correction that you make. If a sentence is correct, write C beside the sentence number.

1. She laid down for an afternoon nap.
2. If the new tax bill is passed, it will lay the heaviest burden on the poorest people.
3. Mrs. Johnson laid the baby in its crib for a nap.
4. A manufacturer cannot afford to let his machines lay idle for long.
5. When I passed the house, Mr. Walters was laying the bricks for a garden wall.
6. How long have you laid there in the sun?
7. The three silver dollars were laying on the counter.
8. I never have the time to lay down during the day.
9. He laid the foundation for his career by working in summer theaters during vacation.
10. The trash has laid in the alley for a week.
11. I had just laid down for a little rest when the telephone rang.
12. It was time to start for the station, but Tony still lay asleep under the tree in the yard.
13. A foreign ship has laid on its side in the harbor for two weeks.

14. This field was laying fallow when I was here last year.
15. On weekends the cove was bright with sails, but during the week the boats laid quietly at anchor.

EXERCISE 22

In the following sentences, correct errors in the use of *sit* and *set* in the way that you corrected the sentences in Exercise 21.

1. If I set here much longer, I'll go crazy.
2. I wanted to sit out a row of plants this morning.
3. Set the basket on the table and come here.
4. Those women will set on the porch all day.
5. I was afraid the jelly wouldn't set because I hadn't used enough sugar.
6. Let's sit where we can see the harbor.
7. In Shakespeare's day, the people sometimes brought boxes to the theater to set on.
8. The sun had set long before we got back to the house.
9. I sat my bundle on the ground and went after the boy.
10. Jervis used to set for hours listening to the water flowing into the cave.
11. While setting in his wheel chair with his drawings by his side, he collapsed.
12. Did you set the plants in straight rows?
13. I have never been so tired of setting in one place.
14. I had just set down to sew when Albert arrived.
15. He sat on the porch and rocked for two hours.

16. TENSE OF VERBS

Tense shows the time of the action expressed by a verb. Unless the tenses are carefully used, the reader or listener will not understand what happened first or how long the action continued. (See Section 3f.)

16a. The present tense is used to show action happening now.

He *hits* the ball.
I *see* Sally coming across the campus.

This tense is also frequently used for statements that are true, or likely to be true, at all times.

> In *As You Like it*, Shakespeare *presents* the question of love at first sight. (Permanently true; the question continues to be presented whenever *As You Like It* is read or seen.)
>
> I was disappointed to find that people in Europe no longer *wear* their national costumes, but *dress* just like Americans.

CAUTION: Although the present tense is occasionally used to make dramatic something that happened in the past, the tone of the material is often cheapened by the use of this device. *Never* tell a story by saying, "Then he says to me. . . . Then I say. . . ." Use, "He *said* to me. . . . Then I *said*. . . ."

16b. The past tense shows action that was completed in the past.

> We *won* the game.

Be careful when you tell a story not to shift from past to present.

> When Judy *appeared*,¹ she *was dressed*² in a filmy blue dress cut very low. We all *thought*³ she *looked*⁴ beautiful. In a few minutes the doorbell *rings*⁵ and in *comes*⁶ Stanley. (Verbs 1, 2, 3, 4 are in the past; 5 and 6 are in the present.)

NOTE: For the use of *can, may, might*, see Glossary of Words and Expressions Often Misused, page 295.

16c. The present perfect (*have seen, has done*) is used for action that began in the past and has continued.

> Bob *has written* to us every week for several years.
> The ice *has been* too thin for skating.

CAUTION: Use the present perfect tense, not the simple present tense, to indicate time starting in the past and continuing to the present.

Wrong: He *is studying* French for several years, but he cannot speak a word of the language.

Right: He *has been studying* French for several years, but he cannot speak a word of the language.

16d. The past perfect (*had written, had finished*) indicates action that occurred in the past before some other action that happened in the past.

All the roads were blocked because the snow *had fallen* fast. (It *had fallen* before the roads were blocked.)

In April they repaired the streets which *had cracked* during the storm.

Notice the three different tenses required in the following sentence:

I *wrote* (past tense) to Helen to tell her that Edith *had been* (past perfect) very ill, but I *have heard* (present perfect) nothing from her.

16e. To express a simple future (expectation) use *shall* with *I* and *we* and *will* with all other subjects. (*Should* is usually used like *shall*, and *would* like *will*.)

Be careful; the fireworks *will* burn your hand.

I *shall* be twenty in July.

I *should* be very glad to come for an interview at your convenience.

To express strong feeling, determination, promise, command, on the part of the speaker, use *will* with *I* and *we*, and *shall* with all other subjects.

He *shall* not go to the party unless he has finished his work.

I *will* not go to that school; I don't like it.

I *will* see that the book reaches you tomorrow.

NOTE: In informal English *will* is frequently used with all subjects in the future tense.

16f. *Should* **is used with all subjects to express obligation or duty or to express a condition in an *if* clause.**

> I *should* read more than I do.
> If I *should* win the contest, we could go to Bermuda.
> If he *should* win the contest, he would have a good career ahead.

16g. Use *would* with all subjects to express habitual action.

> He *would* go to the gardens day after day.
> When we were in Paris, we *would* always have coffee at a little sidewalk café.

16h. The future perfect tense is used to indicate that an action or a condition will have been completed by some time in the future.

> I *shall have learned* to ride by the time that you come.
> The snow *will have melted* before we start.

16i. Use a present infinitive unless you wish the infinitive to express time before the main verb.

> I intended *to see* (not *to have seen*) you about the exam.
> I should have preferred *to tell* her. (Not *to have told*)

16j. A present participle expresses action which takes place at the same time as the action expressed in the main verb. The perfect participle usually expresses action which began before the action in the main verb.

Illogical: *Starting* school at eight, he finished at eighteen. (He did not start at the same time at which he finished.)

Logical: *Having started* school at eight, he finished at eighteen. (Perfect participle)

Illogical: *Moving* to Charleston, we found the town delightful.

Logical: *Having moved* to Charleston, we found the town delightful.

EXERCISE 23

In the following sentences, correct any errors in verb tense by writing the correction and the reason for the correction beside the sentence number on your paper. If a sentence contains no error, write C beside the sentence number.

1. My son rushed into the room, grabs his coat, and goes dashing down the hall.
2. A few minutes elapsed; then as suddenly as the storm appeared, it disappeared.
3. It has been very cold since we are here.
4. I am waiting for this dance for three weeks.
5. When we entered our cabin, we found some thief made off with our supplies.
6. Terry lives in New Mexico now. He is there for nearly two years.
7. I expected to have gone to Richmond for the holidays.
8. On Saturday I discussed with Mr. Kelpert the material which he presented to the committee on Friday.
9. From 1954 until now, he was director of the James Newell Hospital.
10. After some discussion, we decided that real happiness did not lie in material things, but in things of the spirit.
11. Leaving the Capitol, we went to the National Art Gallery.
12. Lady Castlewood thought that her husband's coldness was due to the fact that she lost her beauty.
13. If they realized how ridiculous it was to believe in superstitions, people could save themselves many worries.
14. When I reached home yesterday, I was greatly surprised to find the pair of ice skates you sent me.
15. If anyone had found out what Samuel Pepys said in his diary, the writer would have been beheaded.
16. When Alex came of age, the Cossack society of free people was no longer so free as it once had been.
17. People in white seemed to be everywhere in the hospital, but no sound is heard.
18. When the respirometer started, the surgeon nods to the nurse, and she hands him the instruments.

19. Being built a hundred years ago, the hotel was finally considered unsafe.
20. I fed the lost dog as I fed my country dogs ten years ago, and he came along all right.
21. I preferred to have told her nothing, but she dragged the information from me.
22. Since the days of Adam, one of the most common of human pastimes is the criticism by old people of the habits of the young.
23. Starting out on foot, Sue reached Tampa at dusk.
24. Today is Sarah's birthday. I intended to send her a card.

EXERCISE 24

In current English usage, many people now use *will* with all subjects to indicate future time. If you wish to practice formal usage, refer to Section 16e. Many sentences below depart from formal English usage in the use of *shall* and *will*. On your paper, write the number of the sentence and any corrections necessary. If the sentence is correct, write C beside the number.

1. I think I shall see Doris tomorrow.
2. If you are not careful, you shall burn your fingers.
3. John will be present tomorrow if I have to drag him to the meeting.
4. I am determined that he will not go to the game.
5. I would be very grateful for any assistance which you can give me.
6. I am sure that my committee shall present a sensible bill to the Senate.
7. I promise that I shall write to you every day.
8. We will be pleased to discuss the plans whenever you are ready.
9. I will be very happy to make an appointment for you with the Governor.
10. Before we move, we will have a sale of all the stock in our old store.
11. I assure you we shall do everything in our power to make your visit in our hotel a memorable one.

12. If there is any special service that will make your stay pleasant, I will be happy to arrange for it.
13. I would think that you would find it very pleasant to live in the hotel where you work.
14. We will send your order as soon as possible.
15. As soon as the shoes are repaired, we shall send them to you with the bill.
16. We will be very glad to have you consult with us at any time.
17. We would like to ship your order at once, but we will have to wait until our shipping room has handled previous orders.
18. If you will write your name and address on the enclosed card, I shall send you a copy of our booklet.
19. We will need some information concerning your credit standing before we can open an account for you.
20. I am afraid that I will fail in French.
21. We would be very grateful for your prompt payment.
22. Since I am familiar with the apparatus used in a dentist's office, I should not have to be taught how to use it.
23. We will be pleased to place your name on our mailing list.
24. I would like to apply for the job advertised in yesterday's *News*.
25. I shall consider it a personal favor if you will permit me to send you samples of our merchandise.
26. We hope that we will hear from you and wish to assure you that we will give you our best services on all occasions.
27. We would like to see you; so why not pay us a visit?
28. If you cannot get tickets for the first balcony, get them in the orchestra; and I shall pay you when I see you.
29. If we win the game this afternoon, I will receive a star to place beside my major letter.
30. I shall definitely stick to tennis this summer, and maybe in the fall I will be able to enter the club tournament.

EXERCISE 25

The following paragraph contains errors that are a result of two things: (1) a shift in verb tense; (2) an illogical relationship to the basic tense. Review Section 16a–d. Then rewrite the paragraph, keeping a basic tense and making all verbs show a logical relationship to that tense. When you begin to write, decide whether the story is to be presented with the past tense or the present tense as the basic one. All tenses used in the exercise should show a relationship to that basic tense.

When we visited Washington last year, we had a marvelous time at the zoo, which contained many interesting animals sent from time to time as gifts to various Presidents. As we walk along, suddenly we see a bear wearing a hat. My sister is so excited that she rushes right up to the cage. The guard grabbed her arm and pushed her aside. Then he tells us that this is the bear that appears on all the posters warning us against forest fires. As a cub he was rescued from a forest fire in New Mexico. The U. S. Forestry Service thought he would be a good symbol and had used him to urge us to be careful about fires in the woods. He was wearing a hat when we saw him because he has just had his picture taken.

17. MOOD

The mood of a verb indicates the manner in which a statement is made. Every verb has three moods—the indicative, the imperative, and the subjunctive. (See Section 3e.)

17a. Use the indicative mood to state a fact or to ask a question of fact.

> Who *started* the rumor? (Question of fact)
> Alfred *told* the story first. (Statement of fact)
> The whole story *is* false. (Statement of fact)

17b. Use the imperative mood to express a command or a request (go, open, shut, sing).

> *Shut* the door.
> *Open* a window.

17c. Learn to recognize the subjunctive forms.

PRESENT INDICATIVE		PRESENT SUBJUNCTIVE	
I am	we are	(if) I be	(if) we be
you are	you are	(if) you be	(if) you be
he is	they are	(if) he be	(if) they be

PAST INDICATIVE		PAST SUBJUNCTIVE	
I was	we were	(if) I were	(if) we were
you were	you were	(if) you were	(if) you were
he was	they were	(if) he were	(if) they were

PRESENT INDICATIVE		PRESENT SUBJUNCTIVE	
I come	we come	(if) I come	(if) we come
you come	you come	(if) you come	(if) you come
he comes	they come	(if) he come	(if) they come

NOTE: There are only three differences in form between the subjunctive mood and the indicative mood: (1) the third person singular present subjunctive has no *-s* ending; (2) *be* is used with all persons in the present subjunctive of the verb *to be;* (3) *were* is used with all persons in the past subjunctive of the verb *to be.*

Although the subjunctive does not appear in current English very frequently, there are some constructions that still require it, especially in formal English.

17d. Use the subjunctive *were* to express a wish.

> I wish I *were* a good driver.
> He wishes he *were* tall.

17e. Use the subjunctive *were* to express a condition contrary to fact.

> If I *were* you, I'd refuse to let her use my car.
> If we *were* at home, we could consult our unabridged dictionary for the derivation of the word.

(I am not you. We are not at home. Hence the statements in the preceding examples are contrary to fact.)

130

NOTE: The subjunctive is used also to suggest a condition that is improbable, though not completely contrary to fact.

> Suppose he *were* to tell the whole story!

CAUTION: Not every clause that begins with *if* requires a subjunctive.

> If he *was* out late last night, he is probably still asleep. (The speaker thinks he probably was out late.)
> If she *was* there, I didn't see her. (The speaker is willing to accept the fact that she was there even though he did not see her.)

17f. Use the subjunctive *were* after *as though, as if* to express doubt or uncertainty.

> He talks as if he *were* the only intelligent person in the group.
> She looked as though she *were* completely exhausted.

NOTE: Do not use the subjunctive after *though* when it is not preceded by *as.*

> Even though he *is* deaf, he doesn't have to shout.

17g. Use the subjunctive in *that* clauses expressing necessity, mild command, or a parliamentary motion.

> I move that the committee *be appointed* by the president.
> It is essential that he *appear* at the meeting.
> The committee insisted that he *tell* the whole story.
> I suggest that the topic *be considered* at our next meeting.

17h. In parallel constructions, do not shift the mood of verbs.

> *Wrong:* If I were in your position and *was* offered a trip to Europe, I'd certainly go.
> *Right:* If I were in your position and *were* offered a trip to Europe, I'd certainly go.

EXERCISE 26

Correct errors in the mood of verbs in the following sentences. On your paper, write beside the sentence number the correct form of the verb and the reason for the correction. If no correction is necessary in a sentence, write C beside the sentence number.

1. If I was Sandy, I'd train that spaniel.
2. Many times he wished he was back in his old job.
3. If her mother was well, Ellen would go with us to the picnic.
4. If I was transferred to the Polytechnic Institute, I could get the algebra I need.
5. If I was you, I'd stay away from Jane.
6. I could do the job more quickly if I was not constantly annoyed by my neighbor's radio.
7. I move that he is reinstated at once.
8. My neighbor, who is eighty-five, dresses as if she was a woman of thirty.
9. She looked as if she was frightened to death.
10. The law requires that every operator of a motor vehicle has a driver's license.
11. If I was the principal, there would be some changes made.
12. The lawyer insists that he signs the papers.
13. He acted as if he was president of the university.
14. If your work was done carefully, you would get a promotion.
15. The company wishes that it was able to fill the order at once, but the materials are not available.
16. If Mother's health were better, we could make some plans for the summer.
17. He wrote his autobiography just as if he was writing about somebody else.
18. If he was disappointed, why didn't he tell me?
19. I demand that he gives me a written apology.
20. I often wish I was able to sing as Todd can.
21. If only this was next Thursday, I could pay you what I owe.
22. Every time I see a ship sailing for Europe I wish I was on it.

23. Even though I was exhausted, I kept on studying.
24. I move that a committee is appointed to study the problem.

EXERCISE 27

Follow the directions in Exercise 26.

1. If Howard was a college student, he would be accepted by the medical school.
2. The company requests that he pays his bill at once.
3. Though he works hard, he does not get promoted.
4. I am sure that Catherine is not married. Her mother would tell us if she was.
5. If I was not so nervous, I should not mind speaking before an audience.
6. Mr. Sommers asks that action is delayed until more information can be obtained.
7. The man's face was so red that he looked as if he was going to have apoplexy.
8. Eloise insists that her sister is told the news at once.
9. I wish Elinor was taller than she is.
10. If the President were given a free hand and was sent to negotiate, you would see some action.
11. If he is such good company, why don't you invite him to the party?
12. It was so warm today that I felt as though it were summer.
13. If our committee were more serious-minded, we should accomplish more than we do.
14. As the people looked out over the Mediterranean, it seemed as if Corsica was rising from the sea.
15. If the country is interested in wise laws, it must send men of wisdom to its lawmaking body.
16. If I was sure to fail, I think I should have been told.
17. If he was sorry for Ed, he showed no evidence of his feeling.
18. If he was sorry for Ed, he would help the boy in some way.
19. If the machine was shipped on Tuesday, I should have been notified.
20. If the situation seem a bit improbable, remember that there are stranger things in life than in novels.

133

18. ADJECTIVE AND ADVERB USAGE

Most errors in the use of adjectives and adverbs are the result not of ignorance, but of carelessness. They are made because people develop bad speech habits as a result of what they hear among careless friends or coworkers. Remember that whenever you want a word that tells *how* something is done, you need an adverb.

> The President acted *wisely* in the crisis.
> Scientists have worked *tirelessly* in their search for new drugs.
> We must walk *rapidly* if we are to reach the station in time.

18a. An adjective modifies a noun or pronoun.

> A *free* ticket.
> A *careless* speaker.
> *Tired* but *cheerful*, we reached the top of the mountain. (The adjectives *tired* and *cheerful* modify the pronoun *we*.)

18b. An adverb modifies a verb, an adjective, or another adverb.

> We want you to speak *freely*. (Modifies infinitive)
> He spoke *carelessly*. (Modifies verb)
> Sue has a *very* free manner. (Modifies adjective *free*)
> Morton spoke *too* carelessly. (Modifies adverb *carelessly*)

18c. Do not use an adjective to modify a verb or another adjective.

Wrong: I *sure* am glad to see you.
 Right: I *surely* am glad to see you.
Wrong: He's *some* fat.
 Right: He's *very* fat.
Wrong: Tell the children to play *quiet*.
 Right: Tell the children to play *quietly*.
Wrong: The poor fellow looked *real* happy when he saw us.
 Right: The poor fellow looked *very* happy when he saw us.

NOTE: Not all words ending in *ly* are adverbs. *Lovely* and *holy*, for example, are adjectives.

EXERCISE 28

In the following sentences, correct errors in the use of adjectives and adverbs. Write the sentence number on your paper. Then write the correct word and the reason for the correction. If no correction is necessary, write C beside the sentence number.

1. Some people take life too serious.
2. Everything went off perfect, but we sure were worried.
3. He rides a horse real wild.
4. A student must watch his grammar very close.
5. Why don't you speak plain?
6. We tried to bring the plane in and have it land smoothly.
7. The women were dressed poor and unattractive.
8. We are afraid that Tom won't make the team because he doesn't play very good.
9. I think she sings lovely.
10. Doesn't Carol skate beautiful?

EXERCISE 29

Follow the directions in Exercise 28.

1. Who do you suppose told my father I was doing terrible in physics?
2. Even when Sidney spoke extemporaneous, he was very interesting.
3. The Shimerdas lived very poor in a little hut on the prairie.
4. When they came to the prairie, they thought it would be heaven; but they changed their minds complete.
5. Any criticisms that you give will be treated confidential.
6. Why don't you give the assessment board the facts straightforward?
7. The course is supposed to be extremely hard, but I think you will do good in it.
8. Jane played the part of the blind woman very realistic.
9. If I don't reply to a letter quick enough, I forget what to write.

10. We didn't do so good in football this season.
11. The poor people in India were near starving.
12. Dickens's purpose in writing was to show how wretched the poor people in England lived.
13. A number of us are working real hard to make the pep assembly a success.
14. You sure do play the piano good.
15. On Sunday night Ethel and I did our act at the Woodholme Country Club, and it turned out real good.
16. Since I worked for my money, I thought I could spend it wise or not as I pleased; but my mother thought different.
17. Your merchandise will be shipped as quick as possible.
18. At the edge of the fairgrounds was a row of clumsy built stalls.
19. My brother has been extraordinary successful in advertising.
20. Do come to see us next summer when the bass and trout are biting good.
21. My feet hurt terrible in these shoes.
22. After her success on the stage, she treated her old friends very indifferently.
23. The Burdens, who were early pioneers, learned to live in their simple home as comfortable as anybody could.
24. She hasn't very good manners. She eats noisy.
25. Mrs. Kropotkin acted very rude toward her neighbor.

18d. After verbs such as *smell, taste, feel, sound, look, appear, become* **(used intransitively), use an adjective if the word describes the subject and an adverb if the word describes the action in the verb.**

> He looked *cold* standing in the snow. (Adjective describes *he*.)
> He looked *coldly* at me and left the room. (Adverb tells how he looked.)
> I feel *awkward* when people look at me. (Adjective)
> I felt *awkwardly* in pocket after pocket. (Adverb)
> The cake tastes *good*. (Adjective)
> He tasted the mixture *cautiously*. (Adverb)
> The flower smells *sweet*. (Adjective)

NOTE: *Badly* is often misused after *feel.*

Right: I feel *bad.* (*Sick* or *wicked*)
Right: Arthur spells *badly.*

Some words may be either adjectives or adverbs: *cheap, fast, deep, wrong, well, tight, hard, fair, first, slow, loud.* Some of these also have forms in *ly: slowly, loudly.* The *ly* forms are preferred as adverbs in formal English. Do not say *firstly, secondly; first* and *second* are preferable. *Well* is an adjective when it means the opposite of *sick.* It is an adverb when it tells how something is done. Never use *good* to tell how something is done.

Right: You acted *well* in the play.

18e. Be accurate in the use of comparatives and superlatives. (See also Section 67.)

Most adjectives and adverbs change their forms to show a greater or smaller *degree* of the quality they indicate. This change is called *comparison.* There are three degrees of comparison: *positive, comparative,* and *superlative.*

POSITIVE DEGREE	COMPARATIVE DEGREE	SUPERLATIVE DEGREE
cool (adj.)	cooler	coolest
soon (adv.)	sooner	soonest

In comparisons that indicate *less* of a quality, the words *less* and *least* are used with all adjectives and adverbs that can be compared.

POSITIVE	COMPARATIVE	SUPERLATIVE
weak	less weak	least weak
honest	less honest	least honest

This construction, however, can be avoided if it seems awkward.

Formal: She is less weak than she was yesterday.
Better: She is not so weak. Or,
She is stronger.

Most adjectives and adverbs of one syllable form the comparative degree by adding -er and the superlative degree by adding -est.

POSITIVE	COMPARATIVE	SUPERLATIVE
tough	tougher	toughest
small	smaller	smallest
fast	faster	fastest

Adjectives of two syllables usually add -er for the comparative and -est for the superlative. Sometimes, however, such adjectives have two forms for both comparative and superlative.

POSITIVE	COMPARATIVE	SUPERLATIVE
heavy	heavier	heaviest
lovely	lovelier	loveliest
handsome	more handsome	most handsome
	or	or
	handsomer	handsomest
deadly	more deadly	most deadly
	or	or
	deadlier	deadliest

Adverbs that end in *ly* and adjectives of more than two syllables usually form the comparative and superlative by prefixing *more* and *most*.

POSITIVE	COMPARATIVE	SUPERLATIVE
carefully	more carefully	most carefully
quickly	more quickly	most quickly
steadily	more steadily	most steadily
beautiful (adj.)	more beautiful	most beautiful
competent (adj.)	more competent	most competent

Some adjectives and adverbs are compared irregularly.

good (adj.)	better	best
bad (adj.)	worse	worst
badly (adv.)	worse	worst
well (adv.)	better	best

1. The comparative is used when two persons or objects or actions are compared; the superlative is used when more than two are compared.

> I bought two new dresses. Which do you think is *more becoming?*
> Which of your eyes has *better* vision?
> The sorrel horse galloped *faster* than the bay.
> He is the *most brilliant* student in the class.

In informal English, the superlative is often used when only two things are compared.

2. Avoid double comparatives and superlatives; that is, do not use *more* or *most* before a word to which *-er* or *-est* has been added to form the comparative or the superlative.

Wrong: He is more happier than his brother.
 Right: He is happier than his brother.

3. Choose the comparative form carefully. Do not confuse the comparative of an adjective with the comparative of an adverb.

Wrong: He learns things easier than Gertrude does.
 Right: He learns things more easily than Gertrude does.

4. A few adjectives like *round, square, unique,* and *equal* are logically incapable of comparison because their meaning is absolute. An object is either round or not round. It cannot logically be rounder. However, because these words have, in a measure, lost their superlative force, they are often compared in informal English, and even good writers use adverbs like *quite* or *completely* before them.

5. Avoid including the subject compared if the subject is part of a group with which it is being compared. Use *other* or *else* in such cases.

Illogical: Butte is larger than any city in Montana.
 Better: Butte is larger than any *other* city in Montana.
Illogical: My brother is taller than anyone in our family.
 Better: My brother is taller than anyone *else* in our family.

139

18f. These and those are plural forms and should not be used to modify singular nouns.

Illogical: These kind of dogs are fine for hunting.
  Better: This kind of dog is fine for hunting.
  Better: These kinds of dogs are fine for hunting.

Do not use *here* or *there* after the adjectives *this* or *that*.

Wrong: This here man is guilty.
  Right: This man is guilty.

The use of *a* or *an* after *this kind* or *this sort* is not desirable in formal English.

Undesirable: This kind of a day always depresses me.
  Better: This kind of day depresses me.

NOTE: *These kind of people* is accepted by some writers as standard informal English.

18g. Be careful of the adjectives *fewer* and *less*.

Less refers to quantity and is used with singular nouns (*less money, less food, less sugar*). *Fewer* refers to number and is used with plural nouns (*fewer people, fewer animals*).

18h. In formal English *due* is used as an adjective modifying a noun.

> The old woman said that her good health was *due* to careful exercise. (*Due* modifies *health*.)
> The woes of the world are *due* to poor thinking. (*Due* modifies *woes*.)

The expression *due to* is often used as a preposition, especially in news reports, radio talks, and business letters.

Informal: We have been unable to ship your order *due to* a strike in the factory.
Informal: The business has expanded *due to* the energy and hard work of our salesmen.

18i. Be careful not to overuse adjectives or adverbs.

The overuse of adjectives and adverbs will weaken your writing. Try to choose verbs which will express your meanings without the help of too many modifiers.

EXERCISE 30

Follow the directions in Exercise 28.

1. My dog Smoky sure has cost me a lot of money this summer.
2. In Sicily a message can be delivered quicker by foot than by telephone.
3. This here picture is not very clear.
4. He looked steady; so we gave him the job.
5. Esther looked steady through the window at the snow-covered fields.
6. I sure have felt bad all day; I didn't sleep good last night.
7. In the Romantic Period the poets were able to write more freer than in the Classical Period.
8. Gertrude works faster than any beautician in the shop.
9. An engineer must do his planning thorough in order to avoid all sources of weakness in the finished structure.
10. Rachel is more patient than anybody in her class.
11. One of our big problems today is whether the schools are educating young people satisfactory.
12. There would be less absentees if the students took their work more serious.
13. When Antonia worked in the fields with the men, she became more and more rougher.
14. The personnel manager hired Gloria because her letter was typed more neater than mine.
15. Our sales campaign has been extraordinary successful.
16. I was entertained wonderful at your home, and the experiences are still vividly in my mind.
17. Jimmy draws better than any boy in the art class.
18. Mother tasted the dessert careful to see whether it was too sweet.
19. She added some sugar because she found that the frosting didn't taste sweetly enough.

20. I have always wanted a real good record player, and the one you sent me sure does make me happy.
21. Matilda looked uneasy; I'm sure something was worrying her.
22. Ted looked around uneasy as if he thought he was being watched.
23. An owl sees much clearer at night than a hawk does.
24. These kind of people are always ready to criticize others severe.
25. I don't know which I enjoy most, opera or ballet.

EXERCISE 31

Follow the directions in Exercise 28.

1. The surgeon performed the operation as skillful as he could.
2. My cousin's manners improved considerable during his stay in camp.
3. He spoke very condescending to anyone under thirty.
4. The most favorite book of George Eliot was the Bible.
5. The success of a democratic nation is dependent upon citizens who vote intelligent.
6. We wish to educate our voters to think independent and not to be attached secure to the political bosses.
7. I think this paper is arranged much neater than yours.
8. The store has ordered these two types of materials. Which do you consider most durable?
9. Every year there are less opportunities in the business world for people over fifty.
10. By now, I suppose the Florida sun has tanned you wonderful and given you a real healthy appearance.
11. Stephen has been extraordinary successful with his engineering experiments.
12. I'm not near so tired as I was yesterday.
13. I was brought up so strict that I never had a date until I was twenty.
14. The cantaloupes of our state are uniform good fruit, but they are not always graded careful.
15. I didn't realize how much my mother hated moving to the city, because I was real young at the time.

16. Your invitation sounds very pleasantly, but Mother has felt badly all day and I cannot leave her.
17. I feel very strong about all questions involving the relationship between labor and capital.
18. My violin sounds different from yours.
19. One of the salespeople was reprimanded because she was acting impertinent to customers.
20. The milk tastes sour because it was left out of the refrigerator.
21. The cook tasted the soup careful and then added more pepper.
22. The Italian lecturer spoke English plainer than some of my friends do.
23. The posters used by the advertising department of our competitors are not near so attractive as ours.
24. I can understand that the decision must appear sudden to you.
25. When I had my paper route, I always kept a careful watch for the McDermotts' dog, which had a habit of attacking strangers unexpected.

19. PREPOSITION AND CONJUNCTION USAGE

The most common errors in the use of prepositions and conjunctions are made in two ways:

1. By confusing a preposition with a conjunction in usage. The choice between *like* and *as,* or between *without* and *unless,* is an example.

2. By choosing the wrong preposition to accompany certain words. Use *different from,* not *different than,* for example.

19a. In written English use *like* as a preposition or a verb, not as a conjunction.

Although *like* is frequently used as a conjunction in colloquial, casual English, the best speakers and writers still prefer to use *as* or *as if* when a clause follows.

143

Colloquial: The aviator opened his parachute and dropped to the ground *like* he had wings.

Formal: The aviator opened his parachute and dropped to the ground *as if* he had wings.

Colloquial: Sarah's friends were interested in books and travel *like* she was.

Formal: Sarah's friends were interested in books and travel *as* she was.

Colloquial: Our main objection to Miss Kay is that she treats us *like* we were children.

Formal: Our main objection to Miss Kay is that she treats us *as if* we were children.

Right: Jane looks *like* her father. (Preposition)

Right: You are behaving *like* a baby. (Preposition)

As is a preposition when it means "in the role of." Notice, however, the difference in meaning:

Right: He acts *like* a madman.

Right: He acts *as* the madman in the play.

Right: He acts *like* the chairman of the club.

Right: He acts *as* the chairman of the club.

Like should not be used in place of the conjunction *that*.

Wrong: I always felt *like* Roger would be successful.

Right: I always felt *that* Roger would be successful.

19b. Use *unless* as a conjunction, *without* as a preposition.

Right: The crops will die *without* rain.

Right: The crops will die *unless* we have rain soon.

Right: We will not rent the apartment *without* a redecoration.

Right: We will not rent the apartment *unless* you redecorate for us.

19c. Use the appropriate preposition with certain words.

A good dictionary will show the correct prepositions to be used with many words. (See Section 43.)

NOTE: In casual English, it is all right to use a preposition at the end of a sentence, but it should not be an unnecessary preposition.

Wrong: Where are you going to?
 Right: Where are you going?
 Right: What are you writing with?

EXERCISE 32

From each pair of words or expressions in parentheses in the following sentences, choose the correct word or expression and write it on your paper beside the sentence number. Write also your reason for each choice.

1. He cannot pitch well (without, unless) he warms up thoroughly.
2. Did you have my suit cleaned (like, as) I told you to do?
3. We didn't feel (like, that) this city was large enough to handle the convention.
4. The Sewells were really only neighbors, but they acted (like, as if) they were part of our family.
5. We were treated (like, as) kings during our visit.
6. The poor man never answers (without, unless) he first knows what his wife is going to say.
7. The team is shaping up nicely, but it doesn't yet look (like, as if) it will be a championship team.
8. The doctor says that the patient will die (unless, without) he has an operation.
9. The awnings will be torn to pieces (without, unless) you pull them up at once.
10. Your answer to the problem looks (like, as if) it should be correct.
11. Joel was eighteen, and (as, like) most boys of his age, he was looking for excitement.
12. The scenery in Puerto Rico was different (than, from) anything I had ever seen.
13. He feels (like, that) the world is against him.
14. We rode the first five waves (like, as if) we were on a roller coaster.
15. My Canadian friends at camp were very much (like, as) me.

20. ACHIEVEMENT TESTS IN USAGE

20a. Achievement Test I (Sections 11–14).

Write on your paper the number of each sentence. Beside the number, write the correction or corrections necessary and give the reason for each correction. Write the whole sentence only when a complete revision is necessary. If a sentence contains no errors, write C beside its number.

Examples:
1. Every one of the students have their own lockers.
2. Hazel lives near Bernice and I.

Correction:

1. has	1. subject and verb agreement
his own locker	pronoun and antecedent agreement
2. me	2. object of preposition *near*

1. One of my favorite actors is Alfred Lunt, whom you know often performs with his wife.
2. The violinist who I should select as my favorite was a child prodigy.
3. Since the cause of many diseases are unknown, a number of medical men is kept busy in research.
4. There's many ways to solve a problem, but everybody thinks that their way is the right one.
5. The company announced that every employee could obtain their bonus by stopping at the cashier's desk.
6. To help the depositor keep their account straight, we send you a statement at the end of each month.
7. The only way in which disease among cattle and domestic animals have been stopped are by quarantine.
8. I am sure that the party will be a success and everyone will enjoy themselves.
9. Why don't you come to spend a few days with Mother and I?
10. The business, including the shop, the goods on hand, and all the fixtures, were sold for fifty thousand dollars.
11. I don't know who he could be.
12. You are expected to send the papers to Mr. Henderson and I at once.

13. Members are requested to give the secretary the names of any guests who they intend to bring to the dinner meeting.

14. The transit company is replacing cars with buses and therefore have many more vehicles to keep in repair.

15. This is my old coat. I always wear it when it rains.

16. We cannot accuse the man unless we are sure it was him who you saw enter the room.

17. The Bastille played an important part in the French Revolution because it was a symbol of their suffering.

18. The congressman who we elected from our district is a man of absolute integrity.

19. The garden has been completely rearranged, which ought to give Jane and I a chance to win the contest.

20. Dan went with his brother to the office, where he told the whole story to the principal.

21. A teen-ager's opinion, like their problems, are often taken for granted.

22. When Mother plays bridge with Mrs. Summers, she argues about every trick.

23. Mr. Sherwood is studying the question of who we should appoint as director.

24. Every one of us were told that we must pay for the laboratory materials that we broke.

25. Her and Anthony left the prairie and went to the town to live.

26. Mother decided to let Carol and I go to the circus.

27. The nationally advertised price of these stunning trays are double the sale price that we offer to customers who we have placed on our A-1 credit list.

28. The beautiful scenery with its snow-capped mountains, green pastures, and blue lakes remind him of Switzerland.

29. The number of people who attended the meetings regularly were only fifty.

30. The electron, as well as the proton, were shown to carry electrical charges.

31. The privilege of voting is ignored by many people, and consequently there is in many legislative bodies corrupt politicians sent there by the bosses.

32. If between you and I no compromise is possible, there seems little chance of us doing any business.

33. The prize will be given to whoever makes the largest number of sales.

34. Enclosed is some of our business reply envelopes on which is printed our new address and the name of our new manager.

35. Fred does not want Henry and I to go with him.

36. Of all the contestants, Bert is the only one whom we think have followed the directions exactly.

37. Please do not refer to us, Emma and I, as stage-struck juveniles.

38. I am sure that one of the men who is present is the guilty person.

39. George's father, whom I understand once led a band, taught Frank and I to play.

40. It wasn't until last evening that everyone knew their parts and Jack and myself breathed freely again.

41. When the ballots have been counted, please send a report to the principal, who will forward same to the secretary of the Youth Commission.

42. I was told to give the message to whomever was in the office.

43. It is economical to purchase it in a large bottle.

44. Cataloguing and arranging our specimens for the exhibit has kept my brother and I busy during the whole summer.

45. Mr. Harrison thinks that either you or I are to be selected for the new position.

46. After three months in this business, I begin to feel at last like one of the people who really belongs to the organization.

47. An inspection has been made in order to determine whether the new arrangement of the stacks in the library are likely to contribute to efficiency.

48. The insignia of the Medical Corps consists of a winged staff with two serpents twined around it.

49. If each of the members of the committee do their work carefully, we shall have an excellent report.

50. The results of the inspection, as covered by the attached report, indicates that the buildings of the plant is in satisfactory condition.

20b. Achievement Test II (Sections 11–19).

Follow the directions for Achievement Test I.

1. Every cat and dog in five counties were quarantined.
2. If it had been necessary, Jim could beat any of the men.
3. The party at Goldie's house was better than any party we have had.
4. Sarah has not been well; so she don't go downtown like she used to.
5. This heat would be dreadful if a breeze wasn't blowing.
6. When the Crimean War broke out, the techniques of nursing were dreadful out of date.
7. The doctors worked valiant, but they needed the assistance of nurses very bad.
8. Joan says she has felt badly all day.
9. I could of gone if I had knew that you were going.
10. I'm afraid his foot is froze.
11. The gadgets which we invent makes life more and more simpler.
12. If I was him, I'd try a new job.
13. After we helped put up the tents, we carried water for the circus animals.
14. I drunk a huge glass of milk when I come home from school.
15. The lifeguard said that the boys almost drownded because they swum out too far.
16. We did not think that the experiment would turn out very good.
17. He told Mr. Kenworthy that he was sure to be on the committee.
18. Each of the forty-eight samples were placed in a separate jar.
19. Headlines in the newspaper is arranged so that it attracts attention.
20. Since the T-formation has been used successful, many school teams have adopted it.
21. The old man's eyes reflected the kindliness that laid in his heart.

149

22. I wish I was able to tell Jack and she the whole story.

23. Neither Mother nor I are surprised to hear that Edith failed; she don't do her work careful at all.

24. When I left, after being with the board for ten years, I felt like a piece of my life was gone.

25. When you consider that neither of us have did any shooting for a year, we are not doing so bad.

26. It is always Mr. Peters and me who is reprimanded if things go wrong in the office.

27. Digging a hole ten feet deep, the boys went away and left it.

28. A strange man whom, we learned later, knew Gertrude at one time, enters the house and joins the party.

29. He shall not use my money. I will see that he does not.

30. The conference will probably last until five o'clock; so there is no point in you waiting any longer.

31. Since you invited Paul and I for a visit, our father has been terrible sick; so we will not be able to accept your invitation.

32. A first prize of an expense-paid trip to Europe will be given to whoever can solve the puzzle.

33. Everybody said he acted as a fool at the wedding.

34. New cars don't jump direct from the drafting board to the production room like some people think they do.

35. We recommend that there be appointed an experienced superintendent of waterworks.

36. Losing his fortune in an investment in oil, he begun life anew at fifty.

37. It was not wise for you to have given him the key.

38. The prize was to be given to whomever made the highest mark in German, but I never thought it would be me who would win it.

39. I worked at the job only two months when I was obliged to leave in order to have accompanied my family to Nebraska.

40. Because of the heat wave, air conditioning sold very satisfactory last summer.

41. Every night there has been some sort of party; and although I would have loved to have gone to all of them, it was physically impossible.

42. It says in this article that the average married person is more healthier than the average single person because they have their meals more regular.

43. Since a good picture can sell a product, advertisers are turning to them to improve business.

44. If you won an election against John Cameron, you have did very good indeed.

45. The directors wish to express their appreciation for your cooperation during the year and welcomes this opportunity to wish you a Merry Christmas.

46. The firm objects to me studying Spanish because every man and woman in the office have spent a good deal of time on some similar subject that have not helped their work.

47. I have always felt like I'd like to be a dancer.

48. This school is different than all of the other schools I have attended.

49. The beach was so pleasant I could of laid for hours in the sun.

50. One of the most interesting sights in Seattle are the Cascade Mountains.

Capitalization

21. USE OF CAPITAL LETTERS

A piece of writing in which capitals are scattered about freely or omitted where they should be used gives the impression almost of illiteracy. It is true that some modern writers have ignored the rules of capitalization, but it is not wise for students to be careless about these rules.

21a. Capitalize the first word of every sentence and the first word of a direct quotation.

> Our new car is dark blue.
> He asked, "Is your new car blue?"

21b. Capitalize the first word of a line of poetry.

> Shall I wasting in despair
> Die, because a woman's fair?

21c. Capitalize the word which follows *Resolved* or *Whereas* in formal resolutions.

> Resolved: An automobile driver's license should be granted to no one under twenty-one.

21d. Capitalize the important words in a title of a book, poem, play, magazine, magazine article, or musical composition. (See Sections 27i and 34a.)

> *Harper's Magazine, Romeo and Juliet, The Moonlight Sonata, Death of a Salesman*

NOTE: Capitalize prepositions, conjunctions, or articles (*a, an, the*) only at the beginning or end of a title or when they consist of five or more letters.

21e. Capitalize the first word in each topic of an outline and the first word in each item of a list.

    1. Causes of slums
      A. Crowded conditions
      B. Poor housing

Our investigation shows the following:

      1. Poor sanitation
      2. Lack of parks and recreation space
      3. Unpaved streets

21f. Capitalize the pronoun *I* and the interjection O.

    Usually I find the first ripe chestnuts on the tree.
    O mighty river, flow on!

NOTE: *O* is rarely used. The more common interjection *oh* is not capitalized unless it begins a sentence.

21g. Capitalize all proper nouns and words derived from proper nouns. (See Section 1.) They include the following:

    1. Names of holidays, months, and days of the week (*Christmas, February, April, Monday*).

    2. Names of persons and titles accompanying these names, but usually not the titles alone unless the title is used in place of a name. *Mother* and *Father* are capitalized only when used as names.

    Fred, Helen, Mr. Brown, Dr. Anderson, Captain Wharton, Aunt Helen, the doctor, the captain, my aunt
    Can you hear the whistles, Father?

NOTE: The words *President* and *Vice President,* referring to

153

the President and Vice President of the United States, are always capitalized.

3. The names of races, languages, nationalities.

> Caucasian, the French language, Chinese lacquer, Japanese cherry blossoms

4. The names of cities, states, counties, countries, continents, bodies of water, mountains, constellations, and planets (except the earth).

> Tucson, Arizona, United States, North America, Mississippi River, Rocky Mountains, Orion, Jupiter

5. Names of streets, parks, buildings, ships, trains, planes, hotels, orchestras.

> Hollywood Boulevard, Yellowstone Park, Equitable Building, the Ritz-Carlton, Philadelphia Symphony Orchestra, *Super-Chief, S. S. American Scout*

6. Points of the compass (North, South, East, West) when they mean sections of the country or when they precede the name of a street, but not when they mean direction.

> We moved to the South when I was a child.
> When I saw the thief, he was running south toward the river.

7. The names of political parties, religious groups and their members, and particular organizations or groups.

> Democrats, Catholics, Methodists, Bender and Company, American Historical Society

8. Schools, colleges, clubs, departments of the government.

> Edison High School, Drake University, East High School Glee Club, Department of Agriculture

9. Events in history, historical periods, documents.

> War Between the States, Middle Ages, Declaration of Independence

10. Names of school classes when the word *class* accompanies them.

> Junior class, juniors

11. Names of school subjects when they refer to languages or specific classes.

> English, Latin, Algebra II, algebra

21h. Capitalize words referring to the Deity and sacred books, but not the word *god* or *goddess* referring to pagan gods.

> Lord, Savior, Master, Bible, Koran, Jehovah, gods of the Romans

NOTE: Pronouns used in reference to the Deity are capitalized.

> We can be sure that He will care for us.

21i. Capitalize the first word in the salutation and the complimentary close of a letter.

> Dear Mr. Evans: Dear Sir: Sincerely yours,

NOTE: Any word used in place of the name of the person to whom the letter is written is also capitalized, but not any intervening words.

> My dear Sir: My dear Sister:

21j. Capitalize the abbreviations of titles and academic degrees.

> A.B.   Ph.D.   Lieut.

NOTE: *Do not capitalize the following:*

1. The name of a worker in a particular job.

Wrong: He is the Assistant Foreman of the bindery.
Right: He is the assistant foreman of the bindery.

2. The names of school subjects unless they are names of languages or specific names of courses.

French, physics, mathematics, Journalism II

3. Any word but the first in the complimentary close of a letter.

Wrong: Your loving Nephew,
Right: Your loving nephew,

4. The word *dear* when it follows *my* in the salutation of a letter.

Right: My dear Dr. Harlow:

5. The names of chemical substances.

Right: We used some sulphur.

6. Terms referring to school, if the name of the school is not mentioned.

Right: I go to the junior high school.
Right: I go to Edgar Allan Poe Junior High School.

7. Names of diseases.

Right: He has measles.

8. Nouns such as *father, mother, aunt* when they are preceded by a possessive.

Right: My father is a fishing enthusiast.

9. The names of the seasons and *earth, sun,* and *moon.*

Right: To me, autumn means blue leaf-smoke.
Right: This is the best place to watch the rising moon or sun.

EXERCISE 1

The following sentences from students' themes contain errors in capitalization. On your paper, rewrite each sentence, using the correct capitalization.

1. At the head of the Student Government, we have a Student President and a Student Vice President.
2. Plutarch discussed a Roman Statesman and then a Greek Statesman and compared them.
3. We studied Sulphur and Hydrogen Sulphide in Chemistry.
4. The author lived for many years in a small cottage in devonshire, England.
5. The President of our organization appointed a committee to consult with the Executive Secretary.
6. I want to go to Business College for nine months and then get a job.
7. We asked the advice of James Hannibal, but he referred us to judge rhynhart.
8. I wish to apply for the position of Counselor at camp coxton.
9. Of all the good times that I had during the Spring vacation, I enjoyed most the dance given by the North High glee club.
10. Marie Curie studied radium and won the nobel prize in physics.
11. The lawyer has his office in the fidelity building at 10 east lexington street.
12. I think that easter comes on april 8 this year.
13. They moved to the west and settled on an iowa farm.
14. Mother sent me to visit aunt sally, who lives in paducah, kentucky.
15. Horace has always done well in physics and mathematics, but he cannot master spanish or french.
16. The chamber of commerce is going to publish a pamphlet called "what to see in cleveland."
17. We took a boat down the danube river from vienna to budapest.
18. If you go west for two blocks, you will find the office of the president of the company at 712 charles street.
19. The renaissance was a period of great development in art and literature.

20. Have you ever read the declaration of independence or the bible completely?
21. The seniors wanted to get an advertisement for their year book from snedden, driscoll and company.
22. The gods of the romans were very human in many ways.
23. There are as many baptists in our town as there are catholics.
24. She was employed as chief file clerk, but she often has to act as secretary to the President.
25. An eclipse of the sun occurs when the New Moon passes directly between the Sun and the Earth.

EXERCISE 2

The following paragraphs contain errors in capitalization. On your paper, write with a capital each word that requires capitalization.

Samuel johnson, one of the most colorful figures of the eighteenth century, was born in lichfield on september 18, 1709. His father, a bookseller, permitted the boy to read the books in the shop so that samuel became very well-read. during this period, many people were quite superstitious. they believed that a sick person could be cured by the touch of the queen. consequently, when samuel began to suffer from scrofula, he was taken to queen anne, but the supposed power of a queen to cure the disease failed. the affliction remained with johnson and gave him trouble for years.

because the johnsons did not have enough money to educate their brilliant son, a neighbor sent the boy to pembroke college, oxford. there johnson began his writing career by translating some latin verses. he later wrote *taxation no tyranny,* which argued against the points taken by the american colonists in the revolutionary war and showed johnson as a firm supporter of the tory party.

today we remember johnson chiefly as the author of the first dictionary, a book which showed great prejudice against the scotch, and as the organizer of a famous group called the literary club. members of the latter included the most important intellectual people in london. david garrick, the actor, sir joshua reynolds, the artist, edmund burke, the statesman, oliver goldsmith, the writer, were all members. when johnson was finally granted a pension by the king, he showed great kindness to a number of poor people, whom he kept in his house on fleet street.

EXERCISE 3

Rewrite the following letter, using correct capitalization:

4315 Aldrich avenue
Minneapolis 9, Minnesota
October 31, 1960

Marston Brothers
52 east sixteenth street
chicago, illinois

dear sirs:
    please send the following books with bill:
        1 copy preston, *the growth of american ideals*
        1 copy anderson, *new criticism*
        2 copies jackson, *big league baseball*

very truly yours,
howard sachs

Punctuation

Punctuation is an aid to meaning; but if it is carelessly used, it may distort meaning. The following sentence was dictated by a businessman not long ago. The poor punctuation used by his secretary distorted the meaning and caused the firm some embarrassment. She wrote:

> The house was bought on Monday for five thousand dollars. We can put it in excellent condition and resell it.

Her employer had expected her to write:

> The house was bought on Monday. For five thousand dollars we can put it in excellent condition and resell it.

Sometimes careless omission of a comma can lead to humorous results, as in the following sentence:

Wrong: When we cooked the woman in the next apartment complained that we rattled pots and pans.

A first glance at the sentence might tell the reader that we cooked the woman.

Right: When we cooked, the woman in the next apartment complained that we rattled pots and pans.

Literary artists sometimes use punctuation in a very free fashion; but in business and the professions, clarity is important, and following a few simple rules is imperative.

How good is your punctuation? Do your sentences always convey to your reader exactly what you mean to say? Try the diagnostic test to see what you need to study. Then turn to the practice exercises that will help you with your problems.

22. DIAGNOSTIC TEST ON COMMAS, SEMICOLONS, COLONS, APOSTROPHES, QUOTATION MARKS

On your paper, rewrite the following sentences, supplying the necessary commas, semicolons, colons, apostrophes, and quotation marks. If unnecessary marks have been used, omit them in your correction. After each sentence write an explanation of each correction that you have made in that sentence. If a sentence needs no correction, do not rewrite it, but write C beside its number.

1. If you desire any information about the city we suggest that you call on our Personal Service Bureau.
2. When I came home after a years course in business my father gave me Mr. Simmons old job.
3. Lawrence Biddison the Hopkins lacrosse star was chosen for the Olympic team.
4. The streets were narrow and cobblestoned not paved as they are today.
5. Our prices are always fair Mr. Hathaway said the manager we try to please our customers.
6. How many *ts* are in your last name Davy?
7. The adding machine which the First National Bank has just installed is a real timesaver.
8. The road outside Miami was long and straight only now and then did we round a curve.
9. Yes the flowers were from the Allens'.
10. A person applying for a job must be sure to wear inconspicuous clothes and to see that they are clean and neatly pressed.
11. Shelley and Keats poetry occupies a high place in English literature.

161

12. He is famous however chiefly for his autobiography which people call the best of its kind.

13. In the days of horse-drawn cars fire engines and milk wagons Sam Smith kept a bookshop on Center Street and we boys often went there to talk about literature and politics.

14. We must show that we have grown intellectually that we have increased our interests in current problems and that we can be tolerant of others.

15. Our chef has been in our employ for nearly twenty years and has an excellent staff to assist him as a result we are always sure that the meals will be good.

16. In modern times when one speaks of a fool he is usually referring to a person who has not good sense but in medieval days the fool was a professional jester in the kings court.

17. Pepys' tells in his diary of the bubonic plague that swept England and of the great fire that destroyed a large part of London.

18. My father does not approve of James driving so rapidly but he does not want to forbid him to use the car.

19. The author of the book states no despot however benevolent can rule the people as well as the people can rule themselves.

20. William Harlow who plans to build a large number of prefabricated houses has begun his work in our city.

21. I took the boys to see the Orioles play against Rochester said Uncle Jack and although these teams cannot compare in playing ability with those of New York the game was very enjoyable.

22. Mark Hallam born in Peoria Illinois May 22 1899 traveled to India Persia Java and many other exotic places in order to get information for his book.

23. Gross neglect of his work resulted in Mr. Blacks being discharged said the manager.

24. Major John Perry son of Mr. and Mrs. Henry Perry of Madison Wisconsin won three decorations for bravery in combat.

25. The report submitted by Mr. Arnold showed that the southwest corner of Fleet and Exeter Streets will be an excellent location for our business consequently we shall begin building the new plant next month.

26. One thing is certain this is not the kind of bill which should be rushed through Congress without serious thought.

27. A ladys purse containing five one-dollar bills a silver ring and some change was found in the employees rest room.

28. The management aware of efforts among its employees to set up a closed shop feebly endeavored to nullify them by promoting an independent company union.

29. The Mutual Insurance Company which now occupies one floor of the building will be obliged to move to make room for government offices.

30. We planned to have the party at the Kings house but on the day of the party Mrs. Kings mother was ill.

31. Most of the cars in the parking lot are new roadsters sedans and convertibles although a few are old secondhand buses.

32. There are five kinds of phrases prepositional participial gerund verb and infinitive.

33. There is a sale of ladies and misses dresses and mens suits at Goodman and Canes new store.

34. The children were playing with some pretty little pink seashells which they had found on the beach.

35. A business which is unwilling to change its practices to suit new conditions will never be very profitable.

36. When Ellen heard the lecturer speak with great enthusiasm about antiques she rushed out and bought a lovely Chippendale sofa.

37. When we received Henton and Hawkins acceptance of our plan for the reorganization of their business we began the job by moving the credit managers office to the third floor.

38. Hettie born in 1821 after the death of two other children was a source of great happiness to her parents.

39. Harry Manners who was a war correspondent gives in his short story The Voice Speaks a realistic picture of soldiers in action.

40. The steps creaked as I walked on them and the air smelled stale and musty.

41. The no-smoking provisions do not of course apply to the outer lobbies of theaters to restaurants or to other places designated with the approval of the Fire Department as places where smoking is permitted.

42. When the quarantine on dogs was lifted dozens of dogs began scampering around renewing old acquaintances visiting scenes of former revelry and showing how happy they were to be free.

43. A person who wants to build a hot rod must watch several things careful grinding of crankshaft bearings removal of metal from the bearing surface and reshaping of bearings.

44. As we approached the house said Peter we heard a man say Ill get him if you leave the job entirely to me and we fled without waiting to hear more.

45. Here is a painter who draws his inspiration directly from life and nature.

46. When the scientist sent the beam of his torch toward the tree he saw suspended from a branch a curious little animal which was hanging upside down.

47. It looked something like a Teddy bear but as it moved along the branch of the tree the scientist could see a row of spines projecting from its neck.

48. This animal the potto can double up with its head between its legs so that it is in excellent position to use those spines on any attacker that comes too close.

49. Because I love animals reading Sandersons *Animal Treasure* was one of the most pleasant experiences that I have ever had but I should not have enjoyed the rats snakes and frogs that the scientist met everywhere.

50. Flying squirrels scaly anteaters and whistling skinks were animals new to me until I read of a scientists trip to the jungle but I soon became acquainted with them and learned much about their habits.

23. THE COMMA

23a. Use a comma before the coordinating conjunction that joins two independent clauses.

The coordinating conjunctions are *and, but, for, or, nor*. A compound sentence has at least two independent clauses, which are usually joined by a coordinating conjunction. To determine whether a sentence is compound, read what comes before the coordinating conjunction and see if the thought is complete standing alone; then read what follows the conjunction and see if it is complete. If there are two complete thoughts, place a comma before the conjunction. If there are not *two* complete thoughts, no comma is needed.

> There was an elevator for the use of visitors, but we decided to walk up the steps. (Two complete thoughts)
> Norris darted around the corner and halted abruptly. (No comma is needed because the words following *and* are not complete in themselves; they are part of the compound predicate used with the subject, *Norris*.)

NOTE:

1. If the clauses are short, the comma may be omitted. This statement, however, immediately brings up the question "How short is short?" If the independent clauses consist of only subject and verb, then they are obviously short, and the comma may be omitted. Examples: *John studied and Mary played. I laughed and I cried.* Sometimes lack of punctuation between short clauses may cause momentary misreading. In reading the sentence that follows, your first thought may be that the boys ate the hired man.

> The boys ate bacon and the hired man ate sausage.

2. If the clauses are long and contain other commas, a semicolon is used before the conjunction. (See Section 24c.)

> When he arrived at college, he was invited to join two different fraternities; and it was only after much discussion with his father, his brother, and his friends that he was able to decide which one to join.

EXERCISE 1

Most of the following sentences from student themes and letters contain errors in the punctuation of compound sentences. On your paper, write the number of each sentence. Beside it, write the word after which a comma should be used and the comma. If no comma needs to be added to a sentence, write C beside the sentence number. As an example, the correction for the first sentence is given below:

1. late,

1. Often the mother had to work late and the child was left to take care of himself.
2. The commercials are very elaborate and sometimes take three minutes of a fifteen-minute program.
3. Almost everybody has his pet superstition but some people take the matter entirely too seriously.
4. A senator from Mississippi and one from Georgia were discussing the poll tax.
5. Most of the critics received the book very coldly but the public loved it.
6. The new art museum is a beautiful structure and some of the paintings are exquisite.
7. His trip on the ocean was pleasing to Joe for he rested most of the time.
8. Suddenly dark clouds appeared on the horizon and the sea became rough and wild.
9. We wish to thank you for this opportunity to be of service and to assure you of our desire to please you.
10. We tried to get in to see Toscanini conduct but we didn't have the strength to fight through the mob.
11. His clothes were old and ragged but his spirit was as haughty as ever.
12. We should like to welcome you to Indianapolis and to express a sincere hope that you will enjoy your residence here.
13. We could drive into town in the evening and see a show at one of the small-town movie houses.
14. It's been a long time since we've seen each other and you've probably forgotten all about me.
15. The shouts of the people grew louder and louder for the two wrestlers had entered the ring.
16. The living room is comfortably proportioned and has a large fireplace at one end.
17. A banquet has been arranged for the evening and many other feasts and festivities will be held during the three-day holiday.

18. I do hope that you haven't made any plans for the summer and will arrange to spend July with us.
19. The family intends to drive to my aunt's summer lodge in Oakland for a few weeks and we'd love to have you join us.
20. Last summer I played tennis almost every day and found that I improved quite a bit.
21. I was assigned the task of examining the methods and procedures used by other companies and also the job of adapting these findings to our use.
22. One thousand dollars has already been paid and the balance of seventeen thousand will be paid within sixty days.
23. We are able to obtain adequate chemical supplies but we cannot get enough equipment of other types.
24. She was proud of her beauty and spent much time keeping herself attractive.
25. The sun had now vanished completely and the silver moon peeped through a break in the deep blue clouds.

EXERCISE 2

Follow the directions in Exercise 1.

1. We are holding the freezing units for you and should appreciate your letting us know when you would like to have them delivered.
2. It was interesting to see the Indian dances but I was disappointed to find the costumes of the witch doctors were not like those in the pictures.
3. Streetcars clanged as they traveled to and fro on their daily trips and grass grew between the stones on the street.
4. The story has been told far and wide and will forever be a legend in these mountains.
5. The Trinity River broke through the levees in several places and many people were forced out of their homes.
6. Lucy had many music teachers but scales and rhythm simply would not sink into her head.
7. Calls for service received before 1:00 P.M. were acted upon the same day and those received after 1:00 P.M. were scheduled for the next day.

8. I invited him for lunch and we discussed the present situation in the stainless steel industry.

9. The Metal Products Company has a supply of stainless steel and has been trying to persuade Mr. Paulson to cancel his order with us and buy from it.

10. Some of the homes were on magnificent estates but most of them were the simple houses of workingmen.

11. The relations between labor and management in the company grew steadily worse and an open clash was prevented only by the intervention of the Governor.

12. The early evening was the best time to walk to the top of the hill and look at the little valley below.

13. Practically every firm states that its machinery costs have been reduced by 25 percent and some claim a reduction of 35 percent.

14. I have not had any experience in the business of selling but I will give the job my best effort and feel certain that I can learn it quickly.

15. He subscribes liberally to the Associated Charities and no good object or worthy enterprise fails to receive his support.

16. He made many speeches from the truck and was so well received everywhere that his political party rewarded him with a good job.

17. Virtually all cottages here are reported rented for the summer and hotel reservations are said to have hit an all-time high.

18. We have usually gone to Carmel for the summer but this year we have taken a cottage at Santa Barbara and hope that you will join us for July.

19. Surf bathing and all kinds of water sports are offered and the resort has a background of pine forests and picturesque bays.

20. The cause of a united Ireland is one which arouses flaming passions and causes violent arguments.

23b. Use a comma to separate an introductory phrase or dependent clause from an independent clause.

The fact that the element is *introductory* means that it precedes the independent clause. Often it is at the very

168

beginning of the sentence. The introductory element may be a clause, a phrase, or, occasionally, merely a word. Failure to punctuate it will interfere with the clearness of the sentence. If the introductory element is a clause, it will probably begin with a subordinating conjunction—for example, *if, as, since, because, although, while,* or *when.*

> When she finished high school, she determined to be an artist.
> If no dormitory rooms are available, I'll inquire about rooms off the campus.
> Although summer is months away, the girls have started to make plans for their vacation.

If a sentence begins with a phrase containing a participle or an infinitive and used as an adjective or an adverb, a comma should follow the phrase.

> Acting on the advice of Mr. Crawford, we bought some stock in the company. (Participial phrase used as adjective)
> To win the game, you must watch each card that is played. (Infinitive phrase used as adverb)

A long prepositional phrase is usually followed by a comma if it begins the sentence. Even a short prepositional phrase must be followed by a comma if the meaning would otherwise be confused.

Common prepositions are *to, for, from, with, between, in, over, under, by, across, after.*

> *In a little country store nearby,* we bought some bread and cheese. (Prepositional phrase)
> *After a long walk in the brisk air,* we were glad to rest before the fire. (Prepositional phrase, in which the object of the preposition is modified by a second phrase)

CAUTION:

1. Sometimes in a compound-complex sentence the in-

troductory phrase or clause comes in the middle of the sentence. In the sentence which follows, the clause *before anyone could get it* is considered introductory because it precedes the independent clause *he had reached second base.* Therefore, a comma is used after *it.*

> Bill Tucker hit a ball into the hole between short stop and third base; and before anyone could get it, he had reached second base.

2. A gerund or infinitive phrase used as the subject of a sentence is not separated from the rest of the sentence by a comma.

> Planting a garden requires skill and care.
> To spend a month at the seashore was her chief desire.

EXERCISE 3

Most of these sentences contain errors in the use of the comma after an introductory phrase or dependent clause. On your paper, write the number of each of the sentences. Beside it write the word after which a comma should be placed and the comma. If no comma needs to be added to a sentence, write C beside the sentence number. As an example, the correction for the first sentence is given below:

1. yesterday,

1. While walking home from school yesterday she lost her physics book.
2. Should you desire an interview I can be reached at home.
3. Because you are one of our best customers we want you to have advance information about the sale.
4. If you expect to attend the convention please mail the enclosed card for your reservation.
5. Through the purchase of a retirement policy, you can assure yourself of security in your old age.
6. If you purchase a cottage at Shelby Cove you will own property in an exclusive summer colony.

7. During the years of the German occupation Athens suffered indescribably.

8. As she was coming back from the well with a pail of cool water she noticed a strange movement of the bushes.

9. Thinking that the figure was a ghost we ran as fast as our legs could carry us.

10. To make a good model airplane you must follow the directions exactly.

11. Although I have not had any training as a counselor I have gone to camp for many years and know what a counselor should do.

12. To run a mile a person must first of all be in good physical condition.

13. In order for the laboratory to function properly we need two additional technicians.

14. Under his expert direction the symphony orchestra grew to be one of the most famous in the world.

15. During the past month 6 percent of the work hours was required for machinery repairs.

16. Because he had no parental guidance or home life he began to run wild.

17. Complying with your request of March 10 we are mailing you a membership application blank.

18. After an examination of our easy payment plan you will be sure to want a house in Shelby Cove.

19. If you come to Portland may we have the pleasure of reserving a room for you?

20. Since the capacity of our hotel is limited to one thousand guests you must place your reservation now.

21. Sucking the cool juice of the oranges into their dry throats, the boys discussed the ways of getting home that evening.

22. In addition to the attractive features already outlined Shelby Cove is a paradise for children.

23. Although I have had little experience I can assure you that I am very much interested in the work.

24. Since the establishment of the company in 1921 there have been several reorganizations.

25. As I threw open my window I could see a mass of flames rising from the building across the street.

EXERCISE 4

Follow the directions in Exercise 3.

1. As I look back on the five years which I spent as a clerk in a drugstore I see that I learned a great deal.
2. For some reason that we have not determined Friday seems to be our busiest day.
3. To supply a city like this large power plants are needed.
4. Noticing that it was becoming very dark and thinking that our parents would be worried, we began to gather our bats and balls in order to leave.
5. Having gone without ice cream and candy for two whole months Theresa had finally saved enough money to buy the gloves that she wanted.
6. If you will have your secretary type your name on the enclosed card and mail it to me I will see that you receive one of the first copies.
7. I assured him that as soon as we receive our shipment of 24-gauge steel we will fill his order for 100 water coolers.
8. We guarantee that if you do not find the materials satisfactory you may return them at our expense.
9. We have notified our customers that since the materials are not available we shall be unable to fill their orders until May 10.
10. As the zoologist and his group moved through the jungle, the bushes suddenly parted; and there, in front of the astonished scientists, stood a huge baboon.

23c. Use commas to separate words, phrases, or clauses in a series.

A series consists of three or more words, phrases, or clauses in the same construction.

> *Nouns:* The crowd consisted of *men, women,* and *children.*
>
> *Verbs:* Mr. Brewster *reads, writes,* and *speaks* French like a native.
>
> *Adverbial phrases:* He ran *down the steps, across the street,* and *into the park.*

> *Noun clauses:* They asked me *how I had arrived in Siam, what I intended to do there,* and *when I should return to the United States.*

Some writers omit the commas before *and* in a series; but because in some sentences this omission may cause misunderstanding, it is better to use the comma before *and*.

CAUTION: Do not place a comma before the first member of a series or after the last member.

Wrong: We put, apples, peaches, and pears, into the basket.
 Right: We put apples, peaches, and pears into the basket.

23d. Use commas to separate two or more adjectives when they are coordinate modifiers of the same noun.

> Tall, slender, graceful girls modeled the clothes.

If the last adjective modifies the noun and the one preceding it modifies the combined idea, the adjectives are not coordinate and no comma is used.

> At the ticket window stood a man carrying a large, shabby leather suitcase.

In this sentence *leather* modifies *suitcase. Large* and *shabby* are coordinates with each other, but not with *leather;* they describe the *leather suitcase.*

It is sometimes difficult to determine whether or not the adjectives are coordinate. One way of testing is to insert the conjunction *and* between the adjectives; if the *and* fits naturally, use a comma when it is omitted. In the sentence above, we can say, "The leather suitcase was large and shabby," but "The suitcase was large, shabby, and leather" does not sound natural. We therefore use a comma between *large* and *shabby* but not between *shabby* and *leather.*

CAUTION: If a word modifies the following adjective rather than the noun, do not separate the two words by a comma.

> Yesterday I bought a combed cotton pullover.

173

Here the word *combed* modifies *cotton,* not *pullover.* Hence we do not have two adjectives modifying the noun.

EXERCISE 5

These sentences contain errors in the punctuation of a series. On your paper, write the number of each of the sentences and beside it write the word or words after which a comma should be placed. Include the comma. If a sentence is correct, place a C beside the number. As an example, the correction for the first sentence is given below.

1. students, teachers,

1. The members of the society were students teachers and clerks.
2. We are sure that there are many things which you would like to purchase for yourself your family or your home.
3. A short fat girl came into the room.
4. In my history classes I have learned about my country its government and its people.
5. The tight black silk cap had gay shiny buttons sewed around the crown.
6. The candidate was elected on a platform of slum clearance tax reform and economy in government.
7. At the auction sale she bought a beautiful inlaid rosewood table an antique highboy and a wrought-iron lantern.
8. The courses in science taught us to question to reason and to experiment.
9. The pale yellow porch chairs had dark green cushions.
10. He mixed sodas delivered prescriptions and made himself generally useful in the store.

EXERCISE 6

Follow the directions in Exercise 5.

1. The book tells of her romances her many famous friends on and off the stage and her war adventures.
2. The girl uttered a piercing scream dropped her pail of water and ran for the house.

3. Early in the morning we milk the cows churn the butter and pick berries or peaches and string beans.
4. It was fun to make new friends to take part in the various activities of the school and to join a few clubs.
5. I believe that the school has taught me to think clearly to converse intelligently and to appreciate beauty.
6. Franklin pioneered in the study of the common cold the conduction of heat by various substances and the prediction of the weather.
7. The club has made arrangements to have on display the newest boat models engine equipment and safety devices.
8. The strike shut off the country's power closed its mills and stopped the wheels of industry.
9. Within a few years, the J. M. Salten Company was doing a million-dollar business had purchased the plants of two competitors and was planning to establish a branch office in Pittsburgh.
10. The children came to the vacant lot on warm spring afternoons and played long intense games of dodge ball speed ball or volley ball.

EXERCISE 7

Follow the directions in Exercise 5.

1. The attic was hung with clusters of bats the wooden structure was rotten and the whole effect was gloomy.
2. They needed to cut down the weeds erect new fences and repair the roof in order to make the place habitable.
3. The girl wore a fleecy, dull green coat and hat brown shoes with high narrow heels a beige silk muffler and beige gloves.
4. Standardization of the size of the paper will save space in the main store room in individual office storage cabinets and in file cabinets.
5. The clerk is trained to write legibly to show the necessary information in the proper columns and to add and extend the amount of the sale accurately.
6. Members of the Home Service Corps of the Red Cross receive patients handle case correspondence and assist the professional staff in nontechnical duties.

7. According to some statistics, individuals today spend an average of one hour a week at the motion pictures twenty-five hours listening to the radio or watching television and five hours reading.
8. The book profits by the author's ability to visualize the eighteenth-century scene to describe it convincingly and to bring to life the men who made our history.
9. Scientists all over the world will perfect new weapons improve present weapons and make ready the instruments of destruction that man will turn against himself.
10. The investigation is to cover the kinds of samples analyzed by each laboratory the methods used in analyzing the samples and new methods which may save time and money.

EXERCISE 8

This exercise reviews the use of capital letters and the use of the comma in a series, after an introductory element, and before the coordinating conjunction in a compound sentence. On your paper, write this paragraph, placing commas and capital letters where they should be. Number each correction that you make. At the end of the paragraph list the numbers and beside each number write the reason for the correction.

Last Saturday the northern high school played polytechnic a championship game in football. when we arrived at the benton stadium the stands were filled with girls waving pennants boys shouting for their team and gay parents and teachers. swinging along in perfect time our band entered the field marched once around and then took seats in the reserved section. for the first half we played well. then skippy broke his ankle and our chances of winning declined. when they saw that skippy was out of the game the boys seemed to lose heart. the quarterback miscalled a signal the right tackle pulled out of the line at the wrong time and the ball carrier fumbled as he was tackled. then the opposing team recovered the fumble and scored on the next play. I still hoped but my hopes were in vain. the game ended with a score of 13–7 in favor of poly.

EXERCISE 9

Follow the directions in Exercise 8.

A few summers ago judith went with her mother and father on a cruise to the west indies. it was a beautiful trip. mrs. nolte lay lazily in a deck chair and read most of the time but judith and her father were active. they played deck tennis and shuffleboard sat on the top deck to get a good sun tan and danced at night. when the boat stopped for a day at port of spain in trinidad the passengers had an opportunity to see a new kind of life. because her father had a business acquaintance in this town judith was able to see the inside of a charming tropical home. it was built around a patio where palm and banana trees surrounded a fountain. when judith came home she talked of nothing but trinidad. I was so enthusiastic that I planned to visit the west indies myself.

23e. Use commas to separate parenthetical words, phrases, or clauses from the rest of the sentence.

A parenthetical expression interrupts a thought and is not necessary to the meaning of the sentence. Although it often makes the sentence smoother or adds a bit of additional information, the thought is complete without it. Some expressions frequently used in a parenthetical sense are *however, for instance, of course, as we said, for example, to tell the truth.* If these expressions or any others are used parenthetically, they should have a comma before them and a comma after them.

The task, it is true, is not a difficult one.

The words *it is true* interrupt the thought *the task is not a difficult one.* The sentence is complete without this expression. Hence the expression is separated from the rest of the sentence by commas.

The parenthetical expression may be a rather long clause or phrase. Such expressions frequently give interesting information. If, however, they interrupt the main thought, they are considered parenthetical.

> Kenneth, evidently taking his cue from his brother, answered affirmatively.
> Many professional men, even if they have plenty of time, will have nothing to do with politics.

CAUTION: The conjunctive adverbs *however, moreover, nevertheless, consequently, therefore, thus, then, so, yet, otherwise* are sometimes used as parenthetical expressions. But if one of these conjunctive adverbs joins two independent clauses, it must be preceded by a semicolon.

> Jane, however, stayed at home. (Parenthetical)
> John went to school; however, Jane stayed at home. (Two independent clauses)

23f. Use commas to separate from the rest of a sentence nouns or pronouns used in direct address.

> Mr. Henderson, may I see you for a moment?
> I asked you, Ronald, not to come here today.

23g. The words yes and no are usually followed by a comma when used at the beginning of a sentence.

> Yes, I have studied French.
> No, nobody was there.

EXERCISE 10

The following sentences involve errors in the uses of the comma shown in Section 23d–f. On a piece of paper, write the number of each of the sentences, and beside it write each word after which a comma should be used, with the comma. As an example, the correction is given for the first sentence:

1. believe, Doctor,

1. I cannot believe Doctor that the disease is so serious.
2. Have you by any chance a suggestion as to our lodgings?

3. Yes it will seem strange I suppose to go to the beach and not come to the old cottage.
4. Your delivery promise you may recall was for the first week in April.
5. Billy after realizing what had happened gave a long wail and began to sob bitterly.
6. King Saul fearing the loss of his throne drove David from the palace.
7. No Helene I don't need money, but will you do something for me?
8. Our present Governor will I am sure be reelected by a large majority.
9. New York as we all know has developed many successful writers.
10. Come here Rex and do your tricks.

EXERCISE 11

Follow the directions in Exercise 10.

1. Don't make so much noise Herbert.
2. These price increases effective immediately apply to moderate-priced shoes.
3. His whole life in fact might have been changed if he had accepted the job.
4. My little sister, bravely concealing her disappointment, relinquished her seat to Aunt Sarah.
5. Boys and girls you will have an unusual opportunity this year.
6. At present for example we have only three thousand of the five thousand test tubes which we need.
7. Jenny glad of a chance to make the trip tried hard not to think of the unpleasant company that she would have.
8. Some of the evidence it is said by the defense counsel concerns military secrets and cannot be presented at this time.
9. The house designed I believe by Carter and Wells is a French Provincial cottage with a charming outdoor terrace.
10. The new airport has three runways two of which are 3,000 feet long and a large, impressive administration building.

EXERCISE 12

Follow the directions in Exercise 10.

1. Our research program begun last year in the interest of improved passenger service has now been completed.
2. Pepys though not entirely an egoist never lost interest in himself.
3. Many perhaps the majority of the people traveling to Europe this summer will go by air.
4. One of the greatest crowds in the history of American golf estimated to be from sixteen to twenty thousand fans saw the United States Open Championship yesterday.
5. Four good-looking American girls hailed by everybody as the best-balanced U.S. team ever sent to England won the Wightman Cup matches yesterday.
6. Some travel organizations proceeding on the premise that there will be too many travelers to share existing accommodations have planned all-expense tours.
7. The unsuccessful actors unwilling to admit defeat by accepting other employment sank into abject and hopeless poverty.
8. The river swollen by thirty hours of continuous rain swept over its banks and flooded the town.
9. The blunt, straight-speaking chairman, opening a discussion of the committee's plans for the year, said that nothing would be accomplished unless each member did his share.
10. The first two years of high school gave me in addition to increased factual knowledge an appreciation of the value of an education.

23h. Use commas to separate nonrestrictive clauses and phrases from the remainder of the sentence.

Clauses and phrases are *restrictive* when they limit the meaning of the word they modify by identifying the particular one that is meant. They answer the question "which?" or "what kind?"

> John Mackay, *who is our postman,* is a former aviator.
> The man *who is our postman* is a former aviator.

I like books about people who have had eventful lives.

In the first of these sentences, *who is our postman* merely provides additional information about John Mackay; he is already identified by name. In the second sentence, the clause identifies the man we are talking about. It answers the question "which man?" In the third sentence, the clause answers the question "what kind of people?"

The *context* sometimes determines whether a clause or phrase is restrictive or nonrestrictive.

> Ellen and Sarah entertained us while Louise and Mary were busy in the kitchen. After lunch the girls who had prepared the meal rested, and the others washed the dishes.
>
> Ellen and Sarah drove to Crystal Lake with Jim and Alan for a picnic. After lunch the girls, who had prepared the meal, rested while the boys washed the dishes.

In the first pair of sentences, *who had prepared the meal* tells which of the girls rested; it is therefore restrictive. In the second pair, there can be no mistake about which girls are meant. The clause simply gives additional information.

Sometimes only the writer of a sentence can tell whether a modifier is restrictive or nonrestrictive. If he punctuates such a sentence incorrectly, he will mislead the reader.

> Our camera club has a new projector. The members who worked during the summer paid for it out of their earnings.

The omission of commas before and after the clause *who worked during the summer* indicates to the reader that the clause is restrictive—that is, that it tells which of the members paid for the projector. But the writer meant to say that all of the members had contributed and that all had worked during the summer. Commas before and after the clause would have made this meaning clear.

If you are uncertain whether a modifier is restrictive or

nonrestrictive, try reading the sentence without it. If the sentence still expresses the meaning you had in mind, the modifier is nonrestrictive and should be set off by commas; if the sentence now means something different, the modifier is restrictive and no commas should be used. Study these sentences:

With modifier: Tourists, who can usually be recognized by their cameras, seem to outnumber the native population.

Without modifier: Tourists seem to outnumber the native population.

With modifier: Tourists who fail to declare dutiable goods must, if detected, pay the duty plus a penalty.

Without modifier: Tourists must, if detected, pay the duty plus a penalty.

With modifier: All men who have family responsibilities should carry life insurance.

Without modifier: All men should carry life insurance.

The first sentence means exactly the same with or without the modifying clause; the clause is therefore nonrestrictive. The next is pure nonsense when the clause is omitted. The last makes sense without the clause, but not the same kind of sense; the meaning is greatly changed by the omission. In these two sentences, therefore, the clauses are restrictive.

EXERCISE 13

Some of the following sentences require correction by the addition of commas, usually to punctuate nonrestrictive expressions. Other uses of the comma are also required. Some of the sentences are correctly punctuated. On your paper rewrite any incorrect sentence, adding the necessary commas. If a sentence is correct, write C beside the number; do not rewrite a correct sentence.

1. The fifteen dollars that I had so carefully saved was spent in one evening on a date with Sandra.

2. Grandfather who was a huckster wanted to get a stall in the market.

3. Her knees which were normally strong and firm were now weak and shaky.

4. I tried to find a vacation spot which would give me something different from the usual thing.

5. Mrs. Seaman's husband who is in the printing business has promised to print the tickets free of charge.

6. It was suggested by Mrs. Bruce that a committee be appointed to call on members who are ill.

7. Our team which has lost four first-string men through injuries can hardly expect to win.

8. Basketball players who are more than six feet tall have a real advantage over their shorter teammates.

9. I have been reading about the labor problem which was until recently a complete blank to me.

10. Parents who do not provide a home where there is love affection and guidance are to blame if their children become delinquents.

11. My favorite in the play was Alexander Harding who played the role of the prince's tutor.

12. The second and third floors which were formerly showrooms are now used as storage space.

13. The other blouse of similar style that I have to offer can be seen on page 372 of our catalogue.

14. The school which I attended was not far from our new house but the mountain road was poorly constructed.

15. He became friendly with the Governor who offered to help him start his business.

16. The suit which you ordered Mr. Scott has been shipped by express.

17. One of the counselors whom you employed last year has told me of a vacancy in your office.

18. When I heard the price which I think is outrageous I decided not to buy the house.

19. Everybody who goes to Exeter thinks it is one of the finest schools in the country.

20. Taking her "over-month" bag Grandma went to Lynchburg to see her favorite cousins who have a small farm.

21. Our plan was to visit the site of the bridge which was being constructed about four miles from our home.
22. After two long weeks she found herself walking up the gangplank of the ship which was to take her to America.
23. Although I have learned many things which will help me I value my English training above all others.
24. During this interview which was very interesting I learned many things about the business the city and the county.
25. My aunt who was living in Denver at the time wrote to us of an amazing experience which she had had.

EXERCISE 14

Follow the directions in Exercise 13.

1. The meeting was called to order by Mrs. Ford who called on the chairman of the banquet committee for her report.
2. My father's hunting lodge which is set high on a mountain overlooking a lake is as quaint as a picture in a book.
3. The bully was a strong husky fellow of seventeen who spent his time beating the small boys.
4. We knew Roger as a little boy who used to follow other boys around when they wanted to be rid of him.
5. The success of the organization under my leadership made me impatient with my successor who was a slow easygoing boy.
6. All of a sudden without any warning in advance the truck which we had been following went out of control and turned over completely.
7. The machine will cut office expenses and give employees who operate it an easier day.
8. When Joseph had finished the article which he read with great interest he stood up folded the magazine and began to lecture us.
9. The second flood in that area within a week followed a heavy downpour of rain which felled telephone wires sent trees crashing upon parked automobiles and backed up sewers.
10. Mr. Reever who called on me yesterday had some interesting samples but he was unable to get me any of the fine English wool that I wanted.

23i. Use commas to separate appositives from the rest of the sentence.

An appositive is a substantive (noun or pronoun) joined to another substantive that means the same thing.

> Jones, an *Englishman,* was an excellent sailor.
> Robert Frost, the *author of "Birches,"* is one of the finest American poets. (*Jones* and *Englishman* are the same; *Robert Frost* and *author of "Birches"* are the same.)

A comma or two commas should be used to separate the appositive from the rest of the sentence. If the appositive is at the end of the sentence, it is preceded by a comma and followed by a period.

CAUTION:

1. An appositive which is part of a name is not separated by commas.

> Richard the Lion-Hearted was an English king.

2. Sometimes an appositive is restrictive; that is, it identifies or limits the meaning of the word with which it is in apposition. If the appositive answers the question "which?" it is restrictive and should not be separated by commas. (See Section 23h.)

> The phrase *to my house* is adverbial.
> My brother *Sam* is sick.

In the first sentence, *to my house* tells which phrase the writer means. It is therefore restrictive and requires no commas.

The second sentence is a special case. Names in apposition with words like *brother, sister, friend* are now written without commas. Even if one has only one brother or sister or friend, so that the appositive does not tell *which,* the name is considered so closely related to the preceding noun that no commas are needed.

EXERCISE 15

On your paper, write the following sentences, placing commas where they are needed to punctuate an appositive, a series, a term of address, a parenthetical expression, or an introductory dependent clause.

1. Bob Coleman the coach at Southern High expects his team to win the cup this year.
2. *Good Night, Sweet Prince* is the biography of John Barrymore a well-known much-admired actor.
3. City and Polytechnic our two keenest rivals have lost several of their outstanding players.
4. Mr. Andrews a man of long experience in selling tools will tell you the advantage of buying our products.
5. He sold the business to J. P. David Company an old reliable firm.
6. Dan did you know that the author of the book Dr. Baumgarten was once a teacher?
7. One of the persons whom she met was Celeste Armiger an author of considerable reputation.
8. Dr. Nils Peterson director of the hospital is greatly worried about the increased expenses.
9. He opened the icebox and saw something that caught his fancy immediately a dish of macaroni and cheese.
10. When I reached the waiting room I was greeted by Mrs. Sheldon the director of the volunteer workers.

EXERCISE 16

Follow the directions in Exercise 15.

1. The first wrestler a mere youth looks small and insignificant beside the other a rugged large heavy-set man.
2. The speech marked a historic moment the turning of the tide.
3. She was happy because she was leaving Russia and going to America the land of opportunity.
4. Joan's father an important businessman worked for one of the large expensive department stores.
5. Student government gave me a chance to learn public speaking an art which will be valuable to me in later life.

6. When Joanne married Bob a tall handsome marine she did not expect to settle down on a farm.
7. Last week at our Spanish club two guests one from Uruguay and one from Cuba spoke to us in Spanish.
8. In two games yesterday the sixth and seventh of the season Northern High the champion of last year was badly defeated.
9. When he visited The Poplars a neighboring farm he found the people greatly disturbed by news of a robbery.
10. Elizabeth became interested in Mr. Darcy an arrogant haughty and conceited person.

EXERCISE 17

Follow the directions in Exercise 15.

1. We landed first on the southern end of the island that part where most of the fighting took place.
2. Winston Churchill British wartime Prime Minister and later leader of the Conservative opposition rebuked the Labor Government for its food policy.
3. In your course Dr. Davis I have learned to distinguish between fact and opinion.
4. Pope the man is far different from Pope the poet.
5. Some scientists have been working on an interesting new product a DDT wallpaper which will kill moths flies and mosquitoes.
6. Henry Bronson one of the most wealthy farmers in the county was married to a kind-hearted pert engaging woman of thirty.
7. Godfrey was often led into doing foolish things that would never have occurred to him had it not been for Dunstan his thoroughly dishonest brother.
8. I have a reasonably good command of two important languages Latin and Spanish about which I had no knowledge before I entered high school.
9. Doing two term papers one on labor problems and the other on the development of American railroads has given me a fine opportunity to develop a technique for handling reference materials skill in using the library and a method of organizing facts.

10. Surrounded by three hundred distinguished guests the regally robed monarch ascended the throne in a ceremony which lasted fourteen minutes the climax of one of the most important days in the history of the country.

23j. Use commas before and after the name of a state or country when it follows the name of a city, and before and after the year when it follows the month or the month and day.

John left on July 8, 1959, to go to Peoria, Illinois.

23k. Use commas before and after the abbreviations *Jr.* and *Sr.* and abbreviations of academic degrees.

James Norman, Ph.D., and Frank Hale, M.D., are the authors of the book.
George Madison, Jr., is the owner of the building.

EXERCISE 18

On your paper, write the following sentences, placing commas where they are needed. Most of the commas will be those called for in Section 23i–j, but some commas will be needed for other uses.

1. On February 12 1809 Abraham Lincoln was born in a log cabin in Hardin County Kentucky.
2. Mr. Saunders testified that on May 9 1943 he was in Athens Ohio on business.
3. Good Friday April 10 1868 was the birth date of a great actor George Arliss.
4. The writer studied at the Sorbonne Paris from September 10 1933 to May 30 1934.
5. On July 20 1942 the first group of women to join the United States Army showed up at Des Moines Iowa.
6. At the age of seven my father spent his first vacation away from home in Chestertown Maryland where he had relatives.
7. Simon Bolivar the great South American patriot was a native of Caracas Venezuela.
8. Florence Nightingale famous for her works in nursing and

in hospital reform was born in Florence Italy and took her name from that town.

9. It was in April 1775 that the American Revolution began.
10. Your advertisement in the Denver *Post* of Thursday March 12 interested me.
11. On April 12 1865 Abraham Lincoln was shot by John Wilkes Booth a Shakespearean actor.
12. One night fifteen years ago in Windsor Ontario Martin Banner a steelworker bade his wife good-by and went to a lodge meeting. He was never seen again.
13. Elizabeth Benson one of the pioneers in the movement to educate women visited Hastings Nebraska on May 10 1908.
14. Henry started to school with his cousin Pauline Henderson who lived next door to him on Linwood Boulevard Kansas City.
15. On January 9 1834 in Boston Massachusetts a book by John Carrington was published.

23l. Use a comma to separate contrasted coordinate elements.

> My name is John, not Henry.
> He struck forcefully, but wildly.

23m. Use a comma after the salutation and complimentary close in a friendly letter.

> Dear Harold,
> Sincerely yours,

NOTE: The colon is generally used after the salutation in a business letter and may also be used after the salutation in a friendly letter.

23n. Use a comma before a direct quotation that is introduced by a verb such as *said, exclaimed, thought*. (See Sections 25b and 27a.)

> Morgan said proudly, "I am a Texan."

If the sentence does not end with the quotation, a comma

is required before the closing quotation marks unless the quotation ends with a question mark or an exclamation point or the structure of the sentence itself calls for some other mark of punctuation. (See Section 27f.)

> The stranger said, "This is the end of our trail," and dismounted.
> "Did you hear me?" he asked.
> He wrote, "I shall expect you at five o'clock"; but whatever he might expect, I had no intention of going.

23o. Use a comma or commas to separate an absolute expression from the rest of a sentence.

> The tide having risen, Ferris floated the sailboat.
> On the island, the fog having lifted, he saw the lighthouse.

23p. Use a comma before a final phrase or clause which introduces a new idea.

> I am grateful for everything you have done for me, *especially for your kindness during my illness.*

EXERCISE 19

On your paper, rewrite the following paragraph, placing commas where they are needed. Number each comma in sequence. At the end of the paragraph, list the numbers and beside each number write the reason for the use of the comma indicated by that number.

Not long ago some of our newspapers reported the development of jet-propelled automobiles and we all thought of the great development that has taken place since the first horseless carriage. Although it seems impossible now to think of a life without cars our grandparents remember those carriage days very well. Grandpa climbed into his buggy took the reins in his hand gave old Dobbin a gentle slap and set off to see his girl. The first horseless carriage was built by Charles and Frank Duryea in Springfield Massachusetts in 1892. It was the Duryeas also who won the first road automobile race ever held in the United States. The other day Jane came to me with a photograph album and said "If you want to see something really amusing look at the clothes worn by those early drivers." Long loose coats big goggles and visored caps were used by the men. The ladies not to be outdone added to this costume long veils which tied their hats on securely. With a speed of seven miles an hour the cars caused a great wind a cloud of dust and wild excitement.

EXERCISE 20

Follow the directions in Exercise 19.

Since television has become so popular the average person reads less according to a recent report. If this is true then the average person is missing a great experience that could be his. In the first place reading offers us a chance for vicarious experience. It may be adventure in distant lands the problems of raising chickens on a far-from-modern farm or the struggle to establish a business that pays. However one of the greatest satisfactions that the average man can obtain from reading is the mental stimulation of sharing the ideas of great men. Anyone who has read widely knows what fun it is to meet challenging ideas to broaden one's own outlook to grow intellectually.

EXERCISE 21

Follow the directions in Exercise 19.

As Ichabod approached the stream his heart began to thump. He summoned up however all his resolution gave his horse a kick in the ribs and attempted to dash briskly across the bridge. Instead of starting forward the perverse old animal ran broadside against the fence. Ichabod whose fears increased with the delay jerked the reins and kicked the horse lustily. It was all in vain. His steed started it is true but it was only to plunge to the opposite side of the road. Ichabod now bestowed both whip and heel upon the ribs of Old Gunpowder who dashed forward sniffling and snorting. In a moment he stopped as suddenly as he had begun. In the dark shadow of the grove Ichabod beheld something huge black and towering. As he looked he realized with horror that the figure was headless; but his horror was still greater when he observed that the head which should have rested on the shoulders was carried before the rider on the pommel of his saddle.

—Adapted from *The Legend of Sleepy Hollow*
by Washington Irving

EXERCISE 22

Follow the directions in Exercise 19.

A moment later a throng of people came pouring round the corner. There could not have been fewer than five hundred and they were dancing like five thousand demons. At first they were a mere storm of coarse red caps and coarser woolen rags but as they filled the square some ghastly apparition gone raving mad rose among them. They advanced retreated clutched at one another spun round in pairs until many of them dropped. While those were down the rest linked hand in hand and all spun round together. No fight could have been half so terrible as this dance. It was so emphatically a fallen sport a healthy pastime changed into a means of angering the blood bewildering the senses and steeling the heart. This was the Carmagnole.

—Adapted from *A Tale of Two Cities*
by Charles Dickens

24. THE SEMICOLON

The semicolon is a stronger mark of punctuation than the comma. It signifies a greater break between sentence parts. It is used chiefly between parts of a sentence that have equal rank.

24a. Use a semicolon to separate independent clauses not joined by a coordinating conjunction (*and, but, nor, for, or*).

> Please close the window; the room is cold.
> I entertain my friends by playing the piano; Ellen does tap dancing.

24b. Use a semicolon to separate independent clauses connected by a conjunctive adverb (*however, moreover, nevertheless, consequently, therefore, thus, then, so, yet, otherwise, still, likewise*).

> They were of opposite characters; yet they remained friends for many years.
>
> We regret that we have sold all of the blouses in blue; however, we have the same style in pink.

NOTE: Do not use a semicolon every time that you see a conjunctive adverb. Be sure first that you have two independent clauses.

> John, however, has failed to do the work. (This sentence has no semicolon because *however* is a parenthetical expression and does not connect two complete thoughts.)

24c. Use a semicolon to separate independent clauses joined by a coordinating conjunction if the clauses are long or contain commas.

> When the scorpion stung the man, he felt a sharp pain in his foot; but since there was no swelling, he thought that he had not been injured.
>
> Roberta, a very good friend of mine, wants me to go to camp with her; but because I have been to camp for three years in succession, I am undecided.

CAUTION: Usually no semicolon appears between an independent clause and a dependent clause or an independent clause and a phrase. A semicolon joins only those things which are in the same form structurally.

Wrong: Whenever I hear from one of the old crowd; memories rush to my mind. (The first clause is a dependent clause. It would not express a complete thought if used alone. The second clause is an independent clause. It would express a complete thought if used alone.)

Right: Whenever I hear from one of the crowd, memories rush
to my mind. (See Section 23b.)

Wrong: Everything that you sent me is beautiful; especially the
white doeskin gloves.

Right: Everything that you sent me is beautiful, especially the
white doeskin gloves.

24d. Use a semicolon before explanatory expressions like *for example, namely.*

The government has given to veterans some special considerations; namely, college training, trade training, and
insurance.

24e. A semicolon is sometimes used to separate the members of a series if any of them contain commas.

Down the field came the newly organized, somewhat incompetent band; three drum majorettes in white
spangled skirts; and the team, muddy and wretched.

EXERCISE 23

Some of the following sentences are correctly punctuated;
others are not. On your paper, rewrite the latter, using
commas and semicolons where they are required. Write
your reason for each correction. If a sentence is correct, do
not rewrite it, but write C beside its number.

1. It is painful for me to recall the story I prefer never to think
of it again.
2. When I arrived at the doctor's office I was asked to give the
history of my life then I was ushered into the main office.
3. I can't imagine what he wants; I never heard of him before.
4. Mr. Howells was born on May 30 1903 in Richmond Virginia
but at the age of two he moved to Long Beach California.
5. Heat expands solids; cold contracts them.
6. Our town has many advantages to offer new residents for
example good schools an excellent shopping center and low
taxes.
7. Guests at the wedding included Mr. and Mrs. Jerome

Woodward of Columbus Ohio Mr. Walter Burns of Auburn New York and Miss Ellen Ames of Gary Indiana.

8. Mrs. Smith is interested in purchasing some of our stainless steel products; however, she thinks our prices are too high.

9. Things back home will seem a bit strange to you in fact everything in the old town has changed.

10. Mr. Mayer noticed that Benito was more alert than the average Indian servant therefore he decided to send the child to school.

EXERCISE 24

Follow the directions in Exercise 23.

1. This year I have my last opportunity to win my letter in basketball and if all goes well I shall soon be wearing the emblem of the school.

2. If any fault in our service has caused your long absence from our store we are anxious to correct it for we want you to be entirely satisfied.

3. It was her first transatlantic voyage in fact it was the first time she had ever seen the ocean.

4. Johnson hated to be questioned and Boswell was eternally examining him on all kinds of subjects.

5. I was sure I had no chance of winning the scholarship nevertheless I determined to try.

6. Contributions were received from Henry Lowell, manager of the Sunrise Market Ralph Summers proprietor of the Four Corners Pharmacy and Lillian Moore chief librarian of the Chestnut Grove Library.

7. Farming seemed to be the chief occupation of the section, for everywhere one could see fields planted with corn wheat and potatoes.

8. No one thought until the deadline approached that the men would strike and it seemed inconceivable that they would strike against the government after seizure of the plant.

9. On our side of the street the lawns are neat and the hedges trim on the other side the lawns have tall weeds and ash cans stand in front of the gates.

10. Jane Winters invited me to a party she is going to give for

Mary Lou; and when she heard that you would be in town, she included you in the invitation.

EXERCISE 25

Follow the directions in Exercise 23.

1. For twenty years Boswell continued to worship the master and the master continued to scold the disciple to sneer at him and to love him.

2. When the game started Leroy who had been a great success the week before was not on the field and all of the spectators wondered what had happened to him.

3. In the neighborhood where I lived there were no movies, playgrounds, or nursery schools where children could go for recreation; therefore, the streets and empty lots were used for play.

4. It will in the future not be possible to provide Mr. Schultz with room and board at the building consequently some adjustment in his salary is necessary.

5. The equipment is available for use by anyone that needs it however the laboratory employees are responsible for keeping it in good condition.

6. Not only was there trouble with the chickens but since the farm was far from modern Hilda had to struggle with the stove the plumbing and the heating system.

7. Boswell was very much attracted to Johnson; he made it his business to watch the great man to discover his habits and to remember the remarkable things he said.

8. Salt lowers the freezing point of water that is it causes ice to melt at a temperature below 32 degrees.

9. I explained that it would be impossible to fill the order at once because the current model is out of stock and is not being reordered however I assured the customer that just as soon as the new model is delivered we will make the shipment.

10. There is to be a meeting with the City Council on Monday, June 11, to consider the budget of the Department of Public Welfare; and representatives of this group are planning to appear to show why the funds are necessary.

25. THE COLON

The colon is used chiefly to introduce lists, series, explanations, or formal quotations.

25a. Use a colon to introduce a list.

Please send by express the following:
1 White bathing suit #427, size 14
2 Red beach robes #228, medium size
1 Beach umbrella, red and black, #426

We have notified the following people: Mr. James Montgomery, Captain Richard Stout, Dr. Ezra Watkins, Mrs. Martin Slocum.

The purpose of our trip was threefold: to select a site for the new branch factory, to visit prospective customers, and to enjoy a short vacation in the mountains.

NOTE: Do not use a colon after *are* or *were* when a simple series follows.

The kinds of dogs to be found at the kennels are terriers, bulls, and collies.

25b. Use a colon to introduce a formal statement or a formal quotation.

Robert E. Lee is reputed to have said: "Duty is the sublimest word in the English language."

25c. Use a colon after a statement which is followed by an explanatory clause or expression.

These two things he admired: an honest man and a beautiful woman.

My objection to the plan is this: it will cost a great deal of money, and the returns are likely to be small for many years.

Everything was in good shape for the meeting: chairs placed, pads and pencils ready, and a pitcher of water at the head of the table.

197

25d. Use a colon after the formal salutation of a business letter.

Dear Mr. Henderson:

25e. Use a colon to separate hour and minute figures in writing time, the act from the scene of a play, the title of a book from the subtitle, the verse following the biblical chapter.

7:35
Hamlet I:2
Principles of Geology: A College Textbook
Mark 6:10

CAUTION:

1. When *such as* is followed by a short illustration, usually only a comma is necessary.

He has visited many countries, such as **Italy,** Switzerland, Austria, and France.

2. The words *namely, viz., i.e., that is* are usually preceded by a semicolon unless the material following is very long.

We have studied five parts of speech; namely, nouns, pronouns, verbs, adjectives, and adverbs.

EXERCISE 26

Write the following sentences on your paper. Place commas, semicolons, and colons where they are needed. Give the reason for each correction.

1. Above everything else he hated one thing hypocrisy.
2. He could barely read the sign "Danger, Explosives."
3. The players came from all over the world Germany Italy Japan Russia China and Canada.
4. Howard had little money therefore he had to walk all the way.
5. The lecturer said that we must do three things balance the

budget, go back on the gold standard, and raise tariffs however he would not guarantee an immediate return of prosperity.

6. My father thought that the minister was referring to John 3 16 nevertheless, I was certain that he meant Luke 9 10.

7. This is his program for healthful living drink plenty of milk eat good-sized quantities of fresh, green vegetables take exercise every day, preferably in the open air sleep at least eight hours every night.

8. A football team can be little better than its signal-caller that is to say, its success depends upon the plays it uses.

9. There are three things that I wish to do before I die go to Europe bathe in the warm, inviting waters of Waikiki Beach see the Taj Mahal.

10. Stuart Chase once wrote "For the milk of human kindness the most obvious substitute is soft soap."

11. He has a very sore leg consequently, he cannot make the trip.

12. The letter began "Dear President Smith I intended to answer your last letter more promptly than this however, I have been so occupied that I have not had time to give my answer the thought it deserved."

13. At 12 15 last night our telephone rang loudly but when I answered it, nobody replied.

14. The notice had an ominous ring to it "All lights must be extinguished at 10 15 sharp."

15. You should give that chair at least two coats of flat paint, then you should put on one coat of varnish.

16. It has been our experience that success in college depends to a great extent on one trait namely, the ability to concentrate.

17. There is nothing very original about the street names in our town Main Street, Broad Street, Bank Street, and so on.

18. He used to astound his friends by quoting something and then rattling off the source for it, such as *Macbeth* I 2, or *Romeo and Juliet* IV 1.

19. Please wipe your feet carefully, our front hall is beginning to look like a pigsty.

20. The Johns Hopkins University has six divisions College of

199

Arts and Sciences, College for Engineers, Graduate School, Medical School, School of Public Health, and McCoy College.

21. My itinerary, which I obtained from the travel agent this morning, is certain to do one thing for me, if nothing else it will take me to all the important art galleries in Europe.

22. When he rose to speak, the president of the university threw back his head and began "Ladies and gentlemen, in the troubled times ahead we shall be called upon to make many adjustments, but there is one principle to which we must cling tenaciously it is freedom of speech."

23. In our modern, complicated society, students must do three things they must ask for the source of all information before they believe it they must learn to recognize bad reasoning they must send to their lawmaking bodies only well qualified representatives.

24. The train was scheduled to arrive in Milwaukee at 6 45, but when we left the station at 8 30, there was still no definite news of the time of its arrival.

25. Dr. Isaiah Bowman said in his address "The trade school exists for the admirable purpose of putting practically trained men into jobs the university exists, among other things, to create and expand the sciences that provide the jobs."

EXERCISE 27

On your paper, write these sentences, placing commas, colons, and semicolons where they should be.

1. These are the words of Edmund Burke a fine statesman "A great empire and little minds go ill together."

2. I should like to make this motion that we appoint a committee to study the whole question and report the findings to the Board of Directors.

3. When she gave the girl advice Mrs. Martin quoted this very appropriate line "Gather ye rosebuds while ye may."

4. Edmund Burke objected to force as a means of handling the colonies for these four reasons it is uncertain it is temporary it impairs the object and England has had no experience in using it.

5. One point which you will all concede is this Walt Whitman is one of the greatest figures in American poetry.
6. The framework of the bill is as follows the commission will consist of a chairman and four members appointed by the President subject to the approval of the Senate.
7. We sent him a telegram which said "Meet 8:50 Northern Pacific train from Spokane."
8. The questions which we must decide are these shall we have a committee to plan the improvements and shall this committee be appointed or elected?
9. Scientists do not rely entirely on the evidence of the lie detector for an obvious reason all people are not frightened by a third degree.
10. The train stopped between two white fields ahead the snow had buried the tracks.

26. THE APOSTROPHE: POSSESSIVES AND PLURALS

The apostrophe is used to indicate the possessive case of nouns and of pronouns like *anybody, someone, one, everybody.*

> Carl's book was lost.
> Someone's hat was left in the locker room.

26a. Use an apostrophe and s to form the possessive of all singular nouns.

> boy's, dog's, doctor's, lady's, James's, Dickens's, Mr. Jones's

NOTE:

1. The apostrophe comes before the *s* if the word is singular.

2. Singular nouns ending normally in *s* may omit the second *s*. The apostrophe will then be placed after the *s* which is part of the noun.

> James' or James's (But not *Jame's*)

> Keats' or Keats's (But not *Keat's*)
> Dickens' or Dickens's (But not *Dicken's*)

If the addition of an *s* causes difficulty in pronunciation, add only the apostrophe.

> Aristophanes', princess'

26b. Use an apostrophe alone to form the possessive of plural nouns ending in s.

Most plurals are formed by adding -*s*. Place the apostrophe after this *s*. (See Section 39d.)

> boys', dogs', doctors', soldiers', friends'

Nouns that end in *s* in the singular must add -*es* for the plurals. The possessive form of these nouns has an apostrophe after the final *s*.

> The Joneses' house burned last night.

A few plurals do not end in *s*. These must add *s* to form the possessive.

> men's, women's, children's, people's

26c. When two or more people possess a thing together, the sign of the possessive is added to the last word.

> I'll meet you at Levy and Brown's store.
> Henderson, Sellers, and Company's branch office is on Second Avenue.
> We went into Ed and John's room to see their school pennants.

26d. Add the apostrophe to the last member of a compound phrase.

> somebody else's book
> my mother-in-law's house
> sister-in-law (Singular)

sister-in-law's house (Singular possessive)
sisters-in-law (Plural) I have three sisters-in-law.
sisters-in-law's (Plural possessive)
My sisters-in-law's dispositions are all bright and cheer-
ful.

**26e. Use an apostrophe with each noun when sepa-
rate ownership is indicated.**

Sally's and Helen's dates for the dance are both very tall.
Albert's and Roger's sisters are blondes.

**26f. Use an apostrophe in contractions to indicate the
omission of a letter.**

don't (do not)
can't (cannot)
haven't (have not)
shan't (shall not)

NOTE: Although the *ll* in *shall* and the *o* in *not* are omitted
in *shan't*, only one apostrophe is used.

**26g. Use an apostrophe and *s* to form the plural of a
letter, figure, or word considered as a word.**

There are two *r*'s in my name.
Your theme has too many *and*'s.
He wrote three *2*'s on the paper.

NOTE: Letters, figures, and words used in this way are
italicized. (See Section 34c.)

**26h. The possessive case of a noun or pronoun is used
before a gerund.**

Wrong: I do not approve of John playing football.
Right: I do not approve of *John's* playing football.
Wrong: Has Father agreed to you studying German?
Right: Has Father agreed to *your* studying German?

NOTE: Be careful to distinguish between the gerund and

203

the participle. Although they look exactly alike, the participle is used as an adjective, whereas the gerund is used as a noun. (See Section 3g.)

> I saw John writing a letter. (Correct. John is the object of *saw; writing*, a participle, merely modifies John.)
>
> I do not like John's writing without my knowledge. (Writing is the object of *like* and is therefore a gerund.)

26i. Be careful to use the apostrophe only when it is needed.

1. Usually, in formal English, only nouns indicating living things are used in the possessive case. Some organizations composed of living people may be considered possessive.

Correct: the company's plan
          the city's streets
Informal: the desk's top
Correct: the top of the desk

2. Some expressions of time and some idiomatic expressions may be possessive.

> A week's pay, a month's rest, today's paper, a hair's breadth, for goodness' sake

3. Be sure that the word is completed before the apostrophe is used.

Wrong: Charle's finger, Mr. Jone's hat, Mr. Hopkin's new car
Right: Charles's (or Charles') finger, Mr. Jones's (or Jones') hat, Mr. Hopkins's (or Hopkins') new car

4. Be careful not to use an apostrophe before or after *s* ending a verb.

Wrong: He lives' near us.
Right: He lives near us.

5. Never use the apostrophe to form the nominative or objective plural. (See Section 14.)

Wrong: The Smiths' were present at the party.
   The Jones's have just come home.
   The present was from the Raiders'.
 Right: The Smiths were present at the party.
   The Joneses have just come home.
   The present was from the Raiders.

6. In contractions be sure to put the apostrophe exactly where a letter has been omitted.

Wrong: do'nt, have'nt, whos'
 Right: don't, haven't, who's

NOTE: *Who's* means "who is." The possessive pronoun is *whose.*

> Whose book is this?
> Who's at the door?

7. Do not use an apostrophe with pronouns ending in *-self* or *-selves.*

> Oneself, themselves

8. The apostrophe is never used to form the possessive case of personal pronouns (*hers, yours, ours, his, its, theirs*).

> The dog wagged *its* tail. (Possessive)

Do not confuse the possessive form *its* with the contraction *it's* (*it is*).

> It's a beautiful day.

EXERCISE 28

Most of the following sentences contain errors in the use of apostrophes and the possessive case. On your paper rewrite these sentences, adding apostrophes where they are needed, correcting words in which apostrophes have been used incorrectly, or making any other necessary change. Write your reason for making each change. If a sentence is correct, do not rewrite it, but write C beside its number.

26 THE APOSTROPHE: POSSESSIVES AND PLURALS

1. After Bobs part in the play was over, he collapsed in the dressing room.
2. I like the book because the authors style is clear and stimulating.
3. In music appreciation class we learned about various musicians lives.
4. Any educated persons opinion on the matter would be worth considering.
5. Anne Hathaway was Shakespeare's wife.
6. Dickens books are very popular in our class.
7. James brother Allen is our new clerk.
8. We all like Frances singing.
9. It's nobody's business what I do with my money.
10. Is that hat yours or hers?
11. My sister-in-laws house has just been sold.
12. The stenographers desks have all been painted.
13. The princess clothes were embroidered beautifully.
14. The firemens struggle to save the building was heroic but futile.
15. All requests for tickets must be sent to the womens committee.
16. For pitys sake, do something.
17. My respect for my church and it's beliefs is a result of my home training.
18. Arrangements were made to have the food prepared by the mothers' group.
19. Sue Pinemans parents went to Bismarck last week, and Sue and her brother stayed with us.
20. One of the Tibetan natives dragged away the plane's radio.
21. The Bermans' invited their niece to spend the weekend at Atlantic City.
22. On Thanksgiving Day we have the annual game between the two boys high schools.
23. My parents finally gave in and said I could get my drivers license.
24. The neighbor's considered Dunstan a spiteful person, incapable of interest in another persons welfare.
25. The day's end came so quickly that I couldnt believe I had been working for ten hours.

EXERCISE 29

Follow the directions in Exercise 28.

1. In the Shakespearean theater, the womens parts were played by young boys.
2. Pepys diary gives an excellent picture of the time's in which he lived.
3. Ellen combs the cats fur every day, but she never clips its claws.
4. Who's house is this?
5. The policemens white gloves were spattered with mud.
6. One years work in history and two years work in mathematics are necessary for graduation.
7. This years *Press* is a real students paper, reflecting the ideas and thoughts of the student body.
8. There is no record of that officer having been assigned to the duty mentioned.
9. Mother does not approve of James writing to Charlotte.
10. The nurses' headquarters are next to Dr. Bright's hospital.
11. We were surprised to hear of the citizens decision to call a buyers strike.
12. The government should use it's influence to prevent the man being sacrificed to a local quarrel.
13. When Janes house was robbed last night, the thieves took her mothers fur coat and her two sisters watches.
14. Fifteen years experience in banking makes it possible for us to handle our clients investments with skill.
15. The flowers which came from Hazlitt and Paine's store were sent by the Burtons.
16. Somebodys coat has been left on the Clarks porch.
17. At Mr. Carltons suggestion, I am sending you samples of materials for childrens dresses.
18. I cannot understand Doris refusing to help you.
19. We had Rivers Chambers orchestra, and the girls favors were school seals.
20. Conner and Evans business, including the goods on hand and all the companys fixtures, was sold for $130,000.
21. The United Automobile Companys annual report shows a stockholders dividend of 4 percent.

22. In yesterdays mail there was an order from J. M. Hawkins Office Supply Company.
23. A ladies purse with a monogram of two *T* s was lost in Benton and Kings store on Friday.
24. My sister-in-laws wedding dress came from the new womens dress department at Hughes department store.
25. There have been in the papers a great many articles about Houston getting a football franchise in the All-American Conference.

27. QUOTATION MARKS

27a. Quotation marks are used at the beginning and at the end of the exact words which a person says (direct quotations).

Right: Scott said, "I am going home."
Right: Scott said that he was going home.
Wrong: Scott said "that he was going home."

The second and third sentences contain an indirect quotation. The exact words which Scott used are not in the sentence; therefore no quotation marks are necessary.

The first word in a direct quotation is capitalized. If the quotation is introduced by an expression such as *he said*, a comma must precede the opening quotation marks.

Martin said, "It looks like rain."

If the sentence does not end with the quotation, a comma is required before the closing quotation marks, unless the structure of the sentence or of the quotation calls for some other mark of punctuation. (See Section 27f.)

Martin said, "It looks like rain," but Lana disagreed with him.

If the quotation consists of several sentences, quotation marks do not introduce each sentence. Use quotation marks only at the beginning and end of an unbroken quotation.

> She said, "I have promised to go downtown. Perhaps I could change the arrangements. I'll let you know in a few minutes."
>
> Oliver Wendell Holmes says in *The Autocrat of the Breakfast Table:* "This business of conversation is a serious matter. There are men of *esprit* who are excessively exhausting to some people. They are the talkers that have what may be called *jerky* minds. Their thoughts do not run in the natural order of sequence."

27b. If there is a long quotation which includes several paragraphs or several stanzas of poetry, quotation marks should be used at the beginning of each paragraph but not at the end of each paragraph. They are used at the end of the last paragraph only.

27c. In dialogue, every change of speaker requires a separate paragraph.

> "I've never gone to a better dance," said Jessie.
>
> "It must have been great fun," answered Ida. "Who took you?"
>
> "I went with Ed, and Sally and Paul joined us. Afterwards we all went to Saunders' for a hamburger."

27d. If the quotation is broken by an expression like *he said, Mary answered,* this expression must *not* be included in the quotation marks.

> "If you go," he said, "be sure to let me know."
>
> "No," Andrew objected, "I am afraid that I can't agree that you have found the right solution."

If a quotation broken by an expression like *he said* is composed of more than one sentence, be sure to use a period, an exclamation point, or a question mark at the end of each sentence.

> "It's raining hard," Harold said. "There is no fun on a picnic in the rain. Do you want to go home?"

27e. A quotation inside another quotation is enclosed in single quotation marks.

> "When I telephoned her last night," said Cary, "she told me again and again, 'Don't worry. I won't let you down.'"

27f. Commas and periods are placed inside the closing quotation marks; semicolons and colons are placed outside; question marks and exclamation points are placed inside or outside the quotation marks, according to the meaning of the sentence.

> We heard Phyllis say, "Don't wait for me," and then we heard a sudden cry.
>
> Andrew said, "Don't worry."
>
> The postman said, "I never receive any mail"; he looked so depressed that we shared our postcards with him.
>
> This is what Jim meant when he said, "Bring everything we shall need": food, feed for the horses, bedrolls, cooking utensils, and warm clothing.
>
> He asked, "Who has my knife?" (The question mark is part of the quotation.)
>
> Did Nancy really say, "I won't go"? (The question mark is not part of the quotation.)
>
> Rob cried, "There goes my hat!" (The exclamation point is part of the quotation.)
>
> How amazed I was to hear her say, "You have won"! (The exclamation point is not part of the quotation.)

27g. Use quotation marks to enclose technical terms in nontechnical writing.

> This is a heavily "watered" issue of stock.
>
> A common problem in home aquariums is "green water."

NOTE: Use quotation marks *only* if the term is one which is likely to be unfamiliar to your reader. For example, do not enclose in quotation marks the names of parts of an automobile engine; though they are technical terms, they are familiar to most people.

27h. In formal writing use quotation marks to enclose words which suggest a different level of usage.

> The prevailing opinion is that President Slade informed the Board of Directors that their decision was "cockeyed."
>
> The symphony was conducted by a "stuffed shirt."

CAUTION:

1. Quotation marks *always go in pairs.* Be careful to indicate both the beginning and the end of a quotation.

2. Do not use quotation marks to indicate humor.

27i. Use quotation marks to enclose titles of magazine articles, short stories, and short poems. (See Section 34a.)

> "The Gold Bug," a short story by Edgar Allan Poe, is one of the early classics of detective fiction.
>
> Have you ever read Shelley's poem "To a Skylark"?

EXERCISE 30

On your paper, write the following dialogue, adding quotation marks and other punctuation where necessary, and beginning new paragraphs when required:

Ralph and I had a long talk last night said Betty Lou. He thinks that we should go steady, but my mother is definitely hard to deal with. Parents can be such problems sympathized Jacqueline. My mother always insists upon calling me Jacqueline. Imagine giving a girl such a name. It's only with my own friends, who understand me, that I can be called Jackie. It would be definitely romantic to go steady with Ralph. What did you tell him? What could I tell him? My mother's same old line. Girls should know a number of boys. I'm too young to go steady, et cetera. Jackie sipped her lemonade. It's terrific the way parents behave she said. If you went steady with Ralph you'd always have a good date for every dance. If you don't go steady, a boy can always make a date with someone else. Betty Lou sighed.

Oh well, there's nothing I can do. My mother even invited some friend of hers to bring her son for dinner so that I'd get interested in somebody besides Ralph. I didn't like him at all. Hi, Sonny, she called as a blond youth came into the drug store; what's on your mind? Parents answered the boy, joining the two girls. They give a guy more trouble.

28. ACHIEVEMENT TESTS ON PUNCTUATION
28a. Achievement Test I on commas, semicolons, colons, apostrophes, quotation marks.

On your paper, write the following sentences, placing punctuation marks where they are required. If any punctuation marks have been incorrectly used, make any necessary corrections. Write your reason for each correction. If a sentence requires no correction, do not rewrite it; but write C beside its number.

1. When the lecturer arrived at 8 30 the hall was filled.
2. The sales volume of the company was declining consequently the management increased its advertising appropriation.
3. A business letter should be friendly courteous and conservative in statement.
4. If businessmen are really interested in their government they can improve it in many ways.
5. The speakers manner was pleasing but his enunciation was poor.
6. When Joan arrived we were in the midst of great preparations for my grandparents fiftieth wedding anniversary.
7. According to reports made by R. T. McClintook the commissioner of public roads the proposed highway will greatly aid traffic between Easton Maryland and Charleston South Carolina.
8. We are pleased to notify you that in accordance with your request of February 10 we have opened a charge account for you.
9. Dont get excited said Jane, Mother will bring the books when she comes to see you.

10. Martin Williamson son of Mr. and Mrs. Peter Williamson 918 Wendover Road Dover Delaware was selected for one of the scholarships.

11. Its likely that the club will move into its new quarters next month.

12. When I heard the policemens whistles I thought that something dreadful had happened.

13. Each of the characters' was presented with great care, as a result the novel was very striking.

14. One fact is clear and indisputable the public and avowed origin of this quarrel was taxation.

15. During this period the first organized resistance began and a number of employees looking for a solution of their problems joined labor unions.

16. Im afraid we cant go to the game Sam said David unless you can get your car. My father is going to use ours.

17. In the nineteenth century men worked for long hours in factories and debtors prisons constantly faced the people.

18. Jim had borrowed his father's car for the occasion, and I felt quite smart when he helped me into the new Buick.

19. Dr. Martin Baum president of the society sent letters of invitation to Dr. Hubert Enders Dr. Mark Candell and Dr. Ellen Harrington.

20. Randolph, Brown and Company new store has a sale of mens womens and childrens clothes.

21. Ralph has no regard for other peoples property for instance last night he put his feet up on Mrs. Simpsons new sofa.

22. Gustavus Adolphus of Sweden is often called the father of modern field artillery because he standardized the calibers of his guns brought into existence lighter carriages and placed powder and projectile together.

23. The captain gave orders for everyone to go below and told the sailors to lower the sails.

24. Along the route of the parade people lined the streets filled the windows of office buildings and added a new silhouette to the rooftops.

25. The proposed bridge, which will cost $1,397,000, will be valuable to many businessmen.

28b. Achievement Test II on commas, semicolons, colons, apostrophes, quotation marks.

Follow the directions given for Achievement Test I.

1. I am not sure about Ralph going to college.
2. Fredleys store will be glad to grant credit to new residents who want exclusive tailoring.
3. In Walter Reeds experiment with yellow fever some men were put in perfectly sterile rooms and others slept in a place that contained yellow-fever victims clothing.
4. The pressure groups claimed that if price controls were released production would increase goods would pour into the markets and prices would control themselves.
5. In the final vote, twenty boys expressed a willingness to try the new method; five turned down the plan; and three voted for it with an amendment.
6. As we approached a small desolate farm on the side of a lonely country road we were attracted by the fields which were full of uncultivated cotton and tobacco.
7. Waterview Avenue will play an important part in the city's plans, for Totem Street will be connected to Waterview by a bridge 2,300 feet long.
8. When the bully beat up one of Hanks friends a short skinny fellow who limped Hank rushed to the rescue.
9. A course in critical thinking has taught us the difference between fact and opinion truth and propaganda and good and bad sources of information.
10. As practical as the Greeks were they failed to realize the power of war engines consequently it was not until the time of Alexander that these weapons were developed.
11. In the morning of one of our last days at camp we had a dress rehearsal which was given for the young children who could not stay up late at night.
12. I want to find out if there is any chance of Jack getting a room in the dormitory.
13. The medical clinics occupied the second floor of the dispensary and consisted of rooms for treating diseases of the eyes nose throat and ears.

14. After years of secret work in laboratories and months of limited commercial operation this powerful device was at last ready for the public.

15. My practical experience in selling has been obtained in Green and Hoskins Infant Department and in the offices of the Dalton Motor Company.

16. Among my fellow art majors who shared my zest for art and who liked to spend their free time with the paints and brushes I found the kind of companionship I had longed for since early childhood.

17. At eight o'clock Marion said cheerfully we got dressed in our best clothes and went to the theater.

18. Five-year-old Tommy Lynn and his dog Bozo lost since Thursday in the Coconine National Forest were found this morning but the search continued for his three-year-old sister Estelle who disappeared at the same time.

19. Filled with excitement and joy the child rushed into the living room shouting Uncle John has given me a little white rabbit. May I keep it?

20. I am sending you a sample of Chinese brocade from Nortons shop and should greatly appreciate Helen trying to match it for me Marian wrote.

21. A sale of womens and misses clothes nearly caused a riot at Prestons store yesterday.

22. Simple clear bold and straightforward in mind and action Colonel Settle was one of natures noblemen.

23. While she was restrained by her husband a man of sense and firmness her worst offenses were impertinent jokes little white lies and short fits of pettishness but after his death she did many things which worried her friends.

24. Dr. Phelps who will retire at the end of the month said to the nurses at their graduation exercises some nurses training schools in their eagerness for progress are placing too much emphasis on medication and methods. Remember that the care of the patient as a person is your first concern.

25. Please follow these directions for typing the paper
    Double-space the lines.
    Use a 1½-inch left-hand margin.
    Write all headings in capitals.

29. THE PERIOD

29a. Use a period at the end of every complete declarative sentence.

It was a cold, dismal day.

Although his health was poor, he decided to leave the sanatorium.

You go ahead with your proposed trip; I shall remain at home.

NOTE:

1. Do not punctuate sentence fragments as complete units of thought unless they obviously stand for complete expressions. (See Section 55.)

Correct: "I want to go with you."
"All right."
"When do you leave?"
"Tomorrow."
Incorrect: Walking as fast as he could.
At an early hour when few are awake.

2. Periods are also used after mildly imperative sentences; exclamation marks are used after vigorously imperative sentences. (See Section 30a.)

Look before you leap.
Leave the house at once!

29b. Use a period after a standard abbreviation.

James Smith, Esq., was director of the enterprise.

The envelope was addressed to Paul Travin, M.D.; the postmark was London.

Henry Jones, D.D. (b. 1875; d. 1937)

Dec. 10; bbl.; n.b.; qt.; P.M.

NOTE:

1. Abbreviations of the names of some government agencies and some international organizations are generally

written without periods, especially if the letters form a combination that can be pronounced as a word.

> UNESCO came into being on November 4, 1946.
> Norway and Iceland were among the twelve original member nations of NATO.

2. Although *percent* is an abbreviation of the Latin phrase *per centum*, it is written without a period.

3. No period is used with the ordinal numbers when they are written *1st, 2nd,* and so on.

30. EXCLAMATION POINTS AND QUESTION MARKS

30a. Use the exclamation point to express surprise, command, emphasis, or strong emotion.

> Help! Help!
> What! Are you certain?
> How lucky we are to have such good weather!

30b. Use a question mark at the end of every direct question.

> Do you really know the whole story?
> Why are you so eager to go to Sea Island?

CAUTION: Do not use the question mark after an indirect question.

Wrong: I was asked whether I wanted to go?
 Right: I was asked whether I wanted to go.

30c. Use a question mark enclosed in parentheses to express doubt or uncertainty.

> The ships shown in this painting are the *Washington,* the *Swallow,* and the *Lady Clinton*(?).
> Richardson was born in 1900(?) in Selma.

CAUTION: Do not overuse the question mark for this purpose.

If it is impossible for you to find the exact information needed, you may use the question mark. But do not use it as a lazy excuse for not doing research. Do not use the question mark to express irony or humor.

31. THE DASH

Too frequent use of the dash makes a sensational style. Careless writers sometimes think that the dash makes a chatty, informal style. As a result, they sprinkle friendly letters with dashes. Never use the dash as a substitute for a period, a semicolon, or a colon.

Wrong: When we reached home, the house was completely dark—we opened the door and saw Jo-Jo wagging his tail.

Right: When we reached home, the house was completely dark. We opened the door and saw Jo-Jo wagging his tail.

31a. Use a dash to indicate a break or shift of thought.

Here is a fuller explanation—but perhaps you are not interested.

He is the most despicable—but I should not say any more.

Do we—can we—propose such action to the trustees?

NOTE: Omit the period when a statement ends with a dash.

Well, if that is how you feel—
George began, "May I ask—"

31b. Use the dash to set off sharply distinguished parenthetical matter or to secure emphasis or suspense.

I am unalterably opposed—unalterably, I repeat—to this suggestion.

She was aware—she must have known—that the proposal was hopeless.

I was pleased—delighted, I should say—to hear your excellent report.

NOTE: When the parenthetical material set off by dashes requires an exclamation point or question mark, such punctuation should precede the second dash.

> If I should miss the train—heaven forbid!—I'll telephone you.

31c. Use the dash to indicate the omission of words or letters.

> General B— was an excellent soldier.
> The Civil War was fought 1861–1865.

NOTE: The dash used with numbers is a short dash.

31d. The dash may be used instead of the comma to separate long appositive expressions from the rest of a sentence.

> All the dogs in town—dalmatians, dachshunds, deer hounds—lined up for the animal parade.

EXERCISE 31

On your paper, rewrite the following sentences, placing dashes where they are required:

1. Col. John Hudson from Kansas, you know fought in France in 1942.
2. When I looked up my heart misses a beat even now at the very memory I saw a huge beast before me!
3. You are too how shall I say? too matter-of-fact to do such a hotheaded thing.
4. From 1922 to 1925 perhaps it was 1921 1925 the man made a canvass of the city of Los Angeles.
5. As I was walking along Waverly Place but before that I should mention the sight I saw on Twenty-first Street
6. He was a large man who wore a straw hat and a topcoat a very odd sight, I assure you.
7. The food was excellent, but the boarders
8. I am reasonably certain no, I am positive that you will like this if you will only give it a fair trial.

EXERCISE 32

On your paper, rewrite the following sentences, placing periods, exclamation points, and question marks where they are required:

1. The letter was addressed as follows: "Milton Johnson, M D, Barton, Nev"
2. How feverish you seem Are you certain you are all right Shall I call Dr. Jones You must be ill
3. Ouch Watch where you are going
4. "Why is he leaving Any particular reason" asked Adam
5. Please stop that You know crying only makes you feel worse
6. He asked John if he would go John emphatically said, "Never"
7. Are you quite certain that he holds the degree of M D
8. Fifty percent. of the boys left for the holidays on Dec 20; the others all left on Dec 22
9. Isn't it strange that Dr and Mrs Browne were both born on December 11, 1908
10. Bob is in his fourth year at the University of Minnesota, but he is still not quite certain whether, after college, he will work for his father or try to earn a degree of D D S

32. THE HYPHEN AND SYLLABIFICATION

The hyphen is more a mark of spelling than of punctuation. It indicates that two words or two parts of one word belong together. The hyphen is a mechanical device which is necessary for correct, clear writing. It should be sharply distinguished from the dash, which is longer.

Syllabification is the act or method of dividing words into syllables.

32a. Use a hyphen to join the parts of a compound word.

The use of a hyphen in joining compound words varies greatly. Do not attempt to learn the numerous rules; consult a standard dictionary.

Hyphens are generally used:

1. Between two or more words modifying a substantive and used as a single adjective: *a well-bred person; a never-to-be-forgotten incident.* But when adverbs ending in *-ly* occur in such expressions, the hyphen is not used: *highly seasoned food.* (Do not mistake adjectives ending in *-ly* for adverbs. Write *a lively-sounding tune, a manly-looking boy.*)

2. Between the parts of compound numerals (from twenty-one to ninety-nine): *fifty-two; eighty-four.*

3. Between the numerator and denominator of a fraction: *a four-fifths majority.*

4. Between the parts of certain compound nouns, adverbs, and verbs: *actor-manager;* a *well-nigh* hopeless task; to *dry-clean* a dress.

NOTE: Distinguish carefully between the short mark (period, dot) generally used by dictionaries to divide syllables and the longer mark (hyphen) used to link two words. (See Section 37.)

32b. Use a hyphen to indicate the division of a word broken at the end of a line.

> The rambling old house, it is true, would look considerably better if it were freshly painted.

NOTE:

1. Do not divide a word at the end of a line if you can avoid doing so.

2. Place the hyphen at the end of the first line, never at the beginning of the second.

3. Never divide a word of one syllable. Such words as *purse, through, though, ground, death, grace, quick, asked,* and *breadth* cannot be divided. Write the complete word on the first line, or leave a blank space and carry the whole word over to the next line.

4. Consult your dictionary to determine the correct syllabification of words. It is easier to consult an authority than to learn the various rules for dividing words. The following suggestions may be helpful, however:

Prefixes and suffixes may be written separately.

Compound words are divided between their main parts.

Two consonants are usually divided.

EXERCISE 33

1. With the aid of your dictionary, determine which of the following words are compounds and should be written with hyphens: *notebook, motherinlaw, understand, laborsaving, airtight, bathroom, foregoing, selfstarter, hangeron, blowout, quietspoken, hardworking, thirtynine, offstage, crazyquilt.*

2. Syllabify the following words: *symphony, revolt, delicious, radiation, carefully, torpedo, chemical, heighten, throughout, grounded.*

33. PARENTHESES AND BRACKETS

Do not confuse brackets [ ] and parentheses ( ). Brackets are used to set off inserted matter as extraneous or merely incidental to the context, especially comments made by someone other than the author of the text. Such interpolations may be corrections, comments, or explanations. Brackets are used to set apart the writer's *additions* to *quoted* material; parentheses are used to enclose the original author's *own words.*

33a. Use parentheses to enclose parenthetical material which is only remotely connected with the context.

> This punctuation (I am convinced it is important) should be carefully studied.
>
> If you find any holly berries (surely they must be numerous now), please bring me some.

NOTE: In such constructions the parenthetical material merely amplifies the thought. Thus many writers prefer

dashes to parentheses. The marks may be used inter-changeably, although parentheses are more commonly used when the parenthetical material takes the form of a complete sentence.

33b. Use parentheses to enclose references and directions.

> Agrarianism (see Book I) was the next topic discussed.
> Avoid illogical comparisons. (See Chapter X.)

33c. Use parentheses to enclose figures repeated to ensure accuracy.

> He paid ten dollars ($10.00) for the shoes.
> There were thirty (30) claims for damages.

NOTE: Students often have an idea that a number written out *must* be followed by numerals. This is a mistaken notion; except in legal documents, words or figures alone are sufficient.

33d. Do not use parentheses to cancel parts of your writing. Erase or draw lines through the words you wish to delete.

33e. Use brackets to enclose material interpolated in a passage quoted from someone else.

> "In 1865 he [Lincoln] was a candidate for the Republican vice-presidential nomination."
> "The youth of today [1775] are an unruly lot."

EXERCISE 34

On your paper, write the following sentences, placing parentheses or brackets wherever they are required:

1. It was in December I think it was December that Mrs. Glass became ill.
2. The measurements of the lot 90 by 60 feet were considered small.

3. The mean old ogre he is all of that made the child cry bitterly.

4. "The magazine was first published in the nineteenth century 1878 by Lee and Jones now known as Jones and Bushwick."

5. This article by James Hayes you remember him? has been widely quoted.

6. *Plain Sense* was published in the nineteenth century 1836 by an English firm.

7. Totalitarianism see Chapter 10 was eagerly discussed at the last meeting of the Philosophy Club.

8. This book the one I referred to earlier is an excellent example of sixteenth-century thought.

34. ITALICS

Material that would be italicized in print is underlined in typed or handwritten papers.

34a. Use italics (underlining) to indicate the names of ships, trains, and planes and the titles of magazines, newspapers, books, plays, long poems, and musical compositions.

> From the library of the *Queen Elizabeth* he borrowed a copy of *Life, The New York Times,* and Sherwood's *Roosevelt and Hopkins.*

NOTE:

1. Do not italicize the name of a city used with the title of a newspaper unless the name of the city is actually a part of the newspaper's title.

> The San Francisco *Chronicle* (Name of city is not part of title.)
> *The New York Times* (Name of city is part of title.)

2. Do not omit an article which forms part of the title.

Correct: The Rime of the Ancient Mariner.

3. Do not add an article to a title if none appears in the original work.

Correct: Victory, by Joseph Conrad.

34b. Use italics (underlining) to indicate foreign words or phrases unless continued usage has made these words or phrases part of the English language.

> Henry was really an *enfant terrible*.
> The dodo bird (*Didus ineptus*) is now extinct.
> For dinner we had *arroz con pollo*, a Spanish dish of chicken and rice.

34c. Use italics (underlining) to refer to a word, letter, or number spoken of as such.

> You must note the difference between *whether* and *weather*.
> Your *t*'s look exactly like *l*'s.
> Form your *7*'s and *9*'s carefully.
> I misspelled *miscellaneous* on the test.

EXERCISE 35

On your paper, write the number of each of the following sentences. Beside each number, write correctly any word or words from that sentence which should be underlined to indicate italics or which should be placed within quotation marks. Include the punctuation.

1. Noel Coward's play The Astonished Heart has been received with great enthusiasm.
2. All the way to Europe on the Nieuw Amsterdam Ethel sat on deck reading General Clay's Decision in Germany.
3. In his lecture on Psychology of Humor the dean mentioned an article called National Differences in Humor, which appeared in The American Mercury.
4. The San Francisco Chronicle is a good newspaper.
5. Mr. Samuelson is interested in everything that happens. His chief aim is to be au courant.

6. Don't you ever dot an i in your themes?
7. We enjoyed reading Melville's novel entitled Moby Dick.
8. Henry has written a story called The Vandal.
9. The train we traveled on from Seattle was the Olympian Hiawatha.
10. Robert Frost wrote the poem The Death of the Hired Man.

35. ABBREVIATIONS

35a. Avoid most abbreviations in formal writing.

Incorrect: I asked who the prof. of the lit. class was.
             His train arrives Wed. aft.
             N.J. lies across the Hudson R. from N.Y.
  Correct: Mrs. Scott lives on Primrose Street.
Incorrect: Last wk. I went to see a dr. in the bldg. at Valley & First.

NOTE: Even in informal writing it is best to use abbreviations sparingly, to avoid giving the impression that your letter or theme is not worth your time or trouble.

In formal writing, do not use abbreviations except in footnotes and bibliographies. Especially, do not use the ampersand (&), the abbreviation symbol for *and*.

Certain very common abbreviations are permissible, however; *Mr., Mrs., Dr., Ph.D.* used with proper names are correct.

Incorrect: The Rev. was not at home.
  Correct: The Reverend Dr. Brown was not at home.
Incorrect: Is the Mrs. here?
  Correct: Is Mrs. Anderson here?

35b. Do not use contractions in formal writing.

A contraction is a form of abbreviation: a word written with an apostrophe to indicate the omission of a letter. Such contractions as *won't, don't, can't, shouldn't,* and *wasn't* are usually out of place in formal writing.

In reporting dialogue, contractions are correctly used to

convey the exact words of the speaker. Do not avoid the use of contractions and other colloquialisms to the extent of making your reports of conversation seem artificial or forced.

NOTE: Periods are not used with contractions or with nicknames.

EXERCISE 36

On your paper, write the following sentences, correcting all errors in the use of abbreviations:

1. The sts. run e and w in N. Y C, & the aves. run n & s.
2. The king of Eng. from 1457 to 1509 was Henry VII; he was followed by Henry VIII.
3. The Pres. didn't make any speeches in Jan or Feb because he was taking a vacation in Fla during those two months.
4. Tom. said that the dr. had refused to let him try out for the swimming team.
5. Last mo I went to see Mrs Wilson.
6. The agent asked to see the Rev. Henry Gilman.
7. He said that he would arrive at eight A.M. on Mon.
8. I regret that I shan't be able to accept your kind invit. of Jan. 10.
9. Ga. lies just across the Savannah R. from S C.
10. The dr also serves as a prof. at the univ. across town.

36. NUMBERS

36a. Use words to represent numerals when no more than two words are required.

> Ten; thirty-six; four hundred; eight thousand; three million; one-third
> Betty is *eighteen* years old.

36b. Use figures for numerals when more than two words are required.

> $9.25   1,689   208   165

NOTE: Figures are always used with the word *percent* or with the percent sign except at the beginning of a sentence.

36c. Usually figures are used in dates, street and telephone numbers, chapters of a book, and groups of numbers in the same passage.

> June 14, 1856; 150 Valley View Avenue; Parkhurst 4–
> 1963; Chapter 6, 9, and 15; Track 4; Annex 12
> The dimensions are 4 feet by 9 feet.

36d. Do not begin a sentence with a numeral.

Wrong: 30 boys are playing tennis.
Right: Thirty boys are playing tennis.

CAUTION:

1. Do not repeat a number in parenthetical figures except where great accuracy is desired. (See Section 33c.)

2. Use commas to set off figures in groups of three except in dates and street and telephone numbers: 2,365,189; 365,107.

3. Do not use *st, nd, rd, th* after days of the month or with street numbers.

Correct: May 16, 1911; February 18; 10 West 23 Street

EXERCISE 37

On your paper, write the following sentences, correcting all errors in the use of numbers expressed in figures or in words:

1. He says that the last time he saw the witness was on February 4th, 1959.
2. His telephone number is Hemlock 4,315.
3. 11 players constitute a football team.
4. There are only 500 women in the school, but there are at least one thousand five hundred men.
5. The Blacks have moved to a new home at 8,634 Avondale Street.

6. On March sixteenth his telephone number was changed to Oregon four—six nine six two.

7. 2100 men were at work on the project when the last check was made on April 2nd, 1959.

8. 4 boys and three girls failed the test because they had studied diligently for only ⅓ of the term.

9. In its first year the club had eleven members; at the end of five years it had 63; and now, after 10 years it has a total membership of 134.

10. On March first, 1959, he received a check for $50, but he has received only twenty-two dollars and fifty cents since that time.

11. If I lived only 4 blocks from school, I would never be late either.

12. Additional discussions of this topic may be found in chapters three, seven, and thirteen of the same book.

13. 3 more players are all we need.

14. It is hard for me to believe that Marjorie is only 17 years old.

15. When I was sick last winter my temperature rose to one hundred and five degrees.

The Word

Are you sure of the words you use? The following four examples, all written by high school seniors, show what can happen when you are not careful about the words you select.

> Henry Esmond engaged in literary activities as an *alibi* for his love for Beatrix.
>
> They glanced across the beach trying to *enhance* the entire scene in one glance.
>
> I was surprised and delighted to receive your *lovely* gift for my birthday. The scarf has such *lovely* colors that I can hardly wait to wear it. It was *lovely* of you to give it to me.
>
> A *coma* must follow an introductory subordinate clause.

The writers of the preceding sentences were all having trouble with words. The first student does not know the meaning of the word *alibi*. The second is mistaken in his use of *enhance* and has not listened to his sentence. *Glanced, enhance,* and *glance* sound silly when brought together in this way. The third student seems to know only one word that he can use to describe something that pleases him, and the fourth expects unconsciousness to result from the use of a subordinate clause. These students all need work with words.

The following sections of this book will help you to avoid such errors in your own speaking and writing. You can get much additional help from your dictionary.

37. USE OF THE DICTIONARY

To use words effectively you need to have at hand at least two reference books. One is a good handbook of composition or communication, and the other is a reliable dictionary. If you have not already done so, now is the time to become well acquainted with your dictionary. It will tell you these things about a word: spelling, part(s) of speech, pronunciation, forms (tense, plural, comparative, superlative), syllabification, meaning, origin, synonyms, and antonyms. A good dictionary also shows levels of usage, indicating whether a word is slang, obsolete, colloquial, or dialect.

37a. Choose a good dictionary.

In choosing a dictionary you must be careful, for not every dictionary is reliable. Some pocket dictionaries, for example, are so small that they can be used only as limited guides to spelling and pronunciation. Others, though of good size, may have been so hurriedly and carelessly produced that they are of little value.

When you select a dictionary, be sure that it is one which you and your teachers can trust. Before making a final decision about which one to use or buy, you should ask the following questions:

1. Has this dictionary been recently published or recently revised?
2. What are the qualifications of the people who compiled and edited it?
3. Does the publisher have a good reputation?
4. Is it sufficiently large (approximately 100,000 entries)?

Three good dictionaries, comparable in size and price, are

> *The American College Dictionary* (Random House, Inc., New York)
>
> *Webster's New Collegiate Dictionary* (G. & C. Merriam Company, Springfield, Mass.)

Webster's New World Dictionary (The World Publishing Company, Cleveland)

Larger dictionaries than those listed above provide much more information and a more complete list of words, but they are very expensive and difficult or impossible to carry around. *Webster's New International Dictionary*, *The Shorter Oxford Dictionary* (2 volumes), Funk & Wagnalls' *New Standard Dictionary*, and the twenty-volume *New English* (*Oxford*) *Dictionary* are four such large and complete dictionaries. These can usually be referred to in libraries, offices, or classrooms.

37b. Learn how to use a dictionary.

Dictionaries differ somewhat in their systems of presenting material; therefore, to gain the most from your dictionary you should have a clear idea of the method it follows. First, turn to the table of contents to see what kinds of information and material the editors have included. Second, look over the preface, the introductory sections, and the supplementary material at the back of the book. These will show you what information can be found in the dictionary and will help you understand how to use it.

Your dictionary will contain many words with which you are unfamiliar. When you come upon these words, do not try to guess the sounds of the letters. The pronunciation chart in the front of the dictionary or the key at the bottom of each page will show, with examples, the various sounds that certain letters have.

Each page of your dictionary contains a vast amount of useful as well as valuable information. The reproduction you will find on page 235 of portions of a page from *Webster's New Collegiate Dictionary* gives an example of just how much your dictionary can tell you about words and language in general.

37c. Learn what information a good dictionary will supply.

Most people consult a dictionary merely to look up the spelling, pronunciation, or meaning of certain words. However, the student who realizes that he will want to use these words in the future *studies* each word he looks up. In the long run, such study saves both time and effort.

The following entry* for the word *rescue* in *Webster's New Collegiate Dictionary* shows the kinds of information a good dictionary provides for most of the words it defines.

> **res′cue** (rĕs′kū), *v. t.*; RES′CUED (-kūd); RES′CU·ING (-kū·ĭng). [OF. *rescourre*, fr. *re-* + *escorre* to move, shake, fr. L. *excutere* to shake out.] **1.** To free from any confinement, violence, danger, or evil. **2.** *Law.* To take forcibly from the custody of the law. **3.** To regain, or recover, by force. — *n.* A rescuing; deliverance from restraint, violence, or danger; also, *Law,* forcible removal of a person or goods from the custody of the law. — **res′cu·er** (rĕs′kū·ẽr), *n.*
> **Syn. Rescue,** deliver, redeem, ransom, reclaim, save mean to free from **danger of death,** destruction, or evil. **Rescue** implies release from imminent danger by prompt or vigorous action; **deliver,** release of a person (usually) from confinement, temptation, slavery, etc.; **redeem,** release from bondage or from penalties by giving what is demanded; **ransom,** a release of one enslaved or kidnaped by paying the amount demanded by his captor or owner; **reclaim,** a bringing back to a former state or condition of someone or something abandoned or debased; **save,** a rescue, deliverance, etc., and a continuance in existence or in usefulness.

Vocabulary entry

The *entry* word is usually given in bold-faced type. Also printed in this kind of type are different forms of the same root word, especially when these new forms are another part of speech. For example: *reputed,* which is an adjective, and *reputedly,* which is an adverb, appear in heavy black type within the same entry.

Spelling

The entry word, given in bold-faced type, indicates the correct spelling of a word. When a word has two or more spellings, the preferred form is usually given first. A dictionary will also help with spelling in the following cases:

---

* By permission. From Webster's New Collegiate Dictionary, copyright 1949, 1951, 1953, 1956, 1958, 1959 by G. & C. Merriam Co., publishers of the Merriam-Webster Dictionaries.

1. Vocabulary Entry

The word to be defined is printed in bold-faced type. Spelling, accent, syllabic division, capitalization, and hyphenation are shown.

2. Run-on Entry

Words closely associated with the entry word are also printed in bold-faced type. When the meaning of the run-on can be inferred from the meaning of the entry word, the run-on is not defined.

3. Definition

The meaning of a word is stated in its definition. Different meanings are usually labeled by means of numbers or letters.

4. Pronunciation

The pronunciation of the entry word is shown by means of accent marks, diacritical marks, and phonetic respelling.

5. Part of Speech Label

6. Origin

7. Principal Parts

8. Usage Labels

Labels such as *slang* and *colloq.* (colloquial) show the level of usage in which a word or meaning occurs.

9. Example Contexts

10. Synonym Study

11. Miscellaneous Information

Most dictionaries include entries providing information about important people, places, and events.

12. Subject Labels

Technical or scientific meanings are usually labeled according to the field or branch of knowledge to which they belong.

13. Geographic Labels

Labels such as *Brit.* (British) or *chiefly U.S.* tell where a word or meaning is used.

ges·tic'u·late (jĕs·tĭk'ū·lāt), v. i. [L. gesticulatus, past part. of gesticulari to gesticulate, fr. gesticulus a mimic gesture, dim. of gestus gesture.] To make gestures, esp. when speaking. — **ges·tic'u·la'tive** (-lā'tĭv; -lȧ·tĭv), adj. — **ges·tic'u·la'tor** (-lā'tẽr), n.

ges·tic'u·la'tion (-lā'shŭn), n. **1.** Act of gesticulating, or making gestures. **2.** A gesture, as in representing passion, or enforcing arguments.

ges·tic'u·la·to'ry (jĕs·tĭk'ū·lȧ·tō'rĭ or, esp. Brit., -tẽr·ĭ), adj. Representing by, belonging to, or resembling, gesticulation.

ges'tion (jĕs'chŭn), n. [L. gestio a managing, fr. gerere to bear, manage.] Archaic. Management; conduct.

ges'ture (-tŭr), n. [ML. gestura mode of action, fr. L. gerere, gestum, to bear, behave, act.] **1.** Obs. Carriage; posture. **2.** A motion of the body or limbs intended to express an idea or a passion, or to enforce or emphasize an argument, assertion, or opinion. **3.** The use of motions of the limbs or body as a mode of expression. **4.** [Influenced by F. geste.] Something done or said merely by way of formality, courtesy, or diplomacy.
— v. i. To make gestures or a gesture; gesticulate. — **ges'tur·er** (-tŭr·ẽr), n.

‖**Ge·sund'heit** (gĕ·zŏŏnt'hīt), n. [G.] (To your) health; — a salutation, as when drinking, or after a sneeze.

get (gĕt), v. t.; past GOT (gŏt), Archaic & Dial. GAT (găt); past part. GOT, or (esp. in U.S.) GOT'TEN (gŏt'n); pres. part. GET'TING. [ON. geta.] **1.** To come into possession of; to obtain; acquire; receive. **2.** Hence, in idiomatic uses: **a** To reach by some process, as hunting, sounding, etc.; as, to get a fine stag; to get bottom. **b** Colloq. To receive a sentence of; as, to get three months. **c** Slang. To hit; strike; as, the blow got him in the mouth. **d** To procure as by fetching; as, let me get my hat. **e** To establish communication with, as by telephone. **3.** Specif. Chiefly Colloq. To obtain the mastery over; as: **a** To overmaster; as, a bad habit gets one at last. **b** To capture; as, the police got the thief. **c** To baffle; puzzle; as, this problem gets me; also, to annoy; irritate. **d** To pen; trap; hence, to bring to retribution; also, to kill; as, to get the murderer. **e** In certain sports, to retire, or put out (a player), esp. by making a catch. **4.** With have and had: Pleonastically, Colloq., to be obliged to; as, he has got to do it. **5. a** To cause to be in any position or condition; as, to get one's feet wet. **b** To cause to move or be removed; as, to get him away. **c** To get ready; prepare; as, to get dinner. **6.** To induce; as, to get him to go. **7.** To betake; — reflexively; as, let us get us away. **8.** To beget; — now of animals.
— v. i. **1.** To arrive at, or bring oneself or itself into, a state, condition, or position; as, to get to be friends; to get free. **2.** To make acquisition; to profit.

Syn. Get, obtain, procure, secure, acquire, gain, win, earn mean to come into possession of. Get, a very general term, may or may not imply effort or initiative; obtain suggests the attainment of an end sought for or hoped for; procure, effort in obtaining something for oneself or another; secure, difficulty in obtaining and fixing that obtained in one's possession or under one's control; acquire stresses addition, as by inevitable result, to something already possessed; gain adds to obtain the implications of struggle and, usually, of material value in the thing obtained; win adds to gain the implication of qualities or circumstances that favor; earn implies a correspondence between the effort and what one gets by effort.

— **get ahead of.** Colloq. To surpass.
— n. **1.** An offspring (of an animal); breed. **2.** Begetting; as, colts of Man o' War's get. **3.** In certain games, as lawn tennis and handball, a return of a shot that ordinarily would score for the opponent.

get'–at'–a·ble (gĕt'ăt'ȧ·b'l), adj. Possible to be reached, attained, got, or known; approachable; accessible.

get'a·way' (gĕt'ȧ·wā'), n. The act or fact of getting away, starting, going, etc.

Geth·sem'a·ne (gĕth·sĕm'ȧ·nē), n. [Gr. Gethsēmanē, Gethsēmanei, fr. Aram. gath shemānī(m) oil press.] **1.** Bib. The enclosure outside of Jerusalem, scene of the agony and arrest of Jesus. **2.** [sometimes not cap.] Any place or occasion of great, esp. mental or spiritual, suffering. Cf. CALVARY, 3.

get'ter (gĕt'ẽr), n. **1.** One who gets. **2.** Elec. A substance placed in a vacuum tube to remove traces of free gas.

get'up' (gĕt'ŭp'), n. Colloq. General composition or structure; make-up.

ge'um (jē'ŭm), n. [L., herb bennet.] = AVENS.

gew'gaw (gū'gô), n. A showy trifle; bauble. — adj. Showy.

gey (gā), adj. Scot. Considerable; tolerable. — adv. Scot. Considerably; very; pretty.

gey'lies, gay'lies (gā'lĭs), adv. Scot. Fairly well; very much.

gey'ser (gī'zẽr; gī'sẽr; Brit. also gā'zẽr, gē'-, usually gē'- in sense 2),

1. The plurals of nouns are given if the noun forms its plural in some other way than by adding *s* or *es*.
2. The comparative and superlative degrees of adjectives and adverbs are given when adding *er* or *est* changes the spelling of the root word. (happy—happier)
3. The past tense, past participle, and present participle of verbs are given if there is an unusual spelling change.
4. Compound words spelled with a hyphen, as one word, or as two words are so indicated.

Capitalization

Most good dictionaries will tell you whether a word is usually capitalized. If an entry word is written with a capital letter, that word should always be capitalized (for example, *African*). Occasionally such a word will have one or more meanings which require a small letter. For instance, in *Webster's New Collegiate Dictionary* the third meaning of *Afghan* reads as follows:

> 3. [*not cap*] A kind of worsted blanket or wrap.

Similarly, a word that is usually written with a small letter may have one or more meanings in which it is capitalized. Your dictionary may then add "(*cap.*)," "(*often cap.*)," or "(*sometimes cap.*)" to these particular meanings.

Proper names (people, places) appear either in their alphabetical position within the text or in a special section or sections at the back of the dictionary. Where these proper names are given depends upon the particular dictionary you use.

Syllabification

Most dictionaries use a dot to separate syllables in the vocabulary entry; some replace the dot with an accent mark when a particular syllable is to be stressed. If you look back at the entry for *rescue* on page 233, you will see that it is divided into two syllables, of which the first is accented and the second unaccented. Since all dictionaries do not follow the same method of separating syllables, it is important to read the introductory notes in your dictionary to see what system is being used.

Knowing how a word is syllabified is important for two reasons. It helps you to pronounce the word, and it shows you where you can divide a word if it is too long to be written in full at the end of a line.

Pronunciation

How a word is pronounced depends upon two things: where the accent is placed and how the letters are sounded. Your dictionary has in its opening pages a chart showing the sounds of the various letters and the markings used to indicate those sounds. (See Section 38 for a complete discussion of this topic.)

As with spelling, when two or more pronunciations of a word are used, the more commonly used pronunciation is generally given first. When words are pronounced differently in various localities, the variant pronunciations are usually labeled to show where they are from. If, for example, a pronunciation is labeled as *British* or *Chiefly British*, this indicates that the word is spoken in this way in England.

Part(s) of speech

For almost every entry the "part of speech" (noun, verb, adjective, adverb, etc.) is given. After the word *rescue*, for example, we find *v.t.*, which means that it is a transitive verb. Farther down in the entry is the label *n.*, which indicates that it can also be used as a noun. Following each part-of-speech abbreviation, the particular meaning or meanings are usually given, and the correct usage is explained. Whenever you are in doubt about the meaning of a certain abbreviation, you can quickly check it in your dictionary's table of abbreviations.

Principal parts of verbs

When a verb is irregular in some way, dictionaries spell out the past tense, the past participle, and often the present participle immediately after the part of speech abbreviation. If there are alternative forms, these are given also. Our example, *rescue,* gives the past tense, *rescued,* and the present participle, *rescuing.* The "entry" word itself is the present tense (or the present infinitive). When, as with *rescue,* the past tense and the past participle have the same form, this form is spelled out only once.

If you are unsure about whether a certain verb forms its past tense and past participle with the usual *-d, -ed,* or *-t* endings, your dictionary will tell you. The principal parts of certain regular verbs are also given.

Origin

Frequently your dictionary will tell you how and where a word came into being. It may have arisen through association with the name of a person, such as *derrick,* which was the name of a seventeenth-century hangman; or it may have been derived from an ancestral or foreign language. Old English, Latin, Greek, German, and French have been the heaviest contributors, though many other languages have also played a role in forming our current English vocabulary.

The history of the origin of a word is usually placed within brackets near the beginning or at the end of a dictionary entry. In the case of *rescue,* we are told that the word came from the Old French word *rescourre,* a combination of the prefix *re-* and *escorre* (meaning to move or shake). *Escorre* was derived from the Latin word *excutere* (meaning "to shake out"). This information is often abbreviated. For example, in the entry mentioned above, *OF.* stands for "Old French" and *L.* stands for "Latin"; *fr.* simply means "from."

Meanings

Words have at least one, if not more, of the following meanings: a historical meaning, a traditional meaning, a figurative meaning, a special meaning, or a new meaning. It is a good idea to learn the order in which meanings for words are given in your dictionary; that is, whether the meanings are arranged in order from oldest to newest, from most common to most rare, or from general to specialized. It is also important to know the significance of numbers (1, 2, 3) and letters (a, b, c) preceding various definitions. This information can usually be found in the section entitled "Explanatory Notes."

Whenever you look up the meaning of a word, read through the entire entry and then select the definition which fits most closely into the context where you have come across the word.

Words that are hyphenated and phrases that have an idiomatic, specialized, or figurative meaning are in some dictionaries entered separately in the regular alphabetical listing; in others they are put under the main word. Most dictionaries have now added common abbreviations and foreign words and phrases to the main body of their texts.

Level(s) of usage

The mere fact that you find a word listed in the dictionary does not mean that it is in good use or that some of its special meanings are appropriate in current English. The boy who proudly pointed to *ain't* on a page of his dictionary and said "The word is in the dictionary, so it must be right" hadn't read far enough to see how the word was labeled. Farther along in the entry appear the words: "—now used in dialect or illiterate speech."

Your dictionary will help you to judge the acceptability of a word in various situations by the absence or presence of a "restrictive label." Some words have no labels, and others have labels applying only to certain meanings or to their use as a certain part of speech. All words that are without restrictive labels of any sort may be considered appropriate in formal English. Words labeled *colloquial* are usually acceptable in informal speech or writing, but not in formal writing.

All dictionary labels are guides to the special appropriateness of word usage; generally they can be put into four categories:

1. *Geographical,* which indicates a country or a section of a country where a word or a particular meaning is common. These labels tell whether the word is used primarily in such places as England, Australia, Scotland, or the United States. They may also indicate special regions such as New England, the South, the Southwest, or the West. Since English is the native language of so many people in various parts of the world, it is not surprising that geographical labels are necessary.

2. *Time,* which tells whether a word, or one of its meanings, is no longer used; is disappearing from use; or is still used but has a quaint form or meaning. *Obsolete, obsolescent,* and *archaic* are three possible "time" labels. When a word has no such label attached to it, the word is in current use.

3. *Subject,* which indicates that a word or one of its meanings belongs to a specialized department of knowledge. Examples of this kind of label are *Geom.* (geometry), *Med.* (medicine), *Mus.* (music), *Naut.* (nautical), and *Photog.* (photography).

4. *Cultural,* which tells whether a word or a special use of it is substandard or acceptable as informal English. *Colloq.* (colloquial), *Dial.* (dialect), and *Slang* are three such labels. If no "cultural" label is given in the entry, the word and its various meanings are usually suitable for both formal and informal writing and speaking.

NOTE: Since there is no one authority to decide exactly how and where a word may be used, dictionary editors can only use their best judgment in recording information about words. You should not be surprised, therefore, if you discover that dictionaries sometimes disagree about the labels they attach to certain words or meanings. Such differences of opinion usually arise over labels that indicate levels of usage.

For further study of the different levels of word usage see Sections 41, 42, 44, 45, and 46.

Synonyms and antonyms

Synonyms (words that have the same or similar meanings) are often included in dictionary entries; they usually come at the end and are preceded by *Syn.* If you will look back at the entry for *rescue*, you will note that *deliver, redeem, ransom, reclaim,* and *save,* with their definitions, are all given as synonyms. Though, as in this case, half a dozen words may have similar basic definitions, each one expresses a slightly different shade of meaning. By giving you lists of synonyms, a dictionary not only helps you to understand better the word itself, but also enables you to choose a word which may come closer to expressing a particular idea, concept, or feeling. Finding synonyms is so important that entire volumes have been compiled to help speakers and writers; some of these are *Webster's Dictionary of Synonyms, Crabb's English Synonyms,* and *Roget's International Thesaurus of English Words.*

Antonyms (words that have opposite meanings) can also be found in the entries for certain words in the dictionary. For example, when you look up the word *silent* in *Webster's New Collegiate Dictionary,* you find that *talkative* is given as an antonym. This listing of words which are opposite in meaning will often help you to understand more clearly the word you are looking up.

Other information

In addition to information about words as words, most dictionaries include such useful material as notes on famous people and places, capitals of countries and states, populations of cities, locations of colleges, tables of weights and measures, proofreader's marks, and pictures to illustrate certain words.

38. PRONUNCIATION

Words are mispronounced because of failure to accent the proper syllable or failure to give the letters the proper sound.

38a. Watch the respelling and diacritical marks.

In most dictionaries, words are phonetically respelled to give you the accepted pronunciation. Usually marks are placed over the vowels to indicate the sound. These are called *diacritical marks*. Notice the following example of respelling with diacritical marks.

> **hay′rack′** (hā′răk′)
> ā is pronounced like *a* in *mate*.
> ă is pronounced like *a* in *mat*.

At the bottom of each page of a good dictionary there is usually a key or list of common words written with these marks over the letters. For example:

ăct	āble	dâre	ärt
ĕbb	ēqual		
ĭf	īce		

These words are a guide to the pronunciation of letters similarly marked. If the word that you are examining contains an *a* marked ă, the letter will be pronounced like the *a* in *act*.

If the letter is not explained at the bottom of the dic-

242

tionary page, consult the full key on the inside cover or in the introductory sections of the dictionary.

38b. Watch accent marks.

In your dictionary, the syllable to be stressed will be indicated by a heavy accent mark (′).

mod′el   mis′chief

If the word has two syllables that are accented, the syllable which should be accented more lightly than the other is followed by a light accent mark (′) or by a double accent mark (″).

in′tellec′tual   chor′eog′rapher   Bes″sara′bia

EXERCISE 1

The words in this list are often mispronounced. Consult your dictionary for the correct pronunciation. Then practice saying the words. Use them in your own conversation.

absorb	corsage	hospitable	positively
absurd	cruelly	hostile	preferable
accessories	deaf	humble	ptomaine
alias	diphtheria	influence	quadruplets
almond	dirigible	insane	radiator
athlete	drowned	instead	relapse
attacked	embroidered	Italian	salmon
attorney	escape	italics	since
bicycle	experiment	laundered	souvenir
biography	favorite	length	stomach
candidate	fete	mischievous	strength
caramel	figure	municipal	strictly
champion	film	museum	suite
chic	forehead	orchestra	syrup
clique	genuine	peony	theater
column	government	perspiration	umbrella
contrary	height	pianist	various
corps	heroine	portiere	wrestle

243

EXERCISE 2

If you have a large reading vocabulary, you may understand many words that you do not know how to pronounce. Which of the words in the following lists are familiar to you? Pronounce all the words in the list and check yourself by looking up the pronunciations given in the dictionary. Learn the correct pronunciation of any word that you have mispronounced. Learn the meaning of any unfamiliar word in the list. When you know the correct meaning and pronunciation of all these words, try to use them in sentences in conversation, so that they will all become parts of your speaking vocabulary.

acumen	comparable	incomparable	patronize
amenable	condolence	indisputable	quay
audacious	conversant	inexplicable	reptile
autopsy	debris	intricacy	reputable
bourgeois	decorum	inveigle	sonorous
chastisement	formidable	irreparable	subtle
chiropodist	grievous	irrevocable	syringe
clandestine	grimace	lamentable	ultimatum
combatant	incognito	lingerie	verbatim

EXERCISE 3

Are you sure of the pronunciation of the following foreign words that are in common use today? Consult your dictionary for the accepted pronunciation of each word.

au gratin	boudoir	finis	ravioli
bona fide	chaise longue	per diem	table d'hôte
bon voyage	coiffure	pizza	tête à tête

39. SPELLING

Most poor spelling is a matter of carelessness. Although it is not possible to master the spelling of all words by means of rules, a few simple rules will help a great deal.

39a

39a. Pronounce words correctly.

1. Do not add vowels in pronouncing such words as *disastrous, similar, athletics,* and you will not misspell them.
2. Do not omit consonants in pronouncing such words as *library* and *government* and you will not misspell them.
3. Do not omit syllables in pronouncing such words as *miniature, sophomore, accidentally,* and you will not misspell them.
4. Examine carefully words that contain silent letters: *(p)sychology, (p)neumonia, g(h)ost.*

EXERCISE 4

These words are often misspelled because they are mispronounced. Choose the correct form in each numbered pair and write it on your paper, with its number. Check your choices and make another list of the words that you misspell. Keep the list for study, adding to it other words that you misspell in your written work or correspondence. (See Section 39c.)

1. accidently, accidentally
2. arthritis, artharitis
3. asparagus, asparagrass
4. atheletics, athletics
5. attackded, attacked
6. basicly, basically
7. boundary, boundry
8. canidate, candidate
9. children, childern
10. congratulations, congradulations
11. cruel, crule
12. disastrous, disasterous
13. drasticly, drastically
14. emotionally, emotionly
15. February, Febuary
16. goverment, government
17. grievious, grievous
18. heighth, height
19. hinderance, hindrance
20. hunerd, hundred
21. incidentally, incidently
22. interduce, introduce
23. mischievious, mischievous
24. modern, modren
25. prespiration, perspiration
26. pernounce, pronounce
27. quanity, quantity
28. realisticly, realistically
29. recognize, reconize
30. sarcasticly, sarcastically
31. satirically, satiricly

245

32. sophmore, sophomore
33. strickly, strictly

34. surprise, suprise
35. temperment, temperament

39b. See the words you use.

Poor spellers, especially, should pay particular attention to the appearance of words. The most frequent error in visualizing words is mistaking one for another.

EXERCISE 5

Some mistakes are made because people confuse words that look alike or somewhat alike. Use a dictionary to learn the meaning and pronunciation of the following words. Divide your class into seven groups. Let group 1 write sentences illustrating the correct use of the first ten pairs of words. Group 2 may take the next ten pairs, and so on. When the groups have finished their work, check the results by reading the sentences aloud.

1. accept, except
2. access, excess
3. addition, edition
4. advise, advice
5. affect, effect
6. aisle, isle
7. allusion, illusion
8. ally, alley
9. altar, alter
10. anecdote, antidote
11. angle, angel
12. bath, bathe
13. berth, birth
14. break, brake
15. breath, breathe
16. bridal, bridle
17. capital, capitol
18. censor, censure
19. choose, chose
20. chord, cord
21. cite, site, sight
22. cloth, clothe
23. coarse, course
24. comma, coma
25. conscious, conscience
26. corps, corpse
27. costumes, customs
28. counsel, council
29. descent, decent
30. dessert, desert
31. diary, dairy
32. dual, duel
33. eligible, illegible
34. eliminate, illuminate
35. formally, formerly
36. grate, great
37. hoarse, horse
38. hoping, hopping
39. huge, Hugh
40. idle, idol

41. later, latter
42. led, lead
43. lessen, lesson
44. lose, loose
45. mist, midst
46. moral, morale
47. nauseous, nauseated
48. passed, past
49. peace, piece
50. persecute, prosecute
51. personal, personnel
52. precede, proceed
53. prescribe, proscribe
54. principal, principle
55. prodigy, protégé
56. quiet, quite
57. rain, reign, rein
58. rapped, wrapped
59. respectfully, respectively
60. scene, seen
61. shone, shown
62. sole, soul
63. stationary, stationery
64. steel, steal
65. surely, surly
66. tenants, tenets
67. thrown, throne
68. track, tract
69. trial, trail
70. weather, whether

EXERCISE 6

In each of the following sentences, choose from the parentheses the word that is required by the meaning of the sentence. On your paper, write the number of each sentence and beside it write the word that you have chosen.

1. We did not (accept, except) the invitation.
2. A tall, dark (woman, women) entered the room.
3. I do not know (whether, weather) I can go to the game.
4. Many people were (persecuted, prosecuted) for their religious beliefs in the sixteenth century.
5. Sylvia is such a (quite, quiet) girl that we never learn to know her.
6. Do you understand the theorem about right (angles, angels)?
7. Use a (coma, comma) to separate the items in a series.
8. Jack is much taller (then, than) I am.
9. I was so (scared, scarred) that I ran out of the house.
10. Have you bought any new (clothes, cloths) for Easter?
11. How did you (loose, lose) your money?
12. The man standing on the porch is the (principle, principal) of my school.
13. The (sole, soul) on Bob's shoe is an inch thick.

14. The present was (wrapped, rapped) in silver paper.
15. When we arranged the line, Hazel was to (proceed, precede) me.
16. Please excuse Ellen for not doing her homework. She felt (nauseous, nauseated) all last evening.
17. The business, (formally, formerly) called David Hecht Manufacturing Company, will now be known as Hecht Brothers, Inc.
18. Samuel Pepys wrote a (dairy, diary) that tells of the life he (led, lead) in seventeenth-century London.
19. The (personal, personnel) manager asked me to come to his office for an interview.
20. The motion picture (censor, censure) refused to permit the picture to be shown in the state.

39c. Keep your own list of misspelled words.

Most people learn to spell simply by paying close attention to the appearance of words which they see in their reading, but almost everybody has trouble with a few words that are difficult for him. You save time by keeping a record of the words that you misspell and making a special effort to learn them. Your list will differ from the lists of other students, but there are some common words that give trouble to many people. Exercises 7, 8, and 9 contain some of these words.

EXERCISE 7

These are simple words frequently misspelled. Be able to write these words from dictation. Put in your own list the words which you misspell.

absence	already	anxious	assemblies
absurd	altogether	apartment	audience
accepted	always	apparatus	awkward
across	amateur	argument	beginning
afraid	among	arithmetic	believe
all right	anxiety	arrival	biscuit

brief	foreign	misspelled	riding
business	forty	mortgage	running
buying	fourth	mountain	safety
cafeteria	friend	muscle	seize
captain	frivolous	mystery	sense
certain	fulfilled	necessary	sentence
cheerful	furniture	neighbor	separate
chief	generally	neither	shepherd
choose	governor	niece	shining
coming	grammar	nineteen	shoulder
copies	guard	ninety	similar
courtesy	hammer	ninth	sincerely
cried	handkerchief	oblige	speech
decide	heroes	occasionally	strength
definite	humorous	occurred	stretch
descend	hurried	offered	strictly
describe	imaginary	omission	studying
desirable	immediately	opportunity	summarize
despair	independent	paid	superstitious
destroy	influence	parallel	surely
develop	intellectual	partner	surprise
difficulties	invitation	peculiar	thorough
dining room	itself	perhaps	toward
disabled	jewelry	pilgrim	tragedy
disagree	judgment	pleasant	tries
divide	knowledge	possession	truly
doesn't	laboratory	potato	twelfth
during	ladies	prison	until
easily	laid	privilege	using
eighth	library	probably	usually
embarrass	lightning	pronunciation	village
enemies	loneliness	realize	villain
excellent	lying	really	Wednesday
exercise	magazine	receive	woman
existence	marriage	repetition	women
experience	mathematics	replied	writer
familiar	meant	representative	writing
fierce	messenger	respectfully	written
fiery	minute	rhyme	yacht

EXERCISE 8

The following words are more difficult than those in Exercise 7 and have been misspelled in many students' papers. Write the words from dictation. Add to your own list of words any that you misspell. For rules to help you with spelling, see Section 39d–j.

abandon	changeable	environment	optimism
abbreviate	characteristics	equipped	originally
abundance	chauffeur	exaggerate	pamphlet
accommodate	colonel	explanation	paralyzed
accompanying	committee	extremely	participle
achievement	competent	fascinate	peasant
acquired	competition	fragrant	persistence
advertisement	conceived	grateful	persuade
agreeing	condemn	guidance	polluted
antiseptic	continuous	hygiene	practically
apology	convenient	icicle	precede
appealed	conveyed	immensely	precious
appearance	correspondence	imprisonment	preferable
appetite	couplet	inefficiency	preferred
appreciate	criticism	inevitable	prejudices
appropriate	curriculum	infinitive	prepared
architect	denying	initiative	procedure
ascent	dependent	interfere	proceed
association	disability	interpretation	professor
attendance	disappear	interruption	prominent
banana	disappointment	invariably	prosperous
beneficial	discussion	irresponsible	pursuit
bicycle	distinguish	jealous	questionnaire
brilliant	dormitories	lieutenant	recommend
bureau	economically	literature	reconcile
calendar	eliminate	luxurious	recurrence
campaign	emergencies	maintenance	religion
cancellation	eminent	miscellaneous	reminiscence
carriage	emphatic	mischievous	repaired
ceiling	encouragement	monotonous	repentance
cemetery	enthusiastic	noticeable	resemblance

restaurant	serviceable	temporarily	undoubtedly
sandwich	simile	tendency	unnecessary
scarcity	spaghetti	transferred	valiant
schedule	specialty	unanimous	vehicle
scheme	specimen	unconscious	vengeance
sergeant	sympathizes	undesirable	volume

EXERCISE 9

Some of these words will give trouble to even a good speller. See how many of them you can spell.

abhorrence	conspicuous	imminent	pneumonia
absorbing	contemptuous	impetuosity	preference
accustom	deteriorate	incredulous	prevalent
acknowledge	diphtheria	intentionally	proffered
acquaintance	dirigible	intercede	promenade
aeronautics	discipline	irrelevant	recede
aggravate	dissatisfied	legitimate	recommendation
analogous	dissipate	leisure	reconciliation
apparent	distinction	liquefy	representative
arrangement	ecstasy	mercenary	rescind
artillery	exhilarate	mimicking	reservoir
auctioneer	exorbitant	momentous	rheumatism
authoritative	extraordinary	notoriety	ridiculous
auxiliary	facilitate	occurrence	sacrificing
barbarous	guillotine	parliament	sacrilegious
battalion	harass	particularly	saxophone
carburetor	hesitancy	pasteurization	soliloquy
coincidence	hypnosis	perceive	specifically
colloquial	hypocrisy	perceptible	tyrannically
comparatively	illiterate	perseverance	vacuum
concede	imitation	pervade	vaudeville
conferred	immigration	picnicking	visible

39d. Spelling of plurals.

1. The plurals of most nouns are formed by adding -*s* to the singular.

desks   dogs   boys   chairs

2. Nouns ending in *ch, x, z, sh, s* add *-es* to form the plural.

boss, bosses	sash, sashes	church, churches
tax, taxes	glass, glasses	topaz, topazes

NOTE: Verbs ending in *ch, x, z, sh, s* form the third person singular of the present tense in this same fashion.

pushes   passes   fixes   pinches   fizzes

3. Nouns ending in *y* preceded by a consonant change *y* to *i* and add *-es* to form the plural.

baby, babies	sky, skies
lady, ladies	family, families
dairy, dairies	memory, memories

NOTE: Notice the same change in the formation of the third person singular, present tense, of verbs ending in *y* preceded by a consonant.

try, tries	marry, marries
study, studies	hurry, hurries
worry, worries	justify, justifies

4. Words ending in *ay, ey, oy* add merely *-s* for the plural.

valley, valleys	journey, journeys
donkey, donkeys	attorney, attorneys

5. Musical terms ending in *o* and nouns ending in *o* preceded by a vowel add *-s* for the plural.

studio, studios	soprano, sopranos
radio, radios	piano, pianos

6. Most nouns ending in *o* preceded by a consonant add *-es* for the plural.

potato, potatoes	hero, heroes
mosquito, mosquitoes	Negro, Negroes

7. Many nouns ending in *f* add *-s* for the plural, but others ending in *f* or *fe* have plurals ending in *ves*.

chief, chiefs	wife, wives
dwarf, dwarfs	wharf, wharves
reef, reefs	life, lives
belief, beliefs	loaf, loaves

NOTE: *Believes* is a verb.

Howard *believes* that he is right.
Each religion has its own *beliefs*.

8. Compound nouns usually add *-s* to the most important word of the compound.

brother-in-law, brothers-in-law
commander in chief, commanders in chief
maid of honor, maids of honor
court-martial, courts-martial
man-of-war, men-of-war

9. Some words retain foreign plurals.

SINGULAR	PLURAL
alumnus	alumni
alumna	alumnae
analysis	analyses
crisis	crises
datum	data
parenthesis	parentheses

A few foreign words have two accepted plurals, the foreign plural and an English plural. In the following list, the foreign plural form is given first for each word:

SINGULAR	PLURAL
memorandum	memoranda, memorandums
curriculum	curricula, curriculums
index	indices, indexes
radius	radii, radiuses

10. Some words have the same form in both singular and plural.

deer   sheep   grouse   moose

EXERCISE 10

On your paper, write the plural form of each of the following words:

agony	business	gypsy	pulley
alley	butterfly	hero	quality
ally	calf	lady	radius
alto	canoe	leaf	sky
analysis	cargo	lobby	soprano
apology	casualty	loyalty	stratum
army	cello	mosquito	sympathy
authority	century	mother-in-law	synopsis
baby	comedy	Negro	thesis
balcony	conspiracy	palace	thief
battery	crash	parenthesis	tomato
biography	crisis	pass	topaz
blackberry	crutch	penny	tornado
boss	diary	piano	tragedy
box	echo	potato	valley
buffalo	fox	process	volcano

39e. Words containing *ei* or *ie*.

Write *i* before *e*
Except after *c*,
Or when sounded as *a*,
As in *neighbor* and *weigh*.

believe	deceive
relieve	receive
grieve	perceive
siege	conceive
sieve	conceit

Exceptions often misspelled: *leisure, seize, neither, weird.*

254

39f

39f. Final e.

Words ending in silent *e* usually drop the *e* before adding a suffix beginning with a vowel (*-ing, -able, -ance, -ous*).

resemble	resemblance
believe	believing, believable
interfere	interfering
advise	advising, advisable
hope	hoping
desire	desiring, desirous
care	caring
argue	arguing, arguable
amaze	amazing

Such words keep the *e* before a suffix beginning with a consonant (*-ly, -ful, -ment, -ness*).

pale, paleness	care, careful
sincere, sincerely	amaze, amazement
state, statement	

NOTE: Exceptions often misspelled: *argument, truly, dyeing, canoeing.*

Words that end in *ce* or *ge* drop the *e* only when a suffix beginning with *e* or *i* is added. This rule is easy to remember if you keep in mind that the spelling reflects the pronunciation. Before *e* and *i*, the letter *c* is pronounced like *s* and the letter *g* like *j* (with a few exceptions, such as *tiger*); but before *a*, *o*, and *u* the *c* is pronounced like *k* and the *g* has the "hard" sound as in *go*. Therefore, to keep the "soft" sound of these letters (as in *peace* and *advantage*), we have to keep the *e* after *c* or *g* before adding any suffix beginning with *a*, *o*, or *u*.

notice, noticeable	change, changeable
peace, peaceable	courage, courageous
outrage, outrageous	advantage, advantageous
bridge, bridgeable	

Like other words ending in *e*, these words keep the *e* before a suffix beginning with a consonant.

    arrange, arrangement   strange, strangeness
    resource, resourceful   large, largely

NOTE: Exceptions are *judgment* and *acknowledgment* (preferred spellings).

EXERCISE 11

On your paper, write the words in the following list. Then from each word form as many other words as you can by adding suffixes (*-ed, -ing, -ous, -able, -ible, -ness, -ance, -ment, -ly*). Write these new words beside the words from which they are formed.

adore	debate	hurry	reconcile
advantage	decide	imagine	refute
advise	desire	levy	ride
argue	dine	lonely	sale
arrange	efface	lose	secure
arrive	endure	love	sense
believe	exchange	manage	separate
blame	excite	marriage	service
change	excuse	move	silly
charge	fatigue	note	singe
come	file	peace	store
conceive	force	pronounce	trace
courage	grieve	receive	use
damage	hope	recognize	value

39g. Final y.

Words ending in *y* preceded by a consonant change *y* to *i* before any suffix except one beginning with *i*. Be sure to keep the *y* if the suffix *-ing* is added.

    happy, happiness   worry, worried   worry, worrying
    study, studying   try, tried   mercy, merciful
    steady, steadiness   ready, readied   ready, readying

39h. Words ending in *-ible* or *-able*.

There is no simple rule that will tell you how to spell words ending in *-ible* or *-able*. If you are not sure which spelling is correct, look the word up in a dictionary.

EXERCISE 12

On your paper write the following words, substituting *-ible* or *-able* for the dashes. Consult a dictionary for the correct spelling. Then put on your personal spelling list the ones that you miss.

accept—	convert—	inaccess—	manage—
access—	depend—	incomprehens—	mov—
adjust—	desir—	incred—	not—
admiss—	destruct—	indispens—	notice—
advis—	digest—	inexcus—	plaus—
allow—	discern—	inexpress—	precept—
avail—	divis—	infall—	permiss—
combust—	dur—	insepar—	sens—
commend—	elig—	intang—	suscept—
compar—	excit—	invis—	tang—
compat—	excus—	irrefut—	unbear—
comprehens—	feas—	irresist—	valu—
conceiv—	flex—	liv—	vis—
contempt—	imagin—	lov—	vulner—

39i. Double consonant before suffix.

Double the final consonant before a suffix which begins with a *vowel* if both of the following conditions exist:

1. The word has only one syllable or is accented on the last syllable.
2. The word ends in a single consonant preceded by a single vowel.

> ship (One syllable ending in a single consonant, *p*, preceded by a single vowel, *i*), shipped, shipping.
> shipment (Suffix does not begin with vowel.)

compel (Two syllables with the accent on the final one),
compelled, compelling

quarrel (Two syllables with first accented), quarreled,
quarreling

confront (Two syllables with accent on the final one. Do
not double final consonant *t*, because it is not preceded
by a vowel.) confronted, confronting

NOTE: A few words, mostly adopted from French, end in
a *silent* consonant preceded by a single vowel. In such
words the consonant is not doubled before a suffix, even
though the accent falls on the last syllable.

crochet, crocheted   ricochet, ricocheting

EXERCISE 13

Write on your paper the words in this list. Then add *-ed*,
-ing, *-ment* where possible. Write the whole word each
time you add a suffix.

accuse	develop	plan
acquit	disappear	prefer
admire	disappoint	put
admit	domineer	quarrel
allot	drop	rebel
amuse	equip	recur
anchor	exhibit	refer
assent	fan	repeal
begin	fit	require
benefit	gossip	resent
brag	grab	shine
commit	happen	ship
compel	infer	stop
conceal	interfere	submit
concur	jam	tramp
confer	knit	transfer
confront	occur	travel
control	omit	trip
counsel	permit	whip

39j. Words ending in -ally.

Words ending in *c* do not usually add *-ly* alone to form an adverb. They add *-ally.*

realistic	realistically	drastic	drastically
sarcastic	sarcastically	satiric	satirically
basic	basically	enthusiastic	enthusiastically

NOTE: Watch also *accidentally* and *incidentally.*

40. VOCABULARY GROWTH

Vocabulary growth does not mean simply learning new words. It means also discarding worn-out expressions, using words accurately, learning to suit the expression to the audience and the occasion. It means making language work so that it says exactly what you want it to say. It is important, then, to consider how you can develop a *useful* vocabulary and use it wisely.

40a. Simple words for a growing vocabulary.

No list of words supplied by a book can meet all of the needs of people who wish to understand better what they read or hear. Make your own personal list composed of words which you find in your reading or your listening and which will be valuable to you. Use new words frequently for several days in order to fix them in your memory.

Although nothing can take the place of a personal list, it is sometimes interesting to examine some common words to see whether they are a part of your vocabulary.

EXERCISE 14

Do you know the meaning of the words italicized in the following paragraph? Consult your dictionary for the words that are not clear to you. Be prepared to explain their meaning in the paragraph.

An *eminent* scholar, known for his *eccentricity,* complained

259

recently that he had received a number of *anonymous* letters and had been approached on the street by an *ungainly* creature who made strange *grimaces* and gestures while threatening the learned man. For a time the scholar had ignored the letters because people of refinement do not write anonymous communications or pay any attention to them; but the notes came so frequently that he was annoyed by their *insolence* and decided to try to discover the writer of such *malicious* material. A *magistrate* who was a neighbor of the scholar liked to do a little *sleuthing* as an *avocation*. He agreed to work with the scholar at no *pecuniary* gain. Together they examined the notes and made conclusions. Because the evidence at first seemed *obscure,* the men had to display genuine *acuteness* in working out the problem; but they finally decided to accuse another neighbor, an *uncouth* fellow known in the village as a *misanthrope.* When this man was threatened with a *libel* suit, he was frightened, and the scholar received no more anonymous mail.

40b. Words from newspapers and magazines.

Do you know what a *bipartisan* foreign policy is?

When the paper speaks of a *gubernatorial campaign,* what is happening?

The man was tried for *perjury.* What had he done?

The italicized words in the preceding sentences appear regularly in newspapers. A democratic government depends for its success upon literate citizens, people who know what is going on. Learn the words that are used frequently in the newspapers and magazines.

EXERCISE 15

These words appear regularly in everyday reading. On your paper write the words in the first list. Then write opposite each word the number of the group of words in the second column that defines it.

Example:

1. arbitration   3

1. arbitration	1. working with another
2. collaboration	2. make easier
3. facilitate	3. settling a dispute by discussing and coming to an agreement
4. agrarian	4. mutual exchange
5. reciprocity	5. become worse
6. deteriorate	6. having to do with farm matters
7. dilemma	7. dishonest, cheating
8. strategy	8. belonging to the same time
9. prejudice	9. compensation by a defeated nation for damage after a war
10. amphibious	10. contact between persons or groups working together
11. contemporary	11. skillful management to get the better of an opponent
12. reparations	12. self-governing, independent
13. liaison	13. a difficult or embarrassing situation
14. autonomous	14. capable of working on both land and water
15. fraudulent	15. preconceived opinion

EXERCISE 16

Choose fifteen interesting words from your newspaper and write a definition for each. Arrange words and definitions in two lists as in Exercise 15 and see whether your classmates can match them.

40c. Business words.

Everybody needs to know some business terms in order to manage his affairs.

EXERCISE 17

Here are some common words that will be useful. Match each word and its meaning as you did in Exercise 15.

1. disbursements	1. an addition to a will
2. commodity	2. to reduce, diminish
3. allocate	3. decrease in value through use

261

4. codicil	4. to make payment for expense or loss
5. curtail	5. sum of money paid to shareholders in a corporation
6. amortization	6. amount subtracted from a bill for prompt payment or other special reason
7. assets	7. the amount by which a sum of money is short
8. depreciation	8. security pledged for payment of a loan
9. dividend	9. an article of trade
10. discount	10. property or cash possessed by a company
11. reimburse	11. paid before material is sent
12. deficit	12. to set apart for a special purpose
13. prepaid	13. an itemized bill
14. invoice	14. gradual payment of a debt before the due date
15. collateral	15. amounts paid out

40d. Foreign words in everyday use.

Long ago, the Romans had a little proverb that said:

> *De gustibus non est disputandum.* (There is no disputing about tastes.)

The French say:

> *Chacun à son goût.* (Everyone to his own taste.)

But the Spaniards, with their own sense of humor, say:

> *Cado loco a su tema.* (Every madman to his own obsession.)

Our language has been enriched by adopting from other languages expressions like these. Many terms used in everyday living are from Latin, French, Spanish, Italian, or German.

EXERCISE 18

Write a sentence containing each of the following words or abbreviations and then read the sentence aloud with the correct pronunciation. If you have trouble, consult your dictionary.

A.D.
à la carte
à la mode
alma mater
B.C.
cabana
connoisseur
debris
demitasse
ennui
entrée

espionage
ex officio
finis
gauche
gringo
hombre
hors d'oeuvres
kindergarten
laissez faire
mañana
mantilla

minestrone
patio
post mortem
pronto
répondez s'il vous plaît
(R.S.V.P.)
rodeo
siesta
sombrero
tamale
wanderlust

EXERCISE 19

These foreign words are more difficult than the words in Exercise 18. Follow the directions in Exercise 18.

ad infinitum
ad nauseam
agent provocateur
al fresco
antipasto
au courant
carte blanche
coup d'état

crêpe suzette
esprit de corps
fait accompli
habeas corpus
junta
maître d'hôtel
mare nostrum
milieu

noblesse oblige
persona non grata
peseta
pièce de résistance
savoir faire
savoir vivre
summa cum laude
verbatim

40e. Medical terms.

If your doctor tells you that you have laryngitis, what has happened to you?

What should you do if you need a tonsillectomy?

It is often necessary to know a few medical terms in order to understand what your doctor tells you.

EXERCISE 20

Explain the meaning of the following words:

allergy	appendectomy	metatarsal	neurosis
amnesia	arteriosclerosis	insomnia	sinusitis
anemia	astigmatism	malignant	therapy
anesthetic	benign	myopia	toxic

40f. Musical terms.

Can you read your program at a concert or the newspaper report of a musical event?

EXERCISE 21

What do these terms mean? Pronounce them correctly.

a cappella	coloratura	leitmotif	recitative
acoustics	con brio	medley	scherzo
allegro	concerto	opéra bouffe	sonata
andante	counterpoint	opus	mezzo-soprano
aria	crescendo	overture	staccato
atonal	harmony	percussion	symphony
cadenza	instrumentation	pitch	syncopation

40g. Scientific terms.

Scientific terms appear in newspaper and magazine articles dealing with scientific subjects. Can you understand such terms? The following exercise may help you. As you meet unfamiliar scientific terms in your reading, find out their meaning and pronunciation and add the words to your personal vocabulary list.

EXERCISE 22

Write sentences using these words. Read the sentences aloud, pronouncing the words correctly.

amoeba	bisect	deciduous	horticulture
bacillus	carnivorous	dissect	perennial
bacteria	combustion	erosion	saturated

264

40h. Art words.

Here are a few words used in discussions of art. Perhaps your art teacher will help you to increase the list.

caricature	chiaroscuro	etching	pastel
ceramics	cubism	impressionism	symmetry

40i. Literary terms.

The following are words which you may need if you are going to talk intelligently about literature. Do you know their meanings?

allegory	denouement	lyric	realism
analogy	discourse	nuance	romanticism
blank verse	elegy	pathos	satire
classic	epic	plot	sonnet
couplet	farce	protagonist	symbol

40j. Words for the ambitious.

How good is your vocabulary? Test it by seeing how many of the words in the following exercises you know.

EXERCISE 23

On your paper, write the words in the first column. Then place opposite each word the number of the definition which you think suits that word. Write sentences of your own in which you use these words.

1. abscond	1. able to use both hands equally well
2. adamant	2. improve
3. adroitly	3. to run away to avoid legal process
4. ambidextrous	4. constant in application
5. ameliorate	5. unyielding
6. antipathy	6. able to speak two languages
7. apothegm	7. cleverly
8. assiduous	8. harsh sound
9. bilingual	9. a short, pithy saying
10. cacophony	10. dislike

EXERCISE 24

Follow the directions in Exercise 23.

1. denouement	1. great desire to possess something
2. calumny	2. formal expression of praise
3. commensurate	3. abominable
4. complicity	4. foolish
5. concatenation	5. consisting of similar parts or elements
6. cupidity	6. lasting only a short time
7. cynosure	7. equal or proportionate in measure or extent
8. discrepancy	8. partnership in wrongdoing
9. edifying	9. state of being linked together
10. elucidate	10. the final outcome of a plot or of a complicated situation
11. encomium	11. something that strongly attracts attention
12. ephemeral	12. deviation, variance
13. execrable	13. instructing and improving
14. facilitate	14. slander
15. fallacious	15. a person who has religious beliefs contrary to the accepted form
16. fatuous	16. affectedly grand
17. ghetto	17. make clear
18. grandiose	18. a place in which Jews have been required to live
19. heretic	19. make easy
20. homogeneous	20. logically unsound

EXERCISE 25

Follow the directions in Exercise 23.

1. imminent	1. out of keeping, not harmonious in character
2. incognito	2. essentially, by nature
3. incongruous	3. artless, innocent
4. ingenuous	4. mournful
5. innocuous	5. a hater of mankind

6. intrepid	6. likely to occur at any moment
7. intrinsically	7. a formal expression of great praise
8. invective	8. disgrace or reproach incurred by conduct considered shameful
9. lugubrious	9. having one's identity concealed
10. mendacious	10. coolly unconcerned
11. meticulous	11. characterized by show
12. misanthrope	12. a theory that identifies God and nature
13. misogynist	13. cowardly
14. nebulous	14. faithless, treacherous
15. nonchalant	15. policy of adapting one's actions to whatever circumstances are present
16. onerous	16. impractical, visionary
17. opportunism	17. not harmful
18. opprobrium	18. careful about small details
19. ostentatious	19. fearless
20. panegyric	20. hater of women
21. pantheism	21. vague, hazy, cloudy
22. perfidious	22. not easily excited
23. phlegmatic	23. lying
24. pusillanimous	24. an utterance of violent reproach or accusation
25. quixotic	25. burdensome

EXERCISE 26

Follow the directions in Exercise 23.

1. rationalize	1. done by stealth
2. sanguinary	2. waver
3. sophistry	3. bullying, threatening
4. supercilious	4. great technical skill
5. surreptitious	5. to invent an acceptable explanation for behavior
6. truculent	6. bloody
7. ubiquitous	7. haughtily disdainful
8. vacillate	8. experienced in place of another
9. vicarious	9. present everywhere
10. virtuosity	10. false argument

41. PROVINCIALISMS

When you work to develop a vocabulary, you must not only learn new words, but discard old ones that interfere with accurate, effective speech and writing.

A fundamental requirement of formal usage is that words must be in national, not merely sectional, use. A provincialism, or localism, is a word or phrase used and understood in only a particular section or region of the country. Such words are difficult to detect because a writer or speaker may have come to accept them as reputable and to assume that they are nationally understood since he himself has known them from childhood. Some parts of the United States are especially rich in colorful localisms which add flavor to speech but which may not be immediately intelligible in other areas. Such localisms are appropriate in informal writing and conversation but should usually be avoided in formal writing. Examples: *chunk* and *chuck* for *throw; tote* for *carry; tote* (noun) for *load; poke* for *bag* or *sack; fatback* for *bacon; bunk into* for *bump into; reckon* for *think* or *suppose; choose* for *wish; draw* for *gully; to home* for *at home; loco* for *crazy.*

EXERCISE 27

Make a list of localisms heard in your neighborhood or vicinity. Then decide which ones should be avoided in your formal writing.

42. COLLOQUIALISMS

A *colloquialism* is a conversational expression which is permissible in an easy, informal style of writing and speaking. Colloquialisms are not appropriate in formal writing or speaking.

Dictionaries mark words as colloquial (*Colloq.*) when in the judgment of the editors they are more common in speech than in writing or more appropriate to informal

than to formal discourse. Since editors differ in the inter-
pretations of their findings, the label *colloquial* may apply
to many kinds of words. All contractions, for example, may
be considered "respectable" colloquialisms, whereas some
other kinds should be guarded against even in informal
writing.

The test for the use of colloquialisms is appropriateness.
There is no objective test or exact rule to enable you to
determine when colloquialisms may be used. Certainly it
is better to employ them than to avoid them and make your
writing seem artificial and awkward. But in formal, well-
planned writing they should be avoided unless they are
deliberately used to achieve some stylistic effect. Consult
the dictionary to determine whether a word is considered
colloquial.

Examples of colloquialisms:

ad	flop
along side of	goner (a person lost or dead)
angel (financial backer)	gumption
auto	in back of
brass tacks (facts)	phone
cute	show up
don't	take a try at
fizzle (to fail)	try and
flabbergast	won't

43. IDIOMS

Idioms are forms of expression peculiar to a language.
Many idioms defy grammatical analysis; but because they
are sanctioned by current usage, they are looked upon as
correct. Idioms correctly used make speech and writing
vigorous and picturesque.

Although idioms often cannot be analyzed grammatically,
the careful writer will not therefore assume that he can
change them as he pleases. A good dictionary will contain
a statement of idiomatic usage following words which need

such explanation. Many idioms involve the use of preposititions. A few examples of idioms follow:

UNIDIOMATIC	IDIOMATIC
cannot help but talk	cannot help talking
comply to	comply with
die with (a disease)	die of
different than	different from
doubt if	doubt whether, doubt that
graduated (high school)	graduated from (high school)
identical to	identical with
listen at	listen to
out loud	aloud
plan on going	plan to go
providing that	provided that
to home	at home
wait on	wait for (to await)

Certain words combine with different prepositions to express different meanings.

Examples:

agree
$\begin{cases} to \text{ a proposal} \\ on \text{ a plan} \\ with \text{ a person} \end{cases}$

compare
$\begin{cases} to \text{ something similar} \\ with \text{ something dissimilar} \end{cases}$

contend
$\begin{cases} for \text{ a principle} \\ with \text{ a person} \\ against \text{ an obstacle} \end{cases}$

differ
$\begin{cases} with \text{ a person} \\ from \text{ something else} \\ about \text{ or } over \text{ a question} \end{cases}$

impatient
$\begin{cases} for \text{ something desired} \\ with \text{ someone else} \\ of \text{ restraint} \\ at \text{ someone's conduct} \end{cases}$

> rewarded $\begin{cases} \textit{for} \text{ something done} \\ \textit{with} \text{ a gift} \\ \textit{by} \text{ a person} \end{cases}$

· *In regard to* (not *in regards to*)

The Blank, Rischler Company agreed *to* our suggestion to begin the work on January 1.

Mr. Southern differs *with* you. He thinks that we are not ready for expansion.

This plan differs *from* the first one in many details.

The Hudson River has often been compared *to* the Rhine for its beauty.

When I was on the Rhine, I compared it *with* the Hudson and concluded that it has nothing the Hudson lacks except castles.

NOTE: In casual English, it is all right to use a preposition at the end of a sentence. Sometimes it is acceptable even in formal English, especially in certain idiomatic expressions in which a preposition is retained when the verb becomes passive, with the object of the preposition as its subject.

Active: We cannot think *of* such a thing.
Passive: Such a thing is not to be thought *of*.
Active: Someone laughed *at* him.
Passive: He hated to be laughed *at*.

When you use a preposition at the end of a sentence, make sure that it is not an unnecessary preposition.

Right: What are you writing with?
Wrong: Where are you going to?
Right: Where are you going?

EXERCISE 28

On your paper, write the number of each of the following sentences. Beside the number, write the preposition that should be supplied for that sentence. Consult your dictionary if you have difficulty.

1. This letter means that he will accede _____ your request.
2. I doubt _____ I can go with you.
3. The color of your hat is similar to that of your gloves but is not identical _____ it.
4. The manager did not agree _____ my suggestion for improving the filing system.
5. Now that her salary has been increased, Hilda is completely independent _____ her relatives.
6. This suitcase differs _____ that one only in length.
7. Mrs. Robbins will be _____ home this afternoon.
8. Do you think the snowstorm will prevent him _____ coming tonight?
9. The new family next door is very different _____ the one that lived there before.
10. Jack is now reconciled _____ living on a small salary.
11. I didn't think him capable _____ doing such a thing.
12. Jane is too careless _____ her appearance.

EXERCISE 29

On your paper, write correctly each of the following sentences:

1. What kind of a car did you buy?
2. I can't help but think that Jane has caused all the trouble.
3. When our parents graduated high school, education was different than it is now.
4. We didn't plan on going to the shore so early.
5. If we have to wait on him much longer, we shall be late.
6. I doubt if you will get any help from Ellen, because she is not to home very often.
7. I differ from George about holding a new club election right now.
8. I cannot help but listen when you practice your part out loud.
9. I thought all along that Bill was planning on going with us.
10. I doubt if you can ever find a jacket identical to your old one.

44. VULGARISMS

Vulgarisms (also called "barbarisms" and "substandard" or "illiterate expressions") are words and phrases not accepted in either colloquial or formal language. Since they are used by uneducated speakers, such expressions are always to be avoided in writing unless you put them into the dialogue of people you are characterizing as uneducated. The following words and phrases should be guarded against:

> *hadn't ought, mistakened, this here, anywheres, couldn't of, hisself, being as, concertize, vacationize, still and all, coronated*

45. IMPROPRIETIES

Improprieties are recognized English words which are misused in function or meaning. The word that constitutes an impropriety is acceptable; it is its misuse which causes an error in diction.

45a. Avoid improprieties in grammatical function.

A word may be transferred from one part of speech to another, but the careful writer will not employ such a word in its new function unless it is sanctioned by good use. Examples of improprieties in function:

Verbs misused as nouns:
> *eats,* an *invite,* a *fix,* a *think,* a *combine* (meaning "combination")

Nouns misused as verbs:
> to *suspicion,* to *suicide*

Adjectives misused as adverbs:
> *real* pretty, *sure* pleased, *some* tall

Prepositions misused as conjunctions:
> *like* for *as, except* for *unless*

Avoid: We served eats.
> I suspicioned that the plan would fail.

Use: We served food.
I suspected that the plan would fail.

45b. Avoid improprieties in meaning.

Most improprieties in meaning are caused by the misuse of words similar in form. For example, words in the following groups are frequently misused:

accept, except	formally, formerly
affect, effect	healthful, healthy
all ready, already	ingenious, ingenuous
all together, altogether	irritate, aggravate
allusion, illusion	later, latter
avenge, revenge	liable, likely
complement, compliment	noted, notorious
council, counsel	party, person
disinterested, uninterested	principal, principle
elude, allude	respectfully, respectively
expect, suspect	stationary, stationery
farther, further	than, then

EXERCISE 30

1. Use correctly in sentences each of the groups of words listed in Section 45b.

2. Use each of the following words correctly in a sentence: *continual, creditable, practicable, apt, continuous, vocation, consul, can, may, conscious, conscience.*

46. SLANG

Slang is a particular kind of vulgarism. Formerly the term was applied to the cant of gypsies, beggars, and thieves, or to the jargon of any particular class of society. Now slang is defined as language which consists of widely current terms having a forced or fantastic meaning, or displaying eccentricity. It is sometimes very colorful and forceful, but it is often used with such crudeness that it may offend people who are careful of their choice of words and cause the person who uses it to be considered vulgar.

Note these typical slang expressions:

> grub, to get away with it, bang-up, to get pinched, a bum
> steer, to put it across, so what, spuds, take the count,
> going some, put on the dog, have a heart, a lemon,
> attaboy, cut no ice, fall for it, hard-boiled, get the goods
> on him, talk through your hat, goofy, wacky, off his nut,
> squawk, dead pan, crab, let it ride, you said it, to get hep,
> a rat race, on the beam, sourpuss, cockeyed, good egg,
> mike, croak (meaning "to die" or "to kill"), that's for
> the birds, heap (car), egghead, square, drag

47. TRITENESS

How many times have you heard the following speech?

> On behalf of the team, I should like to present to Mr.
> Anderson this small token of our appreciation.

This is a trite speech. The first time that it was used, it
was acceptable; but the person who uses it now shows
clearly that he is lazy or unwilling to think for himself.

Trite expressions are expressions that have been used too
often. Avoid them. Make your language fresh and interesting. Here are some expressions to avoid. You will probably
notice many other trite expressions in your reading, in public
speeches, or in conversations.

abreast of the times
add insult to injury
all the luck in the world
all work and no play
along these lines
are in receipt of
as big as a house
as luck would have it
at a loss for words
at an early date
at your earliest convenience
be that as it may
be there with bells on

better half
bigger and better
bitter end
bolt out of the blue
brown as a berry (or a nut)
budding genius
busy as a bee
by and large
by leaps and bounds
captain of industry
center of attraction
checkered career
clinging vine

cold as ice
conspicuous by his absence
deadly earnest
deem it an honor and a privilege
deepest gratitude
depths of despair
do justice to a dinner
doomed to disappointment
each and every
esteem it a great honor
exception proves the rule
fair sex
festive occasion
few and far between
filthy lucre
first and foremost
fools rush in
goes without saying
good time was had by all
great open spaces
green with envy
heartfelt thanks
hit an all-time low
hungry as a bear
ignorance is bliss
in this day and age

irony of fate
last but not least
level best
makes the world a better place to live in
meets the eye
method in his madness
milestone on the road of life
needs no introduction
nipped in the bud
none the worse for wear
out of a clear sky
proud possessor
psychological moment
red as a rose
ripe old age
shot heard around the world
take this opportunity
the good life
the weaker sex
the worse for wear
time marches on
time of my life
tired but happy
to make a long story short
too full for utterance
words fail to express

Be careful to avoid trite ideas as well as trite expressions:

> The gift was exactly what I wanted.
> I'll think of you every time I wear it.
> Do not hesitate to call on me.
> All good things must come to an end.

EXERCISE 31

Criticize the English in the following sentences. Which expressions would be acceptable in casual English? Which are trite?

1. Everybody had a ball at the picnic last night. How come you didn't show up?
2. I'd never have won if each and every one of you hadn't helped me.
3. I suspicioned that you weren't coming when I saw Joan with another guy.
4. Now, last but not least, we're happy to present the Nairobi Trio.
5. Well, keep in touch.

EXERCISE 32

Follow the directions in Exercise 31.

1. When I reach a ripe old age, I want to get away from the city and go to the wide open spaces.
2. If this inflation keeps on, you will be down and out when you reach that ripe old age.
3. It's certainly true that prices are going up by leaps and bounds. I've worked like a dog and have nothing to show for it.
4. By and large, I think it's wacky to worry in this day and age.
5. Maybe you're right, but trouble often comes out of a clear sky; and I think we should be prepared for a rainy day.

EXERCISE 33

Criticize the following speech. Then write an introduction of a speaker. Try to make it free of trite ideas as well as trite expressions. Avoid tracing the speaker's background from high school to the present. Select only the details that will show why his speech should be interesting or valuable to the audience that he is about to address.

This morning we seniors are in school for the last time. Soon we shall be sailing the ship of life into the future. I deem it an honor and a privilege to present to you as our speaker, one who needs no introduction. It is fitting that Dr. Edward Benson should speak to us on this occasion. Before I present him to you, I should like to offer him our deepest gratitude for taking time out of a busy day to join us.

48. JARGON

Some inexperienced writers think that they will improve their writing by using long words, elaborate expressions, or technical words understood only by the member of a special trade or profession. Actually, the best writing is simple, direct, clear. Instead of "No," the writer of jargon says, "The answer is in the negative."

Government pamphlets and letters and reports of economists and engineers could often be improved by the omission of jargon. Recently an economist who wished to tell Congress that part of the farm problem is that there are too many farmers said:

"The hard core of the United States farm problem is the surplus of human effort committed to farming."

JARGON	CLEAR WRITING
Pursue his tasks with great diligence	Work hard
Unfavorable conditions	Bad weather
Enter into the state of matrimony	Get married

Business people are often users of jargon. They should avoid expressions such as *along the line of, with regard to, attached hereto, in connection with, enclosed herewith please find.* (See Section 95.)

Sir Arthur Quiller-Couch, in his book *On the Art of Writing,* says the jargoneer makes use of "vague, woolly, abstract nouns rather than concrete ones." Quiller-Couch probably had in mind words like *case, instance, character, nature, condition, persuasion, degree, quality, personality, asset, thing, state,* and *factor.*

Another trick of jargon which Quiller-Couch discusses is "elegant variation," an unwillingness to repeat a word once it has been used. Sports writers often practice elegant variation. To avoid repeating the word *football,* some writers resort to *pigskin* or *oval.* Similarly, such writers strain to invent descriptive nicknames in order to avoid repeating the name of the person they are writing about. Joe Louis, the former heavyweight champion, was known as "The Brown Bomber" and "The Detroit Menace." At best elegant variation sounds affected; at worst it sounds absurd. It is preferable to repeat a word or a name as often as necessary. Often, of course, a personal pronoun can be used.

EXERCISE 34

On your paper, rewrite the following sentences, improving the wording. Substitute other words for jargon.

1. The greatest factor in his success was that he had reached man's estate in a healthy physical condition.
2. In the case of those not present, the nature of their offense will be judged as of a different character.
3. Ruth was one of baseball's greatest assets. He possessed ability to an unusual degree, and thousands of human beings in the environs of New York City thought that no one could ever rival the great Bambino. But by the very nature of things, the Bronx Behemoth entered a declining state over a long period of years. Later the fickle fans were of the persuasion that, with regard to baseball ability, Joe DiMaggio, the former San Francisco star, was of the same stature as the former home-run king.
4. In this instance, his answer in the affirmative was a distinct asset to our business.
5. He was a serious type of student who wished to major in the field of chemistry.
6. Illumination is required to be extinguished before this building is closed for the night.

EXERCISE 35

On your paper, rewrite this business letter in simple, straightforward English. (See Section 95.)

Dear Mrs. Jenkins:

In reply to your letter of January 10 with regard to merchandise along the line of slip covers, we are enclosing herewith samples of three types of materials. We should like to advise that our representative will be in your district on Monday, and we are of the opinion that he will be able to assist you re the slip covers as per your request.

Thanking you for your inquiry, we beg to remain

Very truly yours,

J. A. Henderson

49. CONCRETE AND SPECIFIC WORDS

Words have an exact meaning (denotation) and a suggested or implied meaning (connotation). The denotation of the word *father* is *male parent;* the connotation may be *the kind playmate of my boyhood, the person who always gave me good advice, the stingy fellow who never allowed me enough spending money,* or many other meanings, depending upon the experience of the individual who reads or hears the word. In addition to their special connotations for different people, words also have connotations that are understood by nearly everybody. For example, both *cabin* and *hovel* are applied to a small, rudely built house; but *cabin* may suggest vacations at the seashore or in the mountains, whereas *hovel* always implies poverty and dilapidation.

Some words are richer in connotative values than others; *fragrance* and *aroma,* for instance, suggest more specific ideas than *smell* or *odor.* If you are writing vigorous prose that seeks some response in imagination, words rich in connotation will help. If, however, you are writing a report of a committee activity or a laboratory experiment, the tone should be more objective. You are then concerned with clarity, rather than effect.

Concrete words, however, are important in any kind of writing.

49a. Use specific rather than general words.

Walk is a general word. It gives no definite picture. There are many ways of saying *walk:*

> strut, hobble, stumble, stagger, glide, creep, scurry, stroll, march

These are specific words. Because they show a special way of walking, these words are more descriptive than the general word *walk*.

NOTE: Do not use a specific word like *stumble* for *walk* unless that is precisely what you mean. *Walk* is the word to use if you do not wish to call attention to the *way* a person is walking.

EXERCISE 36

Identify the specific words in the following list.

house	complain	boat	dawdle
laugh	nag (verb)	guffaw	slouch (verb)
freighter	delay	gulp (verb)	drink (verb)

EXERCISE 37

For each of the words in the following list, write three specific words.

Example: opening—window, crevice, peephole

shoes	said	go	food
car	went	old	beverage

EXERCISE 38

On one of the following topics, write a paragraph in which you use specific words:

The Final Touchdown	A Blind Date
A House on the Shore	An Old-fashioned Garden
Enter the Ghost	My First Date
The Beach Party	

49b. Use words that express your meaning exactly.

Distinguish between words whose meanings are similar or related and make sure you are using the one that says exactly what you mean. Your dictionary can often help you make these distinctions. If the word you have in mind is not exactly the word you need, your dictionary may offer a list of synonyms with an explanation of the shade of meaning expressed by each one; or it may refer you to another word under which such a list is given. In this way you can learn, for example, that an automobile mechanic uses *tools,* a farmer uses *implements,* and a surgeon uses *instruments.*

EXERCISE 39

What is the difference in meaning of the words in each of the following groups?

> argue, debate, discuss
> dislike, disgust, distaste
> feature, characteristic, peculiarity
> color, hue, tinge, shade

50. "FINE" WRITING

"Fine" writing is writing that is affected.

50a. Avoid "fine" writing.

The use of direct, simple words to gain effectiveness in writing is mentioned in Section 48. Avoid artificiality, pretentiousness, and affectation.

50b. Use short words.

Short words are usually clearer than long ones. There is a story of a plumber who once wrote to an agency of the United States government that he had found hydrochloric acid good for cleaning out pipes. A bureaucrat replied: "The efficiency of hydrochloric acid is indisputable, but the corrosive residue is incompatible with metallic permanence."

The plumber responded that he was delighted to know that the agency agreed with him. After a further exchange of letters, the government official finally wrote what he should have written the first time: "Don't use hydrochloric acid. It eats the inside out of pipes."

Too many long words will make a piece of writing seem heavy or pedantic. A series of long words will also tend to interrupt the smooth, even flow of a sentence. Compare the effect of the following sentences:

Long words: After liquidating his indebtedness, he was still in possession of sufficient funds to establish a small commercial enterprise.

Short words: After paying his debts, he still had enough money to set up a small business.

This does not mean that long words should never be used. A writer with a mature style will, of course, use many long words; but he will generally use them only to express particular meanings for which shorter words may not exist. There are no short words, for example, to express the exact meanings of *jurisdiction, epilogue,* or *appendicitis.* But compare the following: *repast* and *meal; retire* and *go to bed; epistle* and *letter; ratiocinate* and *think; pulchritude* and *beauty; comestibles* and *food; obsequies* and *funeral.* In these expressions, the simple words express quite clearly what the writer wishes to say and are in better taste.

50c. Use modifiers intelligently.

Too many adjectives or adverbs make a style seem overdone. Notice the overuse of modifiers in the following excerpt from the description of a wedding:

As she swept gracefully down the flower-bordered aisle

of the old, freshly painted church, the bride smiled graciously and kindly into the eyes of her handsome, stalwart husband.

50d. Be careful in using foreign expressions.

A bit of Latin or French sometimes seems impressive, and the inexperienced writer may be tempted to sprinkle his writing with foreign phrases. Actually they are ostentatious and should be avoided except in the very few instances when there is no English equivalent. Businessmen sometimes talk about *per diem* pay when they mean *a day's pay*, or they ship things *via* when they mean *by*. Other people talk of a *faux pas* when they mean a *mistake*.

EXERCISE 40

Rewrite this paragraph in simple language:

Yesterday at high noon Miss Adrienne Sinclair, the lovely youngest daughter of Mr. Gustav Ober Sinclair, was given in marriage to her handsome college classmate, Mr. Spencer Horston-Palmer. The exquisite, radiant bride was begowned in shimmering white satin adorned with old family lace of the utmost delicacy. Her hands, enveloped in spotless white kid, bore a white prayer book, symbol of purity, from which showered fragile lilies of the valley. As the lovely bride moved toward the sanctum sanctorum, she was followed closely by three stunning attendants wearing pale orchid organdy. The tender strains of the wedding march were presented by the talented organist, Eric Feld.

EXERCISE 41

The following letter of eighty-three words can be written in clear, simple language in thirty words. See how close to that number you can come in your revision.

Dear Sir:

We are in receipt of your favor of the tenth instant in re order for five television sets and wish to advise that according to our records your order was shipped on Oct. 19 via Railway Express. In as much as the order was carefully checked on this end, we would ask you to wait for three days. If the material has not been received in that time, we would ask that you use the card attached hereto and give us due notice.

51. WORDINESS

Wordiness, or redundancy, is the use of more words than are needed.

To be effective, writing should be as economical as possible. This does not mean that it must be sketchy or that essential words can be omitted.

Wrong: Shipped order today.
Right: We shipped your order today.

51a. Do not use more words than are necessary.

> I regret that you were not supplied with the necessary information requested by you in order to assure you of the safest means of traveling to reach Cimarron. (Verbose; 28 words)
> I regret that you did not receive information concerning the safest means of reaching Cimarron. (Economical; 15 words)

Be careful not to say the same thing twice.

Redundant: He operates a large 800-acre farm.
Better: He operates an 800-acre farm.
Redundant: The bonds were burned and reduced to ashes.
Better: The bonds were burned.
The bonds were reduced to ashes.

WORDY	BETTER
repeat again	repeat
important essentials	essentials
many in number	many
blue in color	blue
combined together	combined

round in form	round
in my opinion, I think	I think
each and every one	each one
rest up	rest
recur again	recur
in any way, shape, or form	in any way
in this day and age	these days
join together	join
connect up with	connect with
refer back	refer
return back	return

51b. Do not use unnecessary prepositions; for example, do not say _meet up with_ for _meet_, or _fall off of_ for _fall off._

EXERCISE 42

On your paper, rewrite the following sentences, omitting unnecessary words:

1. Maybe I misinterpreted the story wrong.
2. Gabriel was an adjacent neighbor to the Lukes.
3. The Esmonds wished to restore James II back to the throne.
4. I do not wish one which is square in shape; I want one oval in form.
5. The end of the corridor terminates at a small door, green in color.
6. In this day and age any girl with the necessary financial resources can keep her hair neat and attractive in appearance.
7. After his death he received the award posthumously.
8. Although we were many in number, there were a few of us who felt close; and so we decided to correspond with each other in future years to come.
9. It is undeniably true that once you start to study in earnest, your troubles will be lessened and mitigated.
10. The desire to express oneself is a universal craving which is common to all people.
11. The company had a complete monopoly in that territory,

but there were unfavorable climatic conditions which prevented the factory from resuming production again.

12. In the case of those culprits, there are not many people who would judge them solely and completely responsible for their cruel, thoughtless, and heinous misdeeds.

13. In my opinion, I think that the check should be returned to the bank.

14. Each and every one of you must learn to assume responsibility in this day and age.

15. In a department store in our town on Tenth and L Streets, there are always a number of new novelties.

16. I refuse to be involved in his plans in any way, shape, or form.

17. In compliance with your request, we are sending you under separate cover all the pamphlets that we have in connection with agriculture.

18. We wish to state that because we are unable to fill your order which you sent, your check in the amount of $50 is hereby returned.

EXERCISE 43

On your paper, rewrite these sentences in clear, concise English.

1. Through the medium of advertising, we are made to desire more than we can afford.

2. I know it will be a sad misfortune for you if you don't make the Honor Roll.

3. The pioneers struggled through the winter with not even the necessities which they needed.

4. Our modern trains of today have made great improvements for the comfort of the passengers.

5. We should like to take this opportunity to congratulate you on the splendid job.

6. My check in the amount of $75 was sent you in January for the purpose of completing payments on my television set.

7. Each and every one of you is invited to come to the football game which will begin at 1:30 P.M. on Saturday afternoon.

8. Your charga-plate is enclosed; you will find it a great convenience if you will use it when shopping.

9. For those believing ignorance to be an inborn trait, an investigation of facts proves them wrong.

10. During the course of events which encircle my everyday activities, I am able to make contributions to the activities of the community.

11. The program has the aid of a distinguished and reputable physician to impart an explanation of the causes and prevention of disease.

12. The proceeds over and above the expenses of the show and the cost of costumes and scenery will go to the treasury of the Civic Opera Company.

13. I am happy to comply with your request for a petroleum display relative to the oil industry for use in your classroom.

14. We are glad to report that your order has been forwarded to our retail dealer whose shop is near you in Kingsville.

15. We must report at this time that our variety of Golden Rule apple has been discontinued because of an uncontrollable disease that attacks this variety of apple tree.

16. Dear Mr. Norris:

We are sorry to inform you that we are unable to comply with your order for ten hats with 3-inch brims. It is our utmost pleasure to tell you that this model has been replaced by the York hat, which is the product of extensive research and which we are sure will give our customers every satisfaction.

EXERCISE 44

The following paragraphs are wordy. Rewrite them, omitting unnecessary words. Some sentences may require complete rewriting.

I

The granting of home rule to municipalities in our state will be a forward step in the art and science of government. Municipalities have grown rapidly in the last decade in terms of population and industries. Therefore the act of being granted the privilege of making their own charters establishing laws applicable to their needs is conducive to better government. There is no rhyme nor reason to a system that allows a state legislature to spend its time making small decisions for the government and the establishment of laws for each and every town in the state when these towns could handle their own affairs adequately.

II

Tension has become as much a part of the American way of life as have the Four Freedoms. Today we feel it is necessary and imperative to keep up with the Joneses, and as a result we set high goals which are many times impossible to attain and to hold. Not being able to attain these goals, we are beset by feelings of anxiety and failure. Through the medium of advertising and the systems of installment buying we are led to desire more goods and satisfactions for a higher standard of living. This standard of living is often many times more than we can reasonably expect to achieve. As a result we develop discontent and nervousness.

52. EUPHONY

Euphony is pleasant sound. Good writers choose their words carefully and arrange them so that the sound of the sentence is euphonious.

52a. Avoid repetition of the same sound.

> I hope that you will like the *prize* and that it is the right *size*.
> When Mr. Edwards *recovered,* he *discovered* that his money had been stolen.

NOTE: Be particularly careful of words ending in *tion* or *sion.* Several of them used together make a sentence sound heavy.

> After Jack's *explanation,* the principal gave the problem careful *consideration.*

52b. Avoid different forms of the same word.

Weak: The book is covered with a green cover.
Better: The book has a green cover.
Weak: He thought everyone would think his act to be generous.
Better: He thought everyone would consider his act generous.

EXERCISE 45

On your paper, rewrite the following sentences, avoiding faulty repetition:

1. The height of the desk is three feet high.
2. The room has not as much room as my former room had.
3. She had placed the box in another place.
4. Slowly the Indian edged toward the edge of the river.
5. I do mind having you read my mind.
6. Tommy received a birthday present from everyone present.
7. The man loafing in front of the bakery explained that he had come to buy a loaf of bread.
8. He was a likable kind of man, always kind to children and really interested in his fellow man.
9. At the track meet I met my old friend Marshall.
10. If a business has good public relations, people not only want to do business with it but will enjoy doing business with it and will not only continue to do business with it but will recommend it to their friends.

52c. Avoid alliteration and rhyme.

Alliteration is the use of several words beginning with the same sound. It is often used in advertising because it attracts attention, but it should usually be avoided in good prose.

He *f*ought *f*or *f*oreign nations in *f*our wars.

EXERCISE 46

Rewrite these sentences to make them sound better.

1. The balmy winds blew warmly over the bay.
2. The sun rode high in a bright blue sky.

53a-c

3. In high school I developed a yearning to learn.
4. The intelligence service built morale by sending reports concerning support by the home front.
5. Why should I care if you cut your hair?
6. In a blind fury he flew into the fray.
7. Scenes such as these are best seen at sunset.
8. I'm sorry that I was late for the date, but fate just seemed to be against me.
9. When the meetings were resumed, we consumed quantities of refreshments.
10. Misconceptions based on unscientific tradition have resulted in the dissemination of misinformation about nutrition.

53. FIGURATIVE LANGUAGE

Figures of speech help to make writing vivid, but they are not effective if they are forced and strained or if they are mixed. There are many figures of speech, but those discussed in Section 53a–f are among the most important.

53a. A simile is the comparison of two images which are essentially different, but which are alike in at least one respect. The words *as*, *as if*, *like* are used to point to the resemblance.

> He eats like a horse.
> Smoke hung over the city like a great umbrella.

53b. A metaphor is a suggested comparison.

> Money is the root of all evil.
> My cousin Madeline is a cat.
> All the world's a stage.
> The crime investigation committee was told to stop looking for mice and find the breeding place.

53c. Personification gives human qualities to objects that are not living.

> The wind howled.
> A smiling moon looked down on the lovers.

291

53d. Hyperbole is exaggeration.

> I was insane from grief.
> I've told you a thousand times what to do.

Hyperbole should be used sparingly and very cautiously.

53e. Metonymy is the use of one word for another that it suggests.

> The kettle boils. (Water in the kettle boils.)
> She sets a good table. (Good food)

The use of figures of speech, when overdone, makes a style florid. It is important that the figures be fresh and original. Many figures that were once effective have become trite. Avoid these.

53f. Avoid mixed figures.

Students who are striving for effect sometimes mix their similes or metaphors; that is, they start a sentence by making a comparison and finish it with another comparison entirely different from the first.

> The road to success is straight, narrow, and strewn with rocks, but the ambitious man must swim through it. (The way to success is a road; then it is a river.)
> By milking the cow dry, we are going to kill the goose that lays the golden eggs. (Mixing the figures makes the sentence absurd.)

54. GLOSSARY OF WORDS AND EXPRESSIONS OFTEN MISUSED

A, AN. *An* should be used before an initial vowel sound; *a,* before a word beginning with a consonant sound:

> *an adult, a problem*

ABOUT, AROUND. *About* means "approximately"; *around* means "along the circumference of" or "on all sides of."

292

> I live *about* a mile from school.
> I walked *around* the block.

ACCEPT, EXCEPT. *Accept* means "to receive"; *except* (when used as a verb) means "to exclude."

> He *accepted* the nomination.
> The teacher *excepted* from the assignment those students preparing reports.

AD. Colloquial abbreviation for advertisement. In formal writing, avoid such colloquialisms as *ad, exam, phone,* and *prof.*

ADAPT, ADOPT. *Adapt* means "to adjust to new conditions"; *adopt* means "to take as your own."

> The old building could not be *adapted* to today's needs.
> The Romans *adopted* many customs and ideas from the nations they had conquered.

ADVISE. "To give advice." Use sparingly for *inform* or *tell.* (Note that *advise* is used as a verb, and *advice* is used as a noun.)

> *Poor:* We beg to *advise* that our representative will be in Kansas City next week.
> *Better:* We are happy to *tell* you that our representative will be in Kansas City next week.

AFFECT, EFFECT. *Affect* is always a verb; it means either (a) "to influence or produce a change in" or (b) "to put on or assume." *Effect* can be a noun or a verb. As a noun it means "a result or outcome"; as a verb it means "to bring about or to accomplish."

> The sight of so much suffering *affected* him deeply.
> He *affects* a British accent.
> No one could foresee the *effects* of this decision.
> The doctor *effected* a miraculous cure.

ALL READY, ALREADY. *All ready* (two words) means "everything (or everyone) ready" or "completely ready"; *already* means "previously."

> We have looked in that box *already*.
> I was *all ready* to start for school.
> After some delay, the horses were *all ready* to run.

ALL RIGHT, ALRIGHT. *All right* is overworked to mean "very well." *Alright* is not an acceptable word.

ALL TOGETHER, ALTOGETHER. *All together* means "when all are counted" or "everybody (or everything) in one place (or at one time)"; *altogether* means "wholly."

> There were eight of us *all together*.
> That is an *altogether* different problem.

AMONG, BETWEEN. *Among* shows the relation of more than two objects; *between* refers to only two.

> He distributed the prizes *among* the five winners.
> He divided the reward *between* Jack and Joe.
> That is the road *between* Fort Worth and Dallas.

AMOUNT, NUMBER. *Amount* is used with quantities that cannot be counted or in cases where only the size of a thing matters; *number* is used with quantities that can be counted.

> A surprising *amount* of snow fell this spring.
> A record *number* of people attended the first home game.

AND ETC. Redundant. *Etc.* is the abbreviation for *et cetera*, meaning "and so forth." (In formal writing, such abbreviations should usually be avoided.)

ANY PLACE, EVERY PLACE, NO PLACE, SOME PLACE. Faulty. Use instead *anywhere, everywhere, nowhere, somewhere.* Never use *anywheres* or *somewheres.*

BESIDE, BESIDES. *Beside* is a preposition meaning "by the side of"; *besides* is both a preposition and an adverb meaning "moreover," "except," "in addition."

Correct: Jane sits *beside* me.

   Who is going *besides* Harold? (Preposition)

   I don't know the boy; *besides,* I don't want to know
   him. (Adverb)

BRING, TAKE. *Bring* means "to come with something (toward
the speaker or listener)"; *take* means "to carry something
away (from the speaker)."

   Bring me the morning paper.

   Take this note to your homeroom teacher.

BURSTED, BUST, BUSTED. Vulgarisms for *burst.* The principal
parts of *burst* are *burst, burst, burst.* Also used incorrectly
for *break, broke, broken.*

CAN, MAY, MIGHT. *Can* suggests ability, physical or mental.
May implies permission or sanction.

Correct: He *can* make good grades if he tries.

   The teacher says you *may* leave.

The distinction between *can* and *may* is shown in this
sentence:

   I doubt that you *can,* but you *may* try.

May also expresses possibility and wish.

   It *may* rain today. (Possibility)

   May you have a good trip! (Wish)

Might is used after a verb in the past tense; *may,* after
a verb in the present tense.

   He *said* that you *might* go.

   He *says* that you *may* go.

CANNOT HELP BUT. A double negative (*cannot help* and
cannot but).

Correct: I *cannot help* believing the story.

   I *cannot but* believe the story.

CAN'T HARDLY, CAN'T SCARCELY. A double negative.

Avoid: I *can't hardly* hear you.
Correct: I *can hardly* hear you.

CONSUL, COUNSEL, COUNCIL. A *consul* is an official who represents his government in a foreign country. *Counsel* means "advice" or "adviser" as a noun, or "to advise" as a verb. *Council* means "a body of people serving in a legal, administrative, or advisory capacity."

> The class secretary wrote to the Italian *consul* for information about Italy.
> His *counsel* is worthless because he doesn't understand the situation. (Advice)
> The state appointed the defendant's *counsel*. (Adviser)
> The lawyer *counseled* against answering questions. (Advised)
> The student *council* is debating the advantages and disadvantages of the honor system.

CONTACT, CONTACTED. Overworked business terms.

Avoid: We can *contact* Mr. Myers tomorrow.
Better: We can $\left\{ \begin{array}{l} \textit{get in touch with} \\ \textit{reach} \end{array} \right\}$ Mr. Myers tomorrow.

CONTINUAL, CONTINUOUS. *Continual* means "repeated often"; *continuous* means "without a stop."

> These *continual* interruptions prevent me from doing my homework.
> The only sound you can hear at night is the *continuous* pounding of the surf.

CREDIBLE, CREDITABLE, CREDULOUS. *Credible* means "believable"; *creditable* means "praiseworthy"; *credulous* means "gullible."

Correct: The story is not *credible*.
          You have made a *creditable* effort.
          Only a very *credulous* person would believe that story.

DEVICE, DEVISE. *Device* is a noun meaning "a machine, a piece of apparatus" or "a trick, scheme, or plan." *Devise* is a verb meaning "to think out, plan, or invent."

> This new *device* will cut your heating bills.
> It may take years to *devise* a better system.

DISCOVER, INVENT. *Discover* means "to find something that was there before you came along." *Invent* means "to create something new."

> Columbus *discovered* America.
> Madame Curie *discovered* radium.
> Alexander Graham Bell *invented* the telephone.

FAMOUS, NOTORIOUS. *Famous* means "well known for some admirable achievement." *Notorious* means "well known" also, but generally in an unfavorable way.

> Admiral Byrd was a *famous* explorer.
> The *notorious* criminal was captured just as he was leaving the country.

FEMALE. Do not use as a synonym for *woman* or *girl*.

Crude: What kind of *female* is she?
Polite: What kind of *girl* is she?

FEWER, LESS. *Fewer* is used with things that can be counted; it is used with plural nouns. *Less* is used to indicate amount or degree; it is used with singular nouns.

> *Fewer* people attended today's game than yesterday's game.
> I have *less* money this year than last year.

FOLKS. Colloquial for *relatives* or *people*.

FORMER, LATTER. *Former* means "the first of the two mentioned." *Latter* means "the second of the two mentioned."

> Grant and Hayes were both Republican Presidents. The *former* served two terms; the *latter* served one.

GOOD, WELL. *Good* is usually an adjective; it modifies a noun.

> This pie is *good*.

Well may be an adjective or an adverb. When it is used as an adjective, it always refers to health.

> I am feeling *well*. (Adjective)
> This mower doesn't work as *well* as it used to. (Adverb)
> I did the assignment as *well* as I could.

GRADUATE HIGH SCHOOL. Incorrect form. Say "graduate *from* high school."

HEALTHFUL, HEALTHY. *Healthful* means "promoting good health." *Healthy* means "being in good health" or "showing good health."

> The climate in the mountains is *healthful*.
> The nurse said I was perfectly *healthy*.
> He certainly has a *healthy* appetite.

HUMAN, HUMANE. *Human* means "characteristic of man"; *humane* means "kind" or "compassionate."

> To err is *human*.
> They were too *humane* to enjoy the bullfight.

IF, WHETHER. Use *if* in conditional sentences; use *whether* in stating alternatives (expressed or implied).

Correct: *If* he is in, I mean to call on him.
> I don't know *whether* he is ten years old or twelve.

IMPLY, INFER. *To infer* is to draw a conclusion from statements, circumstances, or evidence. *To imply* is to suggest a meaning not explicitly stated.

Correct: The detective *inferred* from the position of the fingerprints that the man who had fired the shot was left-handed.
> What you have just said *implies* that you doubt my story.

IN, INTO. Verbs indicating movement into a place are generally followed by *into*.

> When he walked *into* the room, he found us ready.

In is used to indicate motion within a place.

> She paced up and down *in* the classroom.

INGENIOUS, INGENUOUS. *Ingenious* means "talented, inventive, resourceful." *Ingenuous* means "naive."

> George is *ingenious;* I'm sure he'll find a solution.
> No one expects diplomats to be *ingenuous.*

INSIDE OF, OFF OF, OUTSIDE OF. *Of* is superfluous. *Inside, off, outside* can be used by themselves as prepositions.

> It's warm *inside* the house.
> John has fallen *off* the horse again.
> I'm forbidden to go *outside* the house.

However, when *inside* or *outside* is used as a noun, it is often followed by a prepositional phrase beginning with *of*.

> I painted only the *outside of* the house.
> I spent the morning cleaning the *inside of* the car.

IRREGARDLESS. Incorrect form. Use *regardless.*

LET, LEAVE. *Leave* means "to go away." *Let* means "to permit." "Let me alone" means "Stop annoying me." "Leave me alone" means "I wish to be here by myself."

LIABLE, LIKELY, APT. *Liable* implies exposure to something unpleasant or disadvantageous; *likely* means "expected or probable"; *apt* means "inclined, disposed," "fit, suitable," or "quick to learn."

> The motorist responsible is *liable* for damages.
> It is *likely* to rain.
> She made an *apt* remark.
> He is an *apt* pupil.

299

Apt and *likely* are often used interchangeably; however, careful writers distinguish between their meanings.

MAYBE, MAY BE. *Maybe* is an adverb meaning "perhaps" or "possibly." *May be* is a verb form.

> *Maybe* I won't go after all.
> George *may be* our next class president.

MOST, ALMOST. *Almost* is an adverb meaning "nearly." *Most* is used as a noun meaning "the greatest quantity or number" or as an adjective meaning "greatest in quantity or number" or "nearly all"; it is used as an adverb only to form the superlative degree of an adjective or adverb. (See Section 18e.)

> *Most* of the tickets have been sold.
> We have sold *almost* all of the tickets.
> I believe that *most* people are honest.
> This is the *most* ridiculous story I have ever heard.

NAUSEOUS, NAUSEATED. *Nauseous* means "disgusting, causing nausea"; *nauseated* means "sick at the stomach."

Wrong: I have felt *nauseous* all morning.
Right: I have felt *nauseated* all morning.
Right: The chemical gave off a *nauseous* odor.

NOWHERE NEAR. Colloquial. Use *not nearly.*

Correct: I have *not nearly* finished the job.

O.K. Greatly overused. Use a more exact expression.

PARTY, PERSON, INDIVIDUAL. *Party* implies a group and, except in legal and telephonic language, should not be used to refer to one person. *Individual* refers to a particular or single person. It is not a synonym for *person*; it should be used only when you want to emphasize the oneness of the person as distinct from a group.

> A *party* of young people were on their way to the ski lodge.

> The bridge was so weakened that it could bear the weight of only one *person* at a time.
> The class in sociology is studying the relations of the *individual* with the group.

PERSECUTE, PROSECUTE. *Persecute* means "to annoy, to cause to suffer, to hunt down." *Prosecute* means "to carry out a legal action against."

> Nero *persecuted* the Christians.
> The company threatened to *prosecute* all trespassers.

PLENTY. A noun. As an adverb or adjective, *plenty* should be avoided in formal speech or writing.

Incorrect: He was *plenty* angry.
Correct: The dairy has *plenty* of milk.

PRECEDE, PROCEED. *Precede* means "to go before"; *proceed* means "to go or continue."

> A *precedes* b in the alphabet.
> When the latecomers were seated, the speaker *proceeded* with his lecture.

PRINCIPAL, PRINCIPLE. *Principal* used as a noun is a "sum of money" or "chief executive of a school" and as an adjective means "chief" or "main." *Principle* is used as a noun meaning "a governing rule or truth."

PROPOSITION. Business jargon for "proposal."

RESPECTFULLY, RESPECTIVELY. *Respectfully* means "in a respectful manner"; *respectively* means "each in the order given."

> The letter was signed "*Respectfully* yours."
> In a business letter the salutation and the complimentary close are followed by a colon and a comma, *respectively.*

SAID, SAME, SUCH. *Same* and *such* are adjectives. *Said* is a verb.

Objectionable: Although the *said* plan was feasible, I decided not to adopt *same.*

Use *it, that,* or *this* instead of *said, same,* or *such.*

SUSPICION. *Suspicion* is a noun. Do not use it when you mean *suspect,* a verb.

Incorrect: I *suspicioned* that he was the thief.
  Correct: I *suspected* that he was the thief.
  Correct: I had a strong *suspicion* that he was the thief.

WAIT ON. *Wait on* means "to attend, to serve"; it is a localism when used to mean "wait for."

Incorrect: I *waited on* him for an hour before he came.
  Correct: I *waited* an hour *for* him before he came.

EXERCISE 47

On your paper, rewrite the following sentences, using good diction.

1. I wouldn't except an invite to her party unless she apologized.
2. Some folks still believe that it is not healthy to go without a hat.
3. You're liable to see most anybody you know at those Friday night dances.
4. I couldn't help but feel worried when the principle sent for me.
5. You didn't say you suspicioned him, but your manner inferred that you did.
6. There were five couples beside Frances and me, so that there were twelve of us altogether.
7. I can't hardly believe that Mr. Thompson never graduated high school.
8. Any individual who damages or defaces school property will be persecuted.
9. Please advise me whether you have the machine in stock and how soon you will be able to ship same.

10. These continuous interruptions while I am doing my homework are beginning to effect my grades.
11. I felt so nauseous that I thought I would pass out most any minute.
12. He ran in the house and asked his mother to leave him go swimming, but she said it was nowhere near warm enough.
13. I wish someone would discover a really good device for getting the tops off of glass jars.
14. Henry wasn't feeling very good this morning, but may be he will be alright in time for the rehearsal.
15. I am anxious to know if you are interested in my proposition in connection with marketing your product.

EXERCISE 48

On your paper, rewrite the following sentences, correcting the errors in diction:

1. In spite of the favorable factors in your case, I shall have to answer in the negative.
2. In the sea of ruthless competition, one can climb to success only by seizing the golden flower of opportunity.
3. In connection with the degree of his guilt, I am of the persuasion that we are not certain as to whether we are fully conversant and acquainted with all the facts of the case.
4. The president's attention was arrested by Mr. Blaine's ability to cope with any situation that might arise.
5. Before giving the glass of milk to the little lass, I placed a box of crackers before her.
6. My fellow classmates average in height a height of sixty-eight inches.
7. In these respects, laboratory sciences are of a notoriously trying nature.
8. With bated breath we watched that miserable specimen of humanity go to his doom.
9. As soon as I saw that sleek roadster in the showroom, I felt a weak moment coming on.
10. Those who take rooms in this house will have more than enough room in which to house their appurtenances.

11. The sheer force of his personality beggars description.
12. In connection with her other traits I should mention her pulchritude, which is of a very high order.
13. With regard to gardening facilities, there is an empty, vacant piece of unused land in back of the house.
14. The good benefits one receives from camp are perfectly all right, but excess laziness has a toe hold on the minds of most campers.
15. Ellen is the sort of girl with whom one likes to have a date with.
16. There were many of us who thought that he was an exceptionally unique person.
17. A goodly number of voters, perhaps more sinned against than sinning, wrought havoc by staying away from the polls in droves.
18. Please refer back to the minutes of the last meeting, where you will find a new angle along the lines which we have been corresponding with each other about.

EXERCISE 49

The following sentences contain provincialisms, improprieties, colloquialisms, vulgarisms, slang, and misspelling. On your paper, rewrite the sentences in correct, formal English.

1. We have et every one of the sandwiches.
2. Will you be in the dorm then?
3. The poor student always gets it in the neck.
4. He never let on he knew about it.
5. She was an earthly angle, but one without wings.
6. I could of gone if I had worked on Saturday.
7. They walked up to the alter and got married.
8. What do you reckon he meant by that?
9. Dick had a bad case of the jitters.
10. Please proceed me into the room.
11. She took on when I told her of the accident.
12. I never would have suspicioned it.
13. He had to accompany a dumb bunny to the dance.

14. The latch is broken off the gait.
15. Leave go of me at once.
16. He was peaceful ordinarily, but sometimes his choler rose.
17. Why did you fall for that?
18. Now you will have to work extra hard.

EXERCISE 50

The following sentences contain examples of triteness, "fine" writing, jargon, mixed figures, wordiness, faulty repetition, and lack of euphony. On your paper, rewrite each sentence, keeping as close as possible to the intended meaning.

1. Rod decided to seize the bit in his teeth and come down like a wolf on the fold.
2. At the institution of higher learning which he favored with his presence, he was justly proud of his rugged individualism.
3. After spending much time preparing to leave, and after many fond good-bys, we decided to proceed on our journey.
4. Although he ordinarily liked the succulent bivalve, he picked up one of the delectable morsels in a gingerly fashion and devoured it with a wry smile.
5. Not all widow women regard their lot with apprehension, but those who are left with small children are prone to view their status with alarm.
6. Sitting in his room alone by himself, he repeated her name over again and again.
7. A raging conflagration all too soon destroyed the edifice which with loving hands we had erected.
8. Sweetly scented school sashes worn by the fair sex added to the riot of color on the crowded dance floor.
9. Full steam ahead! In this storm of controversy, you must not let your hand falter on the plow.
10. After serious financial reverses, he attempted to misappropriate funds from the bank.
11. We followed the speaker's line of reasoning to a very great extent.
12. Our gridiron warriors were tendered a banquet at the con-

clusion of their victorious season, and after the sumptuous repast each gladiator spoke a few well-chosen words.

13. The nature of the outside reading in English composition is something of an added attraction.

14. When asked if he wished to be the recipient of our offer of a position, he replied in the affirmative.

15. We beg to state that your valued order will receive prompt attention, along the lines which you suggested.

16. At the groaning table I forgot that I was supposed to have a delicate and birdlike appetite.

17. He was caught in the immutable wheels of fate and never reached the goal of his ambition.

18. I may have gone a little too far, but I was simply impelled to get it off my chest.

19. Among those present were included only a paltry few who voiced the sentiments of the players themselves.

20. All nature seemed engaging, but the sight of the crimson orb setting behind the lofty mountain was a delightful feature which beggars all description.

The Sentence

Do you write *gobbledygook?* This is a type of writing that rambles; it uses ten words where five would do a better job; it is awkward in structure and unpleasant in sound. As a result, the reader must examine it three or four times before he knows what it means. Not long ago the Air Force sent to all its employees a little pamphlet called *Gobbledygook or Plain Talk?* In the pamphlet there are quotations from an article on annual leave and from other military notices—all written in *gobbledygook*. Then the author begs for clear, simple sentences. But the clear sentence is important not only to the military forces. It is vital in business. It is effective in the club and in your social life. The problems of writing good sentences may be considered under three heads: Correctness (Sections 55–58), Clearness (Sections 59–67), and Effectiveness (Sections 68–72).

55. PERIOD FAULT

A sentence is a group of words that expresses a complete thought. Do not write a part of a sentence and put a period at the end. Such punctuation is known as the *period fault*.

Wrong: To a trapper, a fur coat means hours of backbreaking work. Also the joy and thrill known only to the hunter. (The words beginning with *also* do not make a complete thought. They are only part of a sentence.)

Right: To a trapper, a fur coat means hours of backbreaking

307

55 PERIOD FAULT

work; but it means also the joy and thrill known only to the hunter.

Wrong: After a time, I began to find value in the sport. A value appreciated chiefly by the man who follows the trail. (The words beginning with *a value* form an appositive, not a complete thought. They are part of a sentence, not a whole sentence.)

Right: After a time, I began to find value in the sport, a value appreciated chiefly by the man who follows the trail.

Wrong: The hunter sees the beauty of the morning sun. Throwing a path of light across the lake. (The words beginning with *throwing* form a participial phrase, not a complete thought. They are only part of a sentence.)

Right: The hunter sees the beauty of the morning sun throwing a path of light across the lake.

Wrong: The hunter loves life outdoors. Especially in the fall and winter. (The words beginning with *especially* do not form a complete thought. Be careful of expressions beginning with *especially* or *for example*. They should often be joined to the preceding clause.)

Right: The hunter loves life outdoors, especially in the fall and winter.

CAUTION: Don't relax because you are writing a friendly letter. Your correspondent deserves the courtesy of careful work.

Wrong: Was happy to hear of your promotion. (No subject)
Right: I was happy to hear of your promotion.

NOTE: There are two kinds of incomplete sentences which are permissible, elliptical sentences and fragmentary sentences used for stylistic effect.

In elliptical sentences, the complete thought is implied but not stated.

"Did you buy it?"
"Yes."
"For how much?"
"Five dollars."

Skilled writers sometimes obtain special effects by using fragmentary sentences for stylistic effect, but only people skilled in the use of language can use sentence fragments safely. Poor use of sentence fragments gives the effect of illiteracy. High school students, unless they are very talented writers, should avoid the fragment.

EXERCISE 1

On your paper, rewrite the following sentences, correcting the period fault. To correct some of these sentences you will have to guess what the writer had in mind.

1. The room was filled with flowers. Some of which were very expensive.
2. She put on her best clothes and went to the movies. Instead of sitting at home worrying.
3. The airship was put into its hangar. So that curious spectators could not damage it.
4. Have shipped your order and billed you for July 1.
5. First of all, the training which is required.
6. Everything was new and interesting. Mainly the clothes.
7. He told many jokes at the party. Some of which were not at all funny.
8. Swimming and fishing in the ocean in the daytime and dancing on the boardwalk at night.
9. While Julius was in college, he received several academic honors. One of these being a scholarship.
10. Dignitaries of both governments attending in official uniforms and medals.

56. COMMA FAULT

Do not write two sentences with only a comma between them. Such punctuation is known as the *comma fault*. Sentences that are separated only by commas are called *run-on sentences*.

Wrong: I hope that you can get the house that you spoke about, it sounds great.

Wrong: I have some good news for you about the bowling team, we have won three straight matches.

Each of these groups of words is composed of two complete thoughts with only a comma between them. A comma is not a strong enough mark to use between two complete thoughts. Use a period instead.

Right: I hope that you can get the house that you spoke about. It sounds great.

Right: I have some good news for you about the bowling team. We have won three straight matches.

If the ideas are closely related, these run-on sentences may be combined in one sentence. Here are three ways of making one sentence out of them:

1. Use a semicolon.

> I hope that you can get the house that you spoke about; it sounds great.

2. Use a coordinating conjunction (*and, but, for, or*) **and a comma.**

> I hope that you can get the house that you spoke about, for it sounds great.

3. Subordinate one idea.

> Because the house that you spoke about sounds great, I hope that you can get it.

The method that you choose depends upon the emphasis that you wish to make. If both of the ideas are equally emphatic, you may use a period, semicolon, or coordinating conjunction. The two ideas will then stand out with equal strength. The use of a subordinating conjunction makes one idea dependent upon the other. In order to make your style interesting and vivid, you must give some attention to the impression that you wish to make and the type of sentence that will fit that impression.

NOTE: Be particularly careful if the two clauses are joined by a conjunctive adverb (*however, moreover, nevertheless, therefore, thus, then, so, yet, otherwise*). If these words join two independent ideas, a semicolon must precede the conjunctive adverb. (See Section 24b.)

Wrong: You did not complete your work, consequently you will receive no credit.

Right: You did not complete your work; consequently you will receive no credit.

EXERCISE 2

On your paper, rewrite these run-on sentences from student papers. Choose for each sentence the form that in your opinion suits it best.

1. Thank you very much, it was sweet of you to invite me to your party.
2. This is my own fault, if I had done my work in the winter, I should not have to go to summer school.
3. Some shops are using Lucite boxes for a display of jewelry, their tops are transparent.
4. You will have to give the chair at least two coats of white paint, otherwise the dark color of the old paint will show.
5. In some South American countries a businessman must talk sociably for at least fifteen minutes, then he can introduce a business matter.
6. He was not dependable in his former position, therefore we cannot employ him.
7. Do come this weekend to see us in our new home, we have missed the pleasant evenings we used to spend with you.
8. Ten drivers started in the race only eight finished.
9. The next thing to work on is the motor of the car, this is the part of the work that runs into money.
10. There were three political parties in Burke's day, they were Tories, Old Whigs, and New Whigs.

57. FUSED SENTENCES

Do not write two sentences with no punctuation between them. Such sentences are known as *fused sentences.*

If the two sentences combined in this way are both statements, the methods suggested in Section 56 may be used in correcting them. Sometimes, however, an inexperienced writer combines two questions or a question and a statement. Then the only way to correct the sentence is to end one of the complete ideas with a period, a question mark, or an exclamation point. Be very sure that you have *two* complete ideas before you use this method of correction.

Wrong: What kind of yearbook are you going to have will it be anything like ours?

  Right: What kind of yearbook are you going to have? Will it be anything like ours?

Wrong: He is a great lacrosse player don't you think so?

  Right: He is a great lacrosse player. Don't you think so?

EXERCISE 3

On your paper, rewrite the following sentences, using periods, question marks, or exclamation points where they are needed:

1. Are you going so soon I'll walk to the corner with you.
2. Criticizing the candidates gets you nowhere you should vote.
3. Turn out the lights they will see that we are here.
4. Have you been affected much by the water shortage if so, I guess your sister is glad, for she won't have to take a bath every day.
5. On Saturday I saw a movie about the Old South I wish hoop skirts would become fashionable again.

EXERCISE 4

On your paper, rewrite these sentences, correcting the period fault, the comma fault, or the fused-sentence fault. (See Sections 55–57.)

1. Was glad to hear that you made the team.
2. Suppose we had lived long ago when there were no radios just think what we should be missing.
3. In Mexico, the mistress never goes shopping in the market, the maid does the laundry, the cleaning, and the shopping.
4. When they found a piece of ground that suited them. They built a beautiful ranch house.
5. I enjoyed very much seeing June Randall again, she asked to be remembered to you.
6. We drifted down the Grand Canal. Listening to the music and enjoying the beauty of Venice spread out before us.
7. When we took off, not a man knew our destination, we were to be signaled when to jump from the plane.
8. Only one thing will make our project successful. The willingness of all the members to work together.
9. The lie detector does not detect lies, it merely records the emotional excitement of the victim.
10. First cream the butter and sugar thoroughly, then stir in the eggs and milk.
11. I like all the ties. One particularly because it goes so well with my new suit.
12. The most interesting part of the book has to do with the Atlantic Charter. Especially the part in which the Charter permits each nation to choose its own government.
13. There is a great deal of fun in gardening, my neighbor and I always have friendly arguments about whose crops are better.
14. At the age of nine, I was enrolled in The Children's Experimental Theater. A drama group that teaches free expression.
15. When the great day came, I was not too anxious to be in the play, in fact I thought that I was going to be sick.
16. All was quiet, then the man in the glass booth raised his hand and dropped it, we were on the air.
17. There was a tense feeling among the crew. When all of a sudden a cannon shot burst into the air.
18. There was another girl in whom he was interested, she had dark hair and big black eyes.
19. At Garrison Boulevard we didn't see the policeman, it was a dark night, and the street light on the corner was out.

20. Last week was a memorable occasion for me, I purchased my new communications receiver.
21. I surely wish I could get you interested in "ham" radio, it is a fascinating hobby.
22. Last Saturday night the two teams lined up against each other. One like David and one like Goliath.
23. When the crops are sold, not all of the money is profit, a great percent is overhead. Such as labor, repairs to machinery, and freight charges.
24. In the Shakespearean theater, the poor people stood on the ground. While the rich sat in boxes on the side of the theater.
25. To prove my point, let's go back a few years. When Henry Ford started his revolutionary idea of producing cars in great numbers.

58. MISUSE OF DEPENDENT CLAUSES

A child writes simple sentences beginning with the subject; but as a person's style matures, he uses dependent clauses to show the relationship of one idea to another, and he varies the structure of sentences in order to give strength and rhythm to his writing. A knowledge of the proper use of dependent clauses is necessary for the development of a mature style.

58a. Do not use an adverbial clause as a noun clause.

Adverbial clauses beginning with *when* and *where* are often used incorrectly as noun clauses.

Wrong: I read where the weather forecaster said a snowstorm was coming.

  Right: I read that the weather forecaster said a snowstorm was coming.

Wrong: The reason why the automobile stopped was because it had run out of gasoline.

  Right: The reason why the automobile stopped was that it had run out of gasoline.

58b-c

58b. Do not use an adverbial clause in place of a noun.

Wrong: Plagiarism is *where* you take the work of another and pass it off as your own.

Right: Plagiarism is *copying* the work of another and passing it off as one's own.

Wrong: Anemia is *when* the blood is deficient in red corpuscles.

Right: Anemia is an *illness* in which there is a deficiency of red corpuscles.

58c. Do not use an independent clause as the subject of *is* or *was*.

Faulty: There is too much homework is my brother's main complaint.

Better: That there is too much homework is my brother's main complaint.

He complains because there is too much homework.

EXERCISE 5

On your paper, rewrite these sentences, correcting the misuse of dependent clauses:

1. I see in the paper where the weather has been unusually cold this winter.
2. The train left by daylight time is why I missed it.
3. In the game of baseball, a strike is when the player tries to hit the ball but misses it.
4. He did not concentrate was why he failed the course.
5. The reason the mower did not cut the grass was because its blades were dull.
6. Perjury is where a man swears to tell the truth and then tells a lie.
7. Because I bought a new suit is why she thinks I have money.
8. My father was a lawyer was the reason why I studied law.
9. His definition of freedom is when you can look any man squarely in the eye.
10. His home is where you can always have a good time.

59. USING ONLY RELATED IDEAS IN A SENTENCE

In order to be clear, a sentence must have unity and coherence. Sections 59–61 deal with ways of obtaining sentence unity. Sections 62–67 deal with methods of making a sentence coherent. Clear reference of pronouns, which is important in any study of the clear sentence, has been treated in Section 13. A sentence has unity when all ideas in it are closely related and contribute to a single impression.

Wrong: 1. Bill was a basketball player and he is a graduate of Erie High School.

2. Vaslav Nijinsky was one of the greatest dancers the world has ever known, and he was in a mental hospital for many years.

3. I hope that you will visit me next summer and tell June to write to me.

Sometimes unity can be obtained by making one idea subordinate to the other and using a connecting link that makes clear the relationship between the ideas. See the improved form of Sentence 1.

Improved: 1. Bill is a graduate of Erie High School, where he was a star basketball player.

Sometimes, however, the ideas are so completely unrelated that only a complete separation of them can establish unity. Occasionally they should be in another paragraph. See the improved forms of Sentence 2 and Sentence 3:

Improved: 2. Vaslav Nijinsky was one of the greatest dancers the world has ever known. Unfortunately he was in a mental hospital for many years and could not show the world his art.

Improved: 3. I hope that you will visit me next summer. Please tell June to write to me.

EXERCISE 6

On your paper, rewrite the following sentences so that they are unified. If the ideas in any sentence cannot be related, omit one of them.

1. We believe that our club is the best in the school, and it was founded ten years ago.
2. *The Saturday Evening Post* is my favorite among weekly magazines, and it is published in Philadelphia.
3. I made 93 in the last history test, and I decided to go to the movies instead of studying.
4. Last Saturday, I went on my first blind date, and I lost my school ring.
5. My sister wants to be a florist, and she is only twelve years old.
6. He is a much better dancer than his brother, who took lessons for several years and works in a grocery store.
7. Woodrow Wilson was an eminent statesman, and he had a prominent chin.
8. People in North Carolina like hot breads, and the largest city is Charlotte.
9. The father of the family was a physician, having studied at Jefferson Medical College in Philadelphia, the third largest city in the United States.
10. He is a very clever person, his sister having studied in Paris for several years.

60. RAMBLING SENTENCES

Avoid rambling sentences which introduce too many details.

Rambling: Beethoven, who is considered one of the great masters of music, was the son of a court musician and a cook, and he became deaf at thirty-two, but he composed some magnificent symphonies.

Revised: Beethoven, one of the great masters of music, was the son of a court musician and a cook. Although he became deaf at thirty-two, he composed some magnificent symphonies.

EXERCISE 7

On your paper, rewrite the following selection in unified sentences:

1. Nijinsky was a great dancer. 2. His tremendous leaps seemed to defy gravity, and his grace, probably inherited from his mother, who was a dancer, especially in *Scheherezade*, in which he danced the part of a slave in love with a princess, caused him to be applauded by throngs of people in all countries. 3. One of his greatest successes was his debut in New York in a dance called *Specter of the Rose*, now a part of the repertoire of several ballet companies, in which thousands of rose petals floated over the stage as the great dancer performed. 4. Later he danced in Paris with the famous Pavlova and came to England in 1948 with his wife, a Hungarian actress, and his daughter lives in Rome and is also a dancer.

61. CHOPPY SENTENCES

Students who have been taught not to write rambling sentences sometimes go to the opposite extreme. They become afraid to join any ideas in one sentence. As a result, they write each thought as a separate unit. This procedure, however, can destroy unity as thoroughly as rambling sentences do, for in choppy sentences, you cannot see how the ideas are related.

Choppy: Many trees die each year. They have had bad treatment. In our neighborhood, some people whitewash the trunks. They think that whitewash will keep insects away. Tree doctors say that whitewash will damage the bark. In some states there are laws against stripping blossoming trees like dogwood. Every spring a few people evade the law. They want to please themselves. They have no thought for the beauty of the woods. They are unconcerned about the destruction of a tree. They break off large branches. Then the tree dies. Their selfishness deprives many other people of pleasure.

EXERCISE 8

On your paper, revise the choppy paragraph in Section 61 by making sentences that show the relationship of one idea to another.

EXERCISE 9

On your paper, rewrite the following selection in unified sentences:

1. We are bombarded on all sides by propaganda. 2. We don't know what to believe. 3. We have been taught a few ways in which to test what we hear on the radio or read in the newspaper, and it is important to know who the speaker or writer is and what he knows about his subject. 4. Some people try to make us act by stirring our emotions. 5. They do not think clearly themselves. 6. They expect to make us do what they want done. 7. They don't give us logical reasons for acting. 8. Some people present only one side of the question discussed, and no question has only one side; so we suspect those people of being prejudiced and we do not put too much faith in what they say because if they were honest, they would tell the whole story, not simply a part of it. 9. It is important also to know what methods a speaker or writer used to gather his facts because sometimes investigations are carelessly made and the conclusions drawn are not valid. 10. In a democratic country, it is important for people to think.

62. INCOMPLETENESS

To be coherent, a sentence must be complete. Sometimes words are omitted when the writer understands so well what he wants to say that he thinks he has made his meaning clear to the reader.

62a. Be sure to include all necessary verbs.

Doubtful: The lawn is mowed and the hedges trimmed.
  Correct: The lawn is mowed, and the hedges are trimmed.
  Correct: The lawn is mowed and the fence repaired.

NOTE: The auxiliary verb can be understood when it is in the same form that has been expressed in the sentence. If another form is grammatically necessary, it should be expressed. *Is* can be understood before *repaired* in the above sentence.

Doubtful: He has never done any work and never will.
Improved: He has never done any work and never will do any.

NOTE: If the verb *to be* is used as an auxiliary and as a main verb, it must be expressed both times.

Doubtful: She was a fine girl and liked by everybody.

  main verb   auxiliary
Improved: She *was* a fine girl and *was* liked by everybody.

62b. Include necessary articles, pronouns, and prepositions.

> We needed a clerk and typist. (One person)
> We needed a clerk and *a* typist. (Two persons)

Doubtful: He built an automobile which could go ninety miles an hour and pleased many people.
Improved: He built an automobile which could go ninety miles an hour and *which* pleased many people.
Doubtful: I am neither interested nor concerned about his welfare. (Interested *about* his welfare?)
Improved: I am neither interested *in* his welfare nor concerned about it.

62c. In formal writing, do not omit *that* if the subject of the subordinate clause might seem at first glance to be the object of the verb preceding.

Informal: I know the President of the United States must be an American by birth. (At first glance, the writer seems to be personally acquainted with the President.)
Formal: I know *that* the President of the United States must be an American by birth.

See Section 67 for omission of words in a comparison.

62d. Be sure to express every idea essential to the sense or structure of the sentence.

Do not begin a sentence with one structure and shift, before finishing it, to another structure.

Not clear: An automobile, unless you take good care of it, you will soon have to repair it. (There is no verb to complete the structure begun with *automobile*.)

Improved: An automobile will soon have to be repaired unless good care is given to it.

Not clear: With these eleven men working together as a team is the reason for our successful season.

Improved: With these eleven men working together as a team, we had a successful season.

or

Because these eleven men worked together as a team, we had a successful season.

62e. In formal writing, complete the thought after *so, such, those.*

Informal: I was so bored.

Formal: I was so bored that I left the party.

Informal: He is one of those eccentric philosophers.

Formal: He is one of those eccentric philosophers who prefer to be alone.

EXERCISE 10

Complete the sense of each of the following sentences by adding the necessary words or by rewriting the sentence.

1. I have not spoken to Judith about your decision, nor will I.
2. All the money I spent for repairs, I could have bought a new car.
3. The secretary and treasurer were both so excited by the election.
4. It was a night that if one wore a sweater and skirt, she could feel comfortable.
5. He was such a pleasant man and so universally admired.

6. The soldier asked us would we please tell him the road to Washington.

7. When she went to the mailbox, she found the mail had not yet arrived.

8. Anybody who could get 100 on that history test, the whole class would think he was a genius.

9. I shall always be so grateful and appreciative of his kindness to me.

10. Betty worried would we have so much trouble with the heating system of the new house.

63. WORD ORDER

When you have learned to use modifiers properly, you are beginning to build a mature style. Sometimes the modifier is a single adjective or adverb, but often in a mature style it is a phrase or a clause. If these modifiers are not placed near the word which they modify, the sentence will lack clarity. Sometimes misplaced modifiers make a sentence sound absurd, as you can see from the following examples.

Vague: I hope that you received the road information necessary for your emergency trip from the state police. (Was he escaping from jail?)

Improved: I hope that you received from the state police the road information necessary for your emergency trip.

Vague: Thank you for inviting me to the party on December 31 at ten o'clock in your club cellar. (What time is it at my house when it is ten o'clock in the club cellar?)

Improved: Thank you for inviting me to the party in your club cellar at ten o'clock on December 31.

Vague: In the days of Leeuwenhoek, anyone who was working with science was thought to be "cracked" by the public. (Because the phrase *by the public* is misplaced, the sentence has a ridiculous meaning.)

Improved: In the days of Leeuwenhoek, anyone who was working with science was thought by the public to be "cracked."

63a. Do not misplace words such as *only*, *hardly*, and *even*.

> *Vague:* I *only* want to say a few words.
> *Improved:* I want to say *only* a few words.
>> *Vague:* Since the guarantee on your radio *only* covers the repair of the motor, we are unable to replace the case.
> *Improved:* Since the guarantee on your radio covers the repair of the motor *only*, we are unable to replace the case.
>> *Vague:* We were *even* victorious in our game against Southern.
> *Improved:* We were victorious *even* in our game against Southern.

63b. Place phrases and clauses as close as possible to the words which they modify.

> *Vague:* Stewart lived with a friend whom he trusted *in a small apartment.* (Misplaced prepositional phrase)
> *Improved:* Stewart lived *in a small apartment* with a friend whom he trusted.
> *Vague:* It gives me great pleasure to send you a little souvenir with my compliments, *which I hope you will find useful.* (Misplaced adjective clause)
> *Improved:* It gives me great pleasure to send you with my compliments a little souvenir, *which I hope you will find useful.*

63c. Avoid squinting modifiers.

A modifier is said to be *squinting* when it may refer to either of two parts of a sentence.

> *Vague:* Students who cut classes frequently fall behind in their studies. (This could mean either of two things.)
> *Improved:* Frequently, students who cut classes fall behind in their work.
> *Improved:* Students who frequently cut classes fall behind in their work.

EXERCISE 11

On your paper, rewrite the following sentences, placing modifiers correctly.

1. We can only supply two of the items which you ordered.
2. In an effort to amuse me, the nurse put a hat on my head made of a towel.
3. I worked for the Sewell Company during the entire vacation in the Boys' Department.
4. A small native boy was balancing a basket on his head held down by a stone.
5. He even drives his car the two blocks to the drug store.
6. I prepared for the trip by putting the most comfortable shoes I had on.
7. New houses will be built in our country which will be heated by the sun.
8. I read a story in a magazine about a forest fire.
9. Some of the dancers carried huge baskets on their heads which were filled with bright flowers.
10. Mother bought a coat for my sister with a fur lining.
11. We saw a house that we liked very much last week.
12. You cannot write a good report of an experiment in physics unless you know how to arrange what you have to say in clear sentences.
13. Your reply to our previous letters has not been received concerning the $48.95 that still remains unpaid.
14. One night Silas fell into a mysterious sleep during a prayer meeting which was mistaken for death.
15. The clown was wearing a bright blue and yellow sign on his back advertising the side show.
16. The new manager settled himself behind his desk and told the boys how he had made his fortune after lunch.
17. Most cars have sun visors above the windshield, which can be adjusted to shade the eyes.
18. We have the shirts in stock that you inquired about in your letter of May 15.
19. In order that the job may be done efficiently, large bins are distributed on this floor in which are placed different kinds of cotton.

20. The manufacturer can only use the four pelts which you sent to patch others.
21. I sent invitations to a party on Saturday, two weeks ago.
22. She told us to come at nine o'clock, and at ten she rescinded the invitation.
23. There are three letters in this file which are poorly written.
24. I am sorry that you were refused the information that you requested by a member of our company.
25. A representative is always on the grounds who will gladly show the cottages.

EXERCISE 12

Follow the directions in Exercise 11.

1. I believe that I could fill the job that you offer competently and efficiently.
2. On the night of the blizzard, our representative was swamped by inquiries from the members for assistance.
3. This morning I saw the man whose car sideswiped yours in front of the bank.
4. I'm sure you share the problem of finding the right college with me.
5. Several weeks ago I ordered five records from your company costing $20.70.
6. Thank you for returning the tire purchased recently for our examination.
7. A statement of your account will be mailed to you on the first of each month covering your purchases for the preceding month.
8. The factories in our town manufacture articles of great importance such as airplanes and electronic equipment.
9. You will no doubt want to mail us your check promptly for $135.
10. Only minor damage was found at the time of the inspection, which could be repaired immediately.
11. Since the Clippers have only played two games, it is hard to tell whether they have a good team.
12. You should not keep a dog that is used to a steam-heated apartment in a doghouse.

13. The pioneer family owned a house which was really a cave with a door and two bony oxen.

14. She saw a dress in the window of a department store which she has made up her mind to buy.

15. Please let me know whether you can come to the party as soon as possible.

16. I should like to thank you for the birthday gift with all my heart.

17. We understand the disappointment you felt when you opened the box and found the camera that you had been waiting for broken.

18. In those days certain ideals were established which regulated the pattern of the people's lives such as devotion to home and love of personal freedom.

19. The period was called the Puritan Era because some people had broken away from the Church of England who wanted their religion simplified and purified.

20. The newspaper said: "Thanks are extended to all those who generously gave donations and to the group who helped to serve the refreshments which included four girl scouts."

EXERCISE 13

Follow the directions in Exercise 11.

1. In this new history of art, a number of artists are excluded whom no editor can afford to neglect.

2. The book contains excellent reproductions of paintings by many artists to the great delight of the reader.

3. The growth of the railroads diverted most of the freight from the rivers on which the steamboat men depended.

4. Jane's absence from school was the result of a cold accompanied by a fever the day before yesterday.

5. We cannot stress the advantage of traveling with an established firm too forcibly.

6. Driver-education classes are being taught in high school in which any student may enroll.

7. More than a hundred animals of the city zoo escaped when the attendants went on strike, roaming the streets and terrifying residents.

8. A careful study of these figures shows that there are 7,500,-000 people in this state that use chewing gum.

9. Tests have been developed for some jobs that are indicative of the possibilities of success which an individual may have.

10. We have made a tracing of the signature on the checks you enclosed for our files, and we shall publish a warning about this man's activities in our bulletin.

EXERCISE 14

On your paper, rewrite the following excerpt from a travel itinerary. Place the modifiers in the positions that make the sentences clear.

1. Cars will call at the hotels indicated when booking at about 9 A.M. 2. At the first stop, the party will embark in a "canoa" propelled by the natives of the vicinity with long poles, for a picturesque trip on the canals. 3. Then you will see the famous palace built in 1530 by Cortés which is now the seat of the local government. 4. You are requested neither to touch anything nor sit in the old chairs. 5. The shopper will find something either to please himself or the folks at home, with ease. 6. Each resident of the United States is entitled to bring five hundred dollars' worth of articles free of duty home.

64. SPLIT CONSTRUCTIONS

Parts of a sentence which are closely related grammatically should not be carelessly separated. No strict rule about this principle can be made because sometimes it is necessary to separate these parts. In general, however, these rules can be followed.

64a. Avoid *unnecessary* **separation of the parts of a verb phrase.**

Awkward: After he made a decision, he would, *no matter what the consequences might be,* stick to his point.

Improved: After he made a decision, he would stick to his point, *no matter what the consequences might be.*

Awkward: This tree has, *although you would not think so,* been here for thirty years.

Improved: *Although you would not think so,* this tree has been here for thirty years.

64b. Avoid unnecessary separation of subject and verb, verb and object, preposition and object.

Awkward: He, in one sweeping motion, threw both books and newspapers on the floor.

Improved: In one sweeping motion, he threw both books and newspapers on the floor.

64c. Keep parts of an infinitive together.

Many good writers use and defend a split infinitive. It is true that in some constructions the split infinitive makes a smoother or more emphatic sentence, but it may often make an awkward sentence. Clearness and naturalness must be the test.

Permissible: After we had caught a beautiful rainbow trout, we went home *to proudly display* our prize. (*Proudly to display* or *to display proudly* makes the sentence stiff.)

Unnecessary: The radio announcer told the audience *to vigorously applaud* when he raised his hand.

Improved: The radio announcer told the audience *to applaud vigorously* when he raised his hand.

64d. Keep coordinate sentence elements together.

Awkward: *Although he was a good tennis player,* he never was ranked among the first ten, *although he practiced daily.*

Right: *Although he was a good tennis player and practiced daily,* he never was ranked among the first ten.

EXERCISE 15

Rewrite these sentences, avoiding split constructions:

1. Shirley had, instead of doing her job, kept looking out of the window.
2. When the war was over, Vincent bought a farm, after he had come home.
3. In 1937 we added a new top story which was carefully designed to, both in style and material, follow the original structure.
4. When he, instead of building a house, built a barn, Mrs. Perkins rebelled.
5. One man in the group told, when he saw Corsica, a story of life on that island.

65. DANGLING MODIFIERS

A modifier is *dangling* when it is not clearly attached to the word to which it refers. Many of these dangling modifiers appear at the beginning of a sentence. They may be phrases beginning with the present participle (*arriving late, walking across the campus*), the past participle (*exhausted by the trip, overcome by his trouble*), or the perfect participle (*having missed his train, having been paid*); they may be phrases that contain a gerund (*after copying my schedule, in examining the plans*); they may begin with an infinitive (*to give better service, to finish the job*). Logically, they should be attached to the subject of the clause that follows.

65a. Avoid dangling participial phrases. (See Section 6.)

Dangling: *Opening the door,* the odor of strong perfume struck me at once. (The subject of the clause is *odor,* but the odor did not open the door.)

    Right: *Opening the door,* I smelled strong perfume. (The subject of the clause is *I;* the phrase is connected logically with the word which it modifies.)

As I opened the door, the odor of strong perfume struck me at once. (The dangling phrase is changed to a clause.)

Dangling: *Exhausted after the day's work,* it was difficult for Betty to enjoy the evening. (Phrase with past participle.)

Right: *Exhausted after the day's work,* Betty found it difficult to enjoy the evening.
Because she was exhausted after the day's work, Betty found it difficult to enjoy the evening.

Dangling: *Sung by a good contralto,* we thought that the music sounded beautiful.

Right: *Sung by a good contralto,* the music sounded beautiful to us.

65b. Avoid dangling gerund phrases. (See Section 6.)

Dangling: *On examining the goods,* they were found to be defective.

Right: *On examining the goods,* we found them defective.
When the goods were examined, they were found to be defective.
When we examined the goods, we found them defective.

Dangling: *After convincing Mr. Pressman of my ability,* he hired me.

Right: *After convincing Mr. Pressman of my ability,* I was hired by him.
After I had convinced Mr. Pressman of my ability, he hired me.

EXERCISE 16

On your paper, rewrite correctly any of the following sentences that contain dangling phrases. If a sentence contains no errors, write C beside the sentence number on your paper.

1. After nagging my parents for two months, they agreed to let me learn to drive.

2. Arriving late at night, all the lights in the house were out.

3. Seeing a storm coming, we pulled down the sails.
4. Having examined all the plans with care, the one presented by the Benders Company seemed best.
5. Being Saturday morning, the bus was crowded.
6. Hoping to overcome her awkwardness, Isabel went to dancing school.
7. Walking across the dark road, the driver did not see me.
8. Having lost his fortune in some bad investments, his life seemed completely ruined.
9. Handled carefully, a clever propagandist could make great use of television.
10. After being told to take my morning bath, the clanging trays announced breakfast in the hospital.
11. Looking inland, the first thing that we saw was a church tower.
12. Reserved for high dignitaries, we could not occupy the seats.
13. Instead of realizing a return on our investment, it is costing us money to run the department.
14. By filing our cards according to the new system, another clerk will have to be hired.
15. Before going to bed and upon arising, clothes and shoes had to be examined for scorpions.
16. Established in 1890, the inn has always been owned by the Pembroke family.
17. Pressing the button, the elevator went up to the tenth floor.
18. Respected by everybody who knows him, we shall have as candidate for governor Mr. Jameson Harkness.
19. After forcing all opposition groups to withdraw from the legislature, a new constitution was drafted.
20. Repelled by our army, the enemy withdrew to form a new defense line.
21. Having been named chairman of the committee, a meeting was called by Albert Delton.
22. Being interested in aviation, my course in physics has helped me very much.
23. After seeing the circus, there was always pink lemonade for the children.
24. By locating the factory on the third floor and the repair

department on the second floor, greater convenience can be given to our customers.

25. Drunk with power, it was impossible for the people to curb their leader.

65c. Avoid dangling infinitive phrases.

Wrong: *To avoid scrapping such expensive material,* an adjustment was made in the condenser.

Right: *To avoid scrapping such expensive material,* we made an adjustment in the condenser.

Wrong: *In order to keep the car in good condition,* it was greased every 1,000 miles.

Right: *In order to keep the car in good condition,* we had it greased every 1,000 miles.

65d. Avoid dangling elliptical expressions.

An elliptical expression is one from which the subject or verb or both have been omitted. Many elliptical clauses begin with *while* or *when.*

Wrong: *While swimming in a river near our farm,* my clothes were stolen by a tramp. (The italicized expression means *while I was swimming.* In this sentence the clothes seem to be swimming.)

Right: *While I was swimming in a river near our farm,* my clothes were stolen by a tramp.

Right: *While swimming in a river near our farm,* I had my clothes stolen by a tramp.

Wrong: *When still a small child,* his first appearance was made on the stage.

Right: *When still a small child,* he made his first appearance on the stage.

EXERCISE 17

On your paper, rewrite correctly any sentences containing dangling infinitive phrases or dangling elliptical clauses. If a sentence contains no error, write C beside its number on your paper.

1. While eating his lunch one day, land was sighted.
2. While walking home, her name was frequently mentioned.
3. When startled, the animal will fight fiercely.
4. In order to communicate with the president of the company, a cablegram was sent.
5. Unless desirable, we do not list apartments.
6. While talking to a friend one day, he told me where I could get a summer job.
7. While studying bookkeeping, Elaine was offered a job with Crandon, Wells and Company.
8. To serve our customers more promptly, a new information service has been set up.
9. When ten years old, his uncle died and left him a small fortune.
10. As an employee of the Illinois Motor Club, we expect you to follow the rules.

NOTE: The word *due* in formal English is usually considered an adjective. Some writers today, however, use the expression *due to* as a preposition.

Adjective: His illness was *due* to overeating.
Preposition: He was ill *due to* overeating.

CAUTION:

1. Final participial modifiers beginning with *thus* often make awkward constructions.

Awkward: We have just introduced a new filing system, *thus making everything easy to find.*
Improved: Because we have introduced a new filing system, we can now find everything more easily.

2. The absolute construction (noun or pronoun and participle) is often awkward at the beginning of a sentence if it contains a pronoun.

Awkward: *He being a good salesman,* we sent him to see Mr. Eckels.
Improved: Because he is a good salesman, we sent him to see Mr. Eckels.

3. The participle *being* should not be followed by *that;* nor should it be used as a conjunction.

Wrong: *Being that* it is a clear day, we can go for a hike.
Wrong: *Being* it's a clear day. . . .
 Right: Since it is a clear day. . . .
Wrong: *Being we lived at the shore all summer,* I could practice swimming every day.
 Right: Because we lived at the shore all summer. . . .

NOTE: When a verbal is used to specify a general action, it is not considered a dangling modifier: *Generally speaking, considering everything, judging from past experiences,* and similar expressions are often used without being attached to any specific noun.

EXERCISE 18

On your paper, rewrite any sentences containing dangling modifiers. If the sentence is correct, put C beside its number.

1. Passing the stadium, the place looked as if a football game were in progress.
2. When walking the dog, he should be muzzled or kept on a leash.
3. Coming from the dressmaker's, the bus was held up because of an accident.
4. By going to college and gaining further knowledge, my interests will change.
5. Upon examining the shirts which came back from the laundry, it was clear that they had shrunk decidedly.
6. Knowing the excellent reputation of your firm, my surprise was great when the suit shrank in the cleaning process.
7. Before adding antifreeze to your cooling system, your radiator should be completely drained.
8. While searching through a pile of stage props the other day, many strange objects were found.
9. Looking through the window of the Waldorf at the tall buildings of New York made me think of the strength of our country.

10. The other night while visiting some friends, the hostess served some cookies and an unusual French ice cream.
11. While making a purchase at a drug store, a soft drink was spilled on my coat.
12. If used for pulling plows and wagons, the nerves of these fine horses would break.
13. When summoned, it was too late for him to help.
14. When spoken to, his mind worked slowly.
15. Exhausted by the struggle, his breath came rapidly.
16. Having never before been without transportation, my problem during my first year at art school was how to take my girl to the movies.
17. Before starting out, a check of road conditions was made.
18. Although slightly more expensive, many of our customers tell us that the new model is well worth the difference in price.
19. While still children, our beliefs are borrowed from the adults around us.
20. While looking through a magazine in a doctor's office, a tricky slogan caught my eye.
21. I told your clerk that while not a member of the A.A.A., the information was needed in an emergency.
22. When driven in this condition, the sidewalls of the tires may be damaged.
23. Born into a famous medical family his father wanted George to be a doctor.
24. Sulfanilamide remained unknown until its powers were discovered while doing research on dogs.
25. By employing private detectives for police work at sporting events and using policewomen as traffic officers, a large number of policemen would be available for crime detection.

EXERCISE 19

On your paper, rewrite correctly any sentences containing dangling modifiers. If a sentence contains no error, write C beside its number on your paper.

1. After leaving the ship, the first thing that we noticed was the strange birds.

2. In addition to being interesting work, I feel that I am making a contribution to public health.

3. While walking into the quiet office to apply for a job, my shoes began to squeak.

4. Skilled in all kinds of executive work, it was easy for him to get a job.

5. When making a golf stroke, the backswing is the first motion.

6. In order to progress, it was necessary for the company to go into mass production.

7. After ceaselessly searching the newspapers and getting assistance from several agents, we finally found an apartment.

8. One day while looking at the newspaper, my eyes fell on a page that told of business opportunities in Alaska.

9. Looking back on my years of newspaper work, my last assignment was decidedly the most stimulating.

10. Besides being a beautifully designed car, a businessman with a small business can cut his delivery expenses in half.

11. By teaching an understanding of our government, it will be possible to develop wise voters.

12. Being that the strike has interfered with production, we cannot fill your order until March.

13. Looking at random through the many plans submitted, there is a splendid one offered by the chamber of commerce.

14. He being one of our best customers, I should not want to disappoint him.

15. Overcome by his numerous problems, his health failed rapidly.

16. Acting on the advice of Mr. Sellers, Henry's report was presented to the board of directors.

17. Having grown up in the business, it was hard for him to leave.

18. Before starting to cook, all the necessary ingredients and utensils should be placed within reach.

19. After having checked each item against the order, it is packed in cartons and shipped.

20. She being our best stenographer, we gave her an increase in salary.

21. Everything was measured with great care, being sure not to make the smallest mistake.

22. He was experienced in many kinds of business, thus helping him to manage a business of his own.
23. We believe that by appropriating larger funds for education, the legislature would improve instruction in the schools.
24. Huge lights play like searchlights on the tops of people's heads scampering to their places.

66. MIXED AND ILLOGICAL CONSTRUCTIONS

Every part of the sentence must agree with the other parts in some logical way if the meaning of the sentence is to be clear.

66a. Be sure that the subject makes sense in its relationship to the verbs.

Vague: The first case of smallpox dates back more than a thousand years before the birth of Christ and has gone unchecked until recently. (This sentence lacks logic because it says that the first case of smallpox has gone unchecked until recently.)

Improved: The first case of smallpox dates back more than a thousand years before the birth of Christ, but only recently has the disease been checked.

Vague: The time will be eight o'clock at my home and will be informal.

Improved: The party will be at my home at eight o'clock and will be informal.

66b. Every verb must have a clear-cut subject.

Vague: With a family to support makes his decision all the more important.

Improved: His having a family to support makes his decision all the more important.

66c. Adjust the form of an indirect quotation to the rest of the sentence.

Awkward: The boy asked us would we give him a lift to Easton.

Improved: The boy asked us if we would give him a lift to Easton.

337

66d. Avoid mixed constructions.

> *Mixed:* Despite of what you say, I think you are wrong. (*In spite of* is confused with *despite*.)
>
> *Improved:* In spite of what you say, I think you are wrong.
>
> or
>
> Despite what you say, I think you are wrong.

66e. Avoid double negatives.

Awkward: I can't hardly see you.
Improved: I can hardly see you.
Awkward: He hasn't scarcely any money.
Improved: He has scarcely any money.

EXERCISE 20

On your paper, rewrite the following sentences, making them logical:

1. Seeing youngsters running through the streets in dungarees and loose shirts has become a familiar sight.
2. Eighteenth-century literature was a new and exciting period.
3. Eleanor wanted to know was I ever in China.
4. The book tells the story of a man who lost his money and his struggle against poverty.
5. Her hair is blond, and her eyes are a clear gray with a cute little nose and a dimpled chin.
6. I really don't know how to express the wonderful time I had at your house.
7. During the strike the police force was reinforced with one hundred men and orders to prevent violence.
8. The chairman read a letter from the mayor, who regretted his inability to attend but "offer the class my congratulations."
9. For class day the boys wear blue suits and white carnations in their buttonholes.
10. I think the most interesting job next to a forest ranger would be a game warden.
11. By conquering something, whether it be an opponent or a skill, gives one a feeling of pride.

12. The people in a modern democracy no longer consist of small cities as they did in the days of Greek democracy.
13. It surprised us to find that Napoleon is the person most frequently assumed by the mentally ill.
14. Tomorrow is my sister's engagement party.
15. With increasing size of cars is another reason why we have parking problems.

67. COMPARISONS

The ability to make logical comparisons is often important in achieving clarity in writing. The rules that follow will help you to avoid making confusing or misleading comparisons.

67a. Compare only things of a similar nature.

Illogical: Unlike most seaside places, the food here is very poor. (*Food* is compared to *seaside places.*)
Improved: Unlike most seaside places, this one does not serve very good food.
Illogical: In the new school, the teachers were more friendly than my old school.
Improved: The teachers in the new school were more friendly than those in the old school.
Illogical: I like Kipling's poetry better than T. S. Eliot.
Improved: I like Kipling's poetry better than T. S. Eliot's.

67b. Avoid including within the class or group the object or term being compared, if it is part of the class or group. Use *other* or *else* to exclude the object being compared.

Wrong: Sanderson's *Animal Treasure* is better than any book I have read recently. (Since *Animal Treasure* is one of the books that I have read, I am saying that it is better than itself.)
Right: Sanderson's *Animal Treasure* is better than any *other* book that I have read recently.

67c. Use *all*, not *any*, with the superlative degree.

Wrong: Biology is the most enjoyable of *any* of my courses.
Right: Biology is the most enjoyable of *all* my courses.

67d. Complete the elements of one comparison before another is introduced.

Awkward: Colonel Benton is one of the finest, if not the finest, infantry officer in our army.
Improved: Colonel Benton is one of the finest infantry officers in our army, if not the finest.
Awkward: Ralph is as clever if not more clever than Stanley.
Improved: Ralph is as clever as Stanley, if not more clever.

67e. Be sure that every comparison is clear.

Vague: I missed her more than Florence. (More than I missed Florence or more than Florence missed her?)
Improved: I missed her more than Florence did.

or

I missed her more than I missed Florence.

EXERCISE 21

On your paper, rewrite these sentences, making the comparisons logical:

1. Salt Lake City is larger than any city in Utah.
2. Stanley Moore is one of the most successful, if not the most successful, lawyer in town.
3. Unlike most hotels, the radio reception is powerful.
4. Although the baseball team in Richmond cannot compare with New York, the people enjoy watching it.
5. Our posters are prettier than any posters in the contest.
6. The number of hotel rooms that Boston could offer us for the convention was larger than any city.
7. Marianne learned to love her nurse better than her mother.
8. Flowers from Kirkwood are fresher than any florist in town.
9. Crop conditions in all parts of the country have been more favorable than last year.
10. I think that he is funnier than anybody I've ever seen.

11. I am happy to tell you that the Prisoners' Aid Association is about to enter a period of as great usefulness or greater than any in its history.
12. The food of our merchant seamen is as good as any marine group in the world, but our operating costs are higher than any country.
13. The early settler knew more about planting than the Indians.
14. Edith likes oranges better than any fruit.
15. I have no interest nor desire to learn to play golf.

EXERCISE 22

Many of the following sentences lack coherence as a result of violations of principles explained in Sections 62–67. Review these sections. Then on your paper, rewrite the sentences. If a sentence needs no correction, write C beside its number on your paper.

1. Walking down the hall, my eye was attracted by a painting.
2. The principal asked us were we interested in getting summer jobs.
3. Jim told me that one day last week he stayed in school until 5:30.
4. Walter Reed's work differed from other scientists because he used people instead of animals for his experiments.
5. Her antique furniture is more beautiful than any furniture in our community.
6. The best autobiography of all is Benjamin Franklin.
7. Choose the presents you bring into a hospital with care.
8. I only saw small fish swimming in a fish bowl at first glance.
9. Not being able to read, his only source of news would be through the radio and television.
10. The woman took a sleeping tablet which made her relax completely, in hot milk.
11. Every week the boys would have races to see whose boat was the fastest in a nearby quarry.
12. The game being Friday night, we had to leave Friday noon.
13. In early England, the actors were the monks who performed in the church but later grew into private enterprise.

14. While living in the serene, hospitable atmosphere of New Haven, Connecticut, the minor arts and social graces were cultivated.

15. Preston Sproll is as good if not better than any electrical engineer in the city.

16. We asked Mrs. Hunter would she serve on the committee for the church supper.

17. Sally said, "Oh, Mother, I saw a squirrel coming home from school today."

18. Edmund Burke seems to me greater than any other English statesman of his day.

19. His experiences with the people in China were like all doctors who spend years among alien people.

20. The date has been set and the invitations for the wedding sent out.

21. Mr. Lansdale, as a result of studying for many years, was able to speak five languages.

22. A person who budgets his allowance toward the end of the month has money.

23. Recalled to office by an emergency situation, it was necessary for Mr. Hammond to rearrange completely all his business affairs.

24. After 1666 there was no epidemic of plague in London, though a few cases appear in the records up to 1679, and finally disappeared in 1703.

25. You are so hazy that I can't understand anything very well that you say.

68. PARALLEL STRUCTURE

Sentences may be unified and clear and yet be ineffective. Some of the principles that make effective sentences are discussed in Sections 68–72. See also Section 51 on wordiness.

Parallel structure means the use of "like construction for like ideas." Sentences do not always have to be arranged in an absolutely parallel structure, but such an arrangement often gives clarity and force.

68a. Use the same structure on both sides of a coordinating conjunction (and, but, or).

Ineffective: The movie actress told the reporters that she likes *swimming* and *to drive.* (Here the conjunction *and* joins a gerund, *swimming,* and an infinitive, *to drive.*)

Improved: The movie actress told the reporters that she likes *swimming* and *driving.* (Or *to swim* and *to drive*)

Ineffective: I had the rugs taken up in order *to clean the floor* and *for coolness in summer.* (Infinitive phrase *and* prepositional phrase)

Improved: I had the rugs taken up in order *to clean the floor* and *to make the house cool* in summer. (Infinitive phrase *and* infinitive phrase)

Ineffective: We decided *to telephone you* and *that we could then tell you all the news.* (Infinitive phrase *and* subordinate clause)

Improved: We decided *to telephone you* and *tell you all the news.* (Two infinitives)

68b. Be particularly careful not to join a relative clause and an independent clause by and, but, or. Do not use and which, but which, and who, but who, unless there is a preceding "which" clause or "who" clause.

Ineffective: Jessie is a person of strong will *and who always gets her own way.*

Improved: Jessie has a strong will and always gets her own way.

or

Jessie has such a strong will that she always gets her own way.

or

Jessie is a person who has a strong will and who always gets her own way.

68c. Keep the members of a series in the same construction.

Ineffective: She is tall, slender, *and a girl of great beauty.*
Improved: She is tall, slender, and very beautiful.

Ineffective: He took a job as clerk, salesman, *and mixing sodas.*
Improved: He took a job as clerk, salesman, and soda mixer.

68d. Keep the members of a list in the same construction.

> As a result of its study, the committee recommended the following:
> 1. To move the storage room to the first floor.
> 2. To employ an additional clerk for the filing department.
> 3. To arrange typists' desks in one room.
> 4. We should provide a lounge for women.

The fourth item in the preceding list is a sentence and is therefore not parallel with the infinitive phrases of the other three items. It should read:

> 4. To provide a lounge for women.

68e. Use the same structure on both sides of a correlative.

In a structure involving *neither . . . nor* (*either . . . or*), the same part of speech that follows *neither* (*either*) should follow *nor* (*or*).

Faulty: She had neither *completed* her English nor *her Spanish.*
Improved: She had completed neither *her English* nor *her Spanish.*
Faulty: He is either *lazy* or *he doesn't feel well.*
Improved: He is either *lazy* or *ill.*

EXERCISE 23

On your paper, rewrite the following sentences, using parallel structure where it is required:

1. Dolores has studied filing, bookkeeping, and how to type.
2. Harold is intelligent, honest, and a man of genuine ability.

3. The family decided to rent a cottage at the beach and that Sally and I could use it for a month.

4. I do not know anybody more capable than you or who I feel is better qualified for the job.

5. We suggest either selling the lamps at a lower price or that you return them to the factory.

6. Harris tried to decide whether he should go to college or to enter his father's business.

7. I shall always remember the good times you gave me, the rides, the swims, and especially that you taught me to handle a surfboard.

8. A successful salesman has the following qualities: pleasantness, be courteous, dress properly, be helpful.

9. We regret being unable to ship the order at once and that we must ask you to be patient.

10. I'm sorry that I haven't written to you for some time, but I have been very busy in school and doing my homework at night.

11. To want a new dress for the dance and not being able to get it can spoil a girl's weekend.

12. The housewife is always busy, for she must do the dishes and buy the food as well as sweeping, dusting, and cooking.

13. In department stores there are jobs in buying departments, merchandising, stock management, adjustment managers, bookkeepers, and window dressers.

14. In Shakespeare's day people with well-known names and who had plenty of money would send servants to the theater to save seats for them.

15. Mexican opals are famous for their brilliance and because they are durable.

16. The travelers had many thrilling experiences crossing desert territory and into unknown lands.

17. It is a question of either reducing our overhead, or we must find new outlets for our product.

18. Driver education teaches students to become better drivers by obeying traffic laws, never to exceed speed limits, and always to watch signals.

19. Use your horn to signal other cars that you are about to pass or as a courteous warning to pedestrians.

20. The two soldiers were ordered dishonorably discharged from the army and to forfeit all pay and allowances.

21. Jay's father spent fifteen days teaching him to park a car, the hand signals, and the fundamentals of driving.

22. Since Mr. Emory knows our merchandise very well, he will be able to discuss with you the materials handled by us and which will be usable in your business.

23. A Sunday song festival has been organized by the Mexican government and will be presented in Chapultepec Park as a treat for the strollers and to glorify the folk songs of the country.

24. "Ham" radio operators are always ready to give their services in case of disaster and when normal communications fail.

25. Too many people go to college for football, to have fun, to find a husband, or for the purpose of putting off the evil day when they must go to work.

EXERCISE 24

Follow the directions in Exercise 23.

1. At school I studied history, algebra, and how to cook.

2. The artist is a man of genuine talent and who has had excellent art training.

3. In his youth, Dickens saw people poverty-stricken, hungry, and they were afraid of debtors' prisons.

4. We bought a new ventilator for the kitchen to take away the odors of cooking and for greater comfort for my mother.

5. The lyric passages of the symphony were played poetically and with sensitivity.

6. People leaving school to help support their families and still wish to continue their education should have careful advice from counselors.

7. When Tess moved to a new town, she became careless about her appearance and a sloppy worker.

8. Our representative will show you our new products, assist you with current sales, and an opportunity will be given to examine our advertising.

9. We regret not being able to fill your order and that you were not notified sooner.

68

10. When I asked for highway information, I told your representative of the emergency and that I was not a member of the A.A.A.

11. At our school the method of instruction involves lectures, reading long assignments, and to review carefully for the tests.

12. Statistics show that most women work because of financial need or to raise the living standard of the family.

13. Women often work outside the home with no serious damage to their husbands' happiness, their children's welfare, or how their homes are kept.

14. The modern mother studies budgeting, child training, and how to prepare carefully balanced meals.

15. You will find enclosed an illustrated booklet explaining the art of spin fishing and which contains directions for the proper care of your reel.

16. We can improve the cafeteria by doing several things: less noise, replacing chairs, we should leave the tables clean, and hanging hats on racks.

17. The government publication described the growth habits of poison ivy, how to recognize it, and how to combat it.

18. The pictures taken from the air are indispensable for the study of existing conditions and to improve city planning.

19. Employees with ideas are invited to the meetings so that they can be present during the discussion of their ideas and to get help in the presentation of their materials.

20. During the training week, the new salespeople were taught store policy, methods of selling, proper business manners, and how to write sales checks.

21. Selling merchandise, meeting people from various walks of life, and an opportunity to test my knowledge of sales psychology were a real challenge in my new job.

22. The report recommended the following:
    1. Calling in all 3% bonds
    2. We should build a new plant in Milwaukee
    3. To close out the manufacture of farm machinery
    4. To increase the sales force

23. Our new cutlery, the result of years of research, is guaranteed to retain sharpness, it will not stain, and it cannot rust.

24. The new handle gives these advantages:
    1. No slipping even if hands are wet
    2. Safe to use
    3. Prevents cramping of fingers
25. The mayor says his administration has been responsible for these improvements:
    1. Five low-income housing projects have been constructed
    2. Three new schools
    3. Employment of new director of traffic
    4. Repairing poor streets in downtown area

69. POINT OF VIEW

A sentence loses its strength and confuses the reader if it contains shifts in construction.

69a. Avoid unnecessary shifts in tense.

Weak: Dick *ran* quickly to the end of the beach and *jumps* into the water. (*Ran* is past tense; *jumps* is present tense.)

Improved: Dick *ran* quickly to the end of the beach and *jumped* into the water.

69b. Avoid unnecessary shifts in subject.

Weak: The *garbage* is collected, and then the *city* converts it into fertilizer.

Improved: The *city* collects the garbage and converts it into fertilizer.

Improved: The *garbage* is collected and converted into fertilizer by the city.

69c. Avoid careless shifts in voice.

Weak: I *learned* how to accommodate customers, and the stock *was kept* dusted and orderly. (*Learned* is active voice; *was kept* is passive.)

Improved: I learned how *to accommodate* customers and *to keep* the stock dusted and orderly.

69d. Avoid unnecessary shifts in mood.

> *Weak:* *Make* your decision, and then you *ought* to stick to it. (*Make* is imperative; *ought* is indicative.)
> *Improved:* *Make* your decision and then *stick* to it.

69e. Avoid unnecessary shifts in person or number.

The error here also involves a shift in pronoun reference and violates the general principle that pronouns and antecedents agree in person. (See Section 12.) This error occurs most frequently when the writer shifts from the third person to the inappropriate second person *you.*

> *Weak:* If *one* studies hard enough in high school, *you* will have no trouble with college subjects.
> *Improved:* If *one* studies hard enough in high school, *he* will have no trouble with college subjects.

EXERCISE 25

On your paper, rewrite the following sentences, correcting shifts in construction:

1. Elaine fell in love with Lancelot, but he finally tells her that he could not marry her.
2. In the junior high school, the students were treated like babies; but in the senior high school, we are expected to assume some responsibility.
3. First mix the ingredients carefully; then the pan should be greased.
4. Not only did I go to school in the daytime, studied at night, and worked on weekends, but time was found for athletics.

EXERCISE 26

Some of the sentences in the following selection contain incorrect shifts in the tenses of verbs. On your paper, rewrite such sentences correctly.

1. My first visit to the circus, ten years ago, was a thrilling experience. 2. I loved the smell of roasting peanuts, the sight of

349

the delicious pink and orange lemonade, the crackling popcorn, and the funny old clown. 3. I was so excited that I want to see everything at once, the roaring lions, the clumsy elephants, and the trained seals that acted as if they were almost human. 4. Then there is the fat lady, who must have weighed at least five hundred, or the thin man, who looks as if one could push him over with a little finger. 5. The freaks were really a pitiful sight, but I gaze in admiration at the strong man, who was the image of Atlas. 6. And now I want food, hot dogs, lemonade, peanuts. 7. Somehow, at the circus they taste so much better than when I bought them in the corner store. 8. To top off that perfect afternoon, there is a ride on the Ferris wheel. 9. Everyone was so gay that all troubles are forgotten the minute one walks into the circus grounds. 10. The band keeps playing a cheery tune in order to keep everyone in a gay mood, but no band is necessary to keep my spirits up when the circus tents are near.

70. COORDINATION AND SUBORDINATION

Inexperienced writers have a tendency to join all clauses with *and* or *but*. As a result, their writing is ineffective because it does not show the proper relationship between ideas. Ideas are presented as if they were all statements of equal value. Actually, in any thinking, some ideas are the cause of others; some are the result of others; some exist only *if* others exist. Showing this relationship of cause, result, or condition is called *subordination*. It is important to put in coordinate structure only those ideas which are really equal. Other ideas should be subordinated by means of the appropriate subordinating conjunction.

70a. Avoid too frequent use of coordinating conjunctions. (See Sections 59 and 60.)

Immature: George bought a new automobile, *and* it had free wheeling, *and* there was a radio.

Improved: George bought a new automobile which had free wheeling and a radio.

Immature: The meals in camp were dreadful, *and* how anybody ate them, I'll never know.

Improved: The meals in camp were so dreadful that I don't know how anybody ate them.

70b. Select the conjunction carefully.

Do not use *and* if a contrast is needed.

Weak: All the inhabitants except seven were rescued, *and* timberland valued at $30,000,000 was lost. (Here is a contrast between what was saved and what was lost. Use *but* as the connective.)

Weak: The Severn team was one of the best that we faced, *and* we lost by a score of 35–0. (Use *consequently* as the connective. Remember to use a semicolon when two independent clauses are joined by a conjunctive adverb.)

70c. Avoid inaccurate and false coordination.

Do not use a coordinating conjunction to join an independent clause and a dependent clause. (See Section 68b.)

Inaccurate: The nurse was a pleasant person and was well trained, but *who* was a failure.

Improved: The nurse was a pleasant person and was well trained, but she was a failure.

70d. Avoid too many subordinate clauses in one sentence.

Confused: We talked by phone with our representative in your town who told us that at the time of your recent snowstorm, he received so many inquiries concerning road conditions that since he was the only man in the office, they could not all be handled and information which the people wanted was given to members only.

Improved: Our representative in your town told us that the recent snowstorm brought to his office a great many inquiries about road conditions. Because he was the only man in the office, he was obliged to answer the inquiries of members only.

EXERCISE 27

On your paper, rewrite the following paragraph. Make the sentences more effective by using coordination and subordination and by using conjunctions that show accurately the relationship between the ideas. Make any changes in wording that you think will help to express the ideas logically. If necessary, join sentences that are now separate.

1. Wolfgang Mozart was a great musician and has contributed much to the artistic life of today; but when he was a small boy, his father was eager to have him succeed as a musician and took him on a tour of the capitals of Europe, and here he received great acclaim. 2. He started on this tour when he was only seven years old; so the court and intellectuals praised him highly. 3. Although he wrote his first opera when he was only twelve, he went to Italy when he was thirteen. 4. However, he was honored by the Pope and packed the opera house in this country. 5. On most of these journeys, he was accompanied by his father and who was also a musician. 6. He returned to Salzburg and had trouble with the new archbishop, and no definite job was offered him although many places commissioned him to write music for them. 7. Wolfgang later fell in love with a girl who was the daughter of a musician; and his father, who did not want him to marry at this time, sent him to Paris in order to keep him away from the girl. 8. The young musician had many problems. 9. He composed matchless operas, symphonies, and chamber music.

71. EMPHASIS THROUGH POSITION AND ARRANGEMENT

Not all sentences are meant to be emphatic. A writer must learn to judge the tone of his work and emphasize what he wishes to have stand out in the mind of the reader. If he is dealing with material that should give a chatty, casual, or dreamy effect, emphasis is unimportant. For strength in writing, however, some attention to rules for emphasis is necessary.

71a. Place at the beginning or the end of a sentence words or ideas to be emphasized.

Every sentence, of course, has a word at the beginning and a word at the end. These words are not necessarily emphasized if the sentence follows the usual subject-verb-complement order. For special emphasis a word, phrase, or clause may be taken out of its usual position and placed at the beginning or end of the sentence.

Unemphatic: You are certainly not going skating in this weather.
Emphatic: *Certainly* you are not going skating in this weather.
In this weather you are certainly not going skating.
Unemphatic: People in England drive on the left-hand side instead of on the right-hand side.
Better: Instead of driving on the right-hand side, people in England drive *on the left.*

71b. Repeat words to be stressed.

Occasional repetition of words will emphasize their importance. Do not, however, make a habit of repetition. (See Section 51.)

Give: *Give* money when people are hungry. *Give* sympathy when a man suffers. *Give* time to participate in the affairs of your community. *Give* your whole self to help the ideal of peace.

Repetition is frequently used in business writing.

Do you want comfort? Buy at Oakleigh. Do you want refined neighbors? Buy at Oakleigh. Do you want beauty? Buy at Oakleigh. Oakleigh will satisfy every need of discriminating people.

71c. Use the active voice for emphasis.

Acceptable: The party *was enjoyed* by all of us.
Stronger: All of us *enjoyed* the party.

71d. Use periodic sentences occasionally.

A *periodic sentence* is one in which the meaning is not completed until the end. The type of sentence which could end at one or more places before the actual end of the sentence is called a *loose sentence.*

Periodic: Because city driving is very complicated, it is important to keep in the right line of traffic.

Loose: It is important to keep in the right line of traffic because city driving is very complicated.

Too frequent use of either type of sentence is not desirable. Frequent use of periodic sentences gives a distinctly formal tone to the writing.

EXERCISE 28

On your paper, rewrite the following loose sentences, making them periodic:

1. Florence Nightingale faced problems of official etiquette and red tape when she tried to improve conditions for the wounded soldiers at Scutari. 2. She was months completing jobs that should have been done in days if she had not been obliged to follow an elaborate set of rules. 3. Finally she took things into her own hands and ignored the time-consuming rules. 4. The wounded were made clean and comfortable only after great effort by this brave woman. 5. She is called the founder of the nursing profession because of the great work that she did in the Crimean War.

71e. Use balanced sentences occasionally.

A balanced sentence is one in which several parts are of similar length and structure. This type of sentence is particularly useful as a means of making contrast effective.

> Judith is fat; Marilyn is thin.
> Honesty recommends that I speak; self-interest demands that I remain silent.
> Severity breeds fear, but roughness breeds hate.

EXERCISE 29

On your paper, write a balanced sentence based on the contrast in each of the following pairs:

1. travel by automobile—travel by airplane
2. living in the city—living in the country
3. academic course—commercial or technical course
4. beauty of the sea—beauty of the mountains
5. flower garden—vegetable garden

71f. Arrange ideas in the order of their importance.

Building up to a climax is effective if the device is used only occasionally. It is especially valuable in speeches.

> I call upon you to give your money, your time, your lives, for peace.
> That man has lost his money, ruined his home, destroyed his honor.

EXERCISE 30

On your paper, rewrite each of the following sentences in climactic order:

1. The organization is dishonest, incompetent, and out-of-date.
2. Florence Nightingale found that the wounded soldiers had little care, that the hospitals were filled with a dreadful stench, and that the floors were filthy.
3. She asked for cleanliness, medical care, and ventilation.
4. She appealed to the Minister of War himself, to doctors, to nurses.
5. So great has been her accomplishment for humanity that the simple people have given her memory attention, adoration, honor.

72. VARIETY OF SENTENCE STRUCTURE

Sentences cannot be effective if they are monotonous in structure. A good writer varies the length, the word order, and the form of his sentences according to the mood of the piece of writing.

355

72a. Vary the beginnings of sentences.

The easiest way to write is to begin each sentence with the subject, but a paragraph written entirely in this style would be very dull.

The following examples show different ways of beginning sentences. Notice that there are two sentences in each pair. The first sentence in each pair begins with the subject; the second begins with some other construction.

1. Begin some sentences with a subordinating conjunction.
Sentence beginning with subject:

> Florence Nightingale gave up an easy life of wealth and position when she decided to become a nurse.

Sentence beginning with subordinating conjunction:

> *When* she decided to become a nurse, Florence Nightingale gave up an easy life of wealth and position.

2. Begin some sentences with a prepositional phrase.
Sentence beginning with subject:

> *Women* in those days were expected to spend their time on simple household tasks.

Sentence beginning with prepositional phrase:

> *In those days,* women were expected to spend their time on simple household tasks.

3. Begin some sentences with a participial phrase.
Sentence beginning with subject:

> Miss Nightingale won her point only after struggling, working, and planning for years.

Sentence beginning with participial phrase:

> *Having struggled, worked, and planned for years,* Miss Nightingale won her point.

4. Begin some sentences with an infinitive.
Sentence beginning with subject:

> She found it necessary to fight her family and public opinion in order to carry on her work.

Sentence beginning with infinitive:

> To carry on her work, she had to fight her family and public opinion.

5. Begin some sentences with an adjective. This is a device overworked in some magazines. Use it sparingly.
Sentence beginning with subject:

> Florence Nightingale, a vigorous woman, visited hospitals in many countries.

Sentence beginning with adjective:

> Vigorous and determined, Florence Nightingale visited hospitals in many countries.

72b. Avoid frequent use of *there is, there are, it is.*

Monotonous: In some of the coastal towns, there are very primitive conditions. There are mud huts shaded only by a few sick-looking palms. When there is a breeze, clouds of dust blow through the streets.

Improved: In some of the coastal towns, very primitive conditions exist. Mud huts, shaded only by a few sick-looking palms, are covered with clouds of dust whenever a breeze blows.

72c. Use some relative clauses in the middle of sentences.

Simple sentences: Miss Sauers has just returned from a trip to Paris. She is a fashion expert for the Bentz Company.

Combined: Miss Sauers, *who is a fashion expert for the Bentz Company,* has just returned from Paris.

72d. Use an occasional noun clause. (See Section 7.)

> *That some of the costumes were overloaded with decoration* surprised her very much.
>
> *That she would be able to sell these costumes in the United States* was doubtful.

72e. Use an absolute phrase at the end of a sentence. (See Section 23o.)

> All the men of the small South American town came to meet the boat, *their dogs and pigs following behind them.*
>
> The natives dived from the little boats, *their brown bodies gleaming in the sun.*

72f. Vary the length and form of sentences.

Any type of sentence used too frequently makes a piece of writing monotonous. Use a variety of simple, compound, complex, compound-complex sentences. (See Section 8.) Use some loose, some periodic, and some balanced sentences. (See Section 71.)

EXERCISE 31

On your paper, rewrite the following paragraph to make it effective. Vary the sentence structure, choosing the types of sentences that will suit the mood of the material. If it is necessary to add some connecting links, do so. The order of details may be rearranged.

There are primitive conditions in some of the coastal towns of Venezuela. They are unbelievable. These towns are not far from a sophisticated city like Caracas or a bustling commercial port like La Guaira. In some of these cities there is not a tree except the tall palm. It has only a few sick-looking fronds at the top. Dust blows in clouds whenever there is a breeze. There are one-room houses. They are made of mud. They are painted blue or pink or lavender. They have only dirt floors. Sometimes the dirt is not even leveled off. The walls have simply been thrown up over rough ground. There is little furniture. Every house has a hammock. A hammock is more comfortable than a bed. The heat is very great. Most houses have also a Singer sewing machine. The Singer men must be great salesmen. There are no tables, no chairs. The people wear few clothes. The Singer man still sells his sewing machine. Children are often naked until they are eight or nine years old. Their diets are poor. They run through the dusty streets. Scrawny dogs, pigs, and chickens play with the children. They all live together in the mud huts.

EXERCISE 32

Follow the directions in Exercise 31.

One of the most important writers of the eighteenth century was Samuel Johnson. He was the son of a bookseller. He read many of the books in his father's shop. He was desperately poor when he went to college. He was very proud. Once somebody felt sorry for Samuel and placed a new pair of shoes at the poor boy's door. Samuel spurned the gift. Many things that he did were strange, but he became practically a literary dictator of London. He is remembered today chiefly as the author of a dictionary and the founder of the famous Literary Club. Significant men in art, literature, politics, and economics were members of the club. They dined heartily and talked. The brilliance of Johnson's conversation is recorded in one of the greatest biographies in English. It is *The Life of Samuel Johnson* by James Boswell. Boswell was a member of the club. David Garrick, a great actor, Edmund Burke, a great statesman, Oliver Goldsmith, an important writer, were also members of the club. The literary influence of the club was great. All London speedily knew its opinion of a new book. All London respected its opinion. It is said that these men could cause a whole edition of a book to sell in one day.

EXERCISE 33

Follow the directions in Exercise 31.

A very exciting thing has happened in our town. A circus has set up winter quarters. The animals are being trained here for the show in the spring. The circus owners saw a chance to make some extra money and put some of their animals on a television show. The owner's granddaughter was on television with them. She is an elephant trainer. She is said to be the youngest elephant trainer in the world. Many people saw the television show. They became interested in the place where the animals are trained. They rushed to the winter quarters to watch. The circus people decided to charge a small fee for seats. The circus is making many friends, and we are having a great time.

73. ACHIEVEMENT TESTS ON THE SENTENCE

The first test is easy and deals only with the most important principles discussed in the material on the sentence. Review very carefully Sections 55–72. Then take the test. If you do well, take the more difficult test that follows.

73a. Achievement Test I.

On your paper, rewrite any of the following sentences that need revision. Make the sentences correct, clear, and effective. After each sentence, tell briefly why you have corrected it. A sentence may need more than one correction. Some sentences may be right. If you find a sentence that seems to you correct, write the number of the sentence and then write C beside the number.

Example:
  Sentence: 1. After receiving first aid, the camp officials rushed me to a hospital.
  Correction: 1. After receiving first aid, I was rushed to a hospital by the camp officials. *Dangling modifier.*

  1. The fat man made the commercial announcements then he introduced the master of ceremonies.
  2. I could not believe that I was to have a coat with a real fur collar at the age of sixteen.
  3. Do remind me to show you the picture that I took of the chief of the Indian village when you come to Boston.

4. According to my history book, in some cities the employment situation was very bad. So that many people had to stand in bread lines.

5. Some students do not go to college for the purpose of learning or to prepare for a profession.

6. For the sake of simplifying the handling of our accounts and to keep our records up to date, we should appreciate prompt payment.

7. It was the general opinion that the new law permitted the appointment of influential people to the board who could not participate in its work actively.

8. My cousin's engagement party was better than any party I have gone to.

9. At seven o'clock work begins, and we start filling the molds with ice cream after two and a half hours of steady work, there is a fifteen-minute break.

10. I was the driver of a light tank. One of the ten that were sent immediately to the front.

11. I have learned by experience to try to avoid serious arguments with good friends. Because it is very easy to ruin a friendship by arguing.

12. Even though the old lady behaves in a peculiar way does not prove she is crazy.

13. We cleaned the house and hung the curtains, and in a little while the other tasks were completed.

14. Some people gave up their freedom to gain a degree of protection. To be free from the worry of making decisions.

15. Nothing hurt me except the night before the operation I had pains in my back.

16. After calling for help many times, some coast guards heard the cries and went to rescue the children.

17. During the holidays we entertained not only our relatives but also our friends.

18. The colors are wine, navy, blue, and red. Sizes nine through fourteen.

19. Besides studying bookkeeping, we learned business organization.

20. The light on the table is much brighter than the light on my desk.

21. Being embarrassed at such an unusual situation, her face became red.

22. The first rays of dawn were reflected in the still, calm lake and shone on the rolling, barren hills which supported only dry, burnt grass with occasional groves of pine or blackjack oak which, together with the weather-beaten rocks, gave a strange appearance.

23. Doris's house is larger than any place in the community.

24. Edith, although she was terribly frightened, managed to run to the telephone.

25. In examining our correspondence carefully, there is no record of your letter.

73b. Achievement Test II.

Follow the directions for Test I.

1. The trip in the funicular railroad terrified me, I seemed to be flying in mid-air.

2. In my job I have learned to sell and work with many kinds of people.

3. I agree to drive with Walter to Maine and then that I should return alone by train.

4. Instead of campaigns, bazaars, tag days, and other energy-wasting drives which often did not produce even minimum funds for welfare work.

5. While moving to the next group of cages, a loud bark broke the quietness of the zoo.

6. The manager warned the new employees to be on time, that they should obey orders, and he expected them to be regular in attendance at work.

7. Being made of glued plywood, the life of a prefabricated house is less than a standard frame house.

8. Of the prisoners eligible for parole, sixty-three were not recommended because they were bad risks, no jobs waiting for them, or there were not enough parole officers.

9. When approaching the pylon at night, the safety zone was difficult to see.

10. Stanford's course in clear thinking will help him to evaluate what he reads and to make logical decisions.

11. Passing the stadium, the crowd reminds us of a football day.
12. The purpose of the club is to promote better understanding between the faculty and the students and for improvement of the building and campus.
13. His sources of income consist of the following: owner of a small vegetable market, and for the past four years he has been manager of a produce department.
14. Although it was a beautiful morning with the sun shining brightly, I left the house with a feeling of optimism.
15. The salesman told Mrs. Banks that the factory could not make the pair of shoes that she wanted and would she consider buying another type?
16. The principal asked me to secure for Dr. Brown and the State Department of Education the books on this list.
17. Mrs. Carter was once a great singer and applauded by the whole country.
18. I like Helen better than Eva.
19. Leon is the most popular of any boys in his class.
20. We approached the city with great interest, it was not a small city with narrow streets, as we had expected, but a large city with towering skyscrapers.
21. Although man has been able to invent such destructive forces as the atomic bomb, he has also found some new drugs which are very effective and some instruments that help greatly in wartime like the rheostat, which can locate a bullet in a man which cannot be located in the usual way.
22. Recently I read where plastic surgery really got its start in the Franco-Prussian War.
23. Carefully trained at a special school for dogs, we think that our Irish setter is the best-behaved dog in the neighborhood.
24. The building program of the hospital calls for the remodeling of the operating suite, expanded kitchen and dining room services, and beds arranged with more space between them.
25. The furniture was dusted and the ornaments washed in preparation for the party to be given tomorrow and which will celebrate the fiftieth wedding anniversary of my grandparents.

The Paragraph

A good paragraph is not a vague, haphazard jumble of ideas written just as they come to the writer's mind. It is an orderly arrangement of a number of sentences that develop a single idea. Some inexperienced writers complain that their creative quality is destroyed if they are required to have a sense of order. Actually, successful writers always plan their work carefully and revise many times. In popular magazines, newspapers, or business letters, where emphasis is placed on rapid reading, the paragraph is sometimes very short, a statement rather than a development; but writing for these fields is highly specialized and differs in many other ways besides paragraph length from the type of general writing that we are learning.

74. TOPIC SENTENCE

The first requirement of a good paragraph is that it should have a definite point to make and should include nothing which does not contribute to that point. In other words, it should have *unity*. Think of the one point that you wish to make. Then list the ideas that you will use to develop that point. A sentence which tells the reader clearly what point will be made in a paragraph is called a *topic sentence*.

These are some topic sentences from student papers:

> A big family is fun.
> The Soph Hop was a great success.
> Our city has just built a civic theater.

74a. Use a topic sentence as an aid in gaining paragraph unity.

Your writing will gain clarity if you plan carefully. Write in a clear statement each large point that you wish to make. Each of these statements can be the *topic sentence* for a paragraph. These *topic sentences* will serve as guides for the selection of material to be included in the paragraph. Test each sentence to see whether it really develops the topic sentence. Remove from the paragraph any material which does not develop it.

74b. Vary the position of the topic sentence.

You will probably have greater success if your first pieces of carefully constructed writing use a topic sentence as the first sentence in each paragraph. As you gain experience, you may use other positions for the topic sentence. When you have complete control of your thinking, you may sometimes merely keep the topic sentence in your mind and not express it at all.

1. The topic sentence is often placed at the beginning of a paragraph, as in the following selection:

> *A fire warden has to work hard.* He has an area to patrol, and he has to see that no one builds a fire within that area, except at state-designated camp grounds. You just can't go into the woods and camp anywhere, for obvious reasons of safety. Then if there is a lumbering operation going on, he has to manage to show up in the slashes, unheralded and ghost-like, often enough to deter the men from smoking in the woods. This involves a lot of walking in the course of a week and lots of patrolling around the lakes in a kicker boat. If a forest fire starts in his territory, he has to organize the fighters, and if it's in someone else's territory, he has to go over there and help. He has to cooperate with the game warden in seeing that the game laws are observed, although naturally this is a

reciprocal arrangement, and he can call on the game warden for help whenever he needs it. If someone gets lost, they both have to join the search, along with whatever talent they can scrape up around the countryside.
—From *We Took to the Woods,*

by Louise Dickinson Rich

2. The topic sentence may be placed within the paragraph, as shown in the following paragraph:

On the outer platform I met Zurabeg, an Ossetian, who had been in the steerage, too. *But Zurabeg was no greenhorn coming for the first time.* Zurabeg was an American citizen with papers to prove it, and a friend of Gospadin Buffalo Bill besides. This Zurabeg came first to America twenty years before as a trick show rider, and later he was boss cook on the road with the Gospadin Buffalo Bill. Every few years, Zurabeg, whenever he had saved enough money, went home to find a wife—but so far with no luck.
—From *Anything Can Happen,*
by George and Helen Papashvily

3. The topic sentence may be used at the beginning and at the end of a paragraph. Sometimes when a writer wishes to make his point very strong, he uses a topic sentence to begin a paragraph and says the same thing in stronger words at the end. The following selection is from *Sportsmanlike Driving,* published by the American Automobile Association.

How one uses any power which is placed in his hands discloses just what kind of person he is and the degree to which he has grown up. Any power—whether of money, office, political prominence, or a fine car—makes a foolish man look more foolish and a wise man look wiser. What we do as pedestrians may be mild enough to deceive many people, but when we get behind the wheel of a powerful car, every personal quality we have, good or bad, becomes magnified and easily observable. *Power in your hands shows up the real You!*

4. The topic sentence may be implied. In the paragraph which follows, no topic sentence is stated, but one is clearly suggested.

> Of those who drop out of college, some leave for financial reasons, and this is often tragic because these people in many cases do well in college before they have to leave. Some leave because of poor health. A few are drafted. Many leave for "personal" reasons—marriage, family mixups or just the realization that college is not the place for them.
>
> —From "How to Stay in College,"
> by Robert U. Jameson

EXERCISE 1

Here are some topic sentences which students often use as the basis of a paragraph. On your paper, write a list of the ideas which you would use to develop the topic sentence.

1. Every $\begin{Bmatrix} boy \\ girl \end{Bmatrix}$ needs some privacy.

2. My $\begin{Bmatrix} brother \\ sister \end{Bmatrix}$ and I have a very pleasant relationship.

3. A teen-ager is seldom understood by his family.

4. There are many $\begin{Bmatrix} disadvantages \\ advantages \end{Bmatrix}$ to going steady.

5. We could improve our student government.

6. We are a family of back-seat drivers.

7. Integrity is good business.

8. In an investigation of any kind, nothing can replace carefulness.

EXERCISE 2

The following paragraphs written by students lack unity. On your paper, write the topic sentence of each paragraph. Then write any sentences which should not be included because they destroy the unity. Sometimes the ideas in a paragraph do not seem to be closely related because the writer

has not shown the relationship. A new topic sentence which
would take in all of the details in the paragraph could make
the paragraph unified. If you can correct any of these
paragraphs by writing a new topic sentence, do so.

1. Knute Rockne was really a man builder, not just a football
coach. Although he started his education in Chicago, he went
to high school in South Bend, Indiana. After he was graduated
from high school, he went to Notre Dame, where his great career started. Always friendly toward his players, he frequently
arranged little gatherings at his home where the men would
discuss good sportsmanship and good football. He was always
against smoking, drinking, and swearing and taught his men to
dislike these activities. One day while flying to California, his
plane crashed; and one of our great Americans was lost.

2. A musician, even if he is famous, has little security. Most
of the musicians are uncertain today whether they will have
jobs tomorrow. Although most of them are well paid, they can
seldom save any money because they must travel from town to
town under heavy expense. The leader of an orchestra makes
much more than the players do, but he has to work much harder
for his money. He has a great many responsibilities, but if his
orchestra is a success his name will become famous. In music,
there is always a feeling of beauty and a sense of making other
people happy. The life of a musician may be rough, but there
are many compensations.

3. Some educators have said that the comics are good for children. They point to the strips that teach history or one of the
classics in literature. For a time, I remember, *Silas Marner* and
Idylls of the King were both in comic strips, but of course they
were greatly simplified, and the beauty of style was lost completely. These educators speak also of the development of the
imagination. Yet both the motion pictures and a good book
would be more valuable, for they are more stirring, more exciting. When, finally, they talk of the good habits that can be
developed through the comics, I disagree entirely. In most of
the comics that I have seen, people are involved in crime or in
some stupid, impossible adventure. I do not know one comic
strip that has anything to do with good habits. Many children

read these wild, ridiculous things because their parents read them. Then the parents are surprised if the children develop a taste for crime. There are similar arguments about the effect of television programs on children.

75. SUBSTANCE OF A PARAGRAPH

A paragraph may have details which stick rigidly to the topic sentence and yet be very dull. The details that make the substance of the paragraph should be carefully chosen.

75a. Try to avoid stating the obvious.

Your writing is an attempt to communicate some fact or idea to another person. If the fact or idea is already well known to your readers, there is no point in communicating it. A student recently wrote the following paragraph. He was discussing a newspaper which he read regularly.

> The newspaper has several kinds of headlines. Among them are the main headings and the subheads. The main headlines are found at the top of the page.

Such information is common knowledge. The student has added nothing to his readers' experience by what he has communicated.

75b. Choose interesting details.

Inexperienced writers think that they must state every detail involved in a story or in the discussion of an idea. Choose only the interesting or important details. Then develop them fully.

Dull: When we entered the store, a salesgirl approached us. "May I help you?" she said. I told her that I wanted to buy a coat. Since she had nothing that I liked, we left the store and went to another one.

These details are not interesting, but by using his observation, the writer might have written an amusing or entertaining account of a shopping trip. Colorful details describing the store, the people, and the goods would have been more interesting.

Dull: After a very exciting day, we set out for home. On the way we sang some songs, and Leo told a few jokes. Then we reached my house, and the bus driver let me off in front of my door.

These are dull details. How might the writer have improved on them?

75c. Develop ideas.

A paragraph is usually not simply a statement. It is a development. Neither hazy generalizations nor mere repetition of the central thought builds good paragraphs. After you have phrased the topic sentence, draw upon your own experience and the experience of others as revealed in newspapers, magazines, books, and conversation. Make use of your own imagination, observation, curiosity. Then *discuss* the idea stated in the topic sentence.

76. METHODS OF PARAGRAPH DEVELOPMENT

Paragraphs may be developed in a number of ways, depending upon the subject matter to be presented, the mood of the material, and the effect that the writer wishes to obtain. Using a variety of methods to develop a number of paragraphs is often desirable. Sometimes a whole paragraph will be developed by one method; at other times, the writer may use several methods in one paragraph. Some of the most common methods of developing an idea are explained in this section.

76a. Develop a paragraph by details.

In the paragraph that follows, the topic sentence is the first sentence. After the writer has said that there was considerable ceremony in the [life-saving] course, she presents details to show of what that ceremony consisted.

> There was quite a little ceremony connected with this part of the course. Miss Folgil, and some lucky creature named as timekeeper and armed with a stop watch, rowed the prospective victim out to deep water. The pupil, dressed in high, laced tennis shoes, long stockings, heavy bloomers, and a middy blouse, then stood poised at the end of the boat. When the timekeeper yelled "Go!" the future boon to mankind dived into the water and, while holding her breath under the surface, unlaced her shoes and stripped down to her bathing suit. Miss Folgil never explained what connection, if any, this curious rite had with saving human lives.
> —From *My Sister Eileen,* by Ruth McKenney

76b. Develop a paragraph by definition.

The following paragraph is developed by definition. In the topic sentence, the writer states that there are two kinds of snobbishness. The rest of the paragraph defines these two kinds of snobbishness.

> There are two kinds of snobbishness. That of the man who has had a good many opportunities and looks down on those who lack them is recognized by all. The other kind of snobbishness is rarely understood, yet it is real. It is that of the self-made man who glories in his success in overcoming difficulties and admires greatly people who have achieved the things he considers of importance.
> —From *This I Remember,* by Eleanor Roosevelt

76c. Develop a paragraph by example or illustration.

In this paragraph, the writer is discussing integrity in historians and scholars. As an example of what he means, he tells of an incident in the life of Sir Walter Raleigh.

> Their pattern of delusion (believing rumor) is so brilliant that even the most objective historians and scholars,

attempting to record the sum totals of their own investigations, frequently find themselves hypnotized by startling events which never happened and revealing conclusions which were never drawn. All too few have had the integrity of Sir Walter Raleigh, who, imprisoned in the Tower of London, was writing the second part of his *History of the World* when, one day, his work was interrupted by the noise of a fight in the courtyard below his cell. Through the barred windows, Raleigh carefully watched each detail of the incident. The following day he was visited by a friend who had been in the brawl. And, upon discussing the entire event, Raleigh discovered that his own version of the fight was incorrect throughout. Realizing that he was unable to present an accurate account of one little incident, Sir Walter Raleigh abandoned the writing of his *History of the World* and, in disgust, destroyed the manuscript.

—From *Affairs of Dame Rumor,* by David Jacobson

76d. Develop a paragraph by comparison or contrast.

The following paragraph is developed by contrasting the control of infection among the wounded in World War I with that in World War II.

During World War I, more than three-fourths of the men who sustained abdominal wounds died as a result of infection; but infection was almost completely absent following the Pearl Harbor attack. There were a few amputations required, where limbs had actually been hit by shell or bomb fragments, but none because of infections. Yet during 1914–1918 at one hospital 47 percent of the amputations were caused by infections of gas gangrene alone. In December, 1941, wounds healed quickly and cleanly. Even though their injuries would undoubtedly have been fatal in an earlier period, the men recovered rapidly and were soon anxious and able to join the fight once more.

—From *Science Remakes Our World,* by James Stokley

76e. Develop a paragraph by several methods combined.

In the following paragraph, the second sentence introduces an example to explain what has been stated in the topic sentence. This example is composed of two parts that establish a contrast. The last two sentences contain details.

> Another advantage of fluorescent light is that, when necessary, it can be kept at low intensity, and since the ultraviolet that excites it is invisible, the total amount of light is also very low. For instance, in a motion picture theater, you may want to have a sign giving, possibly, emergency instructions. If the sign is printed in the usual way, the whole card must be illuminated, and a great deal of light is reflected from the background. But the Continental Lithographic Corporation, in Cleveland, has introduced a line of fluorescent inks. A sign thus painted can be flooded with enough ultra violet so that the letters shine with sufficient brightness to be read; but no other light is seen. Such a method is useful for blackouts, as has been demonstrated in England. Road signs, too, or even a guide line down the middle of the road, might be painted with phosphorus.
> —From *Science Remakes Our World,* by James Stokley

EXERCISE 3

In his book, *Mirror for Man,* Professor Clyde Kluckhohn discusses the American character. Some of his topic sentences follow. Using three of these topic sentences, write three unified paragraphs. Develop each one by a different method or combination of methods. In the margin of your paper, indicate which method or methods you have used in each paragraph.

1. All Europeans are struck by American attitudes toward women.
2. Even the most bitter critics of the United States have conceded us material generosity.

3. Americans have been shy about expressing their deepest convictions.

4. Countless European observers have been impressed by enthusiasm as a typically American quality.

5. Griping is a characteristic American trait.

6. Americans are devoted to the underdog.

7. Americans are interested in devices or gadgets.

8. American friends tend to be casual and transitory.

9. In America, having a good time is an important part of life.

10. Americans love bigness.

77. ORDER OF IDEAS

When the writer has selected his ideas, excluding those that will destroy unity, and has decided on his method of development, his next problem is the arrangement of those ideas in some acceptable order. Such an arrangement will aid the coherence of the paragraph. What the arrangement should be depends upon the material itself and the effect which the writer wishes to produce. There is no standard rule. However, there is one essential of order: it requires progress, a forward movement of some sort.

Notice the disorder in the paragraph which follows:

1. A hot rod can also be called a custom-made car. 2. By this we mean that it has a custom-made engine and a special body. 3. Most hot rods are built around stock parts from standard model cars. 4. They can do 90 to 100 miles an hour and get 20 or more miles on a gallon of gasoline. 5. Most of the parts from which they are made are as old as fifteen or twenty years. 6. The car which holds the speed record can go 189 miles an hour. 7. "Souping up" the engine for high speed is the most important step in making a hot rod. 8. The motor is torn down, and the block is adjusted for an easier flow of fuel to the combustion chamber. 9. Ideas which may appear on future automobiles are now being developed by hot rodders. 10. If the car is to be used for ordinary driving, the motor is adjusted to get 140

miles an hour; but if the car is used for racing, the original horsepower is almost doubled. 11. The latter cars do not work well at low speeds, burn gas at a high rate, and wear out in one-tenth of the mileage expected of a stock engine.

EXERCISE 4

The student who wrote the preceding paragraph did not arrange his ideas in logical order. The paragraph deals with three points: 1. details of building hot rods (sentences 1, 2, 3, 5, 7, 8); 2. speed (sentences 4, 6, 10, 11); 3. outlook for the future (sentence 9). On your paper, rewrite the paragraph, putting related statements together in a logical sequence. It will probably be necessary to change the wording in some sentences.

EXERCISE 5

As you did in Exercise 4, group together related ideas in the following paragraph written by a student. If any sentence seems to destroy the unity, omit it.

1. Some people consider jazz the one original contribution that America has made to modern music. 2. Jazz is said to have originated in New Orleans. 3. Some musicians would come together and improvise countermelodies on a clarinet while a pianist or a cornetist played the tune. 4. Europeans never quite caught the secret of playing jazz. 5. The early jazz players performed on river boats, at private parties, and in taverns. 6. To most people, Louis Armstrong is the true king of jazz. 7. He formed a band which he called "Louis Armstrong and His Hot Five." 8. Although many people tried to imitate him, there was only one Louis Armstrong. 9. In the early days of jazz, people thought of it only as a product of the Mississippi delta region. 10. Soon it attracted the attention of serious musicians. 11. When it was taken to Europe, it was frequently looked down upon, but people liked to dance to its fascinating rhythm.

EXERCISE 6

Follow the directions in Exercise 5.

1. One of the most interesting features of eighteenth-century London was the coffee houses. 2. The places were really clubs for men only. 3. Men drank their coffee and talked. 4. If a man was interested in talking about politics, he could find a Tory coffee house or a Whig coffee house; if he preferred conversations on literature, fashions, society gossip, he could easily find the appropriate group of people interested in similar topics. 5. Some of the women objected to the coffee house because their husbands were so often away from home. 6. Out of these coffee houses grew an interest in clever conversation. 7. Soon society and literature were affected by this development. 8. In the coffee house, a man could read, write, or paint to amuse himself. 9. Some coffee houses even had their own glee clubs. 10. The women disliked the coffee house because women could not go out alone, and their husbands were too well entertained in the coffee house to take them out. 11. A few of the coffee houses had gambling and auction rooms. 12. The alehouse keepers disliked the coffee house. 13. They now found that they were losing business. 14. It is said that through this eighteenth-century place of amusement, England developed essays, novels, and poetry.

EXERCISE 7

Follow the directions in Exercise 5.

1. Personal habits can be very disturbing. 2. One year at college I had a roommate who always left her facial tissues wherever she happened to be when she used them. 3. Bits of paper with lipstick on them littered the dressing table, decorated the desk, and even appeared on the bed. 4. Apparently she had never heard of a wastebasket. 5. She was careless about her clothes. 6. Because she was always too tired or in too great a hurry to hang them in the cupboard, dresses were thrown over a chair back or dropped on the bed. 7. They were left in little piles on the floor. 8. Then, with a complete lack of considera-

tion, she played the radio whenever she was in the room. 9. I often found it impossible to study because jazzy music or jokes distracted my attention. 10. She was careless about lipstick and powder. 11. Our furniture always had lipstick stains on it, and a fine mist of powder rose to meet me each time that I put something on the dressing table. 12. When she was ready to go out for the evening, she always wanted to borrow my clothes because hers were too wrinkled to wear. 13. In spite of all this untidiness, she was very clean, but even her methods of keeping clean were offensive to me. 14. Whenever she had a free moment, she would wash a blouse or some handkerchiefs and string them up across the room to dry so that I never came into the room without seeing wash or having wet clothes strike me in the face. 15. She was a great girl for noise. 16. She said she felt lonesome if there was no sound in the room. 17. A background of music from the radio, her own humming, or a constant stream of conversation filled the room at all times.

EXERCISE 8

Don't write a friendly letter carelessly. Courtesy to your friend requires some thought before you write and some attention to the general principles of good writing. The following letter shows haste and carelessness which are a discourteous response to the kindness of a friend. On your paper, rewrite the letter, putting related ideas together, combining sentences, and using connecting links.

Dear Laura,

I never thought I could enjoy a weekend in the country as much as I did. After weeks in the heat of the city, I was glad to feel the country air. It was interesting to watch the animals. I will miss gathering the eggs. It was nice of you to ask Mike to take me to the barn dance. We surely had a wonderful time. I loved your dog and your horse. The dog's tricks are very amusing, and your horse is so gentle that even I could ride him I'll never forget the swimming party and your pleasant friends. Thank you for a perfect visit.

78. TRANSITIONAL DEVICES

An orderly arrangement of details will help to make the paragraph clear. Another method of obtaining clarity is the use of transitional, or connective, expressions. Our own processes of thought are so familiar to us that we are likely to forget that our readers do not understand the relationship between our ideas unless we show them what that relationship is.

78a. Use transitional expressions within the sentence, between sentences, and between paragraphs. Be careful to use the appropriate expressions.

To add some ideas: in addition, moreover, another way, a second method, besides, also
To contrast ideas: but, yet, nevertheless, however, still, in contrast, otherwise, on the other hand
To compare ideas: like, similar
To show purpose: in order to, for this reason
To show result: therefore, as a result, consequently, thus
To show time: then, a little later, immediately, meantime, afterwards, in those days, earlier

Notice the use of transitional expressions in the following sentences:

> There are today, *for instance,* 12,000 more steel fabricators—predominantly small—than there were at the eve of the first world war.
> —Peter Drucker
> Progress, *however,* is only another word for civilization.
> —*Saturday Review of Literature*

78b. Repeat key words.

Notice the repetition of key words, which have been italicized, in the following sentences:

> We Americans are victims of the pernicious notion that good books are beyond the comprehension of the aver-

age *mind.* But millions of average *minds* have compre-
hended them in ages past.

—Milton Mayer

78c. Use demonstrative adjectives *this* and *that*, and pronouns *he, she, they, it* to refer to nouns in preceding sentences.

Pronouns and demonstrative adjectives used to make transitions have been italicized in the following examples:

A farmer should have a thorough knowledge of crop rotation. *This* knowledge will save him money on many occasions.

Unfortunately, our forefathers were destructive of natural resources. *They* moved through a wealthy land and left it ruined to seek still other fields.

Notice the transitional expressions in the following paragraph:

Hot rods are useful in many ways. *First,* they give pleasure to their owners because of their fine performance. *This pleasure* is experienced most keenly in the stock car races in which *hot rod* owners often participate. *Then, too,* they are valuable to police, for their greater power and speed make catching a criminal an easier job. *But speed and power are not their only advantages.* Some West Coast taxi companies use *them* for economy, and a few commercial vehicle operators have found that the cars can move heavier loads on steep grades. *Undoubtedly,* they have contributed something to the efficiency of automobiles.

Notice the italicized sentence in the middle of the preceding paragraph. Here the whole sentence is used as a means of moving from one idea to another.

379

78d. Transitional expressions are especially important between paragraphs. Without these expressions, each paragraph seems a separate unit instead of part of a whole.

Notice the transitional expression (italicized here) in these topic sentences from five successive paragraphs from William Beebe's *High Jungle*.

1. One of the unexpected aspects of the wild life of Rancho Grande was the scarcity of ants.
2. *Nevertheless*, we soon learned that when we wanted *ants*, whether singly or in tens of thousands, it was a simple matter to find *them*.
3. The leaf cutters (*ants*) or attas are vegetarians.
4. The army *ants*, or ecitons, are nomads.
5. The two types of *ants* correspond to similar human aggregations or groups.

EXERCISE 9

Reread one of the revised paragraphs that you wrote in Exercises 5, 6, 7, and 8. Have you used transitional expressions to show the relation of details? Add transitional expressions if they will improve the paragraph. Do not, however, use too many such expressions. The result should be natural, not forced.

EXERCISE 10

Select from these topics three which appeal to you. Write an interesting topic sentence for one phase of each topic. List the points that you wish to make in each paragraph. Write a unified, coherent paragraph for each topic sentence, using transitional expressions where they are needed.

1. Family Reunions
2. Blind Dates

79. PROPORTION AND LENGTH

There is no general rule for the length of a paragraph. In a well-written article designed to give information, the paragraph is the development of a unit of thought, and its length may vary from eighty to two hundred words. If the development seems to run to more than two hundred words, the paragraph will be a bit heavy; and it might be wise to divide it. There must, however, be no arbitrary slicing in half. The division should come at the end of an idea.

79a. Adjust the length of a paragraph to the idea and the purpose.

A series of long paragraphs makes heavy reading. Short, choppy paragraphs, on the other hand, give the reader the feeling that the ideas are not developed. Writers for newspapers and magazines often use very short paragraphs to make the ideas stand out. However, such writers are often simply stating facts, not developing ideas. Businessmen also are likely to use short paragraphs in business letters.

79b. Adjust the length of the paragraph in proportion to its importance in the whole article.

Do not deal at length with unimportant ideas or treat lightly important thoughts. In a five-hundred-word theme,

for example, do not write a long paragraph that is merely introductory. See Section 82a–c for further discussion of the division of material into paragraphs.

80. MECHANICS OF THE PARAGRAPH

Neatness and order are important in every paper.

80a. Indent the first line of every paragraph.

The first line of every paragraph is indented except in business letters that are written in block form. The paragraph then begins at the left margin.

80b. Do not leave part of a line blank unless a new paragraph is to begin on the next line.

Keep the margins to the left and right as symmetrical as possible.

80c. In writing dialogue, use a new paragraph for each new speaker.

Notice the paragraphing in the following dialogue:

> For hours we drove through the beautiful country until finally our chauffeur pointed out the object of the trip.
>
> "That," he said, "is the Great Pitch Lake. When even large quantities are taken out, the holes close right up again."
>
> "Now that solves a problem that has puzzled me all my life," said Jane. "This is just like the streets of Baltimore when the temperature has been ninety-eight degrees for several days. I always wondered why the city government chose that stuff for pavements. Now it's clear. If a hole comes in the street, it closes right up again."
>
> "Oh no, miss," the guide said seriously, "I don't think that will happen on a street."

The Whole Theme

Before you attempt to write a theme, you should master the technique of writing a paragraph; for a theme is simply a number of paragraphs carefully joined to present a unified whole. All of the principles of unity and coherence discussed in the section on the paragraph are important for the theme. First, of course, you must choose an interesting topic.

81. CHOICE OF TOPIC

Students frequently complain that they do not know what to write about. Usually their lack of ideas is a result of the fact that they are not observant. Life is filled with interesting things about which a student could write if he would keep all his senses alert. Every day you see something amusing or exciting or alarming. Every day you hear people express opinions with which you do not agree. Then out of your own experiences, you develop an attitude toward life. All of these experiences may be interesting subjects for writing. The subject that you choose should be one about which you really want to write. For that reason, the topics presented here are only suggestive. Some of them are too broad for a short theme. They have purposely been expressed in broad, general terms so that you may choose any phase of the subject which seems interesting to you.

81a. Use your own thought and experience.

In everybody's life there is material enough for a novel. Here are some general topics which may suggest to you specific experiences or thoughts of your own:

Moving to a new
neighborhood
An embarrassing
moment
Fighting a bully
I learn to read
A travel experience
My family

My ideas of friend-
ship
An unusual neighbor
Observance of Yom
Kippur or Christmas
The young people's
group at church

81b. Use the thought and experience of others.

Talk with your parents and friends about experiences that
they have had. Your parents will enjoy telling you of their
youth. Classroom discussions are also an excellent source of
material. The following topics may suggest subjects for you
to write about:

My mother's girlhood
in ——
An old seaman
Our family doctor

My aunt's education in
Sweden
Love at first sight
Dating customs differ

81c. Use current problems.

Other sources of material are your reactions to newspaper
and magazine articles on such subjects as the following:

A candidate for public office
The new interest in science in the schools
Parity prices in our area
Voting as a duty
Effect of political bosses on elections in ——
Our town's largest problem
——'s problem of slum clearance
Our plans for making our city beautiful
Keeping a clean community
Prizes for gardens
Our town and the arts
We build a civic center

81d. Use a motion picture, a play, a book, or a magazine article that has interested you. Discuss the ideas presented and give your reaction.

The following topics may suggest ways of using your reading or theatergoing as a source of subject matter for your themes:

> Underprivileged children
> New housing
> Social injustice
> Safe driving
> The effect of television on motion picture making
> Figures can lie
> The novel discusses the basis of happiness
> The play deals with jealousy
> The novelist Thackeray once said, "There are no people so cruel as the young."
> The play shows that a marriage faces problems if the husband knows that his wife is superior to him.
> Young people and conformity

81e. Use ideas from the literature read in school.

> Understanding myself
> Loneliness
> Understanding an eccentric person
> Poe's development of mood
> Changing heroes and heroines
> Brutus's mistakes
> Coincidence in novel plots
> Building realistic characters
> Macbeth: the failure of an ambitious man
> Is Lady Macbeth the cause of the tragedy?
> Dickens's use of humor
> Influence of a child on a man's life
> Choosing a husband
> Use of the supernatural in *The Rime of the Ancient Mariner*

81f. Use a quotation from literature.

All the world's a stage.

If winter comes, can spring be far behind?

Many a flower is born to blush unseen and waste its sweetness on the desert air.

To live in mankind is far more than to live in a name.

Heaven gives its glimpses only to those not in position to look too close.

Good fences make good neighbors.

There is properly no history; only biography.

The race is not to the swift, nor the battle to the strong.

81g. Choose a topic which can be handled adequately.

It is impossible to write an effective theme of three hundred words on a subject which would require three thousand words. It is possible, however, to discuss in a short theme one phase of a vital topic or to give one's own reaction to this one phase. A thorough discussion of the topic "Social Injustice," for example, would require a book or several books; but your reaction to social injustice as you see it in your neighborhood could be handled in a short theme. The American Automobile Association has discussed "Safe Driving" in a series of five pamphlets, but you can write a short theme about *Errors in Driving Made by Teen-agers* or *Points for Drivers to Remember* or *Good Sportsmanship at the Wheel.*

EXERCISE 1

Be alert to interesting things that happen in the next few days. Talk to other people about things in which they are interested. Read books, newspapers, and magazines. Then write five titles which you think could be used for themes of two or three hundred words, based on your observation, your reading, and your conversation.

386

82. OUTLINES

No theme can be a success without a plan. We all think haphazardly when we are trying to gather materials for a piece of written work. Related ideas do not necessarily come to our minds in order.

82a. Choose a core thought.

A written discussion sometimes fails to make its point because the writer has not established clearly in his own mind just what point he wishes to present. He has a general notion of the topic he will discuss but has not decided on a specific point of view. In the outline that follows, no clear point is made.

HOUSES I HAVE LIVED IN

I. Our four-room apartment
  A. Location
  B. Things I remember
    1. Strange sounds in halls
    2. The wallpaper in my bedroom
II. Our house in New Jersey
  A. Description
  B. Advantages
    1. Room to play
    2. No noise
    3. Garden
III. My parents and their dream house
  A. Location
  B. Description
  C. My departure for college
IV. The row house
  A. Location
  B. Description
  C. Why it was selected

This outline shows simply four different houses. Nothing ties them together; nor does the reader see any basic point in discussing them. Paragraphs I and II seem to suggest that the paper may deal with disadvantages of apartment living and reasons for seeking a house, but paragraphs III and IV do not pursue this idea. The point might be ironical; i.e., all his life the writer and his parents sought their dream house, but just when it was found, the student went off to college and was obliged to live in one rented room in a row house. Yet this point is introduced incidentally and never mentioned in paragraphs I and II. Other possible core thoughts might be (1) effects of the houses on the writer, (2) expanding and contracting (humorous treatment), (3) the family's approach to an ideal (paragraph IV could not be included).

If a point of view is selected and materials are arranged around it, the writing will be more interesting and much clearer. A statement of the point of view should be written at the top of the outline.

EXERCISE 2

Choose five topics from those listed in the early part of this chapter (Section 81). Write a core thought for each.

82b. Analyze your material.

The second step in making plans is to examine the material to see which points go together and what method of development would be best. In order to remember all of the ideas that come to your mind, use a work sheet. As you think through the topic "Good Sportsmanship at the Wheel," these ideas might come to your mind:

1. Disobeying traffic regulations
2. Consideration of others
3. Careful use of horn
4. Recklessness
5. Knowing the power of a car
6. Tolerance of others
7. Driving when intoxicated or sick
8. Taking chances
9. Showing off
10. Self-control

82c. Arrange related ideas under appropriate headings.°

An examination of the ideas listed in Section 82b shows that they fall naturally under three topics:

 I. Fouls in driving (topics 1,4,7,8,9)
 II. Courtesy in driving (topics 2,3,6,10)
III. Knowledge of the power of a car (topic 5)

82d. Use subtopics under main headings to develop ideas.

I. Fouls in driving
    A. Infractions of traffic regulations
        1. Passing on hill
        2. Going through stop lights
        3. Turning corners without signal

82e. Write the outline.

The following outline is written in topics. It could also be written in sentences. The writer should be careful, however, not to mix the topic and sentence methods.

GOOD SPORTSMANSHIP AT THE WHEEL

 I. Fouls in driving
    A. Infractions of traffic regulations
        1. Passing on hill
        2. Going through stop lights
        3. Turning corners without signal
        4. Taking right of way
    B. Bad behavior on road
        1. Being reckless
        2. Showing off
    C. Driving in unfit condition
    D. Driving in unfit car

° The material for the outline is based on Chapter IV of the *Sportsmanlike Driving* pamphlet "Driver and Pedestrian Responsibilities," published by the American Automobile Association.

II. Courtesy in driving
   A. Consideration of other people
      1. Drivers
      2. Pedestrians
   B. Tolerance of others
      1. Poor drivers
      2. Beginners
      3. Show-offs
   C. Careful use of horn
   D. Self-control
III. Knowledge of the power of a car
   A. Knowing relationship of speed to force of impact
   B. Knowing relationship of speed to stopping distance

82f. Notice the form of a good outline.

1. Write the first word of each topic with a capital letter.
2. Indent headings so that those of parallel rank are under each other. See example of form in Section 82e.
3. Use some consistent scheme like the following to show which ideas are to be used to develop other ideas.

I.
   A.
      1.
      2.
         a.
         b.
   B.
      1.
      2.
         a.
         b.
            (1)
            (2)
II.
   A.
   B.
   C.

4. As far as possible, keep topics of equal rank in parallel form.

> *Weak:* A. Consideration of other people
> B. To tolerate others
> *Improved:* A. Consideration of other people
> B. Tolerance of others

5. Do not permit one topic to overlap another.

> *Weak:* I. History of jazz
> II. The Original Dixieland Jazz Band
> *Improved:* I. Origin of jazz
> II. The Original Dixieland Jazz Band

6. Avoid the following topics:

> I. Introduction
> II. Body
> III. Conclusion

An outline containing specific topics provides a more useful plan than does an outline with these three general heads. In a short theme, the proportion is destroyed if a whole paragraph is used to introduce the subject or conclude it. A sentence or two at the beginning of a paragraph will serve to open the whole topic of the paper.

82g. Avoid using an organization that cuts the topic in half.

> I. Advantages
> II. Disadvantages
> III. My opinion

In this organization "My opinion" really overlaps both I and II and should be discussed as points are presented. When advantages and disadvantages have been given, there is nothing more to say. This is a very loose type of organization.

82h. Check the outline.

Does each subtopic develop the main topic under which it appears?

Does any topic overlap another?

EXERCISE 3

Rewrite these outlines according to Section 82a–h.

GOING STEADY

I. Conveniences of going steady
   A. To the boy and girl
      1. Date sure
      2. Chance to show off before friends
      3. Less expense
      4. Sense of belonging
   B. To parents
      1. No worry about child's friends
      2. Opportunity to encourage good standards of behavior
II. Disadvantages of going steady
   A. To girl involved
      1. No chance to know many boys
      2. Difficulties of establishing new contacts if the relationship is broken
      3. Loss of girl friends when much time is spent with one boy
      4. Loss of outside interests
   B. To parents
      1. Possible dislike of boy or girl chosen
      2. Worry about early marriage
III. Individuals
   A. Types of people who should go steady
   B. Types who should not go steady
   C. Reasons for parental opposition

VARIETY'S THE SPICE OF LIFE

I. My opinion of going steady
   A. Variety's the spice of life

   B. Everyone else does it
    1. A fad
    2. Keeping in the swirl of things
   C. Too young
  II. Defects and disadvantages of going steady
   A. Lack of interest in others
    1. Confides in steady
    2. Loss of valuable friends
   B. Difficulty in meeting new people
   C. Ability to get along with others
   D. Choosing a husband
    1. Familiar with one personality
    2. Type of man wanted
 III. Controversial topic among parents and teen-agers
   A. Parents are against it
    1. Fun to date several boys
    2. In their day
   B. Relationship
    1. Not actually in love
    2. Can become serious
   C. My point of view

THE CONFORMIST AND THE INDIVIDUALIST

  I. Thinking
   A. Conformist
    1. Does not think
    2. Leans toward majority
    3. Accepts anything
    4. Adjusts to group
   B. Individualist
    1. Impression means nothing
    2. Suits himself
    3. Logical
  II. Way of life
   A. Conformist
    1. Copy next person
    2. Not dare be different
    3. Counted out of society
    4. Style

B. Individualist
1. Does what he pleases
2. Not always successful
3. Happier
4. More contributions

III. Opinion
   A. Conformist
      1. Follower
      2. No advancement
   B. Individualist
      1. Leader
      2. Seeks knowledge
      3. Searches for new and better ways

OPTIMISM AND PESSIMISM

I. Optimism—pro and con
   A. Good points
      1. Happy outlook on life
      2. Confidence in the future
      3. Forgiving attitude
   B. Bad points
      1. Overconfidence
      2. Often disappointed
      3. Cannot see the bad things about any person or anything
   C. Danger of extremes
      1. Will accept something on its good points and forget the bad
      2. Will not accept advice when it concerns something happy or sad

II. Pessimism—pro and con
   A. Good points
      1. Seldom disappointing
      2. Promotes cautiousness
   B. Bad points
      1. Dark outlook on life
      2. Seldom take chances
      3. Overcautiousness
   C. Danger of extremes

      1. Distrust
      2. Constant worry
III. Comparison
    A. Both have good and bad points
    B. Danger in going to extremes in either one
    C. Optimism is the better of the two but it is the harder to come by

WHO SAYS THE 1920's WERE BETTER?

  I. Patterns in our culture today
    A. Developments in the past decade
      1. Atomic devices
      2. Modern jargon
      3. Domestic changes
      4. Medical progress and discoveries
  II. Patterns of life in the 1920's
    A. Social conditions
      1. Gang rule
      2. Prohibition
      3. Lack of justice
III. Comparisons or eras
    A. Similar problems in both periods
      1. Unlawful drinking
      2. Hoodlums at war in streets
    B. Other similarities
      1. Dress
      2. Dance
IV. Conclusion
    A. Improper perspective by contemporaries
    B. Superior evaluation by posterity

THE CONFORMING NONCONFORMISTS

  I. The "crime" of nonconformity
    A. Areas of pressure
  II. The conformity of adolescents
    A. Areas of adolescent conformity
III. Conclusion
    A. Hope for the future

EXERCISE 4

Write outlines for three of the topics that you listed in Exercise 1.

EXERCISE 5

Write outlines for some phase of each of two topics selected from Section 81a–f.

83. BEGINNINGS AND ENDINGS OF THEMES

The beginning of a theme should attract attention; that is, make the paper look interesting enough for the reader to want to continue reading. Sometimes a little anecdote or a bit of striking conversation will help. Effective endings summarize the composition.

Beginning: Mark Twain once said, "Always do right. This will gratify some people and astonish the rest."

Ending: After all my efforts, I could only hope that more of my friends were gratified than astonished.

EXERCISE 6

Write the opening and closing sentences for the themes that you outlined in Exercises 4 and 5.

84. MANUSCRIPT FORM

Your teacher may give you special directions for preparing a manuscript. Neatness will always be required. The following suggestions may help you:

1. Write the title in the center of the top line of the first page of your theme. Capitalize all important words. Don't capitalize prepositions, conjunctions, or articles unless they are at the beginning or end of a title or consist of five or more letters.
2. Write in ink or use a typewriter. No teacher should be asked to read a paper written in pencil.
3. Number and arrange the pages in correct order.

4. Unless you are given other instructions, fold the paper lengthwise and on the outside write your name, your class, the date, and the title of the composition.
5. Leave a margin of at least an inch on the left side of each page.
6. Do not use brackets or parentheses to cancel a word. Erase the word.

85. REVISION AND PROOFREADING

No paper should ever be submitted until it has been carefully revised and proofread.

1. Check spelling.
2. Check punctuation.
3. Check grammar.
4. Check unity, coherence, emphasis.
5. Check effectiveness.

EXERCISE 7

Write a theme based on one of the outlines which you made for Exercise 4 or 5. When your teacher has indicated the errors, write a second theme, proofreading carefully in order to avoid the errors which you made in the first one. Remember that the outline is the plan, and the theme should follow it. After making the outline, be sure to follow it when you write your theme.

The Research
Paper

The research paper is also sometimes called a term paper. It is usually from two to six thousand words long and requires reading source materials, taking careful notes, and organizing these notes into a unified whole. The problems of the actual writing are the same whether you write a short theme or a research paper, but the preparation for the writing of the latter requires a different and more involved procedure. Skill in the use of the library and in note taking is necessary. (See Section 88.) This skill will be valuable, too, when you must make a *report* for your club or a business report. Before you begin the work on a long paper, learn to find material in the library.

86. USING THE LIBRARY

In some libraries, most of the books are on open shelves easily accessible to the students. In large libraries, however, it is necessary to store some of the books in stacks away from the main reading room. Usually only the librarian and perhaps some advanced students who have special permission go to these stacks, but the librarian will get books for you if you identify them properly.

86a

86a. Use of the card catalogue.

In most libraries, every nonfiction book has a number that tells the student or the librarian on which shelf the book can be found. These numbers are on library cards (3 inches by 5 inches) in small drawers which have labels in alphabetical arrangement. The cards are filed alphabetically. Many books are listed on three cards: one with the author's name at the top, one with the name of the book at the top, and one with a subject classification at the top. If, then, you want to find books by a certain author, you look for his name in the card catalogue. All of his books will be together in alphabetical arrangement. If you know the title of a book, you can find a card for it. If you have simply a subject on which you would like to find information, you look in the appropriate drawer for the subject. Subject cards often contain references to related subjects.

Notice the three types of library cards on page 400. These three cards are for the same book. The first card has the author's name at the top. The other two show the same book listed by subject and by title.

In an upper corner, usually the left, of each card is the call number. Before you go to the card catalogue, secure some call slips. If you do not see any, ask the librarian to give you some. Write the name of the book, the author, and the call number on a call slip (a separate slip for each book). The slip can then be used to locate the book.

If the library is small, you will notice headings on the shelves. There will probably be a science section with numbers 500–599, a literature section with numbers 800–899, a history section with numbers 900–999. It is not likely that you will learn all the numbers, but you will soon learn the sections in which are found the types of books that you use most frequently. Do not hesitate to ask the librarian to explain the system of the library and the rules by which it operates.

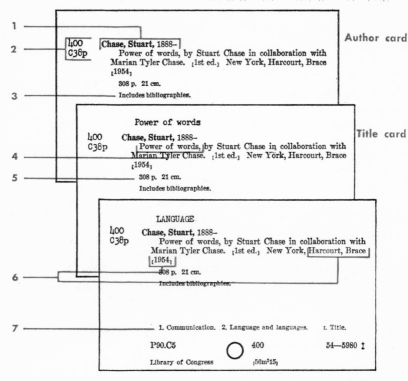

1. Author and date of his birth
2. Call number
3. A bibliography is included
4. Title
5. Number of pages
6. Publisher and date of publication
7. Other headings under which the book is listed

If the library is large, there will be special rooms for books of each type. Ask to see the chart of the library so that you can find the room that you need.

EXERCISE 1

Your teacher may divide your class into four groups, each of which will be responsible for one of the four assignments that follow.

1. (a) Find out what books by Mark Twain are in your library. On a separate index card, write the title of each of these books, the author's name, and the call number or identification used by your library. (b) Find out what books on baseball your library has and list each on a separate card as in (a). (c) List on index cards the titles, authors' names, and call numbers of five French or Spanish books in your library.

2. (a) Copy on index cards the titles, names of authors, and call numbers of five books on history in your library. (b) List as in (a) the books that your library has on conservation. (c) Examine some of the books in the fiction section and list as in (a) three which seem particularly interesting and worthwhile for leisure reading.

3. (a) On index cards, list the titles, names of authors, and call numbers of all books on banking that you can find in the card catalogue in your library. (b) List as in (a) five books on biology in your library. (c) List as in (a) all the books by Sinclair Lewis in your library.

4. (a) What books has your library on airplanes? On separate index cards list their titles, names of authors, and call numbers. (b) List as in (a) five biographies in your library that you think would be interesting to read. (c) Here are the titles of two books that boys enjoy very much; if your library has them, list them on cards as in (a): *Conquest of Space, Under the Red Sea Sun.* If these books are not in your library, find two books on travel or science that would interest your group and list the books as in (a).

86b. General reference books.

Reference books such as encyclopedias and atlases are useful for a summary of information. They are kept together in a special section of the library and, unlike other books, may not be taken out of the library. Among the best reference books are the *Encyclopaedia Britannica,* the *Encyclopedia Americana,* and the *New International Encyclopedia.* A full list of reference books may be found in *Guide to Reference Books* by I. G. Mudge. Since a reference book cannot be revised every year, the encyclopedias publish yearbooks which give more recent information.

It is always important to know the publication date of any reference book because in a field in which changes are occurring, old information must be supplemented or replaced by more recent details. Outstanding events, changes, and progress in the fields of industry, government, literature, and education should be sought in the yearbooks for the period. The *Statesman's Yearbook,* for an example, gives data regarding the government, population, and industries of many nations. Current volumes of both the *Statesman's Yearbook* and the *World Almanac* are valuable for up-to-date information.

EXERCISE 2

Make a list of the encyclopedias and yearbooks in your library. Consult one of them for information on one of the topics that follow. Write the name of the reference book that you use and the date of its publication. In topic form list the main points made in the article.

Advertising	Chemical warfare	Homer
Agricultural	Chess	Horse racing
machinery	Chinese painting	Naples
Alexander the Great	Diving apparatus	New Mexico
Amatitlan	Dresden	Numismatics
Andrea del Sarto	Fingerprints	Tibet
Artillery	Football	Tolstoy
Francis Bacon	Henry Ford	Trade unions
Bavaria	Benjamin Franklin	Treason
Daniel Boone	Heredity	Waterloo
Caveat emptor		

EXERCISE 3

Refer to the *World Almanac* in order to be able to answer the following questions:

1. Who won the British Open Golf Championships in 1946?
2. Name five outstanding motion pictures of last year. Who were the stars?
3. How many homes in the United States have radios?
4. What is the population of Rome, Rio de Janeiro, Moscow?
5. What is the capital of the Republic of Israel?

86c. Reference books on special subjects.

Because general reference books must cover such a broad field, they can give only very limited information. A reference book in a special field will give many more details on the subject. The following list suggests some helpful special reference books.

1. Biography:

> *American Biographies*
> *Authors Today and Yesterday*
> *Current Biography*
> *Dictionary of American Biography*
> *Dictionary of National Biography* (English)
> *Living Authors*
> *Who's Who* (Principally English)
> *Who's Who in America*

2. History:

> *Dictionary of American History*, New York, Charles Scribner's Sons, 1942, 5 vols. and index.

3. Literature—Special Indexes:

> *A. L. A. Index . . . to General Literature*
> Firkins' *Index of Plays, 1800–1926*
> Granger's *Index to Poetry and Recitations*

4. Literature—General Reference Books, Quotation Books, and Guides:

> Baker's *Guide to the Best Fiction*
> Baker's *Guide to Historical Fiction*
> Bartlett's *Familiar Quotations*
> *Cambridge History of American Literature*
> *Cambridge History of English Literature*
> *Oxford Companion to American Literature*
> *Oxford Companion to English Literature*
> Sonnenschein's *Best Books*
> Stevenson's *Home Book of Quotations*
> *U.S. Catalog,* with *Cumulative Book Index*

5. Music:

> Grove's *Dictionary of Music and Musicians*

6. Business:

> *Statistical Abstract of the United States*

86d. Indexes to magazine and newspaper articles.

The most recent information on some subjects may appear in newspapers and magazine articles. There are a number of indexes which make it possible for you to find current information on any subject that has appeared in periodicals. The *Readers' Guide to Periodical Literature* is one of the most useful. When you use an index, it is always important to read the first few pages, which will explain how to use the book and what abbreviations are used.

The *Readers' Guide* is published every two weeks. At the end of the year, all the material for the year is gathered in one volume. If you wish to see whether the last month has produced anything on your special subject, you use the most recent index of the *Readers' Guide;* but if you want to see what last year offered, you consult the volume for the whole year. There are also volumes for periods longer than a year.

Other useful indexes are the following:

Agricultural Index, 1916–
This is a cumulative subject index to a selected list of agricultural magazines, books, bulletins.

Art Index, 1929–
This is a cumulative author and subject index to magazines and bulletins dealing with the fine arts.

Bulletin of the Public Affairs Information Service, 1915–
This is a cumulative subject index to current books, pamphlets, periodicals, government documents, and other material in the fields of economics and public affairs.

Dramatic Index, 1909–1949
This was an annual index to articles and illustrations concerning the stage and players in American and British periodicals.

Education Index, 1929–
This is a cumulative author and subject index to magazines, books, bulletins, and reports in the entire field of education.

Engineering Index, 1884–
With changes over the years, this index has been since 1928 a selective subject-author index to periodicals in all engineering fields. It is published annually, but technical libraries receive weekly cards containing the information eventually published in the annual volumes.

Facts on File, 1940–
This is a weekly world news digest with a cumulative index. It includes world, national, and foreign news in the areas of finance and economics, arts and science, education and religion, politics, military affairs, sports, obituaries, and other miscellany.

Industrial Arts Index, 1913–
This is a cumulative subject index to a selected but extensive list of business, finance, applied science, and technology periodicals, books, and pamphlets.

Music Index, 1949–
    This is a cumulative index to current music periodical literature.
The New York Times Index, 1913–
    This is a cumulative guide to events of national importance by reference to date, page, and column.

All these indexes refer to articles by subject and author, not by title. For example, if you wish to investigate the topic of conservation of natural resources, you would look in the *Readers' Guide* for the topic "Conservation." You might find an entry similar to the following:

> Conservation of resources
>   America faces challenge to live within own means. Science N L 55: 9 Ja 1 49.
>   Country that can feed the world? F. Osborn Atlan. 181: 71–6 Ap '48.

If you consult the list of magazines in the front of the book, you will find that *Science N L* means *Science News Letter.* The article appears in Volume 55, page 9, for January 1, 1949.

The second article was written by F. Osborn. It is on pages 71–76 in Volume 181 of the *Atlantic Monthly.* It was in the April, 1948, issue of this magazine.

EXERCISE 4

Use the *Readers' Guide to Periodical Literature* to find the topics listed below. Copy the entries which seem usable. Then ask the librarian to give you the volumes of the magazines which you need. Since libraries do not have bound copies of all magazines, you may need to limit your choice of articles. Read one of the articles on each subject and write in topic form the main points presented.

Motion pictures	Theater	Conservation
Air travel	Education	Television
Electronics	Housing	Propaganda

87. CHOOSING THE TOPIC OF A RESEARCH PAPER

87a. Choose a topic that interests you.

You have probably discovered that you write better when you are interested in what you are investigating. Since you, like most other students, are likely to be interested in a vocation, you might find a suitable theme topic related to the work you expect to do in the future. You might like to investigate the opportunities in your chosen field, the preparation required, or the salary to be expected. Or perhaps one of these topics for research would interest you.

Rain making
Smog problems
Effects of television on reading
Television rating systems
The use of television in education
Homes of the future
Americans love statistics
Education and the comics
Propaganda as part of our foreign policy
Motion picture censorship
The changing family
Book censorship
False advertising
Women in industry
The war for men's minds
Commercialized college athletics
Trick photography
Municipal support of the arts
Financing a civic theater
Do the large stadiums pay?
The commercialization of amateur sports
Sports car racing
Economic problems of the American theater
Space travel
Establishing a business

407

Must art make money?
Broadway's impact on Hollywood
Jazz as an expression of America
Truth and fiction about Tin Pan Alley
The Stanislavsky method in the theater
Dangers of popular science
Advice columns in the newspaper
The new popularity of ballet
Atomic energy and peace
Influence of Hollywood
The art motion picture
Save our woods

87b. Choose a topic that requires research.

A topic may be very interesting to you but be too narrow or too personal to require an investigation. Which of these topics would require research?

Winning a photography contest	Is my family unusual?
Making a farm pay	A trip to Washington
What do I inherit?	My favorite television actors
Learning to appreciate music	Slum clearance
Activities at Camp X	Hollywood meets the challenge of television

87c. Limit the topic.

Since your first research papers will contain only between fifteen hundred and two thousand words, it is important to limit your topic to an area that can be handled adequately in this space. Limit your topic also to one that you can understand and can make clear to the general reader. Many medical or psychological topics sound very interesting, but can be treated only superficially by people who have not studied medicine or psychology. With topics like "Therapy for the Psychoneurotic" or "The Psychological Needs of the Child" there is danger of using psychological terms glibly without really understanding them or of oversimplifying the material. An encyclopedia article (not a child's encyclopedia) will give a general view of a broad area in which you are interested and may suggest subdivisions of the general area, but this material should be used only to obtain a broad view of the whole topic. Because encyclopedia material must be very general, it is not suitable for actual note taking. Chapter headings of books on your topic will also help you to limit your subject field.

EXERCISE 5

On your paper, write for each of these broad fields several topics which might be handled in two thousand words:

Science	Modern art
Conservation	Plastics
Farming	American education
Ballet	Costume design

87d. Choose a topic on which your library has adequate information.

Keep in mind the resources of the library which you will have to use. Before you decide finally on a topic for a research paper, use the *Readers' Guide to Periodical Literature* (see Section 86d) and the card catalogue (Section 86a) in your library to find available material. Remember that your research paper should be based upon material from different sources: reference books, magazines, books, newspapers, and pamphlets. Unless you have consulted at least five or six sources, you cannot write a satisfactory research paper.

EXERCISE 6

From the lists given in Section 87 or from your own interests, choose a topic which you would like to investigate. Read a summary of the topic in an encyclopedia and bring to class for discussion five or six subtopics which you think might be examined in other sources and used in your paper.

88. TAKING NOTES

88a. Choosing books and articles.

Most term papers will require the use of at least five or six references, including some magazine articles. Which ones to choose will, of course, involve many points, but you can begin your selection when you examine the cards on your subject in the card catalogue. Books with old publication dates may not be useful for the type of subject that you are investigating.

The author should also be investigated. *Who's Who* will help you decide whether he knows the field. Often one good book will contain a bibliography of other acceptable books in the field. The card in the card catalogue will tell you whether there is a bibliography. If a minimum of five books is to be used, you should select at least ten books for examination. Look at the table of contents. Then skim the chapters that seem usable. Gradually the general point that you wish to make will become clear, and you can select for note taking the books that will contribute to it.

88b. Materials for note taking.

Many people have found that the most efficient note taking for a long paper is done on index cards (3 inches by 5 inches), or on larger cards. Some people, however, prefer sheets of paper. The important thing is to use a different card or piece of paper for each fact recorded. You can then move the cards or papers into position so that all notes on one subject are together. Such a procedure will simplify the organization of your paper.

88c. Organization for note taking.

Any project should have a plan. By planning your work, you can save time and also write a better paper. Before you begin to take notes, consider what will be required. Since

all research papers must have a bibliography and footnotes, the information needed to produce them should be gathered as you proceed with the paper. First, make your bibliography.

88d. Preparation of a bibliography.

When you have selected the books and magazines that contain material to be used, make a separate bibliography card for each one. Here is a sample bibliography card. (See Section 92.)

> Da
> 2631.A5
>
> Allen, Hervey, Israfel, the
> Life and Times of Edgar
> Allan Poe, New York:
> Farrar and Rinehart, Inc., 1934

88e. Method of note taking.

1. Use the index and table of contents to see on which pages you will find material that can be used.
2. Take notes on one side of 4- by 6-inch index cards with a separate card for each topic. (This method will save much time later when you are ready to organize your points.)
3. Skim the page before writing anything.

An efficient note taker first skims his material. Well-written books and articles often have topic sentences near the beginning of each paragraph. Let your eyes move quickly down the page picking up these main points.

411

EXERCISE 7

Use your history, geography, or science text to practice skimming. Open the book to a page indicated by your teacher. Skim the page in two minutes and be prepared to list the main points.

4. Record information for footnotes.

Before any notes are taken, copy on the card the name of the author, the title of book or magazine article, and the page from which the note is taken. These details are important for your footnotes and also for any further examination of the source. In the upper right corner of the card, write the topic with which the note deals.

Jacobson, David.   Rumor.
Affairs of Dame Rumor, p.7

5. Condense your notes.

It is a waste of time to copy whole pages from your reference. Notes should be full enough to make the meaning clear, but not so long that every detail is included. Often a paragraph or a page can be reduced to a sentence or two. Notes are often taken in topic or phrase form so that the main idea is retained, but modifiers and articles are omitted. Learn also to abbreviate the words that appear frequently. Be careful, however. Don't abbreviate so much that you cannot read the notes later.

If your main subject is *Propaganda Devices,* you might want to show how rumors or whispering campaigns can be used. Here is a passage on which you might take some notes. The notes taken on it are on the sample card that follows the passage.

> Perhaps the most potent pipe-dream rumors are those which satisfy the yen for financial gain. These morsels, whispered everywhere in the strictest confidence, to be sure, have sent the stock markets and financial exchanges throughout the world soaring and diving. They have set mass migrations in motion. They have sent men crawling about the bottoms of the oceans, searching in the deserts, and scouring the lands for wealth which was to be found only in the imaginative stories.

Jacobson, David   Rumor
Affairs of Dame Rumor, p 7

Most powerful rumors those which
suggest ways of making money. Result of
these: stock markets rising and
falling, mass migrations, searches
in oceans and deserts for wealth
that probably did not exist.

6. Try to use your own words in taking notes.

If you find a striking statement that you wish to quote, copy it *exactly* with quotation marks around it. Be very sure to note the source and the page on which the statement is found.

7. Be careful to distinguish in your reading and in your note taking between facts and the author's opinion.

The value of opinions depends on who expresses them and on the information upon which they are based; therefore, a good paper should tell the reader whose ideas are being presented.

EXERCISE 8

Use your history, geography, or science text to practice note taking. Open your books to a page indicated by your instructor. Skim it first. Then read the sections that will be used in your notes. On your paper write the notes that you would take.

89. PREPARING THE OUTLINE

Before beginning to write the research paper, you should prepare an outline for it. (See Section 82 for outline form.) Because the long paper deals with many more details than the short paper, the outline for the research paper is even more important than an outline for a short paper. If you have followed directions for taking your notes, you now have a large number of cards with a topic written in the upper right corner of each.

89a. Organize the notes.

Put together all of the cards that carry the same topic. These topics can be used in the outline.

89b. Choose a central idea for presentation.

Read your notes carefully and select a central purpose or controlling idea. State this central point in a theme sentence. Referring to it constantly as you make the outline and write the paper will help to keep you on the topic. You will always have notes on material that does not develop the main theme on which you finally decide. Discard the cards containing that material.

89c. Select the main divisions of the central idea.

From the topics in the upper right corner of your cards,

select the ones that will bring out the main supporting points for your general theme. Place these large topics opposite Roman numerals to form the skeleton of your outline.

>   I. Rumors as Propaganda
>   II. Propaganda techniques
>   III. American propaganda in World War II

89d. Subordinate ideas in a logical fashion.

Examine the cards on a single topic. Decide the order in which the points are to be presented. Write the letter *A* beside each note on the first point to be considered; use *B* beside all notes on the second point to be discussed under I. Now fill in the outline skeleton with the subtopics.

89e. Check the finished outline.

1. See that each division indicated by a Roman numeral develops a single topic that does not overlap the point made in another division. (See Section 82.)
2. Examine the material under each Roman numeral to see that points indicated by *A*, *B*, *C*, etc., are of equal value. If the outline is well made, these letters can be the basis of your paragraphing.

90. WRITING THE PAPER

All the directions for writing a theme are again applicable. (See Sections 81–85.) In the long paper, however, it is important to give more careful attention to transitional expressions that will lead from one idea to another and keep the whole closely tied together. Read your notes in the order in which you have planned them so that you will be thoroughly familiar with the subject. Write the first draft with space between the lines in order to have room for revision. When you need a footnote, number the material and write the footnote at the bottom of the page on which you are working. (See Section 91.)

90a. Follow your outline carefully.

Your outline is your plan and will keep your ideas in order. If, as you write, you wish to change your arrangement of details or add some material, make the change on your outline first. Then check it to see that your unity has not been destroyed.

90b. Use a paragraph system.

A research paper is a serious discussion of a topic, though a vivid, lively style is, of course, desirable. Do not paragraph by impulse. A paragraph in this type of writing should be the development of an idea. Writing a topic sentence for each paragraph will help to keep the material unified.

90c. Use an introductory paragraph.

You have seen that in a short paper, a whole paragraph devoted to an introduction may destroy the proportion. In a long paper, however, an introductory paragraph to give an over-all view of the whole topic may be desirable.

90d. Revise what you have written. (See Section 85.)

Read the first draft carefully. Check unity and coherence (Sections 74–80), punctuation, and spelling. Have you used illustrations to clarify your points? Watch your sentence structure to be sure that there is a variety of form (Section 72). Have you used too many simple sentences that are flat statements beginning with the subject or with *There are?* Combine some of these to show the relationship of the ideas and to avoid monotony in your style. Have you used too many or too few footnotes? A full page without any footnotes may need to be reexamined. Yet a great many footnotes on each page may mean that materials need to be gathered together. If you type the final copy, double space and leave a margin of 1½ inches. Always read the final copy for typographical errors.

91. MAKING FOOTNOTES

The writer of a research paper must read what a number of people have said about a topic and present their ideas together with some of his own thinking based on his reading. The reader understands that not all of the ideas presented in the paper are the product of the thinking of the writer, but he wishes to know whose thinking they are. Ideas are often valuable in relation to their source. For an example, ideas presented by a journalist will not have the same value as those offered by an authority in the field. For this reason, the carefully written research paper has a footnote to tell the reader where the information was obtained.

91a. Use a footnote to give the source of information.

The following sentences are not a product of a student's thinking. They contain information which must have been obtained in his reading. The small number (called a superior figure) follows the statements and refers to the same number at the bottom of the page. Following this number is the footnote, which tells where the writer of the paper obtained the information.

> Because politicians have not been interested in the arts, the theater in America has received no state endowment. Its artistic development, however, has been aided by people like Otto Kahn, who helped the Theater Guild over its initial difficulties, and Irene and Alice Lewisohn, who endowed the Neighborhood Playhouse.[1]

[1] Sheldon Cheney, *The Theatre* (New York: Tudor Publishing Company, 1939), p. 505.

If you find in your reading a very striking expression that you wish to use verbatim, copy it exactly as it is in your reference and use a footnote to tell where you found it. Footnotes are not used for information that is generally known.

91b. Use a standard form of footnote and be consistent in its use.

There are various forms for footnotes. The Modern Language Association of America *Style Sheet* favors the following:

1. Books:

Book by one author:

> John R. Tunis, *This Writing Game* (New York: A. S. Barnes and Company, 1941), p. 26.
>
> Henry Louis Mencken, *The American Language*, 4th ed. (New York: Alfred A. Knopf, Inc., 1936), p. 168.

Book by two or more authors:

> John Tasker Howard and Arthur Mendel, *Our Contemporary Composers* (New York: Thomas Y. Crowell Company, 1941), p. 82.

Book of two or more volumes:

> Douglas S. Freeman, *George Washington* (New York: Charles Scribner's Sons, 1948), II, 142.

Book prepared by an editor:

> *Representative English Comedies*, ed. Charles Mills Gayley (New York: The Macmillan Company, 1916), I, xxiii.
>
> Richard Aldington, ed., *Great French Romances* (New York: Duell, Sloan & Pearce, Inc., 1946), p. 17.

A Translation:

> Homer, *The Odyssey*, trans. George Herbert Palmer (Boston: Houghton Mifflin Company, 1929), p. 46.

2. Articles (essays, stories):

From a magazine:

> Walter D. Edmonds, "Arrival of the Lily Dean," *The Saturday Evening Post*, CCX (May 7, 1938), 5.

91c

or

>Walter D. Edmonds, "Arrival of the Lily Dean," *The Saturday Evening Post,* May 7, 1938, p. 5.

>Roger Angell, "A Walk in Washington," *Holiday,* XIX (May, 1956), 37.

or

>Roger Angell, "A Walk in Washington," *Holiday,* May, 1956, p. 37.

>"What to Do About the Draft?" *Life,* XL (May 14, 1956), 69.

or

>"What to Do About the Draft?" *Life,* May 14, 1956, p. 69.

From a collection:

>Katherine Mansfield, "Bliss," *A Study of the Short Story,* ed. Henry S. Canby and Alfred Dashiell (New York: Henry Holt and Company, Inc., 1935), p. 303.
>Burges Johnson, "Campus Versus Classroom," *Reading for Opinion,* ed. Earl Davis and William C. Hummel (New York: Prentice-Hall, Inc., 1952), pp. 79–82.

From a newspaper:

>"Summer's Children," *The New York Times,* June 19, 1954, p. 14.
>"The U. S. and Its Critics," *The New York Times,* April 15, 1956, Section 4, p. 8.

NOTE: The first reference above is to the daily edition, the second to the Sunday edition.

Notice that when the name of the author of an article is not given, the footnote begins with the title of the article.

91c. Use a shorter form for later footnotes on the same source.

1. *Ibid.* If a footnote refers to the same source as the one used in the footnote *immediately* preceding, the abbreviation *ibid.* (from the Latin *ibidem* meaning "in the same place") may be used.

First entry:

> Sheldon Cheney, *The Theatre,* revised edition (New York: Longmans, Green & Co., Inc., 1952), p. 505.

Second entry:

> *Ibid.,* p. 508.

2. *Op. cit.* After the first full reference to a given work, provided that no other work by the same author is mentioned in the paper, succeeding references may be indicated by the author's last name followed by *op. cit.* (from Latin *opere citato* meaning "in the work cited") and the page or pages to which the reference is made.

> Cheney, *op. cit.,* p. 508.

3. *Short title.* Many writers now use a short title for footnote references other than the first. The following example illustrates this form:

> Cheney, p. 508.

If more than one book by the same author is used, the name of the book must be repeated in footnotes after the first.

> Cheney, *The Theatre,* p. 508.

First entry:

> Clifton Fadiman, "Herman Melville," *The Atlantic Monthly,* CLXXII (October, 1943), 88.

Subsequent entry for the same article:

Allowed:

> Fadiman, *op. cit.,* p. 90.

Preferred:

> Fadiman, "Melville," p. 90.

91d. Numbering of footnotes.

Unless your teacher gives other directions, number your footnotes consecutively beginning with *1* on each page.

92. MAKING A BIBLIOGRAPHY

A bibliography is an alphabetical list of books, magazines, and pamphlets on a given subject.

92a. Arrange the bibliography cards alphabetically by last names of authors. (See Section 88d.) If the author's name is not given, list the item according to the first word (except *the, a,* or *an*) in the title. Then type the list.

92b. Arrange all references (books, magazines, pamphlets) in one list unless there is a long bibliography.

92c. Use consistent punctuation.

Punctuation varies in bibliographies, but a simple style is best. Choose the form that you wish to use and follow that form throughout.

This sample bibliography shows books and magazines separated, although in a list of this length, separation would not be necessary.

BIBLIOGRAPHY

Books

Allen, Hervey. *Israfel: The Life and Times of Edgar Allan Poe.* New York: Rinehart & Company, Inc., 1949.

Boyd, Ernest Augustus. *Literary Blasphemies.* New York: Harper & Brothers, 1927, pp. 163–185.

Magazine Articles

Huxley, Aldous Leonard. "Vulgarity in Literature," *Saturday Review of Literature,* VII (September 27, 1930), 158–159.

Wilson, James Southall. "Devil Was in It," *American Mercury,* XXIV (October, 1931), 215–220.

If your instructor wishes to examine your notes, be sure that your cards are included. Do not copy these to make a neat arrangement. Your instructor will want to see the notes as you took them, and he will probably want to know about the method you used to build your outline from them.

The Précis and
the Paraphrase

93. THE PRÉCIS

A précis is a summary. Skill in using it is important in note
taking of any kind. Business and professional people often
ask their secretaries to keep a file of summaries of articles
or reports on new developments in their special fields. When
an executive does not have the time to read the whole report of a committee that has investigated some important
project, he may ask an employee to write a precise summary.

93a. Read the material carefully.

The précis must include *all* of the important ideas. List
these as you read. It must not include your own opinions
or reactions.

93b. Use your own words.

Reduce the important ideas to their bare essentials, making every word count. A word can often be substituted for
a clause. The précis should usually be not more than one-
third as long as the original.

93c. Retain the plan of the original.

Altering the order in which details are presented may
distort the meaning of the article.

93d. Write the précis in exact English.

The condensation must not be a jumble of disconnected words; it must be written in sentences, in precise English. Be especially careful to join the ideas by means of transitional expressions that show exactly the relationship between the ideas.

EXERCISE 1

Write a précis of this selection from William Beebe's *High Jungle:*

It is occasionally advisable and often necessary for an attacked nation temporarily to sacrifice some unimportant portion of its land for better concentrated defense. This temporary national self-mutilation is reflected in jungle warfare by certain long-tailed lizards. Headlong they flee before the onslaught of a swooping hawk. Their race for sanctuary may be a fractional second too slow, and the clutching talons seize the long tail just before it would have vanished to safety. But nature balances delicately her scales of life and death, and for just such a crisis as this have been developed the short, loosely interlaced, proximal tail muscles. Momentarily there ensues a crucial tug of war between lizard legs and hawk talons. The muscles give way, the reptile hurtles to safety down the hole, and the hawk finds meager pickings on the captured tail. The lizard has this advantage over the human nation, in that within a few weeks, a brand-new tail will sprout out from the old stump.

EXERCISE 2

Write a précis of this passage from Louis R. Reid's *American Movies Today:*

Unchallenged is Hollywood's technical supremacy. In such details as photography, sound recording, set and costume designing, the California producers lead the world. Their artistic progress is still hampered by the seemingly inescapable necessity of making their dominant appeal to childish intelligence. Of secondary importance is that production be based upon a

maturity of story and treatment. Upon those occasions when progressive and imaginative directors break away from trite and childish formulae to make pictures of mature intelligence, the result, in many instances, has been astonishingly profitable. Such films have been received with rejoicing among that portion of the public to whom movie-going means something more than a time-passing habit or an escape from realities.

So responsive are the West Coast artisans to this acclaim that they have fallen into the grievous error of copying their newly found formulae to tiresome lengths. Thus has come a succession of films, built upon the themes which had proved refreshingly adult. So impressed is Hollywood by what seems sure-fire that variety and change of pace, the mainstays of all genuinely successful amusement, are neglected.

EXERCISE 3

Write a précis of a selection from a literature textbook that you are now using.

94. THE PARAPHRASE

A paraphrase is a restatement in different words. It is most useful in handling difficult poetry or prose passages that contain involved thoughts or technical language.

94a. Read the passage carefully.

Use reference books to determine the meanings of obscure words and allusions.

94b. Use your own words to present the essential ideas in clear, simple English.

EXERCISE 4

Write a paraphrase of a selection from a literature textbook that you are reading.

Writing for
Special Purposes

Do you want to keep in touch with a new friend who lives in another town? Do you need a job? Do you want some repairs made on your home? Have you purchased something which proves to be defective? Must you discuss your income tax with the government? These and many other problems require letters.

95. BUSINESS LETTERS

Although some business difficulties can be solved by telephone, it is often better to write a letter because you then have a clear record of what has been said. *Always* keep a carbon copy of business communications. A package of Manila folders can be placed in the drawer of your desk or in a small, one-section file and used to keep an orderly arrangement of the business letters that you send and those that you receive.

95a. Plan.

Almost everything is more successful if it has been planned. Letters are no exception. The businessman who dictates his letters without first planning what he wishes to say and how he can make his points effective is seldom as successful as the person who spends at least a few minutes listing the points to be made and considering the language that will carry his message. A good course in business English or careful reading of a book in this field will be invaluable if you wish your business letters to get results.

95b. Appearance.

A good business letter creates a pleasing impression the moment it is taken from its envelope. Physical appearance —quality of paper, neatness of typing or writing, arrangement of letter parts—is almost as important to the total effect as content. Correctness and attractiveness in form reflect a courteous attitude toward the reader.

Business letters should be written on good-quality, white, unruled paper, preferably of the standard 8½- by 11-inch size, although the half-size sheet (8½ x 5½) is acceptable.

Letters should be typewritten if possible, but neat longhand, in black or blue-black ink, is permissible. For typing, a black ribbon fresh enough to ensure legibility should be used. The letter must be neat in every detail. Never strike over or leave a visible erasure.

Leave a good margin on all sides of the paper. If the letter is short, consider carefully the space that it will take and plan the margins accordingly.

95c. Parts.

Heading

The heading includes the writer's complete mailing address and the date. In the block form (see Section 95d), the heading is placed even with the left-hand margin at least two inches from the top of the paper. In the modified block form, the heading appears in the upper right-hand corner. (See Section 95d.) On letterhead stationery, the writer adds only the date. It is placed at least two line spaces below the letterhead, either (1) in the center of the page, (2) even with the right-hand margin, or (3) in the block form, even with the left-hand margin. Abbreviations should be avoided, and -*st*, -*nd*, -*rd*, or -*th* should not follow the day of the month.

Inside address

The inside address contains the name and address of the person to whom you are writing. It usually extends from the left-hand margin. The space between the inside address and the heading varies with the length of the letter but is usually at least three or four line spaces. Some title should always precede the name of the person addressed: *Mr.*, *Mrs.*, *Miss*, *Dr.*, *Professor*. Do not abbreviate the titles *Professor*, *Reverend*, *Honorable*. The full name (not last name only) should follow these titles. The titles *Reverend* and *Honorable* are preceded by *The*.

> The Reverend Carlton C. Lane
> The Honorable Charles M. McLaughlin

Salutation

The salutation should extend from the left-hand margin, two spaces below the inside address. The following are correct forms:

	MEN	WOMEN
Most formal (to address the governor, mayor, president, ambassador, high official of the church):	Sir:	Madam:
Formal:	My dear Sir: Dear Sir:	My dear Madam: Dear Madam:

Less formal:	My dear Dr. Hill:	My dear Mrs. Holt
	Dear Mr. Hill:	Dear Miss Holt:
Friendly:	Dear Ned,	Dear Nelda,

To a firm of men or *men and women:*   Gentlemen:

Ladies:

To a firm of women: Mesdames:

NOTE: Most business correspondence today aims at a friendly, conversational style. Therefore, the *less formal* salutation is frequently used. The salutation labeled *friendly* should be employed only with people with whom you have a very informal relationship.

Body of the letter

The body of the letter should have the following characteristics: clearness, correctness, conciseness, courtesy, and character. Avoid hackneyed expressions like the following:

according to our records	party
acknowledging your letter	per
are in receipt of	prox.
attached hereto	pursuant to our conversation
beg to advise	referring to
beg to inform	state (for say)
by return mail	take pleasure
contents noted	take this opportunity
enclosed please find	thanking you in advance
in re	this is to inform you
in reply wish to state	under separate cover
kindly inform	wish to say
our Mr. Edmonds	you claim
our records show	yours of recent date

Complimentary close

Place the complimentary close slightly to the right of the middle of the page, two line spaces below the last line of the body of the letter. Only the first word is capitalized. A comma usually follows the complimentary close.

Yours truly,   Sincerely yours,
Very truly yours,   Cordially yours,

NOTE: Avoid participial phrases like *Hoping for an early reply, Thanking you in advance.*

Signature

Sign your name in ink. A married woman signs her own name followed by her married name.

> Janet Louise Black
> (Mrs. Henry R. Black)

Miss, Mr., or *Mrs.* is never used as part of a signature. Academic degrees and professional titles should not be used with a signature.

Incorrect: Dr. Samuel White
              Sue Jenkins, Ph.D.

If your letter is typewritten, your name should be typed four line spaces below the complimentary close and in line with it. If you have a particular title or position, this should be placed below your name.

NOTE: For a full discussion of all the various types of letters used in the transaction of business, see *Effective Letters in Business,* by Robert L. Shurter, published by the McGraw-Hill Book Company.

95d. Form.

Styles in business letters have changed a great deal in recent years. Now, the indented heading is seldom used.

The block or modified block form is the accepted one in modern business writing. In the block form, the margins are set. The first line of a pragraph is not indented. Every line of the letter begins at the left margin.

MODIFIED BLOCK FORM

1934 Travis Street
Louisville 8, Kentucky
February 3, 1959

Miss Lucy Irwin
Secretary, Society of Commerce
375 East Boone Street
Arlington, Kentucky

Dear Miss Irwin:

This letter is an illustration of the "modified block" form, since all the parts of the letter, except the heading, complimentary close, and signature, begin flush with the left-hand margin. In the "full block" form, even these parts are at the left.

The paragraphs illustrate block form; that is, each paragraph begins flush with the left-hand margin. Division between paragraphs is indicated by double spaces. Within the paragraphs and within each part of the letter, single spacing is used.

No punctuation marks are used after the lines in the heading, inside address, and signature. Usually a colon (for formal communication) or a comma (for friendly address with first name) is used after the salutation. After the complimentary close, either a comma or no punctuation is used.

Yours truly,
Wilbur Johnson
Wilbur Johnson

516 Tudor Place,
Detroit 22, Michigan,
November 2, 1959.

Rinebeck and Company,
1224 East Denver Avenue,
Chicago 12, Illinois.

Gentlemen:

This letter is an example of the "semiblock" form. The heading, complimentary close, and signature are on the right side of the letter, and the paragraphs are indented. But within the parts the block form is used.

The paragraphs are indented here, but they could be in block form. In fact, blocked paragraphs are always optional. Indented paragraphs can be used, if the writer so desires, with any type of letter, including even the "full block" form.

Closed punctuation is used here: commas at the end of each line in the heading and the inside address except the last, which has a period. Such punctuation, too, is optional, for open punctuation could be used.

Very truly yours,
Rodney R. Rhodes
Rodney R. Rhodes

95e. Content.

Don't waste the first sentence by saying, "I received your letter." The fact that you are answering shows that you have received it. Come directly to the point, or use the opening material to establish rapport with your correspondent. Avoid business jargon such as the hackneyed expressions listed on page 428 and filler phrases like *to the amount of, for the purpose of*. (See Sections 48 and 51.) Be sure

431

that your message is written in language that your correspondent will understand. When writing to people not in
your business, be especially careful not to use business
terms with which you are familiar but which might be
meaningless to the other person.

In business letters, the paragraphs are shorter than in
many other forms of prose, but a letter composed of a series
of one-sentence paragraphs gives a choppy effect. The paragraph is still a unit of thought. A new paragraph should be
used for a new subject, but since *conciseness* is one of the
aims of business writing, ideas are not developed as fully
as they might be in general exposition.

95f. Types of business letters.

Letter of application

An effective letter of application stresses, throughout, the
applicant's desire and ability to be of benefit to the prospective employer. Always emphasize what you, the applicant, with your qualifications, can do for the employer, not
what the employer can do for you. The letter must be
courteous, straightforward, and sincere in tone, offering
services without pleading or demanding.

In the first paragraph, you apply for the position, indicating how you learned of the opening: from a friend, an
agency, a classified advertisement, etc.

Qualifications should follow in the second paragraph. If
you have had experience, tell specifically in the third paragraph of what it consisted and how long you were employed at each place. If you have had no actual work experience, give some school, camp, or church activity that
may have helped you to meet the public, gain poise or
self-confidence, and acquire various necessary skills.

The fourth paragraph presents references. Choose these
carefully. The counselor at your school or some teacher for
whom you have done good work will give you an educa-

tion reference. If you have worked, include the name of someone who knows your work and is willing to recommend you. Failure to supply references from places where you have worked may indicate to your prospective employer lack of success in the position. Give name, title, address, and telephone number of each reference. If you have never worked, character references from the minister of your church or some well-known citizen will help.

Close your letter by requesting an interview at the employer's convenience. Tell where and when you may be reached by telephone.

People who have had much special education or experience often send a data sheet with their letter of application. Under headings such as "Work experience," "Travel," "Publications," etc., they give a full picture of all of their activities. When a data sheet is used, the letter of application simply points up the high lights.

814 Tenth Street, N.W.
Washington 16, D.C.
May 20, 1959

Mr. Alfred Preston, Personnel Manager
Benton, Ward and Company
410 Sixteenth Street, N.W.
Washington 4, D.C.

Dear Mr. Preston:

Your advertisement in the Washington *Post* for a secretary interested me very much. I should like to apply for the position.

In a few weeks I shall be graduated from Central High School, where I have had four years of commercial training. In my senior year I earned an award for typing at the rate of 60 words a minute and made the Honor Roll for receiving a grade of 80 or more in all my subjects.

For the past two years I have been a member of the Business Service Club at school. This is an organization that does typing, mimeographing, and ditto work for the various departments of the school. Since I worked for the club during two study periods each week, I have had some experience in many kinds of office jobs and have learned to work with neatness and accuracy. Last summer I used this experience to obtain a position as relief typist at Denton's Department Store. Here I took dictation, typed, and did some filing.

Information concerning my work and my character may be obtained from the following:

> Mr. Theodore Smart, Denton's Department Store, 31 H Street, S.W., Washington, D.C.

> Miss Hilda Newman, Adviser, Business Service Club, Central High School, Washington, D.C.

> Miss Sarah Burton, Counselor, Central High School, Washington, D.C.

I should be glad to come for an interview at any time convenient to you. My telephone number is CO–4679, and you may reach me there any afternoon, except Tuesday, after 3:30.

> Yours truly,
> *Mary Henderson*
> Mary Henderson

Order letter

If you wish to order seats for a theatrical performance, a room in a hotel, or a new dress, you may write an order letter. Be sure to give *all* information that will help the company to send you exactly what you want: day and date of performance, matinee or evening, price, location (if you have a preference); type of room, price, time of your arrival; size of dress, color, material, etc. Enclose a picture from the newspaper if you are ordering from an advertisement. Be sure to enclose a check or tell how you expect to pay.

311 Patuxent Street
Crisfield, Maryland
October 20, 1959

Harmon Brothers
Connecticut Avenue and F Street
Washington, D.C.

Gentlemen:

Please send me by parcel post the following items advertised in the *Crisfield Mentor*.

2 Colonial style silver candlesticks, @ 7.95	$15.90
1 Colonial style silver platter	5.95
	$21.85
Sales tax	.44
Total	$22.29

A money order and the advertisement are enclosed.

Yours truly,
Jane Holmes
(Mrs. H. R. Holmes)

Inquiries

Most inquiry letters are written to obtain information about the products or services of a business firm. Some may be written to an individual for information concerning a subject on which he is an authority. Always make your request understandable; avoid vague and general questions. Supply any information the reader may need in order to answer your questions definitely.

Routine requests for catalogues, price lists, or other prepared data may be limited to a one-sentence letter clearly identifying the desired material. If your letter is phrased as a question (*Will you please send me. . . .*), it should close with a period instead of a question mark.

Nonroutine inquiries require more detailed letters. For example, a letter asking about an organization's policies must explain the use to which the information will be put. A request stemming from a personal problem must give a clear explanation of the problem and an indication of the type of help needed.

The general plan for the inquiry letter (usually from two to four paragraphs) is as follows: (1) reason for the inquiry, (2) the inquiry, (3) expression of appreciation (*never* a "thank you in advance"). Sometimes material may be included to show the reader how he will benefit by replying. If the inquiry includes several questions, these are more effective when numbered and paragraphed separately.

If the person or firm addressed will eventually profit, no postage should be enclosed. Otherwise, apply this principle: When you ask for that which is of benefit only or primarily to you, enclose a self-addressed stamped envelope.

919 Fowler Avenue
Athens 12, Indiana
September 25, 1959

Secretary-Treasurer
American Institute of Electrical Engineers
33 West 38th Street
New York 18, New York

Dear Sir:

As a student in the College of Electrical Engineering at Athens University, I am interested in eventually obtaining full membership in the American Institute of Electrical Engineers.

Will you please answer the following questions:

1. Is it possible for an undergraduate student of electrical engineering to obtain a junior membership in the A.I.E.E.?
2. What is the cost of such membership?
3. Is such junior membership transferable to full membership upon the student's graduation?

4. Does the junior membership fee include a year's subscription to *Electrical Engineering*?

I shall be very grateful for this information.

> Very truly yours,
> *William Harbin*
> William Harbin

Request for adjustment

A request for adjustment is written not out of a desire to vent your personal anger, but to persuade the company to settle a claim. You cannot hope to obtain adjustment if you antagonize the company. Control your annoyance. Present the facts clearly and concisely, explaining exactly what is wrong. The letter usually contains these points: (1) specific explanation of what is wrong, (2) courteous request for action you would like to have taken, (3) sometimes, the inconvenience you are experiencing. If there is likely to be a struggle for the adjustment, use the first or last sentence to establish rapport by expressing your confidence in the fairness of the firm.

> 311 Patuxent Street
> Crisfield, Maryland
> October 31, 1959

Harmon Brothers
Connecticut Avenue and F Street
Washington, D.C.

Gentlemen:

On October 20, I ordered from you two Colonial style silver candlesticks. When they arrived yesterday, I found that one of them had a decided scratch on the base. Consequently, I am returning it. Please send me a perfect candlestick of the same style.

> Yours truly,
> *Jane Holmes*
> (Mrs. H. R. Holmes)

R.F.D. 6,
Lansom, Pennsylvania,
November 15, 1959.

The Tryco Department Store,
49 East Tenth Street,
New York 10, New York.

Gentlemen:

On November 9, I purchased in your radio department a Vinson radio, table model R–350, with brown plastic case. The radio arrived promptly, but I am disappointed to find that it does not operate on DC. It was my understanding that the model R–350 was designed to operate on either AC or DC, but I find that the accompanying instructions indicate only AC. I am returning the radio at once in the hope that it can be exchanged for a set suitable for DC wiring.

If there has been a misunderstanding and the R–350 does not operate on DC, I shall have to choose another model. In that case I hope that I may have a refund, since I shall not be in New York again for several months. I hope, however, that you will be able to supply an R–350 model which will fill my needs.

Very truly yours,
Edward Paine
Edward Paine

EXERCISE 1

Select an advertisement from the *Help Wanted* section in your newspaper. Write an application for the position.

EXERCISE 2

Order from Hinson, Warner Company, 48 Main Street, Montgomery, Alabama, the following materials: 1 sweater, 2 pairs hose, 1 dozen handkerchiefs. Be sure to specify size, color, catalogue number, material, style. In an order letter, always tell how payment will be made.

EXERCISE 3

Write a letter to a theater in New York, ordering tickets for a current play.

EXERCISE 4

Write a letter ordering a subscription to a magazine to be sent to a friend as a Christmas present.

EXERCISE 5

You have received as a present a subscription to a magazine. For three months the copies of the magazine arrived promptly. For the last two months no copy has arrived. Write a letter to the publisher, explaining the situation and asking for adjustment.

EXERCISE 6

A store with which you have a charge account has sent you a bill listing an item which you did not purchase. Write a courteous note asking for adjustment of the bill.

96. REPORT WRITING

The class activities in any school require simple reports from treasurer, committee chairman, and other class officers. Later, you will need to know how to write reports as officer in a civic group or the Parent-Teachers Association; as chairman of a committee in your union or the organization for which you work; as head of a department or supervisor; as engineer on a project; and perhaps as mayor, traffic director, school superintendent, or president of a board of directors. In fact, report writing will, with letter writing, probably be the type of writing most frequently used and most important to success in your adult life.

From this introduction you can see that we are not talking about book reports, which are really book reviews and have a form of their own; nor are we discussing the report that is a kind of summary on some reading you have done. The reports with which we are concerned are based on an investigation or experiment that will result in recommendations or a summary of the activities of a group over a period of time.

Good books to consult for a full discussion of business reports are the following:

> Aurner, Robert. *Effective Business English.* Cincinnati: South-Western Publishing Company, 1956.
>
> Babenroth, A. Charles, and Charles Parkhurst. *Modern Business English.* Englewood Cliffs, N.J.: Prentice-Hall, Inc., 1955.
>
> Gaum, Carl, et al. *Report Writing.* Englewood Cliffs, N.J.: Prentice-Hall, Inc., 1950.
>
> Saunders, Alta, and C. R. Anderson. *Business Reports.* New York: McGraw-Hill Book Company, Inc., 1957.
>
> Williams, Cecil, and John Ball. *Effective Business Writing.* New York: The Ronald Press Company, 1953.

96a. Types of reports.

A report may be a simple, informal piece of work presented in letter form or two or three typewritten pages of expository writing. It may also be a formal, bound product, containing pictures, diagrams, and graphs.

A good plan for the informal report would be:

1. Tell who asked you to study the problem. Give the date of the request.
2. Explain how the investigation was made (authorities consulted, reading done, number of people questioned, tests made, etc.).
3. Submit results or recommendations.

If the report is to be a long, formal one, a special procedure is necessary. Follow the directions in Section 96b–c.

96b. Gathering material.

When you are asked to consider the problem of safe driving and the means of handling instruction, to study the need for a recreation room at your business, to offer ideas for improvement in handling traffic tickets or parking in your community, to explore plans for pensions on retirement for the members of your union, the first step is to gather information. There are, of course, many ways of doing this. First, use your library. (See Section 86.) Some very careful, competent people may have studied the problem already and have made some sound recommendations which need only to be adapted to your special needs. Examine books, magazines, and pamphlets dealing with the subject. The *Readers' Guide to Periodical Literature* indexes many magazines, but if you are working in a specialized field, you may be able to go directly to the index for that field such as *Industry Index, Agriculture Index, Education Index* and find it very valuable. All of these indexes are used in the same manner as *Readers' Guide.* (See Section 86d.) Use also *Statistical Abstract* and the *Bulletin of the Public Affairs Information Service.*

After you have read what has been done elsewhere and made some careful notes (see Section 88), plan your own investigation. If interviews or questionnaires are to be used, plan the questions carefully and prepare an orderly method of recording the answers. Both the interview and the questionnaire can be used casually and get results that mean nothing at all. To handle them scientifically, proper techniques must be learned.*

If the report is to be a record of work done during a certain period, plans for keeping the information under special headings should be made when the work begins, and other people who will contribute to the report should

* *Surveys, Polls, and Samples* by Mildred Parten, published by Harper & Brothers, gives excellent instruction.

have definite instructions about information that you will need from them.

96c. Plan.

In a formal report or a report of any length, a summary of the methods used to obtain the information and of the results or recommendations appears first. The body of the report discusses these points in detail. The main headings of an outline on the topic *Fraternity Conditions on the Campus* might read:

> SUMMARY
> Members of the committee
> Methods of conducting the survey
> Number and types of fraternities on the campus
> Means of selecting members
> Activities in which fraternities are involved
> Contribution to the school
> Housing
> Fraternities and school elections
> Fraternities and the community
> Effect on student body

96d. General characteristics.

Reports are examples of expository writing; so all of the characteristics of good writing that you have learned are important in reports. Since, however, the aim in report writing is to present a businesslike message in as clear a form as possible, less emphasis is placed on effectiveness, and more stress is placed on correctness, conciseness, and clarity. A discussion of general style characteristics follows:

Objectivity

The first requirement of every report is that it be written without personal prejudice. The investigator who begins his work knowing what answer he wishes to get and uses materials to support his own point of view is of no value to an organization or community and will seldom be asked to work with another group. A report must be approached with a completely open mind, materials assembled in carefully organized form, and recommendations made on the basis of the findings. Even the language of a report is impersonal. The pronouns *I* and *we* seldom appear, and verbs are often in the passive.

> *Avoid:* *We asked* each fraternity to answer the questions on the questionnaire that we are attaching to this report.
>
> *Better:* Each fraternity *was asked* to answer the questions on the questionnaire attached to this report.

Restraint

The report should contain no exaggerations and few superlatives. Avoid expressions such as "remarkably fine contribution to campus life," "exceedingly unsatisfactory," and "perfect for our company." Present the facts and guard the conclusions with expressions like "it seems likely," or "evidence seems to indicate."

Directness

Come to the point at once. Use no unnecessary details. Each paragraph should begin with a topic sentence that will show clearly the point to be discussed in the paragraph. The reader who, after reading the summary, wishes to examine in detail a special part of the report should be able to find that part at once by reading the topic sentences.

Correctness

In a serious business communication, errors in grammar, spelling, sentence structure, and punctuation are inexcusable and will make a very poor impression. With the aid of your handbook and a dictionary, check carefully what you have written. Of course, the information used must be collected and the data compiled with thoroughness and exactness.

Conciseness

Include no unnecessary details or words. Be sure to use no filler words. (See Section 51.) Sometimes a clause can be reduced to a phrase or even to a word.

Wordy: The fraternity which uses the most democratic method when it selects its members is. . . .

Clauses reduced to phrases: The fraternity *using the most democratic method in selecting its members* is. . . .

Reduced to a word: The most *democratic* fraternity method of selecting members is. . . .

Clearness

The first requirement for clarity is a logical plan. If related ideas are not placed together and arranged in order, the report will be unsuccessful. Correctness, of course, contributes to clarity. Particular attention must be given to misplaced and dangling modifiers. (See Section 65.) In order to avoid a number of flat statements beginning with the subject, the writer of reports often uses a participial phrase to open the sentence. Great care must be used to be sure that this phrase is securely attached to the noun that it modifies. Finally, choice of language is important. Consider the background of the people for whom the report is intended and choose words that will be understandable to them. Avoid abstract language and jargon (see Section 48) wherever it is possible to do so.

96e. Form of report.

A formal report should have the following parts: title page, table of contents, summary, report, and diagrams or charts (if they will contribute to the clarity). Very formal reports sometimes also carry a letter of transmittal, in which the author presents the report on a formal basis, and a bibliography.

The report is typed double-spaced with a left-hand margin of an inch and a half. Each new section has a title which is placed either in the center of a line by itself or at the beginning of the first paragraph of the section. In the latter case, it is underlined, as in the following:

> *Housing.* Ten fraternity houses are on the campus itself, and six are located off the campus.

Charts or diagrams should be numbered and given a title. They must always be explained in the text of the report.

EXERCISE 7

Write an informal report on one of the following topics:

> A plan for student patrol of the campus
> How to use student officers effectively
> How to choose cafeteria officers
> Student control in study halls
> Organizing a student government
> Organizing a literary club
> Comparative value of two automobiles
> How to furnish a recreation room
> Plan for using a recreation room effectively
> Report of any committee on which you have worked

EXERCISE 8

Investigate one of the following topics and write a formal report:

> Safety programs in schools
> The effects of fraternities on public high schools
> A plan for protection of athletes injured in school games
> A plan for handling school finances
> A plan for a new civic center
> Improvements in public library services
> Why salaries of ———— should be raised
> Organizing a city manager type of government for ————
> A zoning plan for ————

97. SOCIAL LETTERS

97a. Formal invitations and replies.

Formal invitations are usually written or engraved. They are written in the third person. Full names are used, dates and other numbers are written out, and there is no punctuation at the end of lines. No abbreviations except *Mr.*, *Mrs.*, and *Dr.* are permitted. The message should be centered upon white paper. The letters *R.S.V.P.* mean that an answer is expected. Since invitations permit no expression of individuality or originality, the wording in the model given here may be copied.

Formal invitation

Mr. and Mrs. Frederick Harris
request the pleasure of your company
at a dance to be held in honor
of their daughter Elizabeth
Saturday, February the tenth
at nine o'clock
The Condado Hotel

R.S.V.P.

Invitations should be answered as soon as possible.

The reply is written in longhand, either in the form of the invitation or in a block paragraph. The third person is used, and the exact wording of the invitation is followed as closely as possible.

Acceptance

Miss Catherine Harding accepts with pleasure
the kind invitation of Mr. and Mrs. Frederick Harris
to the dance to be held in honor of their daughter
Elizabeth on Saturday, February the tenth, at nine
o'clock at the Condado Hotel.

Regret

Miss Catherine Harding regrets that she is unable
to accept the kind invitation of Mr. and Mrs. Frederick

Harris to the dance to be held in honor of their
daughter Elizabeth on Saturday, February the tenth,
at nine o'clock at the Condado Hotel.

EXERCISE 9

Write a formal invitation to a dance and a reply to the
invitation.

97b. Informal notes.

All personal notes should be handwritten in ink. Since
these notes are an expression of you, the language should
be the simple, courteous language that you would use in
conversation. For example, don't say, "You are cordially
invited to attend a dance to be given at my house," or "I
should like to take this opportunity to thank you." These
sentences are stiff. They lack personality. The letter that
follows is better form.

Informal invitation

University of Delaware
Newark, Delaware
December 13, 1959

Dear Jack,

Elsa Benson is going to spend the Christmas holidays
with me, and I want to have a little party for her on
Tuesday, December 27. We shall probably dance to some
new records that I bought recently. I should like very
much to have you join us at nine o'clock. Will you?

Sincerely yours,
Gertrude Holtz

Informal acceptance

Madison Apartments
Orange, New Jersey
December 16, 1959

Dear Gertrude,

Nothing could make me miss one of your parties! It will
be fun to see Elsa again and to hear her version of college

life in California. Thank you for including me. I shall be
very glad to join you at nine o'clock on Tuesday, December 27.

> Sincerely yours,
> *Jack Leonhardt*

Informal regret

If you must refuse an invitation, courtesy requires that
you give some legitimate excuse.

> Madison Apartments
> Orange, New Jersey
> December 16, 1959

Dear Gertrude,

Your party for Elsa on December 27 sounds like great
fun. I wish I could be with you. Unfortunately, I shall be
in Washington visiting relatives for the holidays. It will
be disappointing not to see you and Elsa. I do hope that
we can get together when you come back to Orange for
another visit.

> Sincerely yours,
> *Jack Leonhardt*

Thank-you note

Carelessness in acknowledging a kindness is inexcusable.
Whenever you receive a present or someone does a special
favor for you, a telephone call or a note to express your
appreciation is necessary. Brides are sometimes criticized
for not expressing thanks for the presents sent them at the
time of the wedding. Boys and girls graduating from high
school sometimes forget to thank people who are kind to
them. For every present there must be some expression of
gratitude, even if you do not like the gift. A note of thanks
should mention the present, express appreciation of any
special quality that it possesses, and tell how happy you
are to have the gift.

448

McWhorter Apartments
Des Moines 14, Iowa
June 25, 1959

Dear Aunt Jane,

When I came home yesterday and found the lovely string of pearls that you sent me for my graduation, I was so excited that I had to try them on at once with my graduation dress. The dress is soft white net, and the pearls are perfect with it. Thank you for helping to make my graduation day a very happy one.

Sincerely yours,
Adele

Bread-and-butter letter

The bread-and-butter letter is written to a host or hostess who has entertained you away from your home town. If a friend invites you to spend a weekend at her summer place on the beach or to visit her family during a college vacation period, a bread-and-butter letter should be written immediately upon your return to your home or college. Young people usually write a note to the mother of their friend as well as to the friend herself.

August 10, 1959

Dear Sandra,

There is nothing like a beach party at Ocean City. What fun we had! I enjoyed swimming in the ocean, the long hours on the beach with your gay and charming friends, and the dances at night. You couldn't have planned a better weekend for all of us. I know that you will not want to leave Ocean City very soon, but I look forward to seeing you in town and hope that you will have dinner with me when you return.

Thank you again for a perfect visit.

Sincerely yours,
Alan

Note of sympathy

The letter of sympathy is one of the most difficult to write and is often badly done. It should be simple and sincere. Avoid flowery expressions and Biblical quotations.

> Hamilton Hall
> Lake College
> October 28, 1959

Dear Barbara,

The news of the death of your mother came as a great shock to me. Although I have not seen her for several years, I remember well her kindness to all of us when we were children. Her cookie jar made many of us happy.

Nothing that I can say will lessen your grief, but I want you to know that my heart too is heavy with a sense of personal loss.

> With sincere sympathy,
> *Alice Carvel*

EXERCISE 10

Write an invitation to a Christmas party. Then write one reply accepting the invitation and one expressing regret at being unable to accept it.

EXERCISE 11

Write a thank-you note for a present.

EXERCISE 12

Write a bread-and-butter letter to a friend who has entertained you for a weekend. Write a letter of thanks to his or her mother.

EXERCISE 13

Write a letter of sympathy.

97c. Friendly letters.

In these days of easy travel, people make friends in many

places distant from their homes. Good letters help to keep these friends, but a good letter requires careful planning and writing; it cannot be merely "dashed off." Letters can be improved if the following suggestions are practiced.

1. Choose interesting material.

The daily routine of your existence is seldom interesting. Consider the interests of the friend to whom you are writing. One friend may be interested in model airplanes; another, in good motion pictures; a third, in music, art, books, football games. Choose from your experiences those things which will meet the interests of each person to whom you write. Your health or the weather is seldom interesting unless there is something unusual to say about it.

2. Give details.

A full, clear discussion of a football game or a dance is likely to prove far more interesting than a series of choppy notes on a dozen topics. Try to write letters made up of unified details, not random notes which really are only topic sentences needing expansion.

3. Take your time.

If a friendship is worth developing, it deserves the courtesy of time and consideration. "I am sorry that this letter will be brief, for I am in a great rush" is as rude as "Hastily yours."

4. Do not waste time on a statement of the obvious or the trite.

Avoid expressions such as "I received your letter" or "We are all well and hope you are also." Begin the letter, instead, with a reference to something that your friend said in his last letter. Answer some question that he asked or comment on some idea that he presented. Do not close the letter with statements such as "I must close now" or "That's all for now."

5. Avoid participial phrases at the close.

The interesting letter will not close with commonplace expressions such as "Hoping to hear from you soon" or "Wishing you all the success in the world" or "Hoping that this finds you well." These expressions are not complete sentences. They are, in addition, exceedingly trite.

6. Give attention to the appearance of the letter.

Write in ink in a neat, legible handwriting. Use letter paper of good quality. White, cream, or pale gray paper is preferable to that of other colors. Never use lined paper or paper pulled from a note pad. Leave a margin of approximately 1½ inches at the top of the paper and ½ inch at the left. Use the pages in book order. Do not make your friends spend time looking for the next page.

EXERCISE 14

Examine these beginnings and endings of letters. Come to class prepared to discuss which ones are good and which ones are poor. Explain why.

Beginnings:
1. I received your letter Friday and was glad to hear from you.
2. Now that the holidays are over, I have time to write to you.
3. Here's the best news of the season. We beat Polytechnic!
4. Time really flies. It has certainly been a long time since we saw each other.

Endings:
1. Hoping that this finds all of you well and happy.
2. I must close now and do my lessons.
3. Looking forward to seeing you.
4. Be sure to let me know how you get along with your model airplane.

EXERCISE 15

Write five good opening sentences and five good closing sentences for friendly letters.

Listening and Thinking

98. BACKGROUNDS OF WRITERS AND THINKERS

Every day we make mistakes in our purchasing, in our relationships with other people, in our voting, in the development of our attitudes toward life because we have not learned to think clearly. We make these mistakes because we believe whatever we are told without attempting to find out whether the teller knows what he is talking about. Not everything that appears in print or that is presented in a speech is fact. A statement may be based on a few facts and then colored by the author's personal prejudices; it may be deliberately distorted in order to persuade us to accept the author's ideas. Then, too, people often reach conclusions in a field in which they have no information or training, and other people accept these conclusions. The mayor of a city may know a great deal about city government, but his position as mayor does not qualify him as a judge of art. Motion-picture actors and actresses are often asked in interviews to express opinions on economic conditions. Sometimes a newspaper that cannot afford a man trained in the theater uses an ordinary reporter to review a play. Before you accept a conclusion or believe what you read or hear, you should know something about the background of the person who is speaking. A few questions about him will be helpful.

1. Who is he? What has been his preparation for dealing with the subject? A good magazine often carries a section that tells something of the background of the writers for each issue. You might consult *Who's Who?* or Bulman's *Molders of Public Opinion* for information on commentators.

2. What methods did he use to gather his information? If he used a survey, public opinion poll, or questionnaire technique, how many people were involved and how were they selected? We can get nine out of ten people to say they support any idea if we choose the right ten. Some exceedingly careless surveys are made and prove nothing. Unless you know that a survey has been carried out on a scientific basis, it is wise not to be too greatly influenced by its results.

3. Has he a motive for presenting his material? Will he gain a job or money if you act as he tells you to do?

4. Is he prejudiced? Does he present only one side of the question?

5. Does he use oratorical techniques to confuse the audience? Be sure that you distinguish the techniques from the points made.

6. Does he present evidence to support his conclusions?

7. Is his reasoning logical?

EXERCISE 1

Below is a list of commentators and columnists. Using Bulman's *Molders of Public Opinion* or some similar book, read the background of each of these people. Then, on your paper, write a list of his good points and his bad points. Be sure that you include his education and the method used to get information.

> Drew Pearson
> Edward R. Murrow
> Walter Winchell
> The commentator that you listen to most often

EXERCISE 2

In a current issue of *Harper's Magazine* or *The Atlantic Monthly*, read an article on politics, science, or economics. Then turn to the "Personal and Otherwise" pages in the front of the magazine and see what the writer's background is. On your paper, write the name and date of the magazine used, the title and author of the article read, and the facts that you learned about the author. Then state whether you think his background qualifies him to reach conclusions in the area in which he has written.

EXERCISE 3

The sentences in this exercise contain conclusions based on the opinion of another person. On your paper, write a sentence which tells whether you accept the authority presented. Give your reasons.

Example:

This is not a good painting. A friend of ours who is the president of a bank says a child could do painting this good.

I would not accept this authority unless I knew something of his background in art. The president of a bank may know nothing at all about art.

1. I have heard a great deal about the effects of environment, but last night I saw a play that shows that it really has little effect when pitted against heredity.
2. I think I'll take the course on marriage relations because the man who is giving it teaches history in my high school and he's a swell guy.
3. We should eat more potatoes. An article in the paper said that Senator ——— from Idaho thinks they are important in the diet.
4. The salesgirl said this chair would go well with my other furniture, so I bought it.
5. Last week the motion-picture actress, Beryl Chatard, was interviewed about her trip to Rome. She said that there is no evidence of extreme poverty in Italy.

6. Mrs. Manners has been sent as our diplomatic representative to a country where the steel business is important. She is considered well qualified because her husband was in the steel business.

7. The newspapers have recently discussed a piece of sculpture that customs officials refused to admit to this country because they said it was not art.

8. I know that Skinpure is the best face cream because an announcer on the radio said so last night.

9. I am going to take a course in Italian from Sam Serio. He will be able to teach me because he is an Italian himself.

10. Tonight I want to listen to the commentator Eric Sandler. He has just spent six weeks traveling in eight countries and will be able to tell us how the people in those countries feel toward Americans.

11. I have a friend from Boston who is amused at the way we pronounce words in the Midwest. I'm planning to go to college in the East, so I guess I had better learn to speak the way they do there.

12. America ought to have nothing to do with foreign countries. George Washington warned us against entangling alliances.

13. They say that there is rebellion in Russia against the government.

14. Educational television has nothing in common with commercial television; the former is dedicated to the promotion of learning while the latter is dedicated to the promotion of sales.

15. After visiting Stratford-on-Avon, I am convinced that English productions of Shakespearean plays are better than American productions. Being able to perform plays in Shakespeare's birthplace certainly is a great advantage for English actors.

99. TESTING YOUR LOGIC

Thinking is work, but it is important to intelligent living. John Mason Brown once said, "The mind is the muscle most infrequently used." And even when we are willing to use it, we often use it badly. If we want to think intelligently and listen with understanding to the thinking of other people, we must watch certain types of thinking. Your teacher will be looking for these in your writing and speaking, and you should pay attention to them also in the writing and speaking of other people so that you will know what to believe.

99a. Rationalization.

We seldom examine our ideas. Much of our time is spent in finding arguments to support what we have been accustomed to believe or what we want to believe. This type of thinking, in which we reach a conclusion that we like and then try to support it with good reasons, is called *rationalization.* The high school student who wants to go out of town to college when there is an excellent college in his home town often wishes to do so to escape parental control, but he knows he cannot persuade his father to spend an extra thousand dollars just to let him be free from parental decisions; so he rationalizes.

The logical way for a student to solve this problem would be to list honestly those elements of growth that an out-of-town college can give and the home college cannot give; then he would examine the cost and the disadvantages of a college out of town. If the advantages are sufficiently greater than the disadvantages and if his father can afford the extra money, he is justified in going out of town.

Too often, however, the student rationalizes the whole problem; that is, he reaches his conclusion on the basis of desire. Then he looks for reasons to support the conclusion. As a result, he says going out of town will help him to grow independent. A logical thinker might ask how he will be more independent when he will be spending an additional thousand dollars of his father's money.

99b. Oversimplification.

The statement "All women are poor drivers" is a generalization that is false. Everybody knows some women who are excellent drivers. This is a form of oversimplification.

Another form is found in the single solution to a problem: "We can cure juvenile delinquency by keeping children in school." If the problem could be solved as easily as this statement suggests, we'd have no juvenile delinquency. This type of thinking also appears in many predictions: "Give the wage earners social security, and the country will go socialistic" was a common argument thirty years ago. Social security has been in existence for a number of years, and the country is not socialistic. "If the child is not permitted to do as he pleases, he will be frustrated and probably end in a mental hospital" is another oversimplification. Although these things may (or may not) *contribute* to the result suggested, the cause of this result is always much more complicated than the statement suggests.

99c. False dilemma.

The false dilemma is a popular device used by people who wish us to do something. We are offered a choice of two things, one of which is ridiculous or clearly wrong. If we are not thinking, we quickly throw aside the absurd thing and accept the other. Actually, there are usually many more possibilities. Recently a large city ruled that no high school teams might play night football in the city stadium because vandalism had occurred after the games. A city councilman, arguing for night football, said, "Shall our boys play football or tiddlywinks?" This sounds very convincing. Tiddlywinks is a quiet game that even old women can play. By implication, the councilman is adding, "Shall we turn our boys into old women or let them be men playing a vigorous game?" At this point, the clear thinker knows that it is not necessary for him to accept either part of this dilemma. The boys can play football in the afternoon on their school grounds. Numerous other possibilities also suggest themselves.

99d. Non sequitur.

Non sequitur is an old Latin term frequently used in

formal logic. It means "it does not follow." This type of poor reasoning is often a part of many of the other types. A high school student wrote in her composition on teamwork, "If all girls on the team work together, the team will undoubtedly win." This is an example of *non sequitur* and oversimplification. The game cannot be won simply by working together. If all the girls work together, victory does not follow automatically. They may all work together and be such poor players that they lose every game. A newspaper article said recently: "There are more suicides in the English and Scandinavian countries than in Italy. It seems that sunny climates are easier on the spirit." Certainly it is true that Italy has a sunnier climate than these other countries, but we cannot conclude from this fact that the climate affects the number of suicides. The second statement is a *non sequitur.*

99e. Catch phrases.

People are inclined to believe whatever is aptly expressed. *Don't change horses in the middle of the stream* has often been used to persuade people to vote for the man now holding the office. An examination of the statement, however, will show several fallacies in this reasoning. First, a politician is always in the middle of some job; so with this logic we could never get rid of him. Second, if a horse or a man is not doing a good job, the wisest procedure may be to change him.

EXERCISE 4

Many of the following sentences are illogical. Examine each one carefully. On your paper write "Statement 1 is logical" or "Statement 1 is illogical." If it is not logical, write briefly why you consider it illogical.

1. A newspaper recently presented this statement: "Max Sanders compiles football statistics. Occasionally he is urged to give some boy a little push in his record so that the boy

can be all-American. That he has done this only once proves that Sanders is a first-rate statistician."

2. Lanolin is found in sheep's wool. It will surely make hair grow.

3. Some people choose obscene reading material. Therefore books should be censored.

4. Early to bed and early to rise
   Makes a man healthy, wealthy, and wise.

5. When I was at camp last summer, the Governor visited us. He gave me an autographed picture of himself and seems a very nice man; so I am going to vote for him.

6. I heard on the radio last night that there is a new medicine for colds. I think I'll get some of it.

7. I went recently to spend the weekend with a group of scouts who were seeing Navy aircraft, and I can assure you that the Navy is the best of our fighting groups.

8. College teachers are better than high school teachers because the former are better read in their subjects.

9. Nine students elect history for each one that elects a language. Therefore, nine out of ten students on the campus prefer history to languages.

10. We have some friends who came from Germany, but since they know our language, they cannot be cheated in America.

11. Students who do not have enough money to go to college and who want to go should be given state aid.

12. If a person has an easy job, he keeps it.

13. If flowers are watered every day, they will grow well.

14. Mr. Ambrose is a good family man and has two fine sons. I think he will make a good senator.

15. A little folder with the medicine tells how many people the medicine has cured. I think I'll take some of it.

16. Our city should have a new stadium because it would increase the prestige of the city.

17. A survey recently made the following statement: In the United States 30 percent of students who enter high school do not finish. In Belleville's progressive schools only 9 percent do not finish. This record shows the superiority of the Belleville schools.

18. The chart shows that of nineteen feeble-minded inmates

of an institution, fourteen had one parent who was alcoholic. This shows that feeble-mindedness often occurs as a result of alcoholism.

19. Mr. Ashton is a fine person. His friends can always count on him to reward them for any good deed done for him. He is just the man for governor.

20. The politician said, "I am confident we are going to have peace. If the people want peace, there is no reason why we cannot have it."

21. The Chinese do not have high blood pressure. This is probably a result of their diet. If Americans ate more rice, they would have better health.

22. A girl who is destined for marriage wastes her time by going to college. She should study housekeeping.

23. The way to prevent a war is to be prepared for war.

24. There is no reason why men should have a shorter work day. When I was a boy on the farm, I often worked twelve hours a day, and I was not harmed.

25. There have been fewer strikes since the law went into effect. You can see that it is good for the country.

26. This tooth paste will make your teeth white. Buy it.

27. At the tennis matches only two players wore sunglasses. These two were in the semifinals. It must help to wear sunglasses.

28. I'm sure Jay will now be promoted to a big job, for the present treasurer became an executive of the company after he had been in Jay's job for two years.

29. Advertising increases sales. Products cost less when they are made in large quantities. In 1920 an electric refrigerator cost $600. Now the average price is $250.

30. In March we included in our P.T.A. program conferences between parents and teachers, and six hundred parents came. When we had simply a speaker and no conferences in May, only four hundred came. This shows that we should always have conferences.

31. A parent recently said to a teacher, "You have failed my child twice. You cannot be a very good teacher."

32. When a teacher gives 60 in history to a boy with a 120 I.Q., something must certainly be wrong with that teacher.

100. PROPAGANDA TECHNIQUES

The clever use of propaganda by wartime enemies convinced everybody of the need to learn how to recognize it. It also showed many people how in advertising, political speeches, and any argument, certain devices can be used to persuade people to believe what the writer or speaker wants them to believe. We can all learn to recognize a few techniques that will help us to think and act more intelligently. Keeping in mind the types of crooked thinking with which we have already worked will give additional assistance.

Before we can make decisions, we must know the facts. But people who are trying to persuade us to vote in a certain way, to buy a product, or to work for a cause sometimes do not wish us to know the facts. They wish us to see the problem as they do and agree with them. Instead of giving facts and letting us draw our own conclusions, they appeal to our emotions through a number of devices.

100a. Association with something pleasant.

A jar of face cream in an ugly box would have few sales. Medicines are associated with pictures of men in white coats working in a laboratory. A television advertisement presents a happy family watching a television program in an attractive room. You are expected to draw the conclusion that you will be beautiful if you use this face cream, that this medicine has been developed by reputable doctors through careful research methods, that with a television set, husbands, wives, and children will make a happy family circle watching the same program. All of these conclusions may be true, but they may also not be true. A happy family circle does not automatically develop with the purchase of a television set; nor does that advertisement make such a claim. Because the product is associated with something desirable, the purchaser, perhaps even unconsciously, connects the pleasant background with the product.

462

100b. Name calling.

This device has been particularly popular and successful in persuading people who do not think. If a person wishes us to disapprove of something, he calls it *undemocratic* or *radical,* or gives it some other unpopular description. Some of the things referred to may indeed be undemocratic, but many of them have nothing to do with democracy. The speaker knows that if he calls a thing by a name that seems evil to the audience, the listeners are likely to agree with him without asking, *How is it radical?* or *What makes it undemocratic?* On the other hand, if he calls something *democratic* or refers to it as *free enterprise, the American way of life,* he has selected pleasant names and expects his listeners to accept his ideas. In a county education system, a new type of report card was recently devised. Some parents objected to it, and at a meeting between school officials and educators, the leader of the parents said the cards were the beginning of communism for they attempted to level the class, to make all the children equal. Here was an example of name calling where the speaker made no attempt to examine the meaning of his term.

President McKinley defended the protective tariff by saying, "It represents the American family, the American girl and the American boy and the highest possibilities of American citizenship to propose to raise money to pay public expenses by taxing the products of other nations rather than by taxing the products of our own." All of these pleasant names associated with American living tend to make a person believe that any idea with which these are linked is a good one. Sometimes it is indeed a good idea, but we must learn not to accept a thing simply because good names are tied to it, nor reject a plan because bad names accompany it. We need some facts, and we want to know how the idea under discussion is a part of the good name or the bad name. Simply calling a point *democratic* or *undemocratic* does not make it so.

EXERCISE 5

Select from newspapers or magazines ten examples of advertisements showing products presented with attractive backgrounds. Explain what connection the reader is likely to make between product and background.

EXERCISE 6

During the next week, listen to speeches on the radio and read controversies in your newspaper. Select ten examples of the use of unpleasant names. Bring these to class for a discussion. Then write a paper of four hundred words discussing, with examples, how name calling is used, what effect it has on people, and what readers and listeners should do about it.

100c. "Plain folks."

The politician who comes through the crowd shaking hands with everybody and kissing the babies is using the "plain folks" technique. By his behavior, he is saying, "I may be mayor or governor, but I am not snobbish. You can see that I am friendly with everybody, a good fellow." Sometimes he emphasizes the fact that he comes from a simple family and has been obliged to work his way through school. This is a *non sequitur* type of reasoning. A man may be a good governor, no matter from what social class he comes.

EXERCISE 7

Make a list of the people who recommend products in advertisements that you have seen. After each name state whether you would buy the product as a result of that person's recommendation, and give your reasons.

100d. Guilt by association.

This is a particularly dangerous type of thinking. Life is a very complicated process. In carrying on our daily activities, we are sure to be acquainted with people and ideas of which we do not approve. If you receive an invitation to a party, you do not ask the hostess to list her guests and tell their political associations before you accept it. Life will give us associates whom we enjoy for a time because they are superficially agreeable. Later we find that the morals or habits or attitudes toward life of these people cause us to disapprove of them. There is, it is clear, an important time element involved.

Then there is the problem of association of ideas. A belief in public housing, social security, and old-age pensions may be shared by people from all political groups. One does not become a Democrat, a Republican, or a Socialist because he accepts one idea advocated by one of these groups. Here is an excellent opportunity for name calling, but a good thinker asks for the facts.

100e. Statistics.

Nothing is more impressive to the average reader or listener than the use of statistics, and the more decimal places they have, the more accurate and convincing they seem. Darrell Huff has written an interesting book, *How to Lie with Statistics*, which is worth reading completely. He points out that figures can be manipulated to make them present several different points of view. For an example, averages can be obtained by adding together all of the items involved and dividing by the number of items like this:

Salaries in this immediate neighborhood:

$$\begin{array}{r} \$100,000 \\ 20,000 \\ 18,000 \\ 15,000 \\ 12,000 \\ \hline 5)\$165,000 \\ \end{array}$$

Average: $ 33,000

Here the average is $33,000, but only one man makes that much. This kind of average is called the *mean*.

The *median* is also called an average, but it is found by placing the figures in descending order and counting up or down to the mid-point. If we go back to our example, we see that the average is now $18,000, quite a different figure. When we are told, "The average is ———," we shall want to ask, "How was the average found, and how many cases were involved?"

Many other practices that the average man does not understand are involved in statistics. Before we accept the statistics, we should know something about these practices.

EXERCISE 8

Divide your class into groups to read sections of Darrell Huff's book *How to Lie with Statistics*. Plan a panel discussion for the class to teach the students how to think intelligently when statistics are used for persuasion purposes.

EXERCISE 9

Read Mark Antony's speech at the funeral of Caesar. Discuss the techniques that he used to persuade the crowd.

EXERCISE 10

Criticize the following statements from recent speakers or writers:

1. We cannot doubt the enormous disciplinary value of the study of Latin and Greek when we see the admirable intellect of men trained in the English universities.
2. Most of us went barefoot at least sometime or other as children, and as children we had little anxiety. Wearing no shoes or stockings will reduce our anxiety.
3. Since 80 percent of women marry, all colleges should give courses in child care.
4. Either you approve of General Nasser, leader of the Egyptian Nationalists, or you approve of Communist Russia.

5. The man should be discharged from his teaching job because in 1932 he visited Russia.
6. I think the present heat wave has been caused by disturbing the atmosphere with atomic explosions.
7. The speaker said: "Guilt by association is said by some people to be un-American, but my schoolboy copybook says you can know a man by the company that he keeps."
8. Twenty people were recently weighed and then asked about their happiness in marriage. It was found that fat people are happier in marriage than thin ones.

BIBLIOGRAPHY

Allport, Gordon, and Leo Postman. *The Psychology of Rumor.* New York: Henry Holt and Company, Inc., 1947.

Brucker, Herbert. *Freedom of Information.* New York: The Macmillan Company, 1949.

Bulman, David, ed. *Molders of Opinion.* Milwaukee, Wis.: The Bruce Publishing Company, 1945.

Burtt, E. A. *Right Thinking: A Study of Its Principles and Methods.* New York: Harper & Brothers, 1946.

Chase, Stuart. *Guides to Straight Thinking, with Thirteen Common Fallacies.* New York: Harper & Brothers, 1956.

Chase, Stuart. *The Proper Study of Mankind: An Inquiry into the Science of Human Relations.* New York: Harper & Brothers, 1948.

Chase, Stuart. *The Tyranny of Words.* New York: Harcourt, Brace and Company, Inc., 1938.

Dimnet, Ernest. *Art of Thinking.* New York: Simon and Schuster, Inc., 1929.

Doob, Leonard. *Public Opinion and Propaganda.* New York: Henry Holt and Company, Inc., 1948.

Hayakawa, S. *Language in Thought and Action.* New York: Harcourt, Brace and Company, Inc., 1949.

Holmes, Roger. *The Rhyme of Reason.* New York: Appleton-Century-Crofts, Inc., 1939.

Jacobson, David. *The Affairs of Dame Rumor.* New York: Rinehart & Company, Inc., 1948.

Jepson, R. W. *Clear Thinking.* New York: Longmans, Green & Co., Inc., 1956.

Leonard, Jonathan N. *Enjoyment of Science.* New York: Doubleday & Company, Inc., 1942.

Linebarger, Paul. *Psychological Warfare.* Washington, D.C.: Combat Forces Press, 1948.

Lumley, Frederick. *The Propaganda Menace.* New York: Appleton-Century-Crofts, Inc., 1933.

Mackaye, James. *The Logic of Language.* Hanover, N.H.: Dartmouth College Publications, 1939.

Mackenzie, A. J. *Propaganda Boom.* London, England: John Gifford, Ltd., 1938.

Moore, Robert. *General Semantics in the High School English Program.* Columbus, Ohio: The Ohio State University Press, 1945.

What Is Propaganda? (Pamphlet prepared by American History Association for U.S. Armed Forces.)

Appendix

101. TAKING TESTS

Whether you plan to go to college or to take a job after high school, you are likely to encounter a series of tests. These tests may vary in purpose, but they are usually important. A good score may mean a scholarship or advanced standing if you are applying for college, or the job you want if you are looking for work.

Because these tests are important, it is a good idea to familiarize yourself in advance with the kind of questions you will be asked. A number of books providing sample tests are now available for most kinds of examinations. A short bibliography of such books appears at the end of this chapter. You will probably want to examine one or more of these. In the meantime, the exercises in this chapter give you a chance to get acquainted with some kinds of questions common to many different examinations.

101a. Vocabulary tests.

Matching definitions and words

A list of definitions is presented opposite a list of words. You are asked to match each word and its definition. Practice in this kind of exercise can be found in this book in the section on Vocabulary Growth, page 259.

Choosing from several definitions

Each word in a list is followed by five definitions. You are asked to choose the correct one. For example:

> *Equestrian* means most nearly a) statue b) pertaining to the equator c) energetic d) <u>pertaining to horsemen</u> e) diplomatic.

In such a question you merely indicate the correct meaning of the word by underlining, as has been done in the sample, or by using some other method indicated in the directions.

EXERCISE 1

On your paper write the number of each sentence and opposite it your choice (*a, b, c, d*) of definition of the word in capital letters.

Example:

SINISTER means most nearly a) serious b) threatening evil c) gloomy d) sorrowful e) difficult.

1. = b

1. DECORUM means most nearly a) decorate b) peace c) proper behavior d) impropriety e) supposition.
2. EXORBITANT means most nearly a) unique b) powerful c) excessive d) unfair e) carefully calculated.
3. GREGARIOUS means most nearly a) popular b) fond of crowds c) talkative d) subtle e) antisocial.
4. HYPERBOLE means most nearly a) extravagant b) overanxious c) too critical d) great exaggeration e) unusually careful.
5. RACONTEUR means most nearly a) skillful story teller b) orchestra conductor c) curator of museum d) tennis champion e) prize winner.

Choosing the antonym or synonym

An antonym is a word that means the opposite of any given word. A synonym has the same meaning as the given

470

word. These questions are a bit complicated because you are looking for *two* possibilities instead of *one*.

The directions on the test read:

> In each row of five words below, mark the word which means the same as, or the opposite of, the first word in the row.

> Example:
> lethargy: (a) flippancy (b) gravity (c) <u>alertness</u> (d) darkness (e) poisonous.

Here *c* is marked because there is no word that means the same as *lethargy*, but *alertness* is the opposite of *lethargy*.

EXERCISE 2

On your paper write the number of the sentence and then the word or group of words which means the same as the first word in the row or its opposite.

1. BENIGN. (a) blessed (b) modest (c) diffident (d) unkind (e) malignant.
2. INDIGENT. (a) destitute (b) indecent (c) dependent (d) unhappy (e) insufferable.
3. HACKNEYED. (a) cut (b) banal (c) unsatisfactory (d) drowsy (e) strong.
4. IMMACULATE. (a) no consequence (b) blemished (c) immersed (d) washed (e) colorless.
5. INTREPID. (a) pusillanimous (b) extrinsic (c) not rapid (d) careless (e) unworthy.
6. FACETIOUS. (a) fortunate (b) humorless (c) quarrelsome (d) false (e) trustworthy.
7. PRECARIOUS. (a) stable (b) preventable (c) prewar (d) helpful (e) satisfying.
8. EQUIVOCAL. (a) equal to (b) musical (c) nonmusical (d) dubious (e) scarce.
9. DOGMATIC. (a) animal-like (b) dictatorial (c) involuntary (d) automatic (e) efficient.
10. EFFICACIOUS. (a) ineffective (b) talkative (c) double-dealing (d) perfect (e) dynamic.

Filling in blank spaces

The directions on the College Entrance Examination read: "Each of the sentences in this part has one or more blank spaces, each blank indicating that a word has been omitted. Beneath the sentence are five numbered words or sets of words. You are to choose the one word or set of words which, when inserted in the sentence, best fits in with the meaning of the sentence as a whole."

EXERCISE 3

On your paper, write the word or set of words which best completes each sentence.

1. There is in education today an undignified scramble for the student's time, with broad hints on the part of the scientist that the rest of the program is _____.
(a) satisfactory (b) unbalanced (c) folderol (d) cultural
(e) topheavy.

2. Machiavelli said in his book, *The Prince,* "A prince is in the end _____ to all those from whom he takes nothing, and they are numerous; he is _____ to those to whom he does not give, and they are few."
(a) kind—cruel (b) courteous—discourteous (c) liberal—stingy (d) stupid—intelligent (e) royal—plebeian.

3. There have been _____ in all ages, not merely the lethargic masses, but moralists, philosophers, teachers, busily engaged in ratifying existing mistakes and discouraging new ideas.
(a) do-gooders (b) lawyers (c) poets (d) patriots (e) obstructionists.

4. Many athletic programs have a false emphasis. They _____ attention on boys who are varsity material and _____ the large group who need physical activity.
(a) give—discourage (b) place—distract (c) omit—develop
(d) focus—neglect (e) encourage—ignore.

5. Many European countries do not think that education should be wholly _____. Students who cannot pass stiff examinations are not permitted to enter a secondary school.
(a) free (b) democratic (c) academic (d) vocational
(e) completed in lower grades.

6. A whole set of _____ is rapidly developing. We consider ourselves civilized if we multiply the number of motor cars and struggle for the attainment of ends which are not worth attaining.

(a) new beliefs   (b) false standards   (c) cheap manners   (d) important goals   (e) commercial attitudes.

7. Greatly concerned about the supply of pure water in the future, some scientists have been studying _____ control.

(a) pollution   (b) power   (c) irrigation   (d) river   (e) ice.

8. The Germans, we are told, expect a great deal of their theater. It is not a place for _____, good fun after dinner, but must serve a "cultural mission."

(a) comedy   (b) chatter   (c) amateurs   (d) dull performances   (e) casual entertainment.

9. The deplorable nursing conditions which Florence Nightingale found during the Crimean War were the result of petty bungling of minor officials, _____, and fatal exactitudes of narrow routine.

(a) infinite attention to cleanliness   (b) endless ramification of administrative incapacity   (c) unusual concern of the government   (d) too much attention to women   (e) clubs and sororities interested in the work.

10. The pride of an alumnus in his college should be based on the development of intelligence, not on the _____ of the football team.

(a) failure   (b) recruiting   (c) prowess   (d) coach   (e) movement.

Completing analogies

The directions read: "Each of the questions in this part consists of two words which have a certain relationship to each other, followed by five lettered pairs of related words. Select the lettered pair of words which are related to each other in the *same* way as the original pair of words are related to each other." For example:

basket:straw :: (a) dress:stitch   (b) house:room   (c) table:leg   (d) blanket:wool   (e) desk:write.

473

The underlined selection is correct. The important point in exercises of this sort is to establish the *exact* relationship between the first two words before you try to choose the answer. For example, the basket is made of straw. Although in all of the groups of words (a, b, c, d) there is a relationship, only in *d* is the thing named by one word made of the material named by the other.

Many different relationships are used. Sometimes the groups of words are antonyms or synonyms. For example:

> easy:hard :: good:bad   (antonyms)
> easy:simple :: hard:difficult   (synonyms)

Sometimes a word in the first section of the analogy is a member of a class. In the example below, *corn* is a member of the *grain* class. Then in the second section of the analogy, one word must be a member of a class. *Silver* is a member of the *metal* class. For example:

> corn:grain :: silver:metal
> man:mammal :: lobster:crustacean

In some tests, the student is given three parts of the analogy and is asked to supply only the fourth member instead of supplying two words already compared as in the example above.

> embroidery:stitch :: tapestry:
> (a) curtain   (b) wall hanging   (c) weave   (d) fabric   (e) design.

Embroidery is made by stitching; tapestry is made by weaving; so *weave* should be the word selected.

EXERCISE 4

To get practice in establishing relationships, write on your paper the word which will complete each analogy.

1. eye:body :: room:_____   (a) table   (b) house   (c) stable   (d) furniture   (e) carpet.

2. Boy:club :: girl:_____ (a) friend (b) boy (c) dress (d) join (e) sorority.

3. canister:sugar :: drawer:_____ (a) bureau (b) clothes (c) closed (d) food (e) sweetness.

4. abhor:love :: hope:_____ (a) sorrow (b) despair (c) hate (d) like (e) attraction.

5. genial:unpleasant :: liquid:_____ (a) drug (b) pleasant (c) liquor (d) solid (e) medicine.

6. chemist:scientist :: teacher:_____ (a) medicine (b) investigator (c) educator (d) researcher (e) trader.

7. opaque:transparent :: lucrative:_____ (a) translucent (b) helpful (c) prosperous (d) satisfied (e) unprofitable.

8. foolish:inane :: incessant:_____ (a) free (b) continual (c) unfortunate (d) ceasing (e) clever.

9. truncated:cut :: insipid:_____ (a) food (b) flat (c) lively (d) curt (e) interesting.

10. vaccination:smallpox :: caution:_____ (a) accidents (b) disease (c) inoculation (d) diphtheria (e) carelessness.

11. urban:city :: rural:_____ (a) mountain (b) river (c) country (d) suburban (e) healthful.

12. knife:surgeon :: palette:_____ (a) carpenter (b) artist (c) teacher (d) paint (e) sculpture.

13. adamant:inflexible :: erudite:_____ (a) ignorant (b) incessant (c) firm (d) learned (e) clever.

14. bird:whale :: fly:_____ (a) sea (b) soak (c) swim (d) fish (e) air.

15. mendicant:beg :: vicar:_____ (a) sing (b) preach (c) visit (d) hunt (e) eat.

16. Simpleton:fool :: gown:_____ (a) servant (b) dress (c) judge (d) night (e) evening.

17. munificent:philanthropist :: parsimonious:_____ (a) doctor (b) scientist (c) astronomer (d) miser (e) archaeologist.

18. elegy:poetry :: corn:_____ (a) grain (b) bread (c) farm (d) stalks (e) harvest.

19. asylum:orphan :: convent:_____ (a) monk (b) nun (c) rabbi (d) learn (e) religion.

20. nocturnal:diurnal :: external:_____ (a) perennial (b) pastoral (c) superficial (d) outside (e) internal.

21. epilogue:drama :: peroration:_____ (a) sonnet (b) argument (c) prose (d) prologue (e) preparation.

22. deer:sheep :: doe:_____ (a) lamb (b) drake (c) moose (d) ewe (e) buck.

23. eulogy:praise :: penurious:_____ (a) blame (b) poverty (c) stingy (d) opulent (e) helpful.

24. obese:emaciated :: obsolete:_____ (a) new (b) obedient (c) thin (d) absent (e) emanate.

25. she:her :: boy:_____ (a) his (b) boy's (c) yours (d) boys' (e) man's.

Materials similar to those which we have examined are found in a wide variety of tests. Understanding how to handle them will help you to pass tests for college entrance, for scholarships, for jobs.

101b. The College Entrance Examination.

The *College Entrance Examination* itself consists of: 1) a three-hour scholastic aptitude test which includes a verbal section and a mathematical section; 2) three one-hour achievement tests in subjects selected by the candidate such as, foreign languages, English composition, science and history.

The verbal section includes vocabulary questions similar to those which we have examined and a reading test. In the latter the student is given passages to read and is expected to answer questions about content and do some thinking in order to draw conclusions about the material. (See Section 100.)

The English Composition Achievement section often includes (1) sentences in scrambled order to be placed in logical order; (2) a poorly written paragraph to be corrected; (3) an exercise testing the student's appreciation of style.

EXERCISE 5

Assume that the following paragraph is a rough copy

written by you. Copy, rewrite, and proofread the paragraph, correcting grammar, punctuation, capitalization, phrasing, wordiness.

Dissatisfied with life as a member of brilliant society Florence Nightingale's one interest and desire seemed to lay in the field of being a nurse, but many difficulties faced her family and she before she could accomplish it. A true representative of the Victorian era, nursing seemed to Miss Nightingales mother an occupation unfit for a woman of society and who had an independent income. Every effort that Florence made to learn something about hospital work or what was good nursing practice was discouraged by friends and family. Then the Crimean War broke out, and Florence obtained an opportunity to go to Scutari, where dreadful conditions prevailed in English hospitals, from a government official who was a friend of her family. From then on, she worked valiant for better conditions. As a result, nursing became a profession. Today many young women choose this honorable profession.

EXERCISE 6

Follow the directions for Exercise 5.

As I read the book, I felt as if I was actually living the life of the protagonist. Its development, character portrayal, and vivid description adds up to one of the liveliest stories of the postwar years and makes every reader wish they were able to have the experiences presented by the author. Divided into ten chapters, each chapter gives experiences that are stirring, vital, with plenty of "punch," and even with some humor.

Any review would only be half completed if no mention was made of the author's background and how he happened to write the book, which is one reason why the story is so interesting. Born in South Africa, his life was spent in or near the jungle. Here he learned the secrets of the tangled vines, how to deal with the animals, to recognize the poisonous plants and to make even an acquaintance with a little-known tribe that helped him to find the huge warship in a remote section that the Germans had hidden during the war.

Occasionally you may be asked to write a paragraph based on topic sentences such as these:

> Even in societies like ours there is an astonishing amount of unquestioning acceptance of customary behavior patterns, thought patterns, and feeling patterns.

> For a majority of people in the West, purposeless reading, purposeless listening in, purposeless looking at films have become addictions.

> Like every instrument that man has invented, sport can be used either for good or evil purposes.

> How one uses any power which is placed in his hands discloses just what kind of person he is and the degree to which he has grown up.

You may even be asked to choose from a group of topics of wide interest one topic on which you will prepare an outline, write an essay based on the outline, and summarize its theme briefly. The themes which you write for your high school classes will help to prepare you for this kind of assignment.

The last problem, understanding of style, may deal with poetry or prose. It tests the student's appreciation of appropriate tone, imagery, rhythm.

EXERCISE 7

The directions read: "In each of the passages of poetry there is a blank space showing that a line has been omitted. Beneath each passage are four suggested lines which might be inserted in the blank space. One of the lines is appropriate (a); one of the lines is inappropriate in rhythm or meter (b); one of the lines is inappropriate in style or tone (c); and one of the lines is inappropriate in meaning (d). You are to determine the proper category for *each* line."

On your paper write the number of the appropriate line and mark it *a*. Then write the numbers of each of the other lines and mark it with the proper letter.

I

He that loves a rosy cheek,
Or a coral lip admires,
Or from star-like eyes doth seek
Fuel to maintain his fires:
As old Time makes these decay

————— ————— —————

1. His love will waste away.
2. He will seek another way.
3. So his flames must waste away.
4. What, I ask you, wastes away?

II

I did but look and love awhile,
'Twas but for one half-hour;
Then to resist I had no will,

————— ————— —————

1. But you have given power.
2. Now I need some power.
3. Behold, there is no power.
4. And now I have no power.

BIBLIOGRAPHY

Practice exercises based on questions found in both aptitude and achievement tests can be purchased from the Educational Advisory Center, 400 Boylston Street, Boston, Massachusetts. Here the following review materials are available:

College Entrance Reviews in Mathematics Aptitude
College Entrance Reviews in English Aptitude
College Entrance Reviews in English Composition
College Entrance Reviews in Intermediate Mathematics

The Arco Publishing Company, 480 Lexington Avenue, New York 47, New York, publishes the following helps:

How to Pass College Entrance Tests
How to Pass National Merit Scholarship Tests
Vocabulary Builder and Guide to Verbal Tests

Additional information about colleges can be found in:

Karl, S. Donald. *The College Handbook.* New York: College Entrance Examination Board, 1957–58.

Lovejoy, Clarence. *Lovejoy's College Guide.* New York: Simon and Schuster, Inc., 1956.

Turngren, Annette. *Choosing the Right College.* New York: Harper & Brothers, 1952.

102. SENTENCE ANALYSIS AND DIAGRAMING

Theoretically, one who knows grammar should be able to analyze a sentence both by words and by groups of words. Consider the following sentence:

> The little old lady across the street is carefully knitting a sweater for her grandson, who is a freshman.

A grammatical analysis of this sentence is as follows:

The is a definite article modifying the noun *lady.*

little and *old* are adjectives modifying the noun *lady.*

lady is a noun used as *subject of the sentence.*

across is a preposition introducing the prepositional phrase; *the,* a definite article modifying the noun *street; street,* a noun used as object of the preposition *across.* The entire prepositional phrase, *across the street,* is used as an adjective modifying *lady.*

is is an auxiliary verb which with the present participle *knitting* forms the present progressive tense, active voice, and is the *predicate of the sentence.*

carefully is an adverb modifying the compound verb *is knitting.*

a is an indefinite article modifying *sweater,* which is a noun used as direct object of the verb *is knitting.*

for is a preposition; *her,* the possessive pronoun, third person singular feminine, referring to *lady* and modifying *grandson; grandson,* a noun, the object of the preposition *for.* The entire prepositional phrase, *for her grandson,* is used

as an adverb, modifying *is knitting,* if we think of the
phrase as being closely associated with and tied to the
verb phrase *is knitting;* if, however, we think of *for her
grandson* as closely associated with *sweater,* then both by
logic and common sense we can call it a prepositional
phrase used as an adjective, modifying *sweater.*

who is a relative pronoun, nominative case, referring to
grandson and used as the subject of *is; is* is a linking verb;
a is an indefinite article modifying *freshman;* and *freshman* is a predicate noun after a linking verb. The group of
words, *who is a freshman,* is an adjective clause modifying
grandson.

Lacking the skill (or knowledge) needed to analyze sentences as indicated above, many students find diagraming of
value. This is a mechanical device by which you are aided
in identifying words as parts of speech, in identifying
phrases and clauses, and in indicating the uses or functions
in a sentence of these words, phrases, or clauses. These
purposes of diagraming are accomplished through the use
of lines: horizontal lines, perpendicular lines, slanting lines,
curved lines, and dotted lines.

But remember that diagraming, although it seems like a
game, is only a *means* to an end, not an *end* in itself; it is
simply a device to help you identify and see the relationships
between various parts of a sentence.

The important parts of the sentence are put on lines in the
positions indicated in the following skeleton diagram.

481

Filled in, such a diagramed sentence might read:

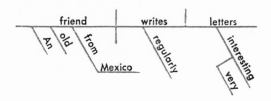

The simple subject, the simple predicate, the direct object, the object complement, the predicate noun (or pronoun), and the predicate adjective are written on the main long horizontal line. Subject and predicate are separated by a perpendicular line intersecting the horizontal line. The direct object is separated from the verb by a short perpendicular line extending up from the horizontal line. The object complement, the predicate noun or pronoun, or the predicate adjective is separated by a short slanting line extending leftward from the horizontal line.

Children	like	candy
subject	predicate verb	object

We	have elected	John	captain
subject	predicate verb phrase	direct object	object complement

This	is	he
subject	predicate (linking verb)	predicate pronoun

Father	will be	glad
subject	predicate (linking verb)	predicate adjective

Dashes or dotted lines (usually perpendicular) are used to join, and the conjunction is written along or across such a line. In the following sentence, notice the compound subject, the compound predicate, and the compound object.

> Freshmen and sophomores read or write stories and essays.

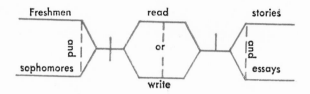

Slanting lines below the horizontal line are used for adjective and adverbial modifiers. Each adjective or adverb is on a separate slanting line.

The old man slowly but carefully signed his name.

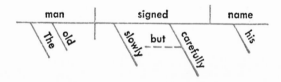

An adverb modifying an adjective or another adverb is written on an additional slanting line (or a stair-step line), thus:

The very old man walked extremely slowly.

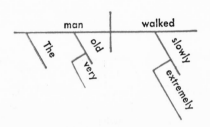

Prepositional phrases are attached below the words they modify by a slanting line for the preposition and a horizontal line for the object of the preposition. Any adjectives modifying this object are, as already indicated, written on a slanting line.

A friend of my father gave me the book with the red cover. (Note how *me*—the indirect object—is diagramed.)

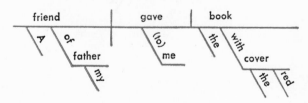

Participial and infinitive phrases (as adjectives or adverbs) are attached to the words they modify by means of a line that curves into a horizontal line. Any objects, adjectives, or adverbs in these phrases are placed as indicated above.

484

The man wearing the brown hat is the man to be nominated for president.

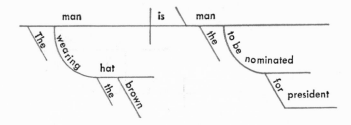

A gerund phrase or an infinitive phrase used as a noun is put on a horizontal line supported by a vertical line placed to indicate whether such a phrase is the subject, object, predicate noun, etc. A noun clause or an infinitive phrase with a subject is similarly supported. Within these phrases or clauses, objects, adjectives, adverbs, and the like, are placed as indicated above.

Gerund phrase as subject of a verb:

Occasionally reading a good book is a worthy achievement.

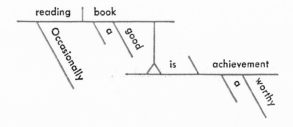

Infinitive phrase as predicate noun:

A precept worthy to be followed by everyone is freely to forgive your enemies.

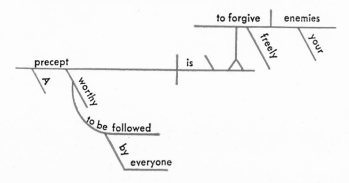

An infinitive phrase with a subject:

Henry asked me to lend him my dictionary.

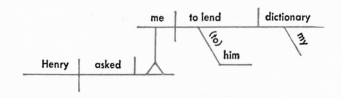

Noun clause as subject:

What you say has convinced me.

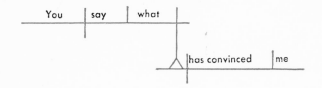

Noun clause as object:

John said that he had studied his lesson faithfully.

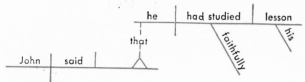

Absolute phrases are similarly placed on a vertically supported line but are enclosed in brackets:

The tire being repaired, we continued our journey.

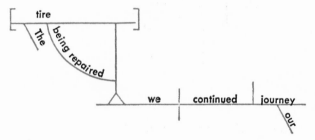

A vertical dotted line serves to link adjective clauses to the noun modified; adverbial clauses to the proper word in the independent clause; and one independent clause to another. Any conjunction expressed is written across the dotted line.

Adjective clauses:

Men who work diligently usually succeed.

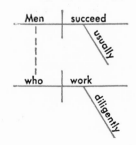

I met a friend whom I like.

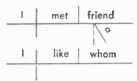

Adverbial clauses:

We won the game because we had the better team.

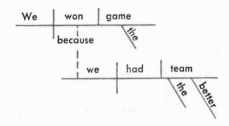

Mary is taller than her mother is.

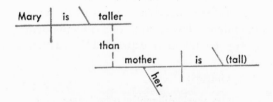

John drives faster than he should drive.

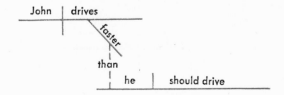

Compound sentence:

I like movies, but John prefers radio dramas.

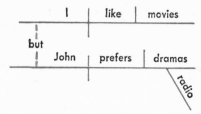

Sometimes a sentence may contain parts in inverted or transposed order; these parts must be put in the proper places in the diagram according to the directions already given.

Never again will John see so exciting a game.

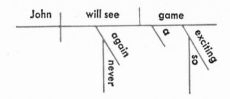

EXERCISE 8

Diagram the following sentences:

1. You may borrow my pen.
2. The Smiths saw many interesting sights on their trip.
3. I am painting my car green.
4. Father has appointed Mary his secretary.
5. You will be our next treasurer.
6. An athletic victory is usually a joyful occasion.
7. The day is becoming colder and more gloomy.
8. Edison has been famous for a long time.
9. Books, magazines, and newspapers are available in the library.
10. Busy people receive and send many letters.

EXERCISE 9

Diagram the following sentences:

1. Henry has worked faithfully to achieve his ambition.
2. Your winning the election so easily surprised everyone.
3. Tomorrow I shall begin taking regular exercise.
4. To recognize one's errors is to take the first step toward improvement.
5. The host invited us to come early and to stay late.
6. That I might have the pleasure of your company is my desire.
7. Father wrote that he would arrive on Friday.
8. We returned to college yesterday, our vacation having ended.
9. The college which I am attending is a small one.
10. To thoughts of love, in the springtime, often turns the fancy of a young man—and that of some old ones, too.

EXERCISE 10

Diagram the following sentences:

1. I am looking forward to your coming to the university in September.
2. John wrote to Mr. Brown, who had promised him a job for the summer.
3. Driving carefully on icy roads is necessary in order to prevent accidents.
4. On this wintry day the weather outside is frightful but the weather inside is delightful.
5. Our first item of business today is to call the roll.
6. I am telephoning what I have to say and then am confirming it by letter.
7. People who make no provision for the morrow are like the five foolish virgins who are mentioned in the Bible.
8. Charles claims to be a better golfer than I am, but I dare him to prove it.
9. When I received your telegram, I dropped everything and came at once.
10. Always to be remembered is that traffic regulations are devised and enforced for the safety of drivers, passengers, and pedestrians.

INDEX

The figures in this index refer to pages.

491